T0384458

The Framework for Innovation

An Entrepreneur's Guide to the Body of Innovation Knowledge

The Management Handbooks for Results Series

Lean TRIZ
How to Dramatically Reduce Product-Development Sosts with This
Innovative Problem-Solving Tool
H. James Harrington (2017)

Change Management
Manage the Change or It Will Manage You
Frank Voehl and H. James Harrington (2016)

The Lean Management Systems Handbook
Rich Charron, H. James Harrington, Frank Voehl, and Hal Wiggins (2014)

The Lean Six Sigma Black Belt Handbook
Tools and Methods for Process Acceleration
*Frank Voehl, H. James Harrington, Chuck Mignosa,
and Rich Charron (2013)*

The Organizational Master Plan Handbook
A Catalyst for Performance Planning and Results
H. James Harrington and Frank Voehl (2012)

The Organizational Alignment Handbook
A Catalyst for Performance Acceleration
H. James Harrington and Frank Voehl (2011)

The Framework for Innovation
An Entrepreneur's Guide to the Body of Innovation Knowledge
*Frank Voehl, H. James Harrington, Rick Fernandez,
and Brett Trusko (2018)*

About the Series

The Management Handbooks for Results™ Series

As Series Editors, we at CRC/Productivity Press have been privileged to contribute to the convergence of philosophy and the underlying principles of Management for Results, leading to a common set of assumption. One of the most important deals with the challenges facing the transformation of the organization and suggests that managing for results can have a significant role in increasing and improving performance and strategic thinking, by drawing such experiences and insights from all parts of the organization and making them available to points of strategic management decision and action. As John Quincy Adams once said, "If you actions inspire others to dream more, learn more, do more, and become more, you are a Leader."

If a good leader's actions inspire people to dream more, learn more, do more, and become more (and those actions will lead to an organization's culture, and if the culture represents "the way we do things around here"), then the Management for Results Series represents a brief glimpse of "the shadow of the leader-manager." This Series is a compilation of conceptual management framework and literature review on the latest concepts in management thinking, especially in the areas of accelerating performance and achieving rapid and long-lasting results. It examines some of the more recent as well as historical contributions, and identifies a number of key elements involved. Further analysis determines a number of situations that can improve the results-oriented thinking capability in managers, and the various Handbooks consider whether organizations can successfully adopt their content and conclusions to develop their managers and improve the business.

This is a particularly exciting and turbulent time in the field of management, both domestically and globally, and change may be viewed as either an opportunity or a threat. As such, the principles and practices of Management for Results can aid in this transformation or (by flawed implementation approaches) can bring an organization to its knees. This Management for Results Series (and the Handbooks contained therein) discusses the relationship among management thinking, results orientation, management planning, and emergent strategy, and suggests that management thinking needs to be compressed and accelerated, as it is essential in making these relationships more appropriate and effective–a so-called "shadow of the leader-manager." As Series Editors, we believe that the greater the sum total of management thinking and thinkers in the organization, the more readily and effectively it can respond to and take advantage of the vast array of changes occurring in today's business environment. However, despite the significant levels of delayering and flattening of structures that have taken place in the last decade or so, some organizational barriers continue to stifle opportunities for accelerating management for results by limiting the flow of experiences and insights to relevant corners of the organization.

The "shadow of the leader-manager" that is present throughout this Management Handbook Series is based upon the following eight characteristics of an effective *leader-manager who gets results*, and provides one of the many integration frameworks around which this Series is based:

Integrity = the integration of outward actions and inner values
Dedication = spending whatever time or energy necessary to accomplish the task at hand, thereby leading by example and inspiring others
Magnanimity = giving credit where it is due
Humility = acknowledging they are no better or worse than other members of the team
Openness = being able to listen to new ideas, even if they do not conform to the usual way of thinking
Creativity = the ability to think differently, to get outside of the box that constrains solutions
Fairness = dealing with others consistently and justly
Assertiveness = clearly stating what is expected so that there will be no misunderstandings and dealings with poor performance

This management book series is intended to help you take a step back and look at your team or organization's culture to clearly see the reflection of your leader-manager style. The reflection you see may be a difficult thing for you to handle, but do not response by trying to defend or to rationalize it as something not being of your making. As difficult as it may be, managers need to face the reality that their team and organization's culture is a reflection of their leadership, leading to the concept of the *leader-manager*. Accepting this responsibility is the first step to change, and as we all know, change begins with ourselves.

As Gandhi said many years ago, we all need to strive to become the "change we want to see in the world"… In the case of *management for results*, we need to be the change we want to see in others!

Frank Voehl and H. James Harrington
Series Editors

Innovation infrastructure™ master plan

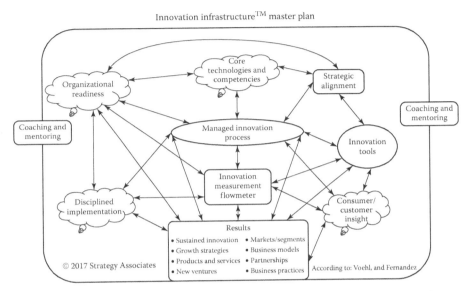

Note: This model, which was developed by Frank Voehl with Rick Fernandez, is the framework around which some of the Sections of the book are organized.

It is discussed in detail in the associated Prologue: Innovation Master Plan Framework.

Please read it before you do any work on the framework itself.

Can you afford to be a dreamer in today's economy? The answer is that you can't afford not to be. This book offers pragmatic solutions to building an innovative organization.

The magic will be up to you.

The Framework for Innovation

An Entrepreneur's Guide to the
Body of Innovation Knowledge

By

Frank Voehl, H. James Harrington,
Rick Fernandez, and Brett Trusko

CRC Press
Taylor & Francis Group
Boca Raton London New York

CRC Press is an imprint of the
Taylor & Francis Group, an **informa** business

A PRODUCTIVITY PRESS BOOK

CRC Press
Taylor & Francis Group
6000 Broken Sound Parkway NW, Suite 300
Boca Raton, FL 33487-2742

© 2019 by Taylor & Francis Group, LLC
CRC Press is an imprint of Taylor & Francis Group, an Informa business

No claim to original U.S. Government works

Printed on acid-free paper

International Standard Book Number-13: 978-1-482-25895-0 (Hardback)

Visit the Taylor & Francis Web site at
http://www.taylorandfrancis.com

and the CRC Press Web site at
http://www.crcpress.com

Contents

Prologue: Innovation Master Plan Framework

Langdon Morris and Frank Voehl

For the existing enterprise, whether business or public-service institution, the controlling word in the term "entrepreneurial management" is "*entrepreneurial.*" For the new venture, it is "*management.*" In the existing business, it is the existing that is the main obstacle to entrepreneurship. In the new venture, it is its absence. The new venture has an idea. It may have a product or a service. It may even have sales, and sometimes quite a substantial volume of them. It surely has costs. And it may have revenues and even profits. What it does not have is a "business," a viable, operating, organized "masterplan" ("present"), in which people know where they are going, what they are supposed to do, and what the results are or should be. But unless a new venture develops into a new business and makes sure of being "managed" with a masterplan, it will not survive, no matter how brilliant the entrepreneurial idea, how much money it attracts, how good its products, nor even how great the demand for them.

Peter F. Drucker
Innovation and Entrepreneurship

In a nutshell: An innovation infrastructure master plan (see Figure 0.1) is only as good as your organization's ability to execute it, and your execution ability depends upon, for the most part, your innovation mind-set. The best-practice innovation framework should be useful to all types of organizations, large and small, public and private, and must necessarily address and organize a very broad range of issues, from the 10,000 foot big-picture perspective of innovation strategy, down to the deep-down inner secrets of creative thought, along with everything in between.

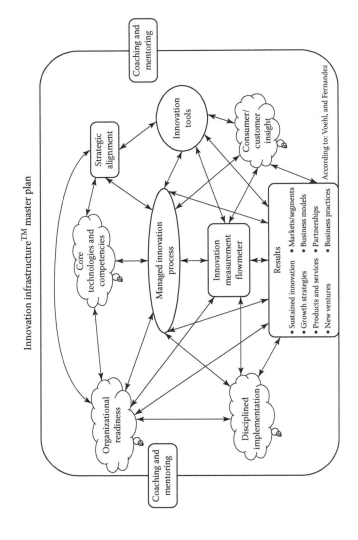

Innovation infrastructure™ master plan

Coaching and mentoring

Strategic alignment

Innovation tools

Consumer/ customer insight

Core technologies and competencies

Managed innovation process

Innovation measurement flowmeter

Results
- Sustained innovation
- Growth strategies
- Products and services
- New ventures
- Markets/segments
- Business models
- Partnerships
- Business practices

Organizational readiness

Disciplined implementation

Coaching and mentoring

According to: Voehl, and Fernandez

FIGURE 0.1

The innovation infrastructure master plan.

OVERVIEW

The innovation infrastructure and master plan described in this book is intended to offer a detailed and comprehensive approach to one of the most difficult and challenging problems: the problem of how to govern your organization's innovation initiatives in the middle of turbulent change. Progress in any field requires the development of a framework, a structure that organizes the accumulating knowledge, enables people to master it, and unifies the key discoveries into a set of principles that makes them understandable and actionable. Law, government, science, technology, business, and medicine have all evolved such frameworks, and each field progresses as new insights emerge that enhance the depth and effectiveness of the principles, and which are then translated into improvements in practice.

This prologue describes a holistic, multidisciplinary framework that will enable your organization and its leaders to take a strategic approach to innovation. The framework combines non-traditional, creative approaches to business innovation with conventional strategy development models. The framework model brings together perspectives from a number of complementary disciplines: the non-traditional approaches to innovation found in the business creativity movement; multiple-source strategy consulting; the new product development perspective of many leading industrial design firms; qualitative consumer/customer research; future-based research found in think tanks and traditional scenario planning; and organizational development (OD) practices that examine the effectiveness of an organization's culture, processes, and structure.

Our framework consists of a well-integrated cohesive set of practices that will look to inspire imaginative innovation teams to look beyond the obvious and explore a broad range of possibilities, in order to identify significant opportunities and make informed decisions about the most promising paths to pursue. Our goal is to create a shared vision for growth, along with defining pragmatic action plans that bridge *from the future back to the present*, while attempting to align the organization around the requirements for success. As Peter Drucker, *Innovation and Entrepreneurship*, once said: *"The earlier changes are discerned, the earlier the opportunities they create can be converted into innovations"*

Our innovation infrastructure model calls for a "whole-systems" approach* that operates on multiple levels:

- It blends non-traditional and traditional approaches to business strategy.
- It deploys the practices of "industry foresight," "consumer/customer insight," and "strategic alignment" as a foundation.
- It supplements them with more conventional approaches and models.
- It combines two seemingly paradoxical mind-sets: expansive, visionary thinking that imaginatively explores long-term possibilities; and pragmatic, down-to-earth implementation activities that lead to short-term, measurable business impacts.

SERENDIPITOUS VS. STRATEGIC INNOVATION

Many organizations rely on serendipitous acts of creativity to foster innovation. Others take an ad hoc, unstructured approach, which often results in only incremental improvements with poor implementation that can lack sponsorship. Our strategic innovation infrastructure is a "whole-systems" systematic approach focused on generating beyond incremental, breakthrough, or discontinuous innovations. Innovation becomes "strategic" when it is an intentional, repeatable process that creates a significant difference in the value delivered to consumers, customers, partners, and the corporation. A strategic innovation infrastructure generates a portfolio of breakthrough business growth opportunities using a disciplined yet creative process.

As Langdon Morris points out in *Agile Innovation*, humanity's understanding of innovation hasn't progressed as much as our understanding of law, because while the intuitively driven practice of innovation is as old as our species, the pursuit of innovation as a systematic, manageable discipline has been practiced for only the last couple of hundred years; systematic research and development began in

---

* When the ancient Greeks explored what constituted the ideal citizen, they identified four qualities: physically fit and strong, emotionally balanced and mature, mentally agile and alert, and having a spiritual or moral order. They saw those qualities as living in the soma – the whole-systems embodiment of the self. The Greeks viewed the living body in its wholeness – mind, body, and spirit as one. The same can be said for the modern-day entrepreneur.

the chemical industry in the 1850s, a mere 160 years ago, so we're still separating the myths or magic from the realities of methodology.

Accordingly, the suggested innovation framework should be a best practice that is useful to all types of organizations. First of all, we need to know how to envision, produce, and manage a disciplined but agile innovation process. Next, how to develop the innovation culture and bring forth the creative spirit from both the managers and the workers in your organization. And we also need tools. And while these are complex topics, it is absolutely necessary that the innovation framework itself remains simple and accessible.

DIMENSIONS OF THE INNOVATION INFRASTRUCTURE FRAMEWORK

- A *managed innovation process* lies at the core of the innovation infrastructure approach. By facilitating the interplay between external perspectives and an organization's internal capabilities and business practices, and by looking beyond what is obvious, it is possible to inspire the collective imagination in the "wisdom-of-the-crowd" fashion to explore a diverse array of innovation possibilities. The process contains an *innovation flowmeter* and is designed and managed to galvanize an organization around shared visions, goals, and actions.
- *Industry foresight* provides a top-down/bottom-up perspective that seeks to understand the complex forces driving change, including emerging and converging trends, potential dislocations, new technologies, competitive dynamics, and alternative scenarios.
- *Consumer/customer insight* provides a "read-the-tea-leaves" perspective, a deep understanding of both the articulated (explicitly stated) and unarticulated (latent or unrecognized) needs of existing and potential consumers and your customers.
- *Core technologies and competencies* is the set of internal capabilities, organizational competencies, and assets that could potentially be leveraged to deliver value to customers, including technologies, intellectual property, brand equity, and strategic relationships.
- *Organizational readiness* may drive or inhibit an organization's ability to act upon and implement new ideas and strategies, and to

successfully manage the operational, political, cultural, and financial demands that will follow.

- *Disciplined implementation*: Success will be enabled or limited by an organization's capacity for effective, disciplined implementation.
- *Coaching and mentoring*: Brings to the table a team of forward-looking external provocateurs and visionary experts to introduce fresh perspectives and insights, challenge established thinking, and collaboratively explore potential growth opportunities, new businesses, new products/services, and innovative business models that may be revealed at the intersection of different worlds and emerging trends.

Our research suggests that after exploring many options and issues, we've found that a powerful framework for thinking about innovation and for defining an innovation master plan can be developed by asking five basic questions around the 5Ws and the 2Hs: Who, What, Where, When, Why, and How and How to measure it.

The goal is to help you achieve a higher level of mastery, and to help guide your organization through the preparation of your innovation infrastructure and associated master plan, in order to help you succeed. For mastery occurs through stages; it proceeds from ignorance to awareness to knowledge of its importance, as shown in Figure 0.2. As you search to

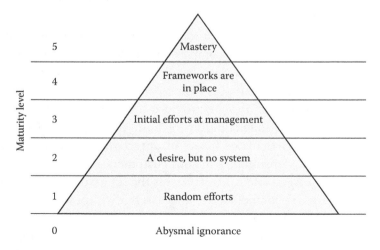

FIGURE 0.2
Maturity level pyramid: From ignorance to awareness.

gather more information, you begin to test your ideas and develop more expertise, while gaining confidence along the way.

1. *Why innovate*: The link between strategy and innovation

    The "why" of innovation is simple: change is accelerating, and we don't know what's coming in the future, but we need to ensure we survive. This means that we must innovate both to prepare for change and to make change in order to improve our position in the market. As we already noted, if things didn't change then your company could keep on doing what it's always done, and there would be no need for innovation. If markets were stable, if customers were predictable, if competitors didn't come up with new products and services, and if technology stayed constant, then we could all just keep going as we did yesterday. But we cannot. Innovation expert Jim Higgins calls it: *innovate or evaporate.*

    But all the evidence shows that change is racing at you faster and faster, which means many new types of vulnerabilities. Technology advances relentlessly, altering the rules of business in all the markets that it touches, which is, of course, every market. Markets are not stable, customers are completely fickle, and competitors are aggressively targeting your share of the pie. So please ask yourself, "Are we managing with the realities of change in mind? And are we handling uncertainty?"

2. *What to innovate*? Over the past 20 years, we have come to recognize that the unpredictable nature of change requires us to prepare for a wider range of innovation options for many, many possible futures. We call these options an investment portfolio. As with any portfolio, some innovation project investments will do well, while others will not. In the case of the innovation portfolio, the disparity between success and failure will often turn out to be very wide because this portfolio is created and managed as a tool for disciplined exploration, and it is by its nature geared toward higher risk in order to successfully meet the continued onslaught of change.

    The alternatives are either to "make change" or to "be changed."

    Since the alternatives are either to "make change" or to "be changed," and making change brings considerable advantages while being changed carries a huge load of negative consequences, then the choice isn't really much of a choice at all. You've got to pursue innovation, and you've got to do it to obtain long-lasting benefits.

3. *Who innovates?* Next, we see that while many people today participate in a robust innovation culture, there are three distinct roles to be played in achieving broad and consistent innovation results. Langdon defines these roles as innovation leaders, who set policies, expectations, goals, and the tone for the innovation culture; innovation geniuses, who come up with great ideas and insights; and innovation champions, who organize the pursuit of innovation and support those who develop great ideas and turn them into business value. The premise is that all three roles must be well played for innovation to flourish, and they must be aligned together in an infrastructure or system that supports success.

4. *Where?* This component of the innovation framework constitutes the basic tools and infrastructure that support the innovation process and the innovating people. Langdon writes* that the four principal elements of this infrastructure are open innovation approaches that engage a broader community in the innovation process; the virtual infrastructure that supports effective remote communication and collaboration; the physical infrastructure, the workplace where people engage together face to face; and the collaborative methods that bring forth the best ideas from all participants, inside and outside the organization, in the most efficient manner possible.

5. *When?* Langdon Morris says that this really is not worth a detailed discussion because you already know the answer: "if you understand that change is accelerating, and if you know how important it is to develop the innovation mind-set and your innovation practice, then the 'when' of innovation is obviously *now*. The market, which ruthlessly demands innovation, and your competitors, who are

---

* Source: *The Agile Innovation Masterplan*, by Langdon Morris et al., Futurelab Press, 2017. Peter Drucker would often say "Is there any doubt in your mind about the importance of innovation? Do you feel that innovation is vital to the future of your company? Then perhaps you've already discovered that the process of innovation is difficult to manage." Langdon Morris calls it "risky, expensive, and unpredictable. Further, some leaders look at the innovations that come from companies like Apple or P&G, and think, 'We don't have people or resources like theirs. We can't do that kind of magic.'" But the truth is that Apple's success, or P&G's, or Toyota's, isn't due to magic; it's because they follow a disciplined innovation process, which we call the innovators masterplan. As innovation coaches, we know that the best way for your firm to become an innovator is to adopt a systematic approach, one that applies the best tools, and also goes beyond tools to help you manage the large-scale risks and opportunities that your organization faces, whether it be a startup or a Fortune 1000. This system elevates innovation to what it really should be, what Drucker defined as a strategic asset to your organization. Defining that strategic asset and system is the intent behind the innovation master plan.

relentlessly creating innovations of their own, wait for no one. You'd better not wait either", he says.

6. *How to innovate?* We know that to answer this question, a rigorous innovation process is both needed and essential. The process must be driven by strategic intent, the "magic-why" of innovation, so in fact the innovation process itself begins with strategy. This is coupled with the "what" of innovation, the design of the ideal innovation portfolio. And while many people tell us that "coming up with ideas" is where innovation begins, we see that to the contrary, ideation actually occurring in the middle, fifth step of a rigorous innovation process.

7. *How to measure innovation?* As this book illustrates, our innovation measurement flowmeter can be helpful here.

The decisions to be made focus on how best to prepare for future markets, and the actions relate to transforming the innovation mind-set into meaningful work throughout the organization, work that results in the development of innovations that impact the market, and improve the position of the organization relative to its competitors. This means, finally, an organization-wide commitment to designing and implementing your version of the innovation master plan.

LINKING STRATEGY WITH INNOVATION INFRASTRUCTURE

Finally, what we're talking about here is the practice of innovation as a vital aspect of corporate or organizational strategy; the rest of this prologue explores how strategy and innovation are intimately linked and should be mutually reinforcing.

A tight linkage between innovation and strategy will certainly be part of your master plan, as innovation by your competitors and by your own firm causes existing products, services, and business models, and indeed entire businesses, to become obsolete. Since innovation is the driver of change, and change is the most fundamentally important driver of business strategy, then it's not an exaggeration to say that innovation is the means of achieving strategy, as we find in the story of Apple's turnaround from the abyss.

When Steve Jobs was asked to return to Apple as chief executive officer in 1997 after an absence of more than 10 years, the company was, to put it bluntly, a mess. If you thought that the PC market was a war between Apple and Microsoft, it was clear that Microsoft had won big. Apple's market share was about 5% and shrinking, and to many observers it seemed that the company was fading away. Its product line was an incoherent collection of 11 different computers, and there didn't seem to be a clear vision guiding the company forward. The board of directors was desperate.*

But did Jobs have a vision for the 21st century, as he had had in the 1970s? Did he still have the magic? We know today that he did, but imagine that it's 1997 and you're Steve Jobs, and you have to figure out how to turn Apple Computer around. What do you do?

Today, Apple's share of the US PC market is growing, although it's still less than 10%. But the iPod is the undisputed MP3 world leader, with 70% of the market; the iPhone became the world standard design for smartphones immediately upon its launch; and the iPad did the same in the tablet market. And now, more than 15 years after Jobs returned, Apple's total market capitalization recently achieved an insider milestone when the company's total stock value surpassed archrival Microsoft, and then another milestone when it became the world's most valuable corporation.

WE SIMPLY CAN'T IMAGINE "APPLE" WITHOUT THINKING ABOUT "INNOVATION"

To summarize, without a focused and successful effort at innovation, Apple surely would not have survived; the quality of its innovative efforts led not only to survival, but to leadership. Innovation was thus essential to the company's strategy, and it was in fact how the strategy was executed, so much so that we simply can't imagine "Apple" without thinking about "innovation."

INNOVATION PLAYS THE SAME ROLE FOR MANY FIRMS

Do you admire Google? Then ask yourself what role innovation plays in Google's strategy. It's obvious that we wouldn't admire Google, and in fact we wouldn't even know about Google if it weren't for innovation.

---

* Source: *The Agile Innovation Masterplan,* by Langdon Morris et al., Futurelab Press, 2017.

The very existence of the company is based on a single strategic insight and on two critical innovations that made the strategy real. The insight was that as the number of web pages grew, the Internet's potential as an information resource was surpassing all other resources for scale, speed, and convenience, but it was getting progressively more difficult for people to find the information they were looking for.

People therefore came to value better search results, and Google's first innovation to address that need was its PageRank system, developed in 1995, an algorithm for Internet searches that returned better results than any other search engine at the time.

The second innovation was a business model innovation, which turned the company into a financial success along with its technical search success. When Google's leaders realized in 2000 that they could sell advertising space at auction in conjunction with key words that Google users searched for, they unleashed a multi-billion-dollar profit machine. The integration of these two innovations provided a multiplicative advantage, and Google's competitors are falling by the wayside as the company continues to dominate.

As a result, in November 2010, Ask.com threw in the towel with only 2% of the market for Internet search after trying for five years to compete with Google following its $1.85 billion acquisition by Barry Diller's IAC/InterActiveCorp. Diller wrote, "We've realized in the last few years you can't compete head on with Google." Yahoo, a much bigger company than Ask, came to the same conclusion earlier in 2010 when it decided to position itself as a media company rather than a technology company, and outsourced its search function to Microsoft's Bing.

What other companies do you like? Do you also admire Starbucks? Or Disney? Or Toyota? Or BMW? They're certainly innovators, and many of us appreciate them precisely because of it. So, the relationship between strategy and innovation is vital, and the important role that innovation plays in transforming the concepts of strategy into realities in the marketplace tells us that none of these companies could have succeeded without innovation. This is the "why" of innovation.

CREATING AND MANAGING INNOVATION PORTFOLIOS

Investors in all types of assets classes create portfolios to help them attain optimal returns while choosing the right level of risk, and innovation managers must do the same for the projects they're working on. Innovation is inherently risky. You invest money and time, possibly a lot of both, to create, explore, and develop new ideas into innovations, but regardless of how good you are, many of the resulting outputs will never earn a dime.

Is that failure or success? It could be both. The degree of failure or success will be determined not by the fate of individual ideas and projects, but by the overall success of all projects taken together. Hence, the best way to manage the risk is to create an "innovation portfolio."

So what do you do? You allocate capital across a range of investments to obtain the best return while reducing risk, and then you manage each project aggressively to make it work.

The underlying principle of portfolio management is that the degree of risk and the potential rewards have to be considered together. In a rapidly changing market, the nature of innovation risk is inherently different than in a slower-changing industry such as, say, road construction, because the faster the rate of change in a company's markets, the bigger the strategic risks it faces. The faster the change, the more rapidly will existing products and services become obsolete, a factor we refer to as "the burn down rate." The faster the burn down, the more urgent is the innovation requirement.

This will necessarily affect the composition of an innovation portfolio by inducing a company to take greater risks in its innovation efforts. Hence, the ideal innovation portfolio of each organization will necessarily be different: Alibaba, Apple, NASA, Genentech, Toyota, Union Pacific, GE, and Starbucks are all innovative organizations, but when it comes to their innovation portfolios it's obvious that they cannot be the same in content or style. *Depending on the questions at hand, senior managers may have tens or dozens of relevant portfolio views to consider.*

A further key to the dynamics of a successful portfolio is described in portfolio theory, which tells us that the components of a portfolio must be non-correlated, meaning that various investments need to perform differently under a given set of economic or business conditions. In the case of innovation, "non-correlated" means that every firm needs to be working on potential innovations that address a wide range of future market possibilities in order to ensure that the available options – and here is the key point – will be useful under a wide variety of possible future conditions.

The need for broad diversity in the portfolio also reminds us that we need to develop all four types of innovation; so what we're really talking about are five different portfolios. There will be a different portfolio for each type of innovation – breakthroughs, incremental innovations, new business models, and new ventures – and a fifth portfolio that is an aggregate of all four. There may also be portfolios for different business units or product lines, so depending on the questions at hand, senior managers may have tens or dozens of relevant portfolio views to consider.

SUMMARY

In summary, we should note that each different type of portfolio will be managed in a different process, by different people, who have different business goals, and who are measured and possibly rewarded differently. Hence, metrics and rewards are inherent in the concept of the portfolio, and the master plan also calls for the design of the ideal metrics by which the portfolio should be measured.

And, because we're preparing for a variety of future conditions, it's obvious that some of the projects will never actually become relevant to the market, and they will therefore never return value in and of themselves. But, this does not mean that they are failures; it means that we prepared for a wide range of eventualities, and some of those futures never appeared, but we were nevertheless wise to prepare in this way. This sort of "failure" is a positive enhancement of our likelihood of survival and ultimate success, so it's not failure in a negative sense at all. By analogy, I carry a spare tire in my car, but it's not a failure if I never have occasion to use it.

Therefore, the process of creating and managing innovation portfolios cannot be overseen by the chief financial officer's office as a purely financial matter. Instead, the finance office and innovation managers are partners in the process of innovation development. Hence, innovation portfolio management is like venture capital investing, early stage investing where it's impossible to precisely predict the winners, but nevertheless a few great successes more than make up for the many failures.

1

Preparing Your Organization for Innovation

A man should never be appointed to a managerial position if his vision focuses on people's weaknesses rather than on their strengths. The man who always knows what people cannot do, but never sees what they can do, will undermine the spirit of the organization. Of course, a manager should have a clear grasp of the limitations of his people, but he should see these as limitations on what they can do, and as a challenge to them to do better. The entrepreneur always searches for change, responds to it, and exploits it as an opportunity using minimal effort in a lean manner.

Peter Drucker
The Practice of Management

In a nutshell: Every idea that is created is usually created for a particular purpose, in order to deliver some sort of value to the entrepreneur/creator. And, for that value to be enjoyed, that "thing" must be utilized by someone or something else. This is obvious enough. And this is what happens, but with an important caveat that is not commonly recognized: *there is always some value left over that is not utilized*. Only if the resource is utilized completely, at the right time and for the right time, absolutely properly, and at the right rate (in other words, perfectly) is all the potential value realized. But, because usually such perfection does not exist, there is always residual value remaining that can be retrieved from that resource. This makes everything around us an *undervalued resource*, a resource that contains untapped, residual value. On the other hand, many people believe that innovation is accidental. Innovation must be something that happens while you are taking a shower, riding your bike, or eating lunch. Of course, innovation can happen in those places, but the chances are that these are just great ideas and the finer points haven't been fleshed out in the shower. This also holds true for organizations, and this chapter deals with getting the enterprise ready in a Lean manner, in order to effectively extract the waiting new ideas fully.*

INTRODUCTION

Think back to when you were in school, lounging around with your friends and solving the world's problems. The problem is that most ideas died before they were fully born. There are many reasons why great ideas never got implemented, but perhaps the most important reason (and something that is changing in the world today) is that there was no infrastructure in place to take a concept and turn it into a marketable product or service.

To a company, this means several things:

1. The enterprise must have a funnel to intake ideas (all ideas, not just the executives').†
2. The enterprise must have the ability to prioritize the ideas that is seen by the employees as fair and impartial.
3. The enterprise must have the funding in place to support individuals in the development of the ideas.
4. The enterprise must have a system that incentivizes individuals to develop the idea inside the company and not feel forced to leave.

---

* Technology, tastes, habits, capabilities, and resources are evolving faster and faster. How many of us knew 10 years ago that we would *need* a portable device that held over 1000 songs? Apple convinced us that we did, and now most of us have at least one iPod. Kodak, whose engineers invented digital photography, is not even in the digital camera game now because leadership did not perceive that the business would evolve in that direction.

† Imagine you are the chief executive officer (CEO) of a small business and your task is to turn around the company, or double revenues over the next three years, or attain any other similarly lofty goal. You aren't going to achieve that objective by doubling down on the strategies that have created the status quo. You need to change course. Perhaps, the answer lies in new products or a new business model. You need to find a new recipe for success that is not only different from what you have done in the past, but you need one that is compellingly different from what your competitors are doing. In short, you need to get the company ready for an innovation.

Consider for a moment university systems; granted, many have been enlightened and have "changed" the way they deal with inventions, most still have not. In most cases, professors who invent new products have to deal with an organization that makes it difficult to get others attention, does not supply much funding for those inventors and then insists on a disproportionate share of the ownership, citing ownership because property was invented during the course of their employment.

To compound the issue, academics tend to be exempt employees, and employers might claim that all of the employees' time is the property of the institution. It is no wonder then, that in the course of our business, one of the most frequent questions asked of us is how to invent; at the same time, how to protect the intellectual property (IP) from the claims of the educational institution for whom they work. In fact, we have many colleagues who have given up and would rather keep an invention to themselves than "give" the majority ownership to their employer. In this case, no one wins – the inventor gets nothing and the institution gets nothing, and worse than that, society loses because many great ideas are never or are underdeveloped. This is the so-called untapped value.

This recognition of the existence of untapped value – the notion of the *undervalued resource* – is fundamental to the creation of an innovation for the entrepreneur. Because there is unused, residual value inherent in any particular resource in the first place – effort that has been previously invested in that resource and that *does not need to be replicated* for that value to be enjoyed – its value is lying there just waiting for you to take advantage of it; provided that you extract that value "cheaply," i.e. with minimal effort concerning the intake of the new ideas.

ON THE INTAKE OF IDEAS

I once knew a chap who had a system of just hanging a baby on the clothes line to dry and he was greatly admired by his fellow citizens for having discovered a wonderful innovation on changing a diaper.

Damon Runyon 1880–1946, Newspaperman/Author

How many of us really look at the world around us? Over the many years that I have been in the business world, I am constantly amazed at what you find out by talking to the rank-and-file employee. In fact, in my consulting practice, I make it a point to get out of the executive suite and spend time in the lunchrooms, break rooms, and other venues in which the "average" employee spends their time. As a consultant, it is amazing the kinds of solutions to corporate problems that you can get straight from the employee. The problem is that when you search for stories such as these on the web, you will have a very difficult time finding any.*

This lack of stories is not because of a lack of ideas, or a nefarious attempt by management to take all the credit (although this scenario isn't out of the realm of possibility). Instead, it is the general inability to capture ideas from the organization and then do something with those ideas. One organization I worked with held a town hall meeting and informed the employees that the only way the organization would survive into the future would be for each and every employee to think out of the box, be innovative, and communicate their great ideas to management. It was a wonderful speech, and it seemed as though the employees left the theater ready to save the company.

In the days following the speech, I approached employees and asked them about whether they had attended the town hall, and what they thought of the chance to submit their ideas to management. First, I found that many of the employees did not bother to attend at all. Seems that once you have heard the propaganda from management, you've heard the propaganda; it doesn't change much. Second, I found that many of the employees who were there, were busy playing with their smartphones and expressed the same concerns as the group that didn't attend. The third group is where I found gold. It seems that this group heard what the executive said and was energized by the whole concept. They asked where they could go to submit their suggestions, and they had a lot of suggestions. This is when I went back to management.

The executive was thrilled that a third of the employees were excited to be a part of the future of the organization. He couldn't wait to see the ideas that came in, and was genuinely enthusiastic about the possibilities that were about to present themselves. Then came the killer ... how were they going to collect and analyze these ideas? We suggested that they build a system that would allow not only employees to submit ideas, but also

---

* As a former chief operating officer (COO) for the Harrington Group International, many clients were well-known brands and a story-based innovation focus is what we always tried to integrate within the groups I consulted with – it was always a significant challenge! The challenge was, and is in many companies, that there is a divide between the "science of IT" and the needs of the business. Meaning that information technology (IT) folks are often enamored with the technology and the science of systematizing business operations, irrespective of the direct value to profitability and nurturing all of the social aspects that go into making a company truly profitable.

customers. We suggested a system that would allow employees to track their ideas and comment on others ideas – an idea management system. We went so far as to recommend a couple of web-based systems that we felt were very good, and would require very little change in the way they did business. So what did they do?

With good intent, he suggested that he already had the solution and that it was already in place throughout the organization. Intrigued, I asked what this solution was and he responded that the company had had suggestion boxes for decades.

Best I can tell, suggestion boxes were introduced at the turn of the 20th century.* As a little piece of history, one of the authors spent his youth as a janitor in a hospital. A common cleanup call was to remove trash, food, liquids, and all other manner of waste from suggestion boxes. Whether the suggestion box was used as a trash receptacle by accident or as a statement to management, we have been struck by the fact that over an entire career (we have better than 100 years of management experience between us), neither of us can ever remember a good idea coming in through a suggestion box.

When I informed the executive that (not the same words I used) his idea was one of the dumbest things I had ever heard, he thanked me, paid my

---

* Some suggest that this was a modern idea introduced by Heinz around 1909, but the actual place or date doesn't matter to this discussion. We do know that it has been a popular mechanism for soliciting comments from employees and customers for over 100 years.

consulting bill, and as far as I can tell to this day hasn't received a single valuable suggestion from any of his 7000 employees.

Ideally, an idea management system requires several important things to be effective:

- Accessibility
- Flexibility
- Graphically appealing
- Crowd based
- Team based
- Ease of use
- Algorithms for weighting
- A Lean approach supporting it
- Adaptability
- Reflection on the future of the business
- Consideration of some rewards

GETTING ORGANIZED FOR INNOVATION

There are two or three basic things that an entrepreneur can use to get the organization ready for innovation: absorb data better and encourage innovation pathways at all levels.

The following advice is from Charles Duhigg's book *Smarter, Faster, Better* (Random House, New York, 2016). In this book are eight key concepts that can be used to ready your organization for innovation: motivation, teams, focus, goal setting, managing others, decision-making, innovation mind-set, and absorbing data.

To Absorb Data Better:

- When we encounter new information, we should force ourselves to do *something* with it. Write yourself a note explaining what you just learned, or figure out a small way to test an idea, or graph a series of data points onto a piece of paper, or force yourself to explain an idea to a friend. Every choice we make in life is an experiment–the trick is getting ourselves to see the data embedded in those decisions, and then to use it somehow so we learn from it.

1. Get smarter. Create an "association-type" database using tools such as SEBIRS or TRIZ.
2. Get quicker with Lean.
3. Get better.

The key to getting an organization ready for innovation is – in today's world – managing how you think, rather than what you think. This shift can transform your life. At the core of *getting ready* are eight concepts – from motivation and goal setting to focus and decision-making – that explain why some people and companies get so much done more innovatively, while others do not.

The way we frame our daily decisions; the big ambitions we embrace and the easy goals we ignore; the cultures we establish as leaders to drive innovation; and the way we interact with data – these are the things that separate the merely busy from the genuinely innovative entrepreneurs.*

---

* Key traits for entrepreneurs in any firm are humility and an open mind. They need to be humble enough that they do not assume customers will want their product or service forever, and that we do not take their loyalty for granted. With that comes an understanding of the necessity to make our own products or services redundant. That is a fundamental characteristic of innovative companies. We also need to be open-minded enough to *see* different paths in the evolution of our business and be willing to invest and uncover where those paths can take us.

Drawing on the latest findings in neuroscience, psychology, and behavioral economics – as well as the experiences of CEOs, educational reformers, four-star generals, airplane pilots, and songwriters – this well-researched handbook explains that the most innovative people, companies, and organizations don't merely act differently; they view the world, and their choices, in profoundly different ways. They know that innovation and productivity rely on absorbing data and making choices.

To Encourage Innovation:

- Creativity often emerges by combining old ideas in new ways–and "innovation brokers" are key. To become a broker yourself and encourage brokerage within your organization:

- Be sensitive to your own experiences. Paying attention to how things make you think and feel is how we distinguish clichés from real insights. Study your own emotional reactions.

- Recognize that the stress that emerges amid the creative process isn't a sign everything is falling apart. Rather, creative desperation is often critical: Anxiety can be what often pushes us to see old ideas in new ways.

- Finally, remember that the relief accompanying a creative breakthrough, while sweet, can also blind us to alternatives. By forcing ourselves to critique what we've already done, by making ourselves look at it from different perspectives, by giving new authority to someone who didn't have it before, we retain clear eyes.

SEBIRS can help you in your business when you need innovative ideas* to

- Save money
- Make money
  Often, you cannot come up with such ideas easily for three main reasons:
  - You don't know where to find an innovative idea or how to develop one.
  - You do know that developing an innovative idea – usually by trial and error – is very time-consuming.
  - You do know that an innovative idea (if you find or develop one) will probably be costly (Figure 1.1).

---

* SEBIRS can help you by providing (1) methods whereby you can use your natural creativity to come up with innovative ideas; and because you borrowed the essence of those innovative ideas from somewhere else, you can probably (2) create an innovative idea relatively quickly, and (3) create an innovative idea at minimal cost relative to the anticipated benefit. Source: http://www.sebir.com/Guide?Length=4.

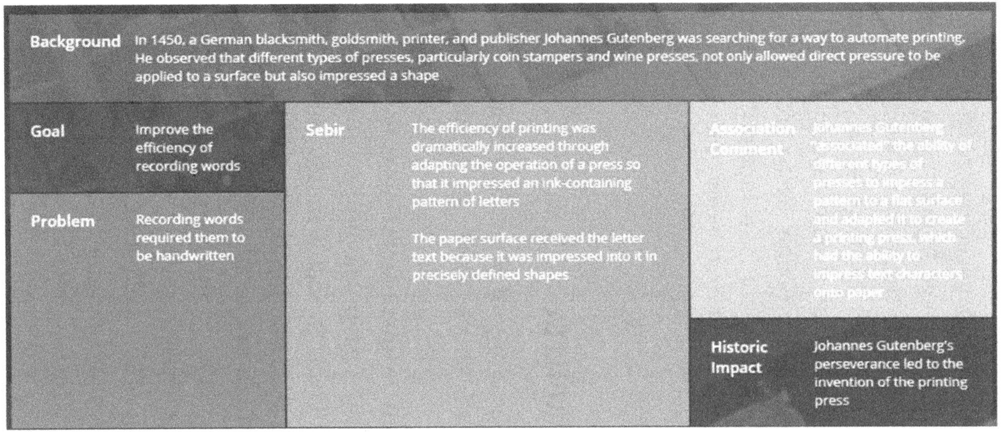

Background	In 1450, a German blacksmith, goldsmith, printer, and publisher Johannes Gutenberg was searching for a way to automate printing. He observed that different types of presses, particularly coin stampers and wine presses, not only allowed direct pressure to be applied to a surface but also impressed a shape	
Goal	Improve the efficiency of recording words	Sebir: The efficiency of printing was dramatically increased through adapting the operation of a press so that it impressed an ink-containing pattern of letters The paper surface received the letter text because it was impressed into it in precisely defined shapes
Problem	Recording words required them to be handwritten	

Association Element	Johannes Gutenberg "speculated" the validity of different types of presses to impress a pattern to a flat surface and adapted it to create a printing press which had the ability to impress text characters onto paper
Historic Impact	Johannes Gutenberg's perseverance led to the invention of the printing press

FIGURE 1.1

Example of a SEBIRS that illustrates the innovation of the printing press in 1450 by Gutenberg.

To make SEBIRS work effectively, the system needs to be accessible by employees (and customers if applicable). For all intents and purposes, the system must be accessible via the Internet or corporate Intranet. Paper-based suggestion boxes offer no tracking to either the organization or the employee. By making the system accessible (preferably from a smartphone as well as a computer), employees can submit ideas on break, while at lunch, or any place else where they feel inspired.*

Yes, accessibility may encourage employees to suggest a lot of crazy things; however, the power of the automated system is its ability for algorithms and peers to sort the serious ideas from the whimsical. An effective idea management system should cost no more than a few dollars per employee per year and is probably best purchased as a cloud-based application. This means that there is no upfront investment other than the cost of customizing the solution to your organization's specific needs.

FLEXIBILITY AND ABILITY

Flexibility refers to the ability of your organization to change what is important to it, without having to hard code a computer system to handle the changing priorities of the organization. Specifically, if you need a system that is weighted to manufacturing this year and the customer experience next year, the system should be easily able to accommodate your needs. Once again, this probably means that a web-based solution is ideal. However, it is possible that due to confidentiality and/or trade secrets, you may want an in-house solution.

Once again, these systems do not have to be overly expensive and in fact may cost you less than installing suggestion boxes conveniently throughout the organization, collecting the suggestions, transcribing them into some coherent system, and then analyzing them. An added benefit is that you don't have to hold a town hall meeting every time the organization changes its priorities.

---

* There is a nice post on Innovate on Purpose, Jeffrey Phillips blog, pointing out that "Nobody ever got fired for failing to innovate." While that's not entirely true (we all have known a few who have), the core message is definitely on the mark. Most of the time, short-term urgencies create pressure that creates an environment that suppresses innovation. It is far easier to do what is needed to nominally meet our performance metrics than to take the perceived risks of finding an innovative way to exceed them.

While you may not think you understand some of the people in your organization, one thing that is becoming universally accepted in the world today, especially in the innovation space, is that applications should not only be functional, but might potentially be "gamified." While this may be a made-up word for this discussion, the point is that people are expecting to get something back from all their transactions and interactions. Why not make it fun to submit and manage innovative ideas. Consider Facebook and the concept of "likes."

What makes someone post something and ask for "likes" from his or her friends? There is no monetary reward and I have found myself liking something that in retrospect I may actually be embarrassed to have been associated with (think cat with a mustache picture). As we all know, many times the majority of the current friends a person has are their colleagues and co-workers. What harm would "likes" do when someone submits an idea? I wouldn't recommend that you bet your business on a popularity contest, but why not build it into an algorithm. What about a voting system where employees could be given a certain number of votes on ideas? Maybe you could reward votes that flow to money-making ideas with cash rewards – an idea makes it to market, makes a billion dollars, and everyone who voted for it gets $100 per vote they placed on the idea? There are a million ways to make the process more fun and exciting. Ways that reward employees for being engaged and working on ideas that are serious and rewarding to the company.

As mentioned in the previous paragraph, crowd-based opportunities allow the company to gather ideas from people who may not have submitted an idea before. Another possibility in this vein is including the crowd. Create groups within your idea management system that allow the collective wisdom of the crowd to shine through. Perhaps you create, or allow teams to create themselves. If there is no limit on the number, you may find that an entire department comes together to work out a problem. Perhaps you could find a way to refine an idea by presenting it to your customers? The possibilities are endless, and completely possible thanks to advances in modern technology.

Encouraging teams creates a comradery that may spill over into other parts of the business. In the past, this was accomplished by having a bowling or softball league. Find any way you can to pull teams together to think about ways to make their team, the company, the world a better place. Don't buy the argument about the boss being above the team.

Just consider Market Basket and CEO Arthur Demoulas.* After his firing by family members, the company faced walkouts by a majority of the employees. Eventually, the company was in such bad shape because of the mass employee walkout that they were forced to hire "Arthur T" back. Last we checked, he had rolled up his sleeves and started to restock the perishables at the company stores – not oversee the restocking – he actually participated in round the clock restocking! This type of teamwork is too seldom seen in modern companies but is a critical component in innovation.

Got an Idea?

There's an app for that! It seems that everyone has a smartphone in their pocket these days. An app connected directly to the idea management system allows employees to submit ideas when they are struck with them. I have heard numerous stories of people who tell me that they were struck with inspiration while performing everyday tasks such as grocery shopping, taking a shower, or working out, but forgot them an hour later. An idea management system should ideally allow an individual to stop for a moment, open the app, dictate in a few details, and either park the idea temporarily or submit for consideration by the system.

Too many systems force you to fill out tens of pages of details, schematics, and cost estimates. Most of your employees and many of the lesser educated might find this process intimidating and a waste of their time. Additionally, a poorly worded proposal is less likely to be considered by a management team who might be evaluating the opportunities. Take away boundaries for submitting ideas and you just might find Einstein on your janitorial team.

Deciding what is important to your organization is one of the most challenging parts of innovation. The "Catch-22" comes from the fact that algorithms require assumptions. Consider that if Apple computers in the year 2000 only entertained ideas about computers, they may have missed the iPod and iPhone. iPad might have still come about, and legend has it that the iPad did in fact precede the iPhone in the research lab, but someone had the great idea that a small iPad would make a really great phone. So, be careful not to limit your thinking to your current line of business.

---

* http://www.bostonglobe.com/business/2014/09/11/after-epic-market-basket-battle-arthur-demoulas-happy-just-being-grocer/Iqd3AyAX6qh36fhldPOyPN/story.html.

Each company is different so it wouldn't be prudent to suggest algorithms in this book. Challenge your innovation team to develop algorithms that give an advantage to the very best ideas without eliminating the unusual or unconventional.

Equal Consideration

A big problem with the suggestion box is the lack of transparency in the process. I know of an individual who went to a company as a consultant and was asked by the CEO what he would do if he were in charge. Naïvely, perhaps, this individual laid out the long-term strategy for the organization in five parts. Thinking that he would be engaged to participate in the development and execution of the strategy, he was surprised to read an interview with the CEO a month later where he outlined to a reputable business paper his five-part plan to change the course of the organization. Apparently embarrassed by his behavior, to this day, he refuses to return phone calls from the consultant.

Too many people have experienced just this kind of behavior in today's business environment. Executives have asked for suggestions just to turn around and take credit for the ideas of an employee. This isn't limited to rank-and-file employees. Professors complain about IP literally taken from them by universities under the auspices of employment contracts. Employees refuse to build anything new on their jobs for fear that the company will take it, claiming that they own it because they give the employee a paycheck. While this may have worked at a time when corporations literally controlled the capital and means of production, this is becoming less and less true every day.

There are probably businesses that you think would be impossible for the average employee to get into, but consider Elon Musk. His biography might include being born wealthy, but not so wealthy that most would consider taking on an entire automotive industry or start to build space planes in competition with a company the size of Boeing. We are also seeing a pronounced shift from internal research and development to outsourcing that functions either through the acquisition of smaller competitors or partnering with universities to develop new ideas.

No matter how you slice it though, it will always be cheaper and probably more effective to keep innovation inside the company. Even the 10,000-pound gorilla of innovation, Google, employed Kevin Systrom (CEO of Instagram), and may have missed out on an innovation opportunity when he left to start Instagram. Apparently, he was interested in photo sharing well before he ever got to Google. Regardless, the startup culture probably isn't that strong in your organization and so your opportunities to reward people with great ideas are simpler and easier to accomplish. Most people have a certain degree of loyalty to the people with whom they work. Almost every employee I have ever had the opportunity to interview would be thrilled to do what he or she can to help out the organization. Unfortunately, many companies do not recognize this and miss opportunities.

Take, for example, alumni giving at a university. Sure, the years spent in college might have been some of the best of your life. For many people though, college is expensive and their careers may not be everything that they hoped for. However, after graduation, many of these people will donate to the alumni association. It's probably likely that they donate because of an affinity to the organization. So, the question is "how much would they give if they had an annuity?" In other words, what would happen to giving if the majority of students graduated from college with an annuity from some product or service they invented?

Your employees are similar. Given the opportunity, most of them will likely give away any good ideas they have, but imagine what you would get from them if you were able to offer them a piece of the action? 1% ownership in a multimillion-dollar innovation is little more than a rounding error to the organization.

Your employees would be thrilled to bring you ideas if they just felt like there was some recognition and reward for their contribution. The company must have the ability to prioritize the ideas that is seen by the employees as fair and impartial.

Internal Venture Capital

In any startup, the biggest hurdle is capital. We can't begin to tell you how many companies profess that they want innovation and will even reward it with a piece of the action. Many universities reward professors with a percentage ownership in the products they invent. The professor is then told to develop it on his or her own time. The problem with this logic is that, while the university justifies the strategy by saying that they pay the professor a salary, they are not actually investing in the product. Accordingly, we talk to many academics who will not develop any new products within their own university, preferring to leave their job than trade a majority ownership in their IP for the rather meager salary of a professor.

This is no different in companies that ask employees to participate in the development of new products while performing their full-time job and offer little or no funding. To perform a simple calculation on the cost-benefit you could imagine:

Annual salary of employee	$50,000
Ownership of product (this is generous)	50%
Sales of new product	1,000,000
Time to develop	2 years

If the employee was able to spend full time on a project for 2 years, the company is out $100,000 (simplified, not including benefits, etc.). The employee knows that the product is worth $1 million and also knows that the company will keep 50% of the ownership. At this point, even a middle school dropout can see that the math doesn't work, and the employee, rightly or wrongly, feels that they are being taken advantage of. The employee takes his or her idea and walks away from the company, in many cases only to sell the new company to a competitor or back to the original company for probably much more than a million dollars.

A problem with our argument is that the company always takes the risk when an employee is taking none – and risk should be rewarded. Granted, this is a viable argument, but at what point does the formula change? All ideas are not equally risky; therefore, a policy of some fixed percentage ownership across the board leads to poor ideas being developed internally while the most promising ideas take a walk.

One solution to this paradox is to deploy internal investment funds and a team of internal venture capitalists to seriously evaluate the viability of each and every idea submitted through the idea management system. A problem that many organizations have today is that IP attorneys instead of businesspeople run the commercialization and/or "innovation" department. One individual we worked with allowed the commercialization department (run by IP attorneys) to apply for a patent on a product he developed, and instantly sold the IP for an amount that 5 years later turned out to be significantly less than they could have sold it for if they had consulted professionals in the field.

In fact, the acquiring company was now charging more for the inventor to use the technology than his organization was paid originally.

Don't get us wrong, attorneys are important players on the team, but creating a small venture capital organization with funding inside your organization can evaluate opportunities and invest in a way that makes sense for each opportunity rather than applying an across-the-board formula that may harbor the worst ideas while chasing the best away.

Incentives

As discussed in many books on innovation, what are the incentives that keep good ideas in your company? How can you be sure that the best ideas do not leave in this day and age when it is easier than ever to file a patent, raise some funds, and become the next big thing? Options include:

- Create an internal mechanism to develop innovation (20% time)
- Promote a separate organization to develop innovation (a lab or accelerator)
- Pay people what their inventions are worth (partner)
- If you love them, let them go ... partner with people with good ideas

Google has had the much-emulated 20% time for many years. The 20% time policy led to products like Google News, Google's autocomplete system (Google Suggest), Gmail, and AdSense, the advertising engine developed to support Gmail financially, now producing about 25% of Google's revenue. The program works something like this:

The company allows its employees to work 20% of their time on projects that they deem promising. This means 1 day per week, 4 days per month, or a couple of months per year. This time is spent on a "Google-related" passion project that is of their own choosing or of their own creation. What one has to remember though is that even at Google, 20% time is not about getting a day a week to goof-off. In fact, there are serious considerations that need to be examined if you are taking 20% time. Considerations such as bonuses, which may not be awarded to people taking time to work on pet projects. There is potential pressure from others on your team if they do not believe in your project and other such potential disincentives.

How you implement a 20% time program is really different from organization to organization. In fact, a very innovative company, 3M, was the first to offer the program at 15% time. LinkedIn has a program, Facebook has a program, as does Apple. The important thing in this space, however, is that there are so many creative outlets for innovation.

There are hackathons and programming marathons that may not be available in other industries such as health care (imagine a surgeryathon in health care or a drillathon in energy), although a bright individual might be able to figure something out.*

In Houston's Texas Medical Center, a model is being built that is not necessarily unique, but is interesting in the many incarnations that exist. By sharing a space for creation, incubation, and acceleration (CIA site) with many companies, there is the potential for a creative outlet for entrepreneurial members of your organization. If you have an individual in your organization with a promising idea, why not allow them to go to the CIA site and create? By doing this, you may or may not leave them on the payroll, but you allow them to go out and work out their idea. These spaces can conceivably be maker space, where needed equipment and labs are available. The space can charge the individual, your company, or take a piece of the ownership. Once again, the possibilities are only limited by the imagination.

One of the models we like is where a space is created and resources are made available. Ideas are brought into the space and deals are negotiated on a case-by-case basis. This is a particularly effective model in a university setting where a business can create a partnership whereby they send employees to the space and allow the university to evaluate the idea, estimate the effort to develop the company, and then dole out an ownership agreement to the three parties (inventor, employer, and university). Given the bandwidth of most large universities (as well as the available space) and the ability to apply for grants, the university can identify the needed resources (engineers, businesspeople, etc.) that will be necessary to bring the product to market and negotiate the ownership depending on how much effort will be required to complete the idea.

For example, a fully functioning prototype may need little more than a business plan, while a vague idea may need engineers, funding, coaching, etc. In the former, the university may take little ownership, while the employer and employee receive the majority. This is also an effective model if the university can be a trusted third-party negotiator (arbitrator) for your employee, with a fair distribution of the IP to all involved.

---

* We should note that there has been much press lately about Google discontinuing 20% time. While some at Google may say that it is discontinued, there are equal numbers that claim that this is not true. It appears instead that Google has simply created a few more boundaries around the practice and therefore it may not be as easy for some employees.

Another option is to simply become an investor in your employee's idea. For example, if an employee has a great idea, but you are risk averse, simply offer to be the angel investor in their organization. You are able to have some say over the day-to-day operations of the company, and maintain ownership at an amount that is considered fair (of course, fairness is subjective) in the initial negotiations. The nice thing about this is that it can be done inside or outside your organization. Consider an employee who comes up with a new product on his or her own. Under the old model, the employee is told that it's a great idea, but since it was developed on company time, the company owns it and you will receive a $500 bonus at the end of the year – thank you very much.

Under the new paradigm, you have several options not previously considered under the old model. You call the employee in and suggest them in a way that gives the employee some power to create their own future. You offer:

1. You can develop the new idea internally under a 20% time option. We would like to offer you the option of working on your product over the next 3 months and at the end of that time, we will make a go or no-go decision. Should the project be accepted, we will negotiate an agreed-upon amount that is fair to both sides – now get to work.
2. You could offer the employee the option to go on a (paid or unpaid) sabbatical for as much time as they need. We will pay for you to take up residence at the local university, where they will supply you with all the needed resources to make your idea a success. In exchange, we will ask for ownership that will be negotiated by the university. After we agree to the approximate ownership percentage, we will give you some agreed-upon time to complete your project. After completion, you may decide to come back to the company or start the new company yourself. We will retain our ownership in the company and possibly become a customer.
3. We will invest some amount of money in your new venture. As an angel investor, we will exercise control based on our investment. This may mean that we will suggest agents from the company work with you on the idea and possibly the launch either inside or outside the company.

As for simple individual incentives, the world has changed. People no longer have lifetime careers and they will change jobs frequently.

Some statistics say that the youngest millennials will only stay in a job for an average of just over 2 years. What this means to you as an executive is that you need to try to get the most out of your creatives as quickly as possible or they will simply take their ideas to the next employer. No longer is it a viable strategy to sue an employee who starts a company shortly after leaving a job – for one thing, there are too many of them. Instead, find ways to partner with them quickly and offer them a "fair share" of the value in their ideas. Doing so may make you an "employer of choice" and keep these valuable creatives on your payroll longer. If you do it very well, you may find that you become a magnet for creative employees and have ideas coming to you unsolicited. The models are changing and the rewards will accrue to those who think differently.

SUMMARY

There are so many competing interests in large organizations that the legitimate business needs and the resources required to support them often get shifted to fulfilling political agendas or are fragmented in such a way that no business objective gets adequate support. These demands for innovation happen all the time in today's ultra-high pressure business climate. We may not see it directly, but the failure to innovate is punished quite severely in the workplace. The next time you read a blurb about a high-profile CEO being replaced by fresh talent, ask yourself on what opportunity to innovate did the outgoing CEO fail to capitalize.

More importantly, as you pursue your own objectives, are you failing to ask yourself what opportunities for innovation you are passing over in the rush to address the daily urgencies. Remember to keep your eye on the important issues as well – these are often where innovation opportunities are hiding.

You may not be overtly punished for failing to innovate. But, the big rewards will come to you only when you embrace innovation as essential to your personal success. I've been checking back through all the great innovation blogs I like to follow, and I found a nice post on Innovation Management by Chuck Frey titled "The Surprising Connection Between Simplification and Innovation."

It seems rather serendipitous to stumble across this article reviewing Matthew E. May's book *The Laws of Subtraction* because just last night a colleague approached me about a new interface in a product update he had just received. He told me how he very much liked the new interface. What my friend didn't know was the debate that had gone on behind the scenes during the design of this interface. The designer had put together a very visually compelling, but very different design for the new interface. The design included many components and provided for a rich interaction model.

Our concern was that users don't always value richness in interaction; they do like directness and ease of function. So, we asked for an alternative design that drew upon familiar data visualization paradigms to provide a simplified interaction model and that the two designs be tested with actual users. In the end, the simpler design was selected based on user preference.

This was no surprise. The value of simplicity in design has long been recognized, as Peter Drucker emphasized* over 30 years ago, along with seven sources of opportunities that drive innovation.† The very essence of this notion is captured in the discipline of value engineering through value equations and is codified in various systematic innovation methods such as TRIZ. Every journey of innovation should include several stops along the way to ask if the current solution can be simplified. This question alone has the power to drive high value innovations.

---

* To be successful, Drucker wrote that an innovation has to be simple and it has to be focused. It should only do one thing or it confuses people and won't work. All effective innovations are breathtakingly simple.
† Drucker identified seven sources of opportunity that will ultimately drive innovation:

1. The organization's own unexpected successes and failures, and also those of the competition.
2. Incongruities, especially those in a process, such as production or distribution, or incongruities in customer behavior.
3. Process needs.
4. Changes in industry and market structures.
5. Changes in demographics.
6. Changes in meaning and perception.
7. New knowledge.

2

Promoting and Communicating

The people who work within industry or public services know that there are basic flaws. But they are almost forced to ignore them and to concentrate instead on patching here, improving there, fighting the fire or caulking that crack. They are thus unable to take the innovation seriously, let alone to try to compete with it. They do not, as a rule, even notice it until it has grown so big as to encroach on their industry or service, by which time it has become irreversible. In the meantime, the innovators have the field to themselves.

Peter F. Drucker

Innovation and Entrepreneurship: Practice and Principles

In a nutshell: We have seen, time and again, that executives who do not "walk the walk" fail. Nothing makes us cringe more than standing in a town hall meeting with a chief executive officer (CEO) who is communicating the newest plan to improve the company, but cannot answer the most basic questions about the new program, preferring to deflect the answer to the expert standing with him on stage. This immediately communicates to the staff that I don't have to do what I am telling you to do. In short, an innovation, to be effective, must be simple and it must be focused. It should do only one thing, otherwise it confuses. The entrepreneur needs to understand that if it is not simple, it won't work.

INTRODUCTION

As we have previously mentioned, this book is a summary of a larger body of knowledge on innovation. It will help you "walk the walk" and "talk the talk" as you create an innovation-oriented organization. This chapter is divided into several sections that will allow you and the organization become more effective at promoting and communicating ideas.* The discussion points include:

- Simple communication concepts
- Audiences
- Top-down, bottom-up communication
- Forums for communication

At its most basic level, communication involves a sender and a receiver. We humans have an added step of coding and decoding the message. Between the sender coding a message and the receiver decoding the message, we have communication channels.

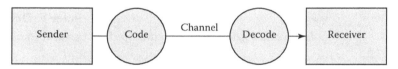

All this is pretty basic. When a computer is involved, the coding and decoding are simple and efficient. Channels are well-defined and miscommunications are rare.

Introduce a human into the equation and we start to see the many problems with how ideas are misconstrued, marginalized, or lost all together. Let's start with my personal problems. I was raised in a household where we felt that we had to speak our minds quickly and efficiently. Perhaps it was because there were five siblings, or maybe it was because both my parents were busy business executives. Regardless, some of you may appreciate this type of communication style while others will believe

---

* Drucker really understood entrepreneurs, an appreciation spawned in part by the work of Austrian economist Joseph Schumpeter. Schumpeter introduced the idea of creative destruction: the necessary collateral damage that occurs when entrepreneurs – whom he called "wild spirits" – breach established markets. Entrepreneurs drive progress and create wealth, Schumpeter believed, a mantra Drucker took up in his own copious writings on innovation. "The entrepreneur always searches for change, responds to it, and exploits it as an opportunity," Drucker wrote.

that I am too focused on the message and not enough on the delivery. This is a classic problem of coding and decoding.

To us, the message is simple and efficient and I rarely use big words when I speak, as we find that many people, even with a large vocabulary, really get confused with the nuances of seldom-used words. We have been fortunate to be able to live and work in many different geographic locations throughout the United States and the world and have found that it is critical to the success of communication to find the right coding for the people, culture, and/or situation in which we find ourselves. A perfect example that many readers will relate to is "academia speak," which essentially means that you take a sentence that can be expressed in simple terms such as

The rain in Spain falls mainly on the plain.

and convert it to something more appropriate to an academic audience such as

The moisture condensed from the atmosphere that falls visibly in separate drops is witnessed predominantly at 40.4000°N, 3.6833°W.*

I don't believe that we need to go into a complete translation to understand that the academic might have just said, in 18 words, what Eliza Doolittle (the fictional character, not the pop star), said in nine. And what Eliza Doolittle the singer might say over the course of several minutes and 100 words through song. The coding is different, the channel is different, but the essence of the message between sender and receiver might be exactly the same thing. One communicates a simple and direct message, one communicates scientific findings, and the third communicates in poetry and music (I suppose in her song 'Let It Rain', she could be in Spain and on a plain, although I suspect I am reaching here). The point is that in the process of communicating ideas, there are many communication channels and many opportunities for problems with the coding and decoding of the message.†

---

* If you are a complete nerd and in pursuit of full disclosure, you will have already calculated that 40.4000°N, 3.6833°W is actually somewhere in Madrid, which may or may not be on the plain in Spain, but is at least in the right country.

† Peter Drucker's first book, *The End of Economic Man*, was a study not of management but of totalitarianism. Living in Germany during Hitler's rise (two pamphlets he wrote – one praising a German-Jewish philosopher and one roundly condemning the National Socialists – were banned and burned by the Nazis), Drucker was achingly aware of the worst that government and society could dish out. His later writing can be interpreted as a lifelong quest for functional, principled institutions.

Taking this to the communication of innovation and ideas, we have all the problems inherent in communications in general. When I speak, I often joke about the need for engineers to learn something about business and businesspeople to learn something about engineering with this simple story. An engineer comes to the director of innovation with a platinum gold computer and proudly states that he has built the perfect computer (now, I am not an engineer so I don't know if platinum would make a great computer, but be patient with me).

The director of innovation says that this is a very nice computer, but there is no way we could find customers for such an expensive computer. The engineer states that it isn't his problem, he made the best computer in the world and a good businessperson should be able to figure out how to package it and sell it. A few minutes later, a businessperson comes in with a crude drawing of a bridge that will enable people to drive across the Atlantic Ocean. When the director tells the businessperson that it is impossible to engineer, the businessperson claims that he has solved a significant problem and the only reason it won't work is because the engineers aren't smart enough. In this case, it is pretty clear that these two individuals are not only communicating, but they are also operating under different paradigms, which leads to the problem of context.

Context in communication refers to the situation in which the message was sent. A problem with computers inferring meaning from speech is that the computer doesn't generally understand the context of the speech. For example, how would a computer interpret the following?

"Let's eat, Grandma" and "Lets eat Grandma"

Obviously, a computer that is reading from text can parse out the comma to understand the comment, but what about the one that translates from spoken language. If you would like a fun example of this, tell Siri "Siri, Let's eat Grandma" and she will tell you about restaurants close to you. I suspect that none of them serves grandma!

Communicating isn't always about what you say. Sometimes it's about what you do (this is the section that comes from Carlos' slides). One of the major problems with innovation today is that too many companies are obligated to stakeholders looking for immediate results (especially in stock values). When an organization wants to change some aspect of their operations such as becoming more innovative, they need to lay out a plan

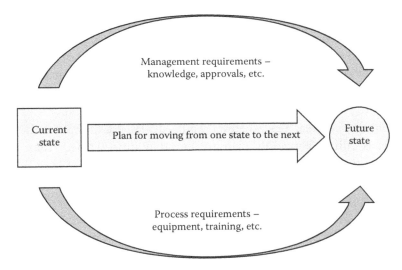

FIGURE 2.1
Management communication requirements.

that outlines where they are, where they want to be, and how they will get there. In their book *The Dynamic Enterprise: Tools for Turning Chaos into Strategy and Strategy into Action*, the creative enterprise, Herman Gyr and Lisa Friedman use a graphic similar to the one shown in Figure 2.1).

The plan for moving from one state to another is fairly self-explanatory and is what most of this book is about. What are the tools and techniques, when do we apply them, and how do we know if we are being successful. One might say that this is where the investment in so-called knowledge workers takes place. People make the plans and people execute the plans. Here is where we retrain our employees to become knowledge workers who are more successful at innovation. They receive training and certification, develop a plan, and execute on that plan.*

The process requirements are essentially about the investments that are required to make the innovation happen. Do we have the right processes

---

* The term "knowledge management" has that PC era aroma about it. However, it is a fact that almost 20 years before the founding of Microsoft, Drucker coined the term "knowledge worker" to describe the growing cadre of employees who labored with their brains rather than their hands. Drucker explained that knowledge workers require a new style of management that treats them more as volunteers or partners than as subordinates. He accurately predicted that the ability of entrepreneurial leaders to "motivate these founts of productivity – the most valuable asset of a 21st century institution – would become a cornerstone of competitive advantage."

in place? Do we need to redesign certain processes?* Should we invest in equipment, hardware, software, and other enabling technologies that we currently do not have? When we talk to senior executives about innovation, new equipment is never the problem. The investment in equipment is generally a given and is always expected as a part of any profound change. Whenever we need to have this talk with an executive, we expect resistance – what we generally get is, "Yea, Yea, whatever we need." Where they show the most concern is with the people, the plan, and how they are to behave in the process.

We are sure that our readers have all experienced this at least once in their career. A senior executive has called a town hall meeting to announce a "new direction" for the company (I have seen this many times with Six Sigma), and are proud to bring the consultant or executive who is in charge up to the stage. "This is going to change the way we do business." "This is the most important program the company has ever done in its history." "The future of our company depends on this." But what happens? The consultant or executive that he or she has called onto the stage is going to take charge, and where so many of these executives get into trouble is they invite questions from the employees.

What becomes clear almost immediately is that the senior person has no clue about how the program is going to work. For a leader to come on stage and announce that the new program is going to be the "most important program the company has ever undertaken," that it is "critical to the company's future," and then not know anything about the program sends a clear message to the employees.† The messages that come across are

1. This is critical, but I am far too busy to know why
2. It's really not that critical
3. It's critical to you, but I can always find another job or
4. Some derivative of these three statements

---

* Thomas Edison would get no pushback from Drucker on his 1 percent inspiration and 99 percent perspiration formula. Drucker believed that innovation – "the specific function of entrepreneurship" – must be methodically ferreted out, and he posited seven likely places to find it: in unexpected occurrences, incongruities, process needs, new knowledge, demographics, perceptions, and changes in industries and markets. The crucial characteristic of innovators is focus. Even Thomas Edison, Drucker pointed out, "worked only in the electrical field."

† In effective organizations, Drucker would say, employees know their roles. "My job is to ask questions," he once informed a consulting client, according to an article in *Business Week*. "It's your job to provide answers." In this Socratic style, Drucker inspired a generation of business leaders to wax introspectively about their organizations. Any journey of self-exploration, he believed, should begin with five essential questions. "What is our mission? Who is our customer? What does the customer value? What are our results? What is our plan?"

As a case in point, one of us once worked in an organization that demanded that everyone take training on Peter's Senge's double-loop learning. A consultant was hired and put on an impressive show in front of the rank-and-file employees. The CEO proudly announced that everyone would be required to take a three-day training course on how to do this, and that it was "critical to the success of the company."

All of this would take place over the next six months and if you did not attend, you would be fired.*

Imagine what employees thought when it got out that several of the key executives in the organization never attended the training. Apparently, they were just too busy to spend any time with the initiative that was to be "critical to the company's future." Additionally, and we know this because one of us who did work at this organization was an executive, it turns out that the executives who were too busy to attend the training also never had time to read the book, and couldn't tell you a thing about the program; this included the CEO who hired the consultant in the first place.

Several things happened as this revelation came out. The first was that the program, for all intents and purposes, died. As new ideas bubbled to the surface, the executives who needed to champion the ideas didn't really get very excited about them. They didn't understand the process and were not personally vested in the concepts. The second thing was that it was clearly communicated that for all the talk and bravado about the program being necessary to save the future of the company, the behaviors of the executives communicated that, in fact, it wasn't that big of a deal.

While we weren't privy to the final cost of the program, we can tell you that a single consultant did all of the training. There were almost 3000 employees in the organization and this was done 120 at a time over a three-day period. Essentially, this consultant was paid for full-time work for more than six months for a project that never actually launched. At the prevailing consulting rates of the day, we estimate that the administration of the organization spent roughly $500,000 for a program that never launched. Given that this was nearly 20 years ago and given the prevailing consultant rates, you are probably looking at twice that today. Since the

---

* The Japanese found much to love about Peter Drucker in the 1960s, as industrial giants like Toyota embraced his theories on the primacy of employees and ideas about marketing – a comparably nascent discipline there. The admiration was mutual, with Drucker praising such Japanese practices as lifetime employment (though he later conceded the need for greater flexibility) and deliberative decision-making followed by quick action. Among Drucker's great passions was Japanese art, which he both collected and lectured on extensively.

company only made about $7 million net income per year, this was about 7% of the net income invested in a program that went NOWHERE, simply because a few executives were too busy to attend the training.*

This would be no different with a program to change your company from where it is today to calling yourself an "innovation leader" in your industry. Perhaps your organization isn't as transparent as a small 3000-person organization, but this makes the stakes even higher. A multi-billion-dollar company that invests heavily in innovation, but fails to convince its employees that it is serious about the program risks a lot more than the cost of a consultant. In today's hyperconnected world, you risk being seen as completely out of touch and your employees and customers will all know that while you put on slick commercials and throw around the term "innovation" without hesitation, when it comes down to really taking a risk, you will flinch. Employees understand this and for all the efforts you make, if they are afraid to take a risk, to introduce new ideas, or to make a mistake because the executive communicates their doubts about the innovation programs they are "supporting," then the ideas will not come. As the saying goes, you must not only "talk the talk, you must walk the walk." Walking the walk is the non-verbal communication that your employees rely on more than any speech or new policy.

So how do you communicate innovation to your employees? First, there are several outstanding individuals who, while not always agreeing, are happy to spend time with you talking about innovation. One of the greatest things about innovation is that the people who are actively involved in consulting and who run companies that are truly innovative are thrilled to talk about it. I am always amazed at how many people continue to be disgusted with the way everyone gives everything away on the Internet. Coders sharing with others, experts blogging about strategies that work, stock tips, recipes, music, and on and on.

What many of my colleagues still believe is that a good idea should have layers of non-disclosure agreements (NDAs) attached to it. When I am asked to sign an NDA, I am always concerned that someone is going to tell me something I already know, but am now forbidden to talk about.

---

* Peter Senge learned much from Peter Drucker, and popularized the concept of "learning organizations" in the 1980s. But learning organizations are predicated on learning individuals. Drucker called teaching people how to learn "the most pressing task" for managers, given the perpetual expansion of skills and knowledge that are products of the information economy. He personally eschewed the designation "guru" – which suggests one who counsels – casting himself rather as a student. True to form, Drucker every year assigned himself a topic about which he knew nothing and made it the subject of intense study.

As someone who is a student of innovation, I am sure someday that I am going to enter an organization, sign an NDA, and then hear about how they invented "Brain Hurricane,"* which is just like "Brainstorming," but bigger. Of course, it is exactly like brainstorming, but now I am forbidden from talking about it with my other clients.

Of course, we are being facetious, but there is always the chance that something similar could happen. The point of the story is that anyone doing good work in innovation is happy to share his or her success stories with anyone who is struggling. In all our contacts with senior executives from companies all over the world, manufacturing processes might not be shared, secret formulas may remain in a vault, or market strategies will only be divulged at the right time, but people will always share what works for them in innovation. Perhaps innovators are a naïve bunch, but most we have come across are interested in making the world a better place. ****Check out – hasn't Tesla made all their patents public? Say something about it!**** To use a sports metaphor, "it aint bragging if it's true." The best companies in the world will invite you in, offer you a cup of coffee, and gladly share with you everything they are doing in innovation. The best will probably even ask you to partner with them in some arcane way you never even imagined.

SUMMARY

Join an online forum and read what people are saying. There are several online forums that concentrate on innovation. Some are the Wild West and anyone can write a piece on what works for them. Others are more academic and tend to wait until something is proven. At the International Association of Innovation Professionals (IAOIP), the focus is on the science of innovation, operating on the assumption that until something can be communicated and tested, you have to take it at face value. In the non-innovation world, you wouldn't hire someone who is stating they have a better way to do accounting or law, so why trust your company's fortunes to someone who posts their innovation methodology on the Internet with

---

* Brain Hurricane is a complete math and literacy program for elementary and middle school students that has helped more than 50,000 students in over 1,000 schools with engaging learning. See www.brainhurricane.com for details. This program has no relationship with the authors and is offered as an example only.

no evidence that it works? Our suggestion is that you join these groups and forums, read about the innovation tools and what people are saying about them, and soon you will be able to identify who is real and who is not.

Lastly, go on innovation tours. Today, there is no shortage of "silicon" this or that out there. There are silicon alleys, silicon prairies, silicon garages, silicon ranches, and silicon villages, with new ones coming online every day. Your participation in a silicon tour will allow you to see what people in other industries and maybe even your competitors' companies are doing. Of course, a great place to start is in the San Francisco Bay Area – the original innovators playground. Visiting with the executives who are driving tomorrow's innovations is a tremendous message to your employees. Don't forget the other great places where innovation is happening – in consumer-packaged goods, in entertainment, and in energy. Go there and find out what the greatest companies in the world are doing – they will be proud to show off their programs.

Finally, probably the most important thing in innovation communication is, as they say, "walking the walk;" leaders actually demonstrating curiosity and an open mind-set. This doesn't mean you have to switch to a black turtle neck and jeans. It means that every day in your actions, both personally and corporately, you show that risk-taking and creativity are things to cherish and embrace, not just talk about. One of the great things about the IAOIP is the conversations we get to have with top-flight innovation practitioners from around the globe. It's exciting exchanging ideas with people who are passionate about innovation and understand the import and impact of innovation when strategy, innovation, and execution converge.

Unfortunately, this convergence is still a rarity. Too many organizations remain trapped in the quagmire of the accidental innovation paradigm. They cling to the misguided notion that simply talking about the need to be more innovative will somehow unleash the torrent of intellectual potential within their companies that years of anti-innovation practice and cultural reinforcement have been so effective at suppressing. This is a sad state of affairs that I am committed to changing. I am glad to say that I am not alone in this conviction.

As we have been writing these books on innovation and entrepreneurship over the past 10 years or so, we authors have been rethinking how to help others to benefit from repeatable innovation best practices. This has been a challenging process, demanding so much energy that it has kept us away from blogging. But, it has also been very rewarding. Recently, we have been talking with innovation leaders in companies around the globe. The response to these conversations has been tremendous.

In the coming months, we will return to posting regularly, and will share with readers what we are seeing on the front lines of innovation in Europe, the Americas, and Asia, and we think you will agree that the outlook is very positive. Despite a continuing economically challenging climate (and sometimes because of it), companies globally are reinvesting in innovation. But, more importantly, these companies want to learn from the mistakes of the past, and relaunch their efforts around innovation.

Innovation continues to be a critical part of driving business success, and we are very fortunate to have the opportunity to explore its boundaries in new ways every day.

3

Personal Creativity for Entrepreneurs

In a nutshell: This chapter presents what we call the essential "top-10" creativity tools and techniques that you can use to develop ideas as an entrepreneur, tools that support creative and imaginative solutions to business problems. The tools in this chapter can help you to become more creative as a businessperson; they will help you determine new and better solutions to the problems you identify; they will also help you find opportunities that you might otherwise miss. Before you continue, however, it is important to understand what the authors mean by creativity. There are two totally different types of creativity. The first is technical creativity – by using technical creativity, individuals create new theories, technologies, and ideas. Technical creativity is the type of creativity that we discuss in this chapter. The other type of creativity is artistic creativity. This second type is beyond the scope of this chapter.

DRUCKER ON CREATIVITY AND THE ENTREPRENEUR

"The entrepreneur always searches for change, responds to it, and exploits it as an opportunity," Drucker wrote. *"Efficiency is doing things right, and effectiveness is doing the right things."* What's true for individual managers is also true for organizations, which often squander time and resources trying to improve processes for products not worth producing. The solution? It was Drucker who first suggested that choosing what not to do was a decision as strategic as its opposite. Drucker's theory of *"purposeful*

abandonment" exhorted business leaders to quickly sever projects, policies, and processes that had outlived their usefulness. *"The first step in a growth policy is not to decide where and how to grow,"* he told author Jeffrey Krames in 2003. *"It is to decide what to abandon. In order to grow, a business must have a systematic policy to get rid of the outgrown, the obsolete, the unproductive."**

INTRODUCTION

While the next chapter discusses corporate creativity, the fact is that corporations cannot imagine (think) or produce new ideas without individuals. The common fallacy of innovation diminishing as individuals' age need not be true. What may be truer is that as one becomes older, one has more to lose. What this can directly translate to is the need for organizations to make it safer for individuals to be creative.

One company I consulted with referred to their innovation program as "prairie dog innovation." When I asked them, they explained the concept. The company had a very public program to solicit innovative ways to deliver health care to patients. They wanted new products, better ways to do things, and new and novel ways to connect with customers and fellow employees. The problem was that employees' felt like they were prairie dogs, and management was a guy with a shotgun. If they stuck their heads (ideas) out of the hole, they better be sure that it was a good one. If not, it was likely that they would get their heads shot off (fired, censured, reassigned, etc.).

In other words, management made it clear by their actions that innovation was only good when the idea was good. So, no one brought forth any ideas for fear that they wouldn't be the ideas that management was looking for. Additionally, in this particular organization, the individual responsible for starting and building a world-class innovation department was not promoted when it was decided that they needed a chief innovation officer. The position was filled by an acquaintance of the chief executive officer (CEO), a person who had no innovation-related qualifications.

---

* "The Wisdom of Peter Drucker from A to Z." Known widely as the father of management, Peter Drucker formulated many concepts about business that we now take for granted. In honor of the 100th anniversary of his birth, we take a look at Drucker's contributions, from A to Z. Written by Leigh Buchanan, editor-at-large, *Inc. Magazine.* Source: https://www.inc.com/articles/2009/11/drucker.html.

BOOSTING YOUR CREATIVITY ABILITY

In their book *Problem Solving for Results*,* authors Bill Roth and Frank Voehl discussed the need to shape the right attitudes and perspectives for creativity to flourish in light of the need to improve creativity in problem-solving in any business operation. Ten years later, in his seminal work on the subject, *Creativity*, Mihaly Csikszentmihalyi said that an effective creative process in almost any type of problem-solving or opportunity-finding situation usually consists of five steps. Picking the right tools and techniques can be divided into four meta-categories:

- Those used to improve creativity and enhance the problem identification skills of the individual.
- General techniques used to improve the creativity of groups.
- Systems-oriented techniques used to work with problem networks or "messes" as systems scientists call them.
- Tools used to specifically measure an organization's productivity and innovation creativity IQ.

The Sweet 16 personal creativity tools and techniques can also be used in groups and are organized within the following five-step method; also, many of the tools can be found in two or three of the steps listed.

The five steps for improving creativity in any organization are

1. *Preparation*: Understanding the problem or issue that peaks your curiosity and has a good chance of being improved.
2. *Incubation*: Letting the initial thoughts and ideas percolate in your mind subconsciously.

---

* *Problem Solving for Results*, by Bill Roth and Frank Voehl, St. Lucie Press, Delray Beach, FL, 1996. Turbulence is not new to the entrepreneur in the business world. In fact, turbulence is increasing and managers are seeing teams spinning their wheels. Management systems are in a state of crisis and operations are more complex. The old top-down operations mode no longer suffices. Today's businesses demand speed and increased accuracy, forcing everyone to re-evaluate chains of command and tear down the walls between functions. Amid the responsibilities of traditional entrepreneurial management lies problem-solving. The push is toward moving decision-making authority down the ladder to all levels. Entrepreneurs are no longer equipped to or capable of making the number and variety of necessary decisions in a vacuum. The current mode is to have employees deal directly with workplace issues and take corrective action without complaint and without management involvement, thus fostering an attitude of personal creativity. Coping with this reality and preparing for these improvements in workplace problem-solving requires interest, creativity, and motivation.

3. *Insight*: Finally knowing that you understand the true essence of the problem and it all starts to make sense. You now have a fundamental understanding of this issue.
4. *Evaluation*: Considering the value that the idea brings compared to the cost and resources necessary to implement the solution.
5. *Elaboration*: Developing an action plan with steps, responsibility, and timing to implement the solution.

We've focused on these five steps and their associated tools, which are covered in this chapter, to provide a clear and practical way for you to think about creativity and to use it every day of your life. Over the years, we have seen as many as 20 steps involving a process for creativity often used with lesser impact and success than the five steps outlined in this chapter. We like the idea of five steps because – in the areas of creativity and directed problem-solving rules and steps – less is more.

> Effective innovations start small, not grandiose. They try to do one specific thing. It may be to enable a moving vehicle to draw electric power while it runs along rails – the innovation that made possible the electric streetcar. Or it may be as elementary as putting the same number of matches into a matchbox (it used to be fifty), which made possible the automatic filling of matchboxes and gave the Swedish originators of the idea a world monopoly on matches for almost half a century.
>
> **Peter F. Drucker**
> *Innovation and Entrepreneurship*

In books about innovation, you'll find no shortage of recommendations to increase personal productivity in your organization. Much of the time, the recommendations include building new offices, adding a coffee bar, changing the furniture, or holding playful retreats. While many of these suggestions can improve personal creativity, the fact is that many companies that are doing the most innovative things have not changed a thing about their furniture, color schemes, or cubicles. In fact, much of the innovation actually happening in the world isn't happening in Silicon Valley. This innovation is happening in consumer-packaged goods (CPG), oil and gas, and automobile manufacturing, just to name a few.

So, how do these companies get innovation from their employees? The answer is actually surprisingly simple. They allow their employees to be unique. Organizations that force strict compliance with rules, chain of command, and rigidity in everything they do, find that employees act the same way.

> Entrepreneurs, by definition, shift resources from areas of low productivity and yield to areas of higher productivity and yield. Of course, there is a risk they may not succeed. But if they are even moderately successful, the returns should be more than adequate to offset whatever risk there might be.
>
> **Peter F. Drucker**
> *Innovation and Entrepreneurship*

If you've ever coached children's sports, you know what this means. Simply telling your kids to play better does not make the score better. Instead, you practice and teach them to play better. When it comes time for games, you encourage them and get excited about what it is that they're doing. Creativity and employees are similar in that you need to give them the tools, teach them the tools, and allow them to be creative. In a recent survey done by the International Association of Innovation Professionals (IAOIP) of executives from around the world, we found that one of the most underserved areas of innovation is creativity.

But face it, all humans are becoming creative. This creativity is what makes us human and different from other animals in the world. Sure, occasionally, we see amazing dog tricks or monkeys perform, but these are trained behaviors, not innovation. This is how we are different when compared to the rest of the animal kingdom. This ability to creatively solve problems is a natural tendency and part of human nature.

Unfortunately, however, 'creativity' and 'innovation' are often used as interchangeable terms or are meshed together as one concept; the difference between the two is an important one that actually helps us to understand each more fully. One way to understand the subtle difference is to think about creativity as a precursor to innovation. Creativity can happen without innovation but innovation seldom happens without creativity. Think about all the wonderful and creative ideas you have had in your lifetime but have never turned them into a product. Now consider all of the innovations that you have come up with in your lifetime, and you would probably be hard-pressed to take creativity out of that equation. You might imagine creativity as a relatively random event. Innovation is the ability to organize these creative thoughts into new ideas, products, processes, and services for the real world. So, if you have a creative workforce that lacks the processes and systems to translate that creativity into innovation, all you have is a creative workforce.

OVERVIEW

If you believe the premise that creativity is separate from innovation and you take personal creativity as a stand-alone topic, then you can begin to sort out creativity from the process of innovating. Creativity is another of those topics where there is much agreement but subtle differences in that agreement. The fact is that there is no universal way to define creativity that makes sense to all of us trying to understand it in the context of our own lives. A standard definition of creativity might look something like this: "creativity is the ability to create original ideas, connections, alternatives, or possibilities for effective problem-solving, communicating with others, and inspiring new and useful ideas in others." Therefore, creativity requires an unrestrained openness of originality that is not always in sync with the organization. When the organization can recognize creativity and see the connections between creative people, ideas, and the problems of the organization, then it becomes inspirational, useful, and enjoyable.

Given these definitions, understanding personal productivity requires us to recognize that creativity as a process needs the organization to recognize and harness it in a way that changes business. In the work of Arin Reeves, she describes research that she has done with dozens of individuals in a multitude of industries and professions. Specifically, she asks questions of how to generate original effective ideas. She states that this requires:

1. Diverse inputs/inclusive thinking
2. Context articulation
3. Divergent thinking
4. Convergent thinking

While conventional thinking on creativity is far from settled, there are certain stereotypes that typify a creative thinker. Examples include behavioral differences, cultural differences, differences in education and intelligence, and natural ability to be creative. While we may imagine an artist as a naturally creative person drawn to a certain field, there are many artists, such as those who create animation for movies, who may be doing it for the money. As an example, we know of several individuals working in film who are more attracted to computer programming in the visual arts. If one were to view their work, they would think the opposite, that they were creative types who are forced to program. And while it is tempting to stereotype different groups of people such as Asians and Indians in math and the sciences, there are no shortages of "creative" in this space.

In fact, it may be that certain people are trained to restrain their creative tendencies because of their job title, training, or background. For example, you may prefer to have your barista or bartender be creative than your certified public accountant (CPA). Does this mean that people who are accountants are not creative? Before you answer that question, consider the fact that one of the authors of this book was a CPA in his first career. As an aside, the reason he left accounting was that the rules and structures did not easily allow for creativity. On the other hand, a tax accountant, especially for a large corporation, is probably encouraged to explore creativity within the law.

Regardless, and getting back to Arin Reeves discussion, an important component of personal creativity, diverse input/inclusive thinking, requires your organization to integrate diverse inputs into your thinking process, especially when groups are nonhomogeneous. In our book *Global Innovation Science Handbook*, we dedicated a chapter to ethnography. While ethnography is a methodology that requires you to look at other groups (race, sex, culture, etc.), you could also consider this in the diversity of inputs and inclusive thinking. Throughout our careers, we have found that spending time with employees who are outside of the executive suite consistently delivers a high return on investment. Many times, those who are closest to the problems have the best ideas for how to solve them.

Unfortunately, it is a rare manager who possesses the humility to communicate that a company-changing idea came from an assistant, a physical plant employee, or the janitorial staff. After all, great ideas are supposed to come from the highest-paid employees. When you do business across national or cultural boundaries (as is the case with most companies these days), it becomes even more critical to integrate diverse inputs into your thinking process. Individuals who can integrate diverse perspectives into their personal creativity are better informed, more competitive, and more effective than individuals who don't.

Our experience, and that diversity of perspectives, engaged in the understanding of creativity must be recognized to capture the variance and how creativity is understood, inspired, and executed. So, whether the objective is personal creativity in a global environment or to be able to personally inspire great creativity in a group of people, it is critically important that you, as a leader, seek out and integrate diverse perspectives into your organization.

From Ms. Reeve's context articulation, we must ask the question of original ideas in context. For example, an innovation classic is the invention of the Post-it note. As scientists at 3M worked on adhesives, they created one that wasn't so effective. As the story goes, an employee who wanted to keep notes in a book and was frustrated with the paper falling out asked if he could use the sticky substance on paper. A legend was born! It's exciting to see in the innovation world how this simple concept is beginning to play out in life-changing ways. Health care has always been a hotbed for innovation; however, sometimes the bench-to-bedside techniques have been less than successful. Highly effective researchers with little or no knowledge related to commercialization techniques have seen their research languishing in obscurity. Offices of commercialization have changed much of this in many organizations. By providing workspaces and breaking down silos so that businesspeople, researchers, companies, and investors can better work together, ideas that may have been locked away in someone's desk have a real opportunity to be seen by people who can make them a reality. Simply put, having another set of eyes look at the opportunity allows the context to potentially change.

Finally, we must recognize the importance of divergent thinking and convergent thinking. In life, there are certain rules that people recognize such as in sports when you must go backward to go forward using the scientific method. In innovation, we could coin a new universal law: that we must be unrestrained to be more effective when we are restrained. To express this more clearly, consider the funnel. The funnel takes a great deal of whatever it is we pour into it. What comes out of the bottom of the funnel is much less. A better analogy would be a water filter. Much goes into a water filter, but what comes out is pure water. If we seek pure water and our answer to creating it is to pour pure water into the filter, then we really haven't done anything special. On the other hand, if we take dirty water and put it into a water filter with the result being clean water, then the filter has done its job. To take this analogy a step further, if all we have is dirty water, but we insist on only pure water going in, we will have no water in the end. Many ideas can be filtered to an organization but without those ideas, the best ideas may never get into the system.

TOOL #1: THE QUICKSCORE CREATIVITY TEST*

Start by taking the MindTools Quickscore 3-Min Creativity Test, which helps you assess and develop your business creativity skills, which is why the authors have listed this as the #1 creativity "tool." Creativity is about sourcing new and innovative solutions to problems. It is also the process of looking for and discovering opportunities to improve the methods that we use in daily life to accomplish everything we do. Lastly, creativity is also about discovering and developing completely new ways of thinking and different ideas and approaches. As such, any one of us can be creative, as long as we have the right state of mind and we utilize the appropriate tools available for the task at hand. This test will quickly assess how creative you are right now. It doesn't provide an absolute measure, but it does give you a sense of your level of creative thinking. We will use the results from this test along with some additional tools to help you develop your level of creativity.

Over the course of writing more than 70 books and consulting with hundreds of client organizations, we have found that there are at least three core alternative attitudes related to creativity found in many organizations.

- *Attitude #1*: Research and development is the only creative area in the organization.
- *Attitude #2*: All employees are creative. We just need to sit back and let things happen.
- *Attitude #3*: We must proactively stimulate and encourage all of our employees to be creative and pursue new and different ideas.

---

* Creativity tests are typically divided into four main components: divergent thinking, convergent thinking, artistic assessments, and self-assessments. Divergent thinking is the ability to consciously generate new ideas that branch out to many possible solutions for a given problem. These solutions or responses are then scored on four components: (1) originality – statistical infrequency of response; (2) fluency – number of responses; (3) flexibility – the degree of difference of the responses, in other words do they come from a single domain or multiple domains; and (4) elaboration – the amount of detail in the response. Source for quickview: "How Creative Are You," article on the MindTools website (https://www.mindtools.com/pages/article/creativity-quiz.htm).

In today's environment, the third attitude is the only one that is acceptable. Our employees are probably the most valuable resource we have in our organizations. Do we make good use of them to help develop new products and services or to solve our problems? We are missing an important opportunity if we are not mining this gold mine of great ideas by not providing an environment that requires our employees to be creative. We must make efficient and effective use of their mental capacity as well as their experiences. It is important to help expand this capability if the organization is going to survive.

In his work on human motivation, Robert E. Franken states that in order to be creative, you need to be able to view things from different perspectives. Creativity is linked to fundamental qualities of thinking, such as flexibility and tolerance of ambiguity. This creative problem-solving test was developed to evaluate whether your attitude toward problem-solving and the manner in which you approach a problem are conducive to creative thinking. The test is made up of two types of questions*: scenarios and self-assessment. For each scenario, answer according to how you would most likely behave in a similar situation. For the self-assessment questions, indicate the degree to which the given statements apply to you. In order to receive the most accurate results, please answer each question as honestly as possible.

To summarize, you have seen other authors refer to the concept that our brain's right and left sides perform different functions. Creative people can integrate those two functions into one solid approach. Combining left and right abilities creates a synergy that no one can compete with when focusing on only one side of the brain.

The left-hand side is the logical reasoning side and the right-hand side is the creative side. They exist within our skull much like Felix and Oscar of "The Odd Couple" existed within the same apartment (see Figure 3.1). Felix, like the left-hand side of our brain, is the functional, logical, technical, and planning individual. He loves lists; he wants everything in order. He's upset in a confused environment. He has a strong desire to please other people. Oscar, on the other hand, is much like the right-hand side of our brain: very creative, very conceptual, tends to get emotional very quickly, and thrives on confusion and

---

* After finishing this test, you will receive a FREE snapshot report with a summary evaluation and graph. To take this test, go to https://www.psychologytoday.com/tests/career/creative-problem-solving-test.

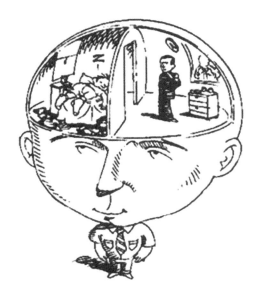

FIGURE 3.1
The Felix and Oscar sides of the brain.

ambiguities. Concepts that Oscar creates, Felix tries to put into a logical, structured order so that they can be implemented, or he rejects the concept outright as being impractical.

The humor in "The Odd Couple" TV show was the problem that these two very different personalities faced in living together without driving the other one crazy. The problem that we face in being creative is how we can get these two different parts of our brain to work together to accomplish previously unattainable results. But creativity alone is not enough. It must be accompanied by innovation. Creativity and innovation are partners, but they are not the same thing.

- Creativity is developing new or different ideas.
- Innovation is converting ideas into tangible products, services, or processes. Creativity without innovation is wasted effort. The challenge that every organization faces is how to convert good ideas into profit. That's what the creative process is all about.

This means that the organization has to have a system in place that will fast-track an individual's idea through the process of getting it approved and implemented. This requires that the creative/innovative process makes a smooth transition from an individual to a team, to all of the impacted individuals. The creative thinking methodology uses the following process for accomplishing this type of organization:

1. Embed creativity into the organization's culture and vision.
2. Assess creativity status. An assessment should be made of the creativity performance level of the organization. Typical questions that would be answered are
   - Does the organization have a measurement of its return on its creativity investment?
   - What percentage of our effort is devoted to creative activities, and is that enough?
   - Does the organization have a chief creativity officer?
   - Do we have creativity goals and targets?
   - What percentage of our employees made a measurable creativity improvement in the past 12 months, and is that percentage high enough?
   - Are resources made available to support the refinement of new ideas?
   - What roadblocks are in the way of the organization becoming more creative?
3. Establish a creative thought process (see Figure 3.2).
   - Train everyone in how to be creative.
   - Set up an idea review system that will quickly bring to upper management's attention the ideas that will have an important impact upon the organization's present and future performance so that these ideas can be implemented quickly. Lower-level review boards should be established to expedite the evaluation of less important ideas and assume the responsibility for implementing them.
   - Budgets should be set up for the review board to fund creative proposals. The review board's return on investment related to its budget should be measured. At the very minimum, the return on investment should be 12:1 if the process is working effectively.
   - Management should recognize and support employees who have an entrepreneurial attitude by having them form possibility teams to explore, develop, and prepare business proposals for good concepts.

- Reward systems that reward both noble failures and crowning successes should be established to reinforce a risk-taking environment throughout the organization.

Example: Figures 3.2 and 3.3 are two flowcharts of different types of the thinking process. Figure 3.2 represents the creative thought pattern and Figure 3.3 represents the conventional thought pattern.

One factor that strongly affects an organization's creativity success rate is its attitude toward creativity and problem–opportunity finding in the first place.

On the creativity spectrum, it ranges from inactive, active, proactive to hyperactive. Regardless of the type of approach, creative people don't just sit around and wait for opportunities or problems to surface. Instead, they

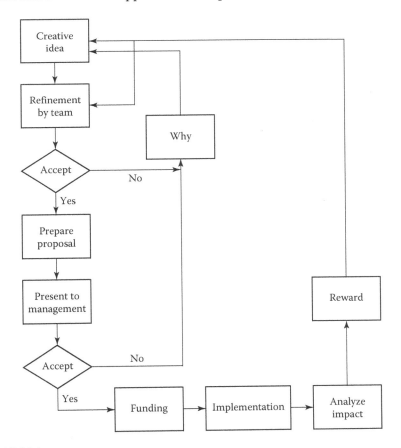

FIGURE 3.2
The creative thought process.

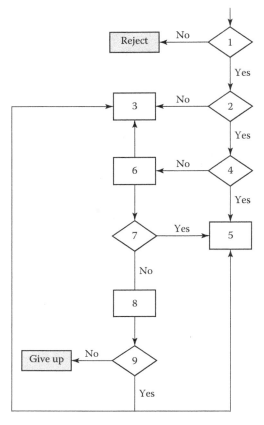

1. Is it important?
2. Does it require action?
3. Store information
4. Do i know what to do?
5. Take action
6. Conduct research
7. Do i know what to do?
8. Create new solution
9. Do i know what to do?

FIGURE 3.3
The conventional thought process.

scan their environment for potential opportunities or issues, and they see this as exercising creativity time well spent, for in actuality they are often excited by the opportunity to change things. They aren't intimidated by the change; rather, they embrace it.

Finding Opportunities and Problems to Solve Requires New Thinking

As you launch the continued innovation side of your organization, you hear many new words and phrases that may not be a common part of your lexicon. Many will be familiar from your business education, but others will be completely new. For this chapter, we will not go into great detail about all of these tools and techniques for personal creativity.

One of the things that makes managers uncomfortable is a shift to the whole brain thinking by members of your organization. For 100 years, employees have been asked to only use their "left brain" when they go to work. As you may recall, the left brain is the side of the brain that is responsible for linear thinking, sequential thinking, analytical thinking, logical thinking, and detailed thinking. These are all important attributes in the industrial era of work. But work has changed and now we ask more from employees. Unfortunately, education and companies have been slow to figure out that what we are asking for and what we are rewarding is not the same thing. When we ask someone to use the "right brain," we are now asking for nonlinear thinking, for them to use their imagination, be more responsive to emotions, think conceptually, and consider a more holistic approach to the world.

A good example of this type of thinking that has stood the test of time is Edward de Bono's six thinking hats. At its simplest, the parallel thinking technique known as the "six thinking hats," challenges organizations to move beyond a linear, one-track way of approaching problem-solving and decision-making. Six thinking hats is a method to teach the brain to look at a problem from multiple perspectives to promote open-mindedness and creative thinking, engage everyone in the conversation, and deter shutting down discussions due to defensive or offensive behaviors. The hats are expressed as follows:

- Analyzing (white hat) represents analyzing facts and data
- Positivity (yellow hat) represents positive feelings and optimism
- Managing and controlling (blue hat) represents the tendency for order
- Intuition and feelings (red hat) represents the tendency to listen to yourself
- Exploration and creativity (green hat) represents curiosity
- Danger spotting (black hat) represents the need to stay vigilant

In fact, many have argued that the world we find ourselves in today will not only benefit from, but will demand right brain thinkers. In Dan Pink's writing, he discusses the need to remain competitive in the face of great change in globalization. He proposed that we find and encourage the other person's terminology and consider it a "higher-level concept." To do so requires the capacity to recognize patterns and identify opportunities, and to combine seemingly unrelated ideas into something new. This new high touch approach involves the ability to empathize with others, to understand the subtleties of human interaction, and to find joy in oneself and to elicit it in others. It is to stretch out beyond the quotidian in pursuit of purpose and meaning*

TOOL #2: KANO ANALYSIS

Kano Analysis is ranked by the authors as the #2 creativity and innovation-enhancing tool and is one of the most useful creativity techniques for entrepreneurial innovators in deciding which features you want to include in a product or service. It helps you break away from the thought process where you must maximize the number of features in a product. By having many features, you must be serving the needs of the customer. In reality, one should think more subtly about the features that you do choose to include. This can make a product or service more or less profitable, depending on the elimination of those features that do not "delight" the customer and only include those that do. Also, the real payoff for this creativity tool is that it helps you develop a product that will truly win your customers' hearts.

When he was at Florida Power and Light (FPL), author Frank Voehl worked with Dr. Kano during the Deming Prize Challenge, as Kano was developing the Kano Model. This model evolved based on the premise that a product or service can have three types of attributes or properties†:

---

* Your challenge as an entrepreneur innovator in this modern world is to undo the damage done by our organizations, including schools and workplaces. By the time we are 25, studies have shown that only 2% of the population can think in "divergent or nonlinear ways," a key component of creativity. If you compare this with children in the age group 3–5, 98% think creatively, while 32% of children of the age group 6–12 do, and down to 10% of children in the age group 13–15, you can see that we are doing things the wrong way, and are loosing ground in our educational systems. Larry Thompson of Ringling College of Art and Design refers this to this as being "brain ambidextrous." Giving employees the opportunity to engage their right brain may be the difference between leaders to succeed and fail in the future.
† When we weigh up one product against another and decide what price we're prepared to pay, we're comparing performance attributes. These are shown as the middle line in Figure 3.4. For example, on a cell phone, performance attributes might be polyphonic ringtones or cameras, although to many teenagers, using polyphonic ringtones may be threshold attributes. Excitement attributes are things that people don't really expect, but which delight them. These are shown as the top curve in Figure 3.4. Even if only a few performance attributes are present, the presence of an excitement attribute will lead to high customer satisfaction.

- *Threshold attributes*: The minimum that customers expect and require in a product.
- *Performance attributes*: Not completely necessary, but will increase the customer's use of the product.
- *Excitement attributes*: Customers don't even know they want, but are delighted when they find them (Figure 3.4).

Threshold attributes affect customers' satisfaction with the product or service by their absence: If they're not present, customers are dissatisfied. And even if they're present, if no other attributes are present, customers aren't particularly happy. If one were to use a cell phone as an example:

- *Contact information*: The ability to store people's names and telephone numbers is a threshold attribute. A cell phone without this function would work, but it would be grossly inconvenient.
- *Making a phone call without dropping the call*: This would be a performance attribute. According to Kano, it is usually on performance attributes that most products compete. Making or receiving a call would be considered a threshold attribute, but not dropping a call while traveling from place to place would be more of a performance attribute.

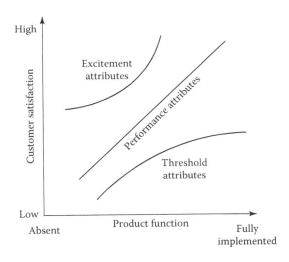

FIGURE 3.4
The Kano Model.

To use Kano Model analysis creatively,* follow these steps:

1. Start by brainstorming all of the possible features and attributes of your product or service, and everything you can do to please and delight your customers.
2. Classify these as "threshold," "performance," "excitement," and "not relevant."
3. Be sure that your program, product, or service has all the appropriate threshold attributes. If necessary, cut out performance attributes so that you can get the threshold attributes included, as you're going nowhere fast if these aren't present.
4. Where possible, cut out attributes that are "not relevant."
5. Next, look at the excitement attributes. Ask yourself how you can include some of these in your product or service. If you need to cut out some performance attributes, that would be alright if you are doing so to have sufficient resources to add an excitement attribute.
6. Select appropriate performance attributes so that you can deliver a product or service at a price the customer is prepared to pay, while still maintaining a good profit margin.

Note that this tool can be used by both individuals (such as R&D scientists) and groups (creativity and innovation teams). This is a great creativity tool for those who develop products and services. It's also something that you can use in most jobs to improve the service that you provide to your stakeholders as the Kano brand of innovative thinking is something we can all strive for.

TOOL #3: NOMINAL GROUP TECHNIQUE

The Nominal Group Technique (NGT) is listed as the #3 top creativity tool because of its use as a powerful and time-tested group ideation

---

* We first encountered the Kano Model and associated analysis techniques while researching ways to measure delight at FPL in the 1980s. Professor Noriaki Kano, a Japanese academic and consultant, disagreed with the prevalent theories on retaining customer loyalty – popular at the time was by addressing customer complaints and extending the most popular features. Professor Kano insisted to the FPL design team and execs that retaining loyalty was far more complicated. He did what researchers do: defined hypotheses and devised a study to substantiate these theories. Professor Kano's work was subsequently expanded upon in the United States by FPL's QualTec Quality Services and other quality management consultants. We translated Kano's original paper from Japanese with help from Productivity Press and Norman Bodek, and the Center for Quality Management with statistician Jeff Sauro and others.

and problem-solving technique involving the "triple crown" of problem identification, creative solution generation, and decision-making. It can easily and consistently be used in groups of many types and sizes – groups or teams who want to make their decision quickly by voting – but who want at the same time everyone's input and all opinions are taken into account. This is opposed to traditional voting, where only the largest group is considered – with the method of tallying being the essential difference and the main focus on establishing priorities rather than synthesizing.

Similar to brainstorming, NGT first generates the ideas just like brainstorming. The difference is that the method used to reduce the ideas to those with the greatest chance of success is by listing, voting with a limited number of votes, sorting by the number of votes, reducing the votes available, and voting again. This is done until a smaller significant list is generated from which the team can work on solutions.

Routinely, the technique involves five creativity-building stages:

1. Introduction and explanation
2. Silent generation of ideas
3. Sharing ideas
4. Group discussion
5. Voting and ranking

TOOL #4: SYNECTICS*

Synectics is regarded by the authors as the #4 creativity and problem-solving technique because it combines a structured approach to creativity with the freewheeling problem-solving approach used in techniques like brainstorming. It's a useful technique when simpler creativity techniques like SCAMPER, brainstorming, and random input have failed previously. Synectics uses many different ways to trigger the ideas that are being generated. It stimulates people to move away from established ways of thinking and helps to steer them into more creative ways of thinking.

---

* The word *synectics* means "bringing different things together to create a unified connection." It began to be used in the early 1960s and developed (in an artistic context) by Nicholas Roukes. The problem is that no two theories explain *Synectics* in the same way. There are two possible explanations for this: one is that the technique is just too complex to be understood by anyone but the "founder." The second is that pioneers in the movement purposefully incorporated this vagueness to enhance the technique's flexibility.

However, given the sheer range of different triggers and thinking approaches used within synectics, using it can take much longer to solve a problem than with, say, traditional brainstorming – hence many experts classify its use as a "second-level tool" when other creativity techniques have failed. The problem is that no two experts view this tool in the same way, largely due to the inventor (William Gordon) purposefully incorporating a sense of "vagueness" in order to enhance its flexibility as a creativity-enhancing tool.

Generating ideas with Synectics is a three or four approach/stage process:

1. *Referring*: Gathering information and defining the opportunity regarding direct analogies.
2. *Reflecting*: Using a wide range of techniques to generate ideas, including personal analogies.
3. *Reconstructing*: Bringing ideas together to create a useful solution using a "compressed conflict" model.
4. *Building fantastic energy*: Users must let their imaginations ramble unrestrained, and to connect and concoct the most bizarre solutions imaginable, often described as the "fantastic analogy."

In the referring stage, you lay the foundations you'll use later for the successful use of the tool. At this stage, you:

• Precisely define the problem you want to solve.
• Properly research the factors contributing to the problem.
• Understand what solutions have been tried up to this point.

Reflecting is where you creatively and imaginatively generate possible solutions to the problem you've defined. The emphasis here is on using a range of different "triggers" and "springboards" to generate associations and ideas. Just as with brainstorming, reflecting is best done in a relaxed, spontaneous, and open-minded way with an emphasis on creative thinking rather than on a critical assessment of suggestions. Where Synectics differs from brainstorming and other creativity methods is formally, and systematically it seeks to spark comparison with other approaches and situations, creating new ideas by making associations between these and the problem being solved. That said, a useful way to start the Synectic idea generation process is to brainstorm inside and around the opportunity or problem. This should generate a range of possible solutions to the problem.

If none of these solves the problem, the next step is to use some of the following 22 possible triggers to try to break free of existing thinking patterns. These triggers reflect things that you can do to transform your current product, service, or approach to try to solve the problem. They are

1. *Subtract*: Remove parts of your current approach, or simplify it.
2. *Repeat*: Duplicate parts of it, or significantly increase resources so that you can take existing approaches to a new level.
3. *Combine*: Mix existing approaches with other approaches.
4. *Add*: Make existing approaches bigger or stronger, or add other elements.
5. *Transfer*: Move existing approaches into different situations, and look at how they would change to cope with these approaches.
6. *Empathize*: Put yourself in the mind of your customers, or pretend that you are the problem: From this perspective, how would you do things differently?
7. *Animate*: Bring the problem to life. Think about it as a living thing.
8. *Superimpose*: Overlay the situation with new meanings or ideas, possibly randomly generated.
9. *Change scale*: Think about what would happen if you radically expanded the scale of the problem, or if you reduced it substantially.
10. *Substitute*: Switch out and replace elements of your current approach. Switch in parts of alternative approaches.
11. *Fragment*: Take the problem or your current approach apart. If you solve some parts of the problem, does this help solve others? Or can other people help you solve parts more effectively?
12. *Isolate*: Is there value in only looking at part of the problem? Are people really that concerned about other parts?
13. *Distort*: Change the "shape" of your current product, solution, or service: extend it or stretch it, think about it as a different, distorted shape.
14. *Disguise*: Think about whether you can eliminate the problem by hiding it or camouflaging it (in some cases this may be a legitimate solution).
15. *Contradict*: Think about doing the opposite of what you want to do (e.g., how you would make the problem worse?), then reverse this.
16. *Parody*: Think about what you'd ridicule about your problem or solution. See if this changes the context or suggests alterations.
17. *Prevaricate*: Fantasize about your service. Think about what it would be like in your wildest dreams.

18. *Analogize*: Think about analogies for your product or service, and what you can compare it to in other disciplines. How do people deal with analogous or similar problems?

19. *Hybridize*: Think about what would happen if you crossed your current approach with something wildly different. Does this suggest any ideas?

20. *Metamorphose*: Think about how your product or service will be affected if current trends continue – will the problem get worse, or will it fade away and become less significant?

21. *Symbolize*: How can you strip your product or service back to its bare essentials? How can you convert it into something that is immediately easy to grasp?

22. *Mythologize*: Taking this further, how could you give it symbolic, "iconic" or some type of imaginary status.

In summary, use triggers as starting points for brainstorming. Again, once you've done this, evaluate whether you have a satisfactory solution to the problem you're addressing. If you haven't, it's time to move to the next stage: Use "synectic springboards" to stimulate new ideas. These are analogies between the current situation and other situations or things. They can be functional analogies (with other products, services, and approaches that do a similar job), analogies with other phenomena (e.g., with an ocean storm, a rainforest, or a mechanical digger), or stretched analogies (e.g., comparisons with emotions or symbols). Reconstructing is where you collect all of the ideas you've created during the "Reflecting" step, and evaluate them rationally, bringing them together to create practical and useful ideas.

—————————————

TOOL #5: OPERATIONAL CREATIVITY*

Most of us have in one form or another experienced the process of brainstorming. Brainstorming can generate many new ideas but they

---

* Operational creativity contends that, with the accelerating dynamics of competition and a movement of entrepreneurial organizations toward more dynamic approaches to strategy formulation and implementation, creativity becomes of key importance for achieving both product and operational excellence. Over the last 20 years or so, entrepreneurial organizations have increasingly adopted team-centered structures to improve the way in which knowledge is developed, disseminated, and applied in organizations. Although this has dramatically improved product and operational performance, organizations now realize that future radical improvements in performance hinge on improving the creative capabilities of individuals as well.

don't necessarily deal with the solutions needed for the problem at hand. Operational creativity was developed as an alternate to brainstorming's apparent superficiality weaknesses. This method was developed by William Gordon. Instead of stating the opportunity or problem, the facilitator begins with a general statement about the opportunity as only the facilitator is aware of the exact nature of the issue.

Once the general steps of brainstorming have ended, the facilitator then asks a more specific question that comes closer to the essence of the issue being explored, and the participants respond. The facilitator then continues to ask increasingly more specific questions, listing the responses until the actual creative issue is addressed in detail. In most cases, brainstorming provides a free and open environment that encourages the whole team to participate.

Because of the inclusiveness of the brainstorming process, it can also help to obtain buy-in from team members for the solution selected. Team members are more likely to be committed to an approach and will do everything they can to make it a success if they participate in developing it. Also, the interaction between the team members during a brainstorming exercise works to create and strengthen the bonds between team members. The team then moves more quickly through the team development process to become a high-performance team. Later, using operational creativity, questions grow increasingly specific until the issue at hand is addressed.

TOOL #6: NEW IDEAS WITH STORYBOARDING*

Standard idea generation techniques concentrate on combining or adapting existing ideas. This can certainly generate results. The Storyboard approach is a creativity-enhancing tool in that it stretches your mind to

---

* In many cases, what passes for brainstorming are idea-killing sessions that leave entrepreneurs thinking they're not innovative. The technique of storyboarding can remove the worst of these habits and surface both great ideas and a plan of action. Having an individual storyboarding session before a group brainstorming session is definitely helpful for many of the entrepreneurs we have worked with. Another value is the time allowed for individual thinking. Many people tend to simply follow others' thoughts when they are allowed to. Having individual storyboarding time will really help those people to develop their own thoughts before being influenced by others. Thus, a higher degree of originality and creativity can be reached if the atmosphere and structure are facilitated in a creative manner.

forge new connections, think differently, and consider new perspectives. The Storyboard technique combines brainstorming and lateral thinking with a studio-type system for developing film plots. The facilitator brings along a flipchart, a corkboard, thumbtacks, and a good supply of 5 × 8″ blank index cards.

The facilitator begins by describing the opportunity or issue to be resolved and the participants name the potential solution categories. For example, suppose the problem is: What should we do with the people who are part of an operation that is being shut down? The categories might include reorientation, relocation, release retraining, reduction to a part-time role, retirement, etc. Each category is hand-printed on a card, which is pinned along the top of the corkboard.

The facilitator then asks a series of idea-generating questions such as: How can these employees be oriented in a way that will profit the company? The individual? The participants then write their ideas on the 5 × 8 cards, one idea per card. The cards are collected, read aloud without naming the author and without criticism, grouped according to common themes, and pinned on the board under the proper category card. Depending on what he or she sees, the facilitator asks related questions to help generate more creativity and ideation.

Remember, the following techniques can be applied to spark creativity in group settings and brainstorming sessions to break and create thought patterns. We tend to get stuck in certain mind-sets and patterns of thought. Breaking through these can help you get your mind unstuck and generate new ideas. One can use several tools and methods to begin using new thought patterns, leaving the old ones behind:

- Challenge assumptions
- Reword the problem
- Think in reverse
- Express yourself through different media
- Mind mapping possible ideas
- Play the "If I were" game: Ask yourself "If I were ..." how would I address this challenge?
- Formations and combinations

These strategies help in creating an atmosphere that lays the foundational groundwork that will allow a significant increase in creativity.

TOOL #7: ABSENCE THINKING*

Absence thinking involves training your mind to think creatively about what you are thinking and also to think what you are not thinking; sort of a yin and yang technique. When you are thinking about a specific something, you often notice what is not there, you watch what people are not doing, and you make lists of things that you normally forget. In other words, you try to deliberately think about what is absent and envision "what is not there." This technique can be used to improve individual creativity as well as when working in groups. You can use it when you are stuck and unable to modify your mind-set or thinking pattern to another mode. Also, you can use it when you want to do something that has not been done before.

How to use it:

1. Fold a piece of paper in half. Write and think about what you are concentrating on the left side of the paper, and then think about the right side and what is NOT there from the left side.
2. Next, when you are looking at something (or otherwise sensing), notice what is not there.
3. You can also watch people and notice what they do not do.
4. Some use it to make lists of things to remember that you normally forget.

In summary, to be really useful, deliberately and carefully think about what is absent.

Tool Summary

Think about an artist who draws the spaces between things, or a manager of a furniture warehouse who wonders about product areas where customers have made no comment. He or she watches them using tables and notes that they leave the tables out when not using them. The creative

---

* Also called reversal thinking by Frank Voehl in his book *Problem Solving for Results* in 1996, he and Bill Roth suggested three ways to introduce it to entrepreneurs and innovators: use it to stimulate new thinking when you are stuck in a rut; use it to reframe a problem, looking at it from a different angle; and use it when you are seeking different views to define the problem.

act is that he or she invents a table that can be easily folded and stored. The psychology of the creative thinking process is such that while we are very good at seeing what is there, we need to do a better job of seeing what is not there. Absence thinking compensates for this by deliberately forcing us to easily do what does not come naturally to us.

Opportunity Exploration (Insight)

Once you've identified and verified your opportunity, you can figure out what's actually going on. Often, the initial issue that you identified will turn out to be a symptom of a deeper opportunity. Therefore, identifying the roots of the opportunity at issue is extremely important. There are six major tools in this area, of which three have already been covered; the remaining three are as follows.

TOOL #8: BREAKDOWN (DRILLDOWN) TREE DIAGRAM*

Breakdown or Drilldown is a simple technique for breaking down complex opportunities and problems into progressively smaller parts. To use the technique, start by writing the opportunity statement or problem under investigation beginning on the left-hand side of a full sheet of paper. This is similar to starting an Ishikawa Diagram. Next, break down the problem to the next level by jotting the items or conclusions with which the next level of detail is composed. These may be factors contributing to the issue or opportunity, information relating to it, or questions raised by it. This process of breaking down the issue under investigation into smaller parts that together make it up is called "drilling down."

Then, repeat the process for each of these parts at the second level, now creating a third level. Repeat this process. Keep on drilling down into the points until you fully understand the factors contributing to the situation

---

* According to the American Society of Quality (ASQ), this is also called a systematic diagram, tree analysis, analytical tree, and hierarchy diagram. The tree diagram starts with one item that branches into two or more, each of which branches into two or more, and so on. It looks like a tree, with a trunk and multiple branches. It is used to break down broad categories into finer and finer levels of detail. Developing the tree diagram helps you move your thinking step-by-step from generalities to specifics.

or opportunity under investigation. Drilling into a question helps you to get a much deeper understanding of it. The process helps you to recognize the contributing factors that affect the issue. Drilling down sequentially prompts you to tie similar contributing factors that had not initially been associated with a problem. It also identifies where to look for additional information, as shown in Figure 3.5.*

This is also similar to the creation of an outline or a structure tree. If you cannot break them down using the knowledge you have, then carry out whatever research is necessary to understand the point. Drilling down gives creative people a starting point in which to begin thinking about the situation and starts prompting their creativity and curiosity. It highlights where they do not fully understand the facts at hand, and shows where they need to carry out further research. "Drilling down" assists in the decomposition of a large and complex opportunity statement into the parts that make it up. This facilitates the development of plans to deal with these components. It also shows you which points you need to research in more detail.

TOOL #9: LOTUS BLOSSOM

The Lotus Blossom technique uses analytical techniques to generate a significant number of ideas. These could provide the best solution to the problem being addressed. The technique was developed by Yasuo Matsumura, director of Clover Management Research in Japan.[†] Six steps are followed in this technique:

---

* In the above example, the owner of a Florida windsurfing club has complaints from its members about the unpleasant quality of the water close to the Biscayne Bay shoreline, which according to many members seems like it has been a huge problem for some years now. The owner brings in a director of creativity who carries out the drill down analysis in the generic figure above.

† Matsumura believed that we were all born as spontaneous, creative thinkers, while a great deal of our education may be regarded as the inculcation of mind-sets, or "thinking ruts." We were taught how to handle problems and new phenomena with fixed mental attitudes (based on what past thinkers thought) that predetermine our response to problems or situations. Typically, we think on the basis of similar problems encountered in the past. When confronted with problems, we fixate on something in our past that has worked before. Then, we analytically select the most promising approach based on past experiences, excluding all other approaches, and work within a clearly defined direction toward the solution to the problem. Source: http://www.innovationman-agement.se/imtool-articles/creative-thinking-technique-lotus-blossom/.

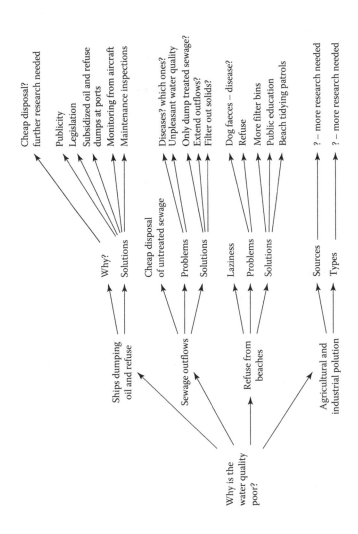

FIGURE 3.5

Drill down into the problem of poor seawater quality.

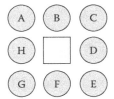

FIGURE 3.6
Lotus blossom.

1. Draw up a lotus blossom diagram (Figure 3.6) made up of a square in the center of the diagram (the pistil) and eight circles (petals) surrounding the square.
2. Write the central idea or problem in the center of the diagram (yellow square).
3. Look for ideas or solutions for the central theme. Then, write them in the flower petals (pink circles).

Example
The mission of the Harrington Institute was to "build a creative atmosphere" within the clients' organizations. The trainers, consultants, and staff wrote this core idea/statement at the center of a lotus blossom to follow this approach. During a debate on how best to address the mission, they came up with eight sub-themes related to the main theme of "build a creative atmosphere":

- Create a challenging atmosphere.
- Generate paths to discover out-of-the-box ideas.
- Make up a creativity board.
- Make the job funny.
- Expand the meaning of job.
- Generate a positive attitude.
- Offer contexts for ideas.
- Organize meetings of creative thinking.

4. These ideas are written in the circles around the main square. Each idea written in the circles becomes the central theme of a new lotus blossom (Figure 3.7).
5. Step 3 is then followed for each of the central ideas.
6. Continue the process until all ideas have been used.

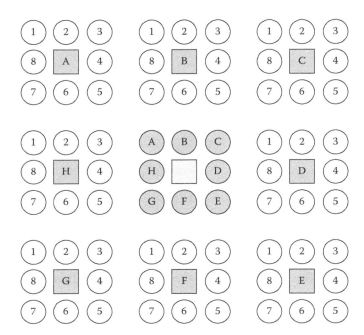

FIGURE 3.7
Lotus blossoms.

This technique has helped the Harrington Institute over the years to create many interesting ideas. Among others, we helped to set up a special empowerment room for creative thinking that was furnished with multimedia creativity books, videos, educational toys, and so on. Moreover, the tool was used with drawings, and the room was decorated with these drawings made by the staff and family members to remind everyone that we are all born innocent and creative.*

When you have clear insight into the essence of the issue, you can move on to generating ideas for a creative solution. Here, you want to generate as many useful ideas as possible. Only some of the ideas generated will be practical to consider implementing. In this step of the creativity process,

---

* The affinity diagram is an associated tool for entrepreneurial innovators to organize ideas and data. This is one of the most useful tools used to improve creativity. This method is commonly used within creativity sessions and allows large numbers of ideas stemming from brainstorming. The cards need to be sorted into groups, based on their natural relationships. Once sorted, they can be more easily reviewed and analyzed. It is also frequently used in creativity contextual inquiry sessions as a way to organize notes and insights from field interviews. With today's IT, the functionality of this tool has been somewhat automated inside algorithms that group data into groups based on their inter relationship. The term "affinity diagram" was devised by Jiro Kawakita in the 1960s and is sometimes referred to as the KJ Method.

you need to decide which criteria you'll use to evaluate your ideas. Without a solid evaluation process, you'll be prone to choosing a solution that is perhaps too cautious.

TOOL #10: FORCE FIELD ANALYSIS DIAGRAM

Force field analysis is a visual aid for pinpointing and analyzing elements that resist change (restraining forces) or push for change (driving forces). This technique helps drive improvement by developing plans to overcome the restrainers and make maximum use of the driving forces.

The force field analysis technique has been used in some settings to do the following:

- Analyze a problem situation into its basic components.
- Identify those key elements of the problem situation about which something can realistically be done.
- Develop a systematic and insightful strategy for problem-solving that minimizes "boomerang" effects and irrelevant efforts.
- Criteria need to be developed and clearly defined for use during the evaluation step such that these can be applied consistently.

The technique is an effective device for achieving each of these purposes when it is seriously employed. The level of activity, to put it differently, is the starting point in the problem identification and analysis. To constitute a problem, the current level typically departs from some implicit norm or goal.* A particular activity level may be thought of as resulting from some pressures and influences acting upon the individual, group, or organization in question.

---

* Kurt Lewin, who developed force field analysis, has proposed that any problem situation – be it the behavior of an individual or group, the current state or condition of an organization, a particular set of attitudes, or frame of mind – may be thought of as constituting a level of activity that is somehow different from that desired. For example, smoking, as an activity may become the basis for a problem when it occurs with greater intensity or at a higher level than one desires. Quality, as another example of an activity level, may become a problem when it is at a less-than-desirable level. Depression or authoritarianism, as examples of attitudinal activity levels, become problems when they are too intense or at higher-than-desirable levels.

These numerous influences Lewin calls "forces," and they may be both external and internal to the person or situation in question. Lewin identifies two kinds of forces:

- Driving or facilitating forces that promote the occurrence of the particular activity of concern.
- Restraining or inhibiting forces that inhibit or oppose the occurrence of the same activity.

An activity level is the result of the simultaneous operation of both facilitating and inhibiting forces. The two force fields push in opposite directions and, while the stronger of the two will tend to characterize the problem situation, a point of balance is usually achieved that gives the appearance of habitual behavior or of a steady-state condition. Changes in the strength of either of the fields, however, can cause a change in the activity level of concern. Thus, apparently habitual ways of behaving, or frozen attitudes, can be changed (and related problems solved) by bringing about changes in the relative strengths of facilitating and inhibiting force fields.

To appreciate just what kinds of forces are operating in a given situation and which ones are susceptible to influence, a force field analysis must be made. As the first step to a fuller understanding of the problem, the forces (both facilitating and inhibiting) should be identified as fully as possible. Identified forces should be listed and, as much as possible, their relative contributions or strengths should be noted.

Once the problem has been recognized and a commitment has been made by the appropriate stakeholders to change the problem situation, four basic steps are used in the force field analysis activity to analyze the problem.

- Define the problem and propose an ideal solution.
- Identify the forces acting on the problem situation and evaluate whether these forces are acting for or against the solution.
- Develop and implement a strategy for changing these forces.
- Re-examine the situation to determine the effectiveness of the change and make further adjustments if necessary.

The first step includes defining the problem and proposing the ideal situation. In defining the problem, it is necessary to say exactly what it is.

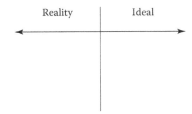

FIGURE 3.8
Reality vs. ideal.

1. Propose an ideal situation in a "goal statement." It can be prepared by answering the question: "What will the situation be like when the problem is solved?" The answer must be tested to determine if it really gets to the heart of the problem.
2. Another possible question is "What would the situation be like if everything were operating ideally?" (Figure 3.8).

Determining the precise goal statement is important because it guides the rest of the problem-solving steps. The second step is to identify and evaluate the forces that affect the problem or that are for or against your implementation of the solution.

1. The facilitating forces tend to move the problem situation from reality toward the ideal. The restraining forces resist the movement toward the ideal state, and, in a state of equilibrium, counterbalance the facilitating forces (Figure 3.9).
2. You can visualize a problem situation by drawing a line down a sheet of paper and listing the facilitating forces on one side and the restraining forces on the other side. Each of these forces has its own weight and taken together they keep the field in balance (Figure 3.10).

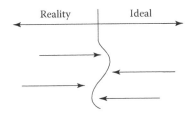

FIGURE 3.9
The as-is state in equilibrium.

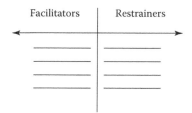

FIGURE 3.10
In balance.

3. In addition to helping make the problem situation visual, force field analysis provides a method for developing a solution. The most effective solution will involve reducing the restraining forces operating on the problem (Figure 3.11).
4. There are two reasons for reducing the restraining forces:
   • To move the problem toward a solution.
   • To avoid the effect of having too many facilitating forces.
     Because the forces on each side of the situation are in balance, removing or reducing the restraining forces will cause movement of the problem toward a solution.
5. On the other hand, adding facilitating forces without reducing restraining forces will likely lead to the appearance of new restrainers. Remember that although you may change the situation by changing a force, you may not have improved the situation.
6. An effective strategy cannot be planned without evaluating the restraining forces for two factors: first, whether and to what degree a restrainer is changeable, and secondly, to what degree will changing a restrainer affect the problem.
7. It is ineffective and a waste of energy to try to change an unchangeable force.

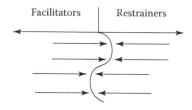

FIGURE 3.11
Reducing the restraining forces.

8. One way to begin planning a strategy is to evaluate each force to see how changeable it is. A simple three-point rating scale is sufficient:
   - A fixed, unchanging force. Example: A contractual item, a law, a fixed budget.
   - A force changeable with moderate to extensive effort. Example: An item that involves the efforts and cooperation of many departments.
   - A change that can be readily performed, perhaps by just revising a procedure and is probably within the control of the group.

9. The change or removal of some restrainers may have little or no impact. You must consider the effect that changing the force will have. It is good, then, to also rate the restrainers for their effect on solving the problem.

10. A three-point rating scale can be used to rate the effect a change will have on the problem:
    - No significant improvement will occur with the change.
    - Some minor improvement will occur with the change – perhaps up to 20% of the improvement needed to solve the problem.
    - A major improvement results from changing this force; that is, from 25% to 100% of the needed improvement.

11. After you have rated all of the forces operating on the problem situation, you can determine a priority for dealing with each force by adding together the numbers with which you rated each of the forces. The highest priority will be the restraining force, which will have the most effect and which is most changeable. After this will come those forces that you judge to have a large effect but are less changeable, and so on.

At this point in the force field analysis, you are ready to begin the third step: developing and implementing a strategy for changing the forces affecting a situation.

1. In deciding the priority, strive for a balance between ease of change and the impact of the proposed change. Often, actions when dealing with any situation will require creative thinking. The balance between the facilitators and the restrainers is a clue to deciding which forces to change.

2. A recommended tool is to remove the restraining forces to allow the point of equilibrium to shift. If the new point is not satisfactory, examine the driving forces and determine which ones you can successfully change.

The fourth step is to examine the situation. If you are still not satisfied with the new situation, determine which facilitating forces can be added.

Each time a change is planned, take the time to estimate and determine whether the change was worth it. Ask these questions:

- Will it produce the desired results?
- Which facilitating and restraining factors will be affected and by how much?
- How will the equilibrium point be affected?
- Is there a better way of getting the same results?
- Does the change have a negative impact on other parts of the process?
- What will be the return on investment?

Force field analysis is a straightforward tool. Using it with diligence and an ongoing evaluation of solutions will ensure that it can work toward the achievement of your desired goal. Force field analysis is valuable because it goes beyond brainstorming by helping to develop plans and set priorities.

SUMMARY

Individual creativity covered in this chapter refers to the process that starts with the identification of a problem until the completion of the work involved in bringing the ideas to reality. From those definitions alone, it is clear that entrepreneurs simply cannot go forward and prosper without at least the smallest degree of creativity. An entrepreneur needs to have all of the following *components of creativity*:

- *Motivation*: Let us say, for example, that the individual has the two basic ingredients of an entrepreneur: creative thinking and expertise. There is still a high probability that nothing will come of it if the individual is not motivated to do anything about it. One thing is for sure: an individual will never become an entrepreneur without a desire to bring forth creative solutions.

- *Expertise*: Covers everything that the entrepreneur knows, particularly in the field or area that he works in. An entrepreneur is expected to have more than a basic knowledge about the line of business that he is planning to set up. Becoming known as an "obvious expert" may be acquired through formal education, trainings, and seminars, or even actual or practical experience.*

- *Skills of creative thinking*: While expertise is largely obtained from external sources, creative thinking is more attributed to one's personality and character. It refers to the capability of the individual to come up with ideas and put them together to arrive at combinations that provide their desired results or goals.

These three components are deemed the main components of creativity. Without any one of them, creativity simply could not exist. But those are not the only elements that are required in order to fully tap or utilize the full potential of an entrepreneur's creativity.

While creativity for the entrepreneur has several meanings, all point to one thing: coming up with something new and fresh, or something that no one has seen before. Individual creativity is a unique ability that is inherent within individuals alone, making them capable of coming up with fresh and innovative ideas. It can also be described as the way that entrepreneurs do things, or their approach toward a problem that needs a solution.

---

* Obvious experts are the *thoughtleaders*, the high-profile professionals who rise above everyone else in their field to become the go-to experts in all forms of media. Follow the "Five Pillars of Thought Leading": (1) publish articles and books; (2) speak regularly to groups and companies; (3) inspire with "fresh" thinking; (4) attract ongoing media attention; and (5) leverage the Internet creatively. Used together, these five pillars offer an unbeatable strategy for positioning your business as the only one to call. Prospects and clients will think only of you when your service or product is needed. Your competitors are left struggling to catch up.

4

Corporate Creativity and Innovation

Entrepreneurship is neither a science nor an art. It has a knowledge base, of course, which this Book attempts to present in an organized fashion, but as in all practices (medicine, for instance or engineering) knowledge in Entrepreneurship is a means to an end. Indeed, what constitutes knowledge in a practice is largely defined by its ends, that is, by the practice. Hence a book like this should be backed by long years of practice.

Peter Drucker
Innovation and Entrepreneurship, Practice and Principles

In a nutshell: Creativity seems to be something that a corporation cannot possess. Essentially, if creativity is one thing, it is passion, and passion is something that a nameless, faceless entity cannot possess. After all, a computer cannot possess passion, or can it? You can improve your company's performance by increasing creativity and by fostering employee innovation. *A great many of the so-called creative acts are unexpected, and herein lies your organization's creative potential. A company is creative when its employees do something new (and possibly useful), without being directly shown or taught what to do.** Creativity can and has the potential to happen in every organization, including companies with highly standardized

---

* Peter Drucker wrote that purposeful innovation results from analysis, systemic review, and hard work, and can be taught, replicated, and learned. Purposeful, systemic innovation begins with an analysis of opportunities. The search must be organized and conducted on a regular basis. It seems that we may be getting hung up on "the fuzzy front end" and other views that make innovation seem really obscure. He taught that *effectuation* is taking action toward unpredictable future states using currently controlled resources and with imperfect knowledge about current circumstances.

procedures. While creativity is intangible, you can see the results of it in your company's improvements and innovations. However, consider an organization such as a sports team. Many times, a team that is completely overmatched by its opponents manages to win, and these wins are highly charged and emotional. So why can't a company develop a winning attitude, or a passion for creativity? In our consulting engagements, we often encounter individuals with a consistent passionate attitude in organizations that, for all intents and purposes, feel that they (the organization) are looking for the white knight to appear in their own organization. This often presupposes that an individual (usually a top executive) will bring both creativity and innovation, if only the culture allows it and the time is right. This chapter will discuss how the "white knight" attitude can be found or brought about.

INTRODUCTION

Having taken a course with Peter Drucker in the late 1970s, one of the authors was struck with how the following corporate creativity notions were introduced by Drucker as innovation and entrepreneurship at the time:

- *Abstract rules*: Those unarticulated, yet essential guidelines, norms, and traditions that people within a social setting tend to follow.
- *Spontaneous order*: A term that Friedrich Hayek uses to describe what he calls the Open Society. It is created by unleashing human creativity generally in a way not planned by anyone and, importantly, could not have been.
- *Affordable loss principle*: Stipulates that entrepreneurs risk no more than they are willing to lose.
- *Lemonade principle*: Based on the old adage, "If life throws you lemons, make lemonade." In other words, make the best of the unexpected.
- *Crazy quilt principle*: Based on the expert entrepreneur's strategy to continuously seek out people who may become valuable contributors to his or her venture.

- *Pilot in the plane principle*: Based on the concept of *control* using effectual logic and is referred to as *non-predictive control*. Expert entrepreneurs believe they can determine their individual futures best by applying effectual logic to the resources they currently control.
- *Creativity and innovation*: Since innovations involve different ways we can solve a problem, we can say that creativity in so many ways is associated with innovation.
  - Creativity is often proven by curiosity.
  - Effective preparation and sincere efforts often produce creativity.
  - Creativity involves the use of pre-acquired knowledge and practices in a whole new way to achieve results.
  - Sometimes, we get unusable or useless results due to creativity.
  - Anybody can be creative.
  - Unpredictable positive results and luck can be achieved via creativity.

Starting around 1980, Drucker first codified the following five principles of corporate innovation:

1. "Purposeful, systematic innovation begins with the analysis of the opportunities. It begins with thinking through ... the sources of innovative opportunities." Drucker was a logical thinker with his feet firmly on the ground and this first principle is a perfect example of this. Opportunity is key, but only a logical and clear-headed analysis will highlight the right opportunity for the individual.
2. "Innovation is both conceptual and perceptual ... successful innovators ... look at figures, and they look at people. They work out analytically what the innovation has to be to satisfy an opportunity. And then they go out and look at the customers, the users, to see what their expectations, their values, their needs are." This is an early perfect example of Drucker's belief that innovation needs to be managed like any other business activity. In other words, there has to be a need that can be fulfilled, and then every aspect of that need – from the product or service through to customer expectations – has to be analyzed. "An innovation that is not handled in this way is nothing more than a 'pipe dream' filled with 'hopium' and not an innovation," he would say.
3. "An innovation, to be effective, has to be simple and it has to be focused. It should do only one thing, otherwise, it confuses.

All effective innovations are breathtakingly simple. Indeed, the greatest praise an innovation can receive is for people to say: 'This is obvious. Why didn't I think of it?'" Simplicity is not a requirement that you might expect from a groundbreaking innovation, but as Drucker explains, it is necessary to ensure that a clear business model can be put in place. Know what you are doing and where your defining lines are and you will then know how to beat any competition.

4. "Effective innovations start small ... they try to do one specific thing." To fill a common need, merely find a solution. If you try to do any more than that, then you aren't solving a problem, you are merely tampering and complicating it. Only once you have successfully filled that need can you expand it into a competitive advantage.

5. "A successful innovation aims at leadership within a given market or industry ... if an innovation does not aim at leadership from the beginning, it is unlikely to be innovative enough, and therefore unlikely to be capable of establishing itself."

For Drucker, an innovation must be both creative and innovative; otherwise, it is simply mimicking the work of others and stealing their thunder without finishing the job. To be the best at what you do is without doubt inspirational talk, but putting it into action is a true work of the entrepreneurial management and only after you have achieved leadership in the industry can you count it a success. Drucker stated that corporate creativity and innovation should be managed like any other business activity, and he highlights the need for functional inspiration to ensure success in a management environment. Accordingly, he identified the following *seven kinds of opportunities*:*

1. *Unexpected occurrences*: "These are productive sources of innovation opportunities because most businesses dismiss them, disregard them, and even resent them. Genuinely entrepreneurial businesses

---

* These seven opportunity areas are summarized in a blog http://www.creativehuddle.co.uk/peter-drucker. Creative Huddle works with individuals, teams, and organizations to help them learn skills for modern business, including creativity, critical thinking, and problem-solving. Their motto is: No matter how brilliant your idea, or how detailed your planning, execution is what matters. By managing yourself effectively, you can make sure you achieve all your aims and tick off all your tasks.

have two 'first pages' – a problem page and an opportunity page – and managers spend equal time on both."

2. *Incongruities*: Look for inconsistency and disharmony to see where an innovation could smooth a process or join it up.

3. *Process needs*: What can you develop that supports another process or product?

4. *Industry and market changes*: "Managers may believe that industry structures are ordained by the good Lord, but these structures can – and often do – change overnight. Such change creates tremendous opportunity for innovation."

5. *Demographic changes*: "Managers have known for a long time that demographics matter, but they have always believed that population statistics change slowly. In this century, however, they don't. Indeed, the innovation opportunities made possible by changes in the numbers of people – and in their age distribution, education, occupations, and geographic location – are among the most rewarding and least risky of entrepreneurial pursuits."

6. *Changes in perception*: "Changing a manager's perception of a glass from half full to half empty opens up big innovation opportunities."

7. *New knowledge*: "They are the superstars of entrepreneurship; they get the publicity and the money. Knowledge-based innovations differ from all others in the time they take, in their casualty rates, and in their predictability, as well as in the challenges they pose to entrepreneurs. Like most superstars, they can be temperamental, capricious, and hard to direct."

EKVALL BUILDS ON DRUCKER

Several research studies have been carried out since Drucker's days to determine factors that are essential to cultivating a creative atmosphere in a company. According to Ekvall's model, the following factors should be available for a creative atmosphere to occur*:

1. *Idea time*: There is need to provide the time for employee idea development. Time is required to develop a creative idea.

---

* The most common reaction to a great idea isn't immediate recognition. For many great ideas, when first presented to an audience, the initial reaction is rejection. The answer to why do great ideas get rejected? According to Drucker and other experts, it all boils down to risk.

2. *Taking risks*: Employees should be able to take certain risks with the company's risk limits. But, there must be a clear indication of the level of risk that employees can take, in order to reduce the fear of taking risks.

3. *Challenge*: Employees who are experts in their field need to feel tested and challenged.

4. *Freedom*: People need to express their abilities, make errors, learn from their errors, and improve in their field of mastery. A few directors have a propensity toward "too early" intercessions and tend to foil the fundamental unlearning and learning process that only first-hand experience can give.

5. *Supporting ideas*: Employees need to feel that their ideas and thoughts align with the interests of the organization. Organizations ought to set up clear targets for employees and communication lines to each idea, and encourage employees to analyze them.

6. *Conflicts*: People should have the capacity to safeguard their inventive thoughts inside the organization's commercial center of thoughts. Ideas should live beyond words on their relative legitimacy in the market hub. Employees ought to be engaged with business case presentation and development that empowers them to sufficiently verbalize their creative ideas while in the commercial setting.

7. *Debates*: Employees ought to be occupied with debates about the benefits of their creative thoughts. Debating fills two essential needs: *It empowers the idea initiator to ponder the conceivable importance and issues concerning the creative idea; and it makes those who participate in the debate have better concepts of their creative ideas.*

8. *Humor*: People regularly get good ideas and do so more immediately when they are permitted to play with ideas in a non-debilitating manner.

9. *Trust, receptiveness*: Transparency and trust are essential for people working to get something done.

10. *Dynamism, exuberance*: Organizations that cultivate open spaces, free-streaming discussions, and unrehearsed talk sessions, and support an energetic work environment buzz are the best among the present most innovative organizations.

Organizations can implement creativity with careful development of the conditions under which creativity normally exists. When employees do not communicate with each other, it causes creativity impediment. Generally speaking, innovation at the corporate level lives and dies according to the culture of the organization. Organizations that are inherently stifling and/or don't really understand their own culture can sometimes create innovation, but it is generally a rare occurrence.

As an example, we have worked with literally hundreds of companies throughout our respective careers. These companies have represented almost every industry in almost every part of the globe. For argument's sake, let's say that half of these companies consider themselves innovative, while the other half are asking for help to become innovative. We can say without hesitation that the dividing line between these two is a pure construct of how the companies feel about themselves and innovation – which is one of the reasons why innovation remains so elusive.

Recently, we have had the pleasure of working with oil companies around the world. Almost without exception, the people we worked with explained that they were not innovative at all. When I explained that fracking seemed to be a pretty innovative technique for extracting oil, and that some of the specialized equipment they used hundreds of feet below the ocean was particularly innovative, they just responded with "that is our main task."

On the other hand, working with technology companies that consider themselves to be the most innovative companies sometimes perplexes us. The company simply takes an existing real-world process, applies computer software that has been around for 20 years, uses objects from previous iterations of programs that they or someone else has written for another project, puts a fancy front end on it – and then brags about how they are the most innovative organization in the world. *What makes this particularly insidious is the fact that many of these companies are considered the most hostile work environments in the business world.*

So, from a corporate innovation perspective, does just saying you are innovative make it so? Accordingly, do many patents actually mean that you are innovative, or just that you can afford many good patent attorneys? Consider a company like IBM, which turns out thousands of patents per year. If corporate innovation is measured by the number of patents that you produce, then we should consider IBM one of the most innovative companies in the world (and at times they are, just think about Watson). Alternatively, we have thousands of companies in Silicon Valley that collectively consider themselves "the most innovative place on earth."

Well, as any parent who has had to endure 45-minute lines in the heat of Florida in Orange County can attest, Disneyworld is definitely NOT the happiest place on earth, regardless of the claims. So, does the declaration of being the most innovative company or region make it so? The answer is yes and no. Being innovative isn't about your declaration of innovativeness; instead, it is about demonstrating it every day in the little things you do. We recently had the privilege of spending time with a technology executive who explained to me that when he considered taking money from investors, he thought about it this way:

> They come to me and tell me that if I want my company to grow to be a multibillion dollar IPO, I have to do this and that to get there. One of the things I need to do is take their money and allow them to have seats on the boards, bring in executives that fit their mold of what a company needs to look like and the kinds of degrees and background that this team needs to contain. I tell them to go to hell – I have a successful product offering that is growing at 300% per year and it seems to me that they need me a lot more than I need them. They need to invest in a company that will give them and their stakeholders a huge return, but I can organically grow, or find investors that will allow me to continue to grow my company in the way that has already made it great in just a few short years.

As consultants to this company, we were inspired and came back a few days later with a recommendation for the executive that turned all the traditional models of how to perform a business process on their ear. In this particular case, the company was struggling to keep up with demand from consulting companies for training on the company's platform – not enough qualified individuals to train the consultants. In the traditional model, the consultants come for training and might even go out to an implementation or two in an effort to become competent in the platform.

The inspiration that he gave us was that his company was growing at 300% per year and the consulting firms needed him much more than he needed them – he was happy with his growth, and his investors trusted what he was doing. Without getting into confidential details, the new proposal called for the consulting firms to start to do the majority of the work in the relationship.

So what does this have to do with innovation? ... the story illustrates the inspiration provided by the chief executive officer (CEO) to think differently and approach the world from a new perspective. Granted, this type of approach to the world can cause problems. It is now widely accepted that Steve Jobs could be difficult to work with and to work for. This had a lot to do with him pushing the envelope and essentially saying that you needed him much more than he needed you.*

> *Working for an innovator can lead to harassment suits, hurt feelings, and unhappiness, but the rewards for throwing out conventional wisdom about how things should be done are awe-inspiring.*

Now, what about the companies that shout from the mountain tops that they are the most innovative (this or that) company, a favorite marketing message for many companies, but particularly automobile manufacturers. It appears that in the case of many of these companies, declarations are more the truth than actual fact. *Consider the case of the faulty ignition switches at GM a few years back.* It seems that an innovative company would have done a few things differently – starting with coming up with an ignition system that was not rooted in 50-year-old technology. An innovative company would not have found it acceptable that the technology hadn't notably changed in 50 years, and the leaders would have been in the engineering department challenging the assumption that an ignition switch needed to be designed in a certain way, because that's just the way they worked.

The executive we wrote about earlier, or perhaps even Steve Jobs, would not have accepted a faulty design and would have likely been in the department with his or her sleeves rolled up, helping change the design. We have stated earlier that it's likely that this kind of behavior in an automobile manufacturing company would have been entirely unacceptable and led to engineers resigning in protest, because the executive was trying to tell them how to do their job. Having an innovative organization is disruptive and sometimes messy, because it tends to be a meritocracy.

---

* For many individuals, this was not acceptable. After all, as someone who graduated from the finest schools and was trained by the best companies, it's hard to accept that an upstart like Jobs, who didn't even complete college, could be better at anything than you. However, the people who accepted that the man might be right were inspired, and became some of the wealthiest people in the world of organizational creativity and entrepreneurship.

In a meritocracy, the person with the best idea gets ahead, regardless of their race, sex, college degree, or social status. Yes, technology and business process innovation is taking place at an unprecedented pace in Silicon Valley, but it is also happening in New York, Israel, Russia, China, and India. In fact, the problems with some companies in regard to females in the workforce isn't as much about meritocracy as it is about a general lack of females going into engineering and computer programming – an issue mostly unrelated to innovation.

As illustrated in the oil companies, innovation is also happening in places that people don't know. Yes, there are companies that use the innovation moniker as a pure marketing ploy, but there are many more that just go quietly about their business, innovating every day of their existence with very few people even knowing it. There are also those that haven't figured out how it works.

Take the case of cybersecurity and cybercriminals. The fundamental flaw in the cybercrime story is that the technology industry has not been innovative. Computer software design is rooted in a foundation that is at least 30 years old. Consider the Y2K fiasco and how that all started. Essentially, in most of the legacy systems that existed at the time, programmers did not include the ability for the computer to go beyond the year "99." These were programs written in the 1960s, 1970s, and 1980s that assumed that the code would be replaced with something better way before it became a problem. What took people by surprise was that a vast number of programs that were specifically designed to be replaced within 10 or 20 years were still the backbone of much of the economy in 2000. Since we were fortunate to be involved in many Y2K projects in the late 1990s, we heard the story over and over that replacing a system when it should have been done was (1) expensive and (2) didn't make sense because the old system worked.

Fast-forward to 2015 and how are we any different? We have systems that are essentially using Java code (written 20+ years ago), MS DOS-based windows computers (DOS has been around since the 1980s), and even the virus-free Windows operating system is based on fairly old technology. The fact is that, with the exception of Linux, we are basing our entire global infrastructure on decades-old computer architecture. So, even the most innovative industry in the world has more than a few warts. Just ask NASA.

So, what are the lessons for your company, and how do you achieve the coveted innovative company status? The first thing is to challenge the way you have ever done anything. As a consultant and industrial engineer, I am often asked how to come up with an innovative idea in this fast-moving world, and my pat answer is to tell my people to invent something that solves a problem that doesn't yet exist. What I mean by this is that by the time you recognize a problem, there is a good chance that someone else has already recognized it and done something about it.

When Apple invented the iPad, it wasn't the first digital music player – it was about the volume and ease of the digital music experience. It was about the iTunes library and it was about solving a problem that we didn't know we had. Tesla Motors knows about the limitations of electric cars, but it also knows that by the time it perfects the car, the batteries will be much better than today.

Is your company solving today's problems or tomorrow's problems? Is the attitude that we are too busy working at solving our current problems and designing the next generation without understanding what five generations should be? If this is the case, can you be an innovative organization?*

These types of business model improvements are not stifling to innovation – and will probably enhance it. The need for trust; trust that paychecks will be delivered on time and that agreements with customers will be fulfilled per agreement are a critical part of innovation. It gets back to Maslow's order of needs. Essentially, unless we know that the basics of food, water, and shelter are being fulfilled, we cannot possibly set our minds free to be innovative. It was a learning process for us to understand that you really don't have to land an airplane to rebuild it, and even if you do need to land it periodically, you better be sure it is only grounded for a very short time.

Finally, don't be scared to annoy some people. In a time of rapid change, there will be people who will keep up and people who will fall behind. There will be people who won't want to fly on a plane while the engines are being changed in flight. This is OK, because there are a lot of companies that will innovate in a slower and more controlled manner. Which leads to another very important point in corporate innovation; corporate innovation is relative.

Some things are already pretty well designed and have such a large infrastructure that massive disruption doesn't make a lot of sense. When

---

* Does your company have a bunch of policies and procedures that mimic the industrial age? Although we hate to admit it, one of our clients hired us to work with the company to make it more attractive to Wall Street and an IPO. Granted, many startup companies need to grow up a little. Wasted money, reinventing the same processes every time a transaction takes place, and not having any consistency from one office to another is counterproductive.

we sit through pitching contests throughout the world, we are constantly amazed at some of the ideas that people come up with. In some respects, with television shows like "Shark Tank" and everyone wanting to be the next Facebook, ideas sometimes sound a bit crazy. In the interest of confidentiality, we are probably prohibited from discussing any of these ideas specifically, but in general, I think we can help the reader to understand the point.

Let's say that an individual invents an improved laptop technology that produces a laptop that is 5% more energy efficient but costs about $1000 more than the current best-in-class laptop. The new design may be more energy efficient, and over the long run could save someone a few cents in overall cost. Let's also admit that less energy consumption means a smaller carbon footprint over the world population of laptop computers. I am sure most readers will admit that a 5% improvement on the battery life of a laptop isn't going to lead to anyone switching laptops, and funding for the project will probably not happen unless the technology is just the beginning of something greater.

A LOOK AT SOME ORGANIZATIONAL CREATIVITY MODELS*

According to K. Ferlic, in studying our inherent creativity, one can come to see that there is an inner creative power and an outer creative power. Organizational creativity is about learning the relationship between inner and outer creative powers and how to use this relationship to create the desired organization or organizational transformation. Depending on what one desires to create, the focus may be primarily on the inner creative power, the outer creative power, or the relationship between the inner and the outer.[†]

---

* *Corporate Creativity: It's Not What You Expect*; Alan G. Robinson, PhD and Sam Stern, PhD. Dr. Robinson is professor at the School of Management, University of Massachusetts at Amherst. Dr. Stern teaches at the School of Education, Oregon State University, Corvallis. They wrote *Corporate Creativity: How Innovation and Improvement Actually Happen*, (Berrett-Koehler, San Francisco, 1997) from which this section is loosely based and adapted.

† See http://www.organizationalcreativity.info/oc_topics.htm. In a relatively short time after starting the journey of *exploration of creativity in the workplace*, the author K. Ferlic came to understand the existence of what can best be described as a *creative spirit* existing within each individual. It was an unexpected discovery for Ferlic and it took him a while to fully understand the implications of living true to our creative spirit.

Organizational creativity captures the concepts, principles, and understanding related to organizational transformation, organizational design, and organizational dynamics resulting from an exploration of creativity in the workplace and subsequent exploration of our individual inherent creativity. Applications of these concepts, principles, and understanding to organizations and groups are discussed in the topics "Transforming the Organization" and "Transforming the Heart of the Organization."*

Managers and executives in most companies are aware that their creative *potential* greatly exceeds their creative *performance*. The issue with this is that they are not aware of how to go about resolving this issue. Most inventive acts are largely unplanned, as they now happen spontaneously, and originate from places where they're not usually anticipated. It's difficult to anticipate what they'll be, whose responsibility they are, and how and when they will happen. This is the genuine idea of corporate inventiveness, and it's here that an organization's creative potential is truly seen. Surprise is the unique feature of corporate creativity.

An occurrence at the Japan Railways (JR) East is a decent example of the energy of sudden creativity. This organization never expected that another bullet train line could be built through the mountains north of Tokyo. The new train required many passages. The one through Mt. Tanigawa had water issues, and JR engineers started to draw up waste designs. In any case, inside the passage, a support laborer thought the water tasted so great that he suggested that as opposed to pumping it away into overflows, JR East should bottle and market it as premium mineral water.

The idea was implemented, and soon the water was available under the brand name "Oshimizu." It turned out to be popular to the point that JR East introduced Oshimizu candy machines at each of its almost 1000 stages. Notices for the water stress the purity of Mt. Tanigawa's snow pack, the wellspring of the water, and the moderate procedure by which it permeates through the mountain, absorbing restorative amounts of minerals. The brand of product has increased over the years, adding frosted and hot teas and espressos. About $47 million was generated from sealing Oshimizu beverages in 1994.

Their ideas were completely unforeseen by their companies. Through our examination of creativity in organizations around the globe, we have come to understand that the greater part of creativity, regardless of

---

* http://www.organizationalcreativity.info/oc_topics.htm.

sensational developments or little changes, happens just like the previously cited examples.

Take, for example, a 2 year research program that had won government awards between 1986 and 1990 for the administration's Science and Technology Agency and the Japan Institute of Invention and Innovation.

The authors were at the same time was seeing similar concepts in of unstopping creativity. All the organizations we studied utilized a planned way to deal with constant change, an approach in which what to enhance, by how much, and by whom was chosen ahead of time; the best staff with the best strategies perpetually set more prominent accentuation on frameworks intended to fortify unplanned creative improvement. Here, as well, the more novel and extensive improvements had a tendency to be the unforeseen ones.

We asked why this unplanned creativity was so hard to uncover. Most organizations don't appear to understand the significance of unforeseen imaginative acts. Maybe a characteristic is the propensity of management to over-trust its more responsible protocols, especially when these historically prompted effective changes and/or new developments. After some time, corporate informal and recorded histories shade out the truly surprising causes of creativity, substituting shortsighted and mismanagement accounts of what really happened.

Six Vital Fundamentals of Corporate Business Creativity

For any enterprise or business to progress and have room to expand in this ever-changing world, it is important to comprehend and implement innovative concepts and essential elements of business creativity. The current business framework is unpredictable and multifaceted. Thus, we all need to be corporately creative. Six features are essential in all corporate creative activities, and these features are believed to be the vital aspect of reliable improvements and advancements in corporate creativity. The results or outcomes of these features are unpredictable, but with these considered features actively implemented, the probability for corporate business creativity improvement is certain. "Managing" – just like managing a casino – creativity is tied in with increasing probabilities and possible outcomes.

Despite the fact that the management of casinos are rarely aware of how gamblers are performing at any given table, they are aware that the more people who come and play for a considerable length of time against all odds is an extremely unsurprising and stable benefit for the business.

When considering a short period of time, the effects are uncertain, while profitability is certain when considering a longer period of time.

This means that organizations can't actually predict the creative feature that will occur or be successful for them, but they can implement strategies to make the ones that do occur become profitable and occur more often.

1. *Alignment*: The term "alignment" in this case means that all employees' activities and interests are directed toward achieving the goals of the company or organization.* This implies that all staff are focused on implementing creative ideas that will positively impact the company. Organizations can exist with little or no alignment; however, they can't be reliably creative until there is noticeable alignment. Most times, alignment is disregarded – it's considered to be negligible or immaterial – but with corporate creativity the effect of alignment is vital and very obvious as soon as it is implemented.

2. *Unofficial activity*†: Considering corporate creativity, an intention by an employee to carry out something beneficial and new for an organization without any official assistance or support is known as an unofficial activity. When a new concept is introduced into an organization, it's frequently opposed and restricted. With unofficial activities, thoughts and ideas have the opportunity to grow until they're sufficiently able to resist opposition. Besides, official requirements for any task raise a wide range of boundaries to innovative creativity and all pre-arranged projects and ideas till they are executed. Employees are allowed to test in an unofficial capacity,

---

* According to Clear Company, goal alignment, or strategic alignment, is the process by which you keep your workforce working toward your company's overarching goals. When company-wide goals are set, steps must be taken to ensure that employees are informed not only as to what they should be working on, but also why. Managers must ensure that their individual goals and work – as well as that of their direct reports – are in line with the overarching strategy. Then, you can ensure that your people are driving progress daily. Proper strategic alignment ensures the work of your best talent is being effectively and efficiently utilized.

† Understanding how individual employee's work ladders up to larger organizational goals allows for an in-depth understanding of progress. Additionally, it ensures your workers understand their value and contributions to the company. This helps improve employee engagement and leads to a happier company culture. Implementing a goal-centric system makes certain your people are working toward the right goals, preventing costly misalignment.

even outside their field of expertise, and frequently come up with surprising ideas during this time. The concept of corporate creativity was achieved at every unofficial experiment examined.

3. *Serendipitous discovery**: Serendipity or, in other words, fortunate insight (astuteness of insight), is the occurrence of a knowledgeable and profitable accidental action. Creativity entails connecting things that seem disassociated. The depth of the associated connection determines the extent of knowledge and expertise required to effectively execute a creative action and likewise how unpredictable the results will be. Serendipity is essential and available in each inventive demonstration, regardless of whether those included remember it or not. Only when serendipity is really comprehended and implemented can organizations fully see its impact.

4. *Diverse stimuli*: Stimulus can help provide new creative insights into an idea that has already been set in motion or it helps to bring in a whole new idea. Nevertheless, it's difficult to foresee how an individual will respond to a specific stimulus, and what stimulates one person might not inspire another person. Organizations ought to put in sufficient effort to convey diverse stimuli to their employees, and also consider that not all efforts are completely effective. Generally, our everyday life as well as our work-related activities comes with diverse stimulus. It's vital that employers give opportunities to their workers to enlighten others concerning the diverse stimulus they've gotten and the potential outcomes. Genuine leverage is achievable at this point.

5. *Self-initiated activity*: In corporate creativity, what makes a self-initiated problem-solving activity so effective is that it enables and motivates workers to pick an issue they're focusing on and feel the need to provide solutions, often for reasons unknown. This implies that their inherent inspiration is significantly higher than it would be if another person had arranged the undertaking. Promoting self-initiated actions that produce corporate creative results is clearly doable and easily achievable.

---

* Stories of scientific discovery abound with lucky coincidences. It's true that serendipity and good fortune are often cited as key factors in making scientific innovations. But look closer. Even when scientists feel that they just got lucky – like Newton being hit on the head with his proverbial apple – the steps leading to a new finding or idea often tell a different story. It takes more than being in the right place, at the right time, to make a serendipitous discovery. Source: Understanding Science at https://undsci.berkeley.edu/article/serendipity.

6. *Company's internal communication**: Organizations regularly carry out planned activities, and it is expected that essential methods of effective communication are set in place. In any case, official channels of communication are effective for corporate creativity. We tend to see more internal communication at smaller organizations; bigger organizations don't usually have effective internal communication. The bigger the organization, the more probable it is that creative activities exist in some areas; however, the more outlandish they are, the more likely they will not be received well without some assistance. Sometimes, communication is effective enough between employees working in a similar section. Not to talk of communication between individuals who work in various sections and may never, in the ordinary course of occasions, meet each other? An organization's creative potential develops quickly with its size; however, without frameworks set up in advance for unforeseen data exchange, this potential will never be realized. The assumption that only smaller organizations can truly exhibit corporate creativity continues to exist.

Organizations are not unlike *people who are creative, in that they have five key psychological features. Five features are curiosity, sensuality, openness, paradox and telling stories; they are reliable across organizational culture, progressive system, and almost all types of situational condition.* There are tools that are accessible by company administrators that anybody can use with only a little training. Keep in mind that most of these tools can be created by an individual or corporately.

The following is a list of the essential parts of the organizational creativity model framework.

- *Curiosity*: A specific positive thought of how things truly are, and not stalling out on how one expect they are or trusts they are, is known as curiosity. Creative organizations are interested in finding out how things really work, and are willing to sit tight until a

---

* The role of good internal communications cannot be underestimated. According to a recent study by Towers Watson, companies that are effective communicators have on average 47% higher returns for their shareholders. What's more, 62% of employees said that accessibility to company information directly affects job satisfaction and creativity. With job hopping and low retention being the new norm, organizations need to do whatever they can to make effective internal communications systems for innovation a priority.

genuine idea arises. Curiosity goes against the concept of business-as-usual. Innovative creativity is different from the norm. Creative organizations feel the need to infiltrate and get a handle on customer insight and feelings, while aching and plotting their own goals, since the buyer's ideas are sometimes the main source of experience that can prompt innovation and achievement of goals.

- *Sensuality*: From time to time, creativity requires being sensitive to your own particular ideas. Creative organizations live on an enthusiastic crazy ride, and like it that way. They endure the plunges since they need the excitement of the rise. In creative organizational cultures, when the innovative spark sets in, the feeling of the dramatic prompts action at the research level.

- *Openness*: Creative encounters can originate from any place and from anybody. Receptiveness to voices and circumstances other than your own are basic grist for the idea advancement process. Creativity is likewise the first to appear as a suspicion or a thought, long before the details have been completely worked out. Creative organizations are energized by new thoughts and need input.

- *Paradox*: In the current complex and ever-changing world, things are no longer straight-forward or of one logical thread. Everything appears to contain intrinsic logical inconsistencies and ambiguities. Nothing is essentially either black or white. Day-to-day life – both professionally and privately – is a mix of cashmere and sawdust, love and despisement. Creative organizations can live on the cusp of this oddity and utilize the apparent predicament as a jolt for advancement and imagination. Gregory Bateson, the famous researcher and scholar, stated "Logic is a very elegant tool, but logic alone won't quite do because that whole fabric of living things is not put together by logic. Metaphor is right at the bottom of being alive." The use of metaphors liberates one from the limits of boundaries. It gives the organization some innovative "breathing room" to toy with thoughts, and to assemble things that – more often than not – don't go together.

- *Making and telling a story*: Creative organizations, like people, analyze things in the form of stories. They don't identify with information as a main focus, but instead take a gander at connections between snippets of data – hidden examples and standards, and surmizings about different outcomes. With this, creative people manage unpredictability and change information into a story that is the basis for development.

More noteworthy, efficiency and improved capacity with regards to idea development should interact with any business endeavor that fosters corporate creativity. Creative ability rules. Also, inspiring leaders make the best administrators, who are creative scholars and brilliant strategists. With each business task, inventiveness is fundamental to taking care of complex issues, growing new methodologies, encouraging advancement, and driving change inside the organization.

Ordinarily, when we talk about development in an organization, we are informed that Bill is accountable for the innovative concepts, or Sue or Frank or some other person. From time to time, you hear that the whole organization is accountable for creativity. With this we understand that everything concerning a company when we hear an individual, or a few people are responsible for the development of the organization. It was earlier stated in this book that with a creative culture, everybody in an organization is committed to being creative. Organizations that fail to meet expectations in creativity have not given their employees the ability to be creative.

- A creative test. It can go a long way in your company's steps to instill creativity into the company's operations and vision. To achieve this, one of the initial steps is to evaluate the creative status of the company, its execution level, and what changes may be expected to enhance it. Ask the following questions:
  a. Is there an estimation of the organization's targets on creative ventures?
  b. Is enough effort invested in creative exercises and analyzing them?
  c. Is there a creativity manager in the company?
  d. How many of our representatives made inventiveness changes in the previous year, and is the rate sufficiently high?
  e. Are assets to refine new thoughts accessible?
  f. What are the barriers impeding the company from improving creativity?

Analysis by Kano Examination

If quality is replaced with innovation in Kano's Model, it can then be used to effectively analyze innovative creativity. For instance, the following figure indicates a normal Kano Model. When we analyze our organization, we consider just four measurements. The first two are that we either carry out a task or we ignore it or we either fulfill clients' requirements or we don't. If we consider the life cycle of the cell phone, we will have a better understand.

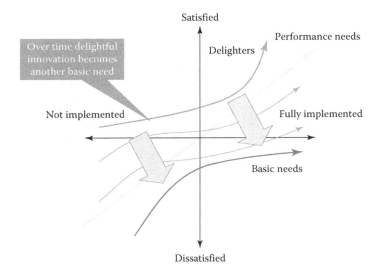

When cell licenses initially ended up accessible to everyone, the all-inclusive community didn't realize that they required a cell phone. All things considered, for what reason would anybody need to stroll around with a telephone in their pocket? At that specific point in time, only a few individuals had the idea.

As telephones became available, individuals gradually embraced them, anticipating that they would only work intermittently but took pleasure in being able to talk anywhere. The first users of cell phones remarked that they could communicate within x to z mile makers, which was not possible from a to c mile-markers. With time, there were improvements, with the so-called 'delighters' becoming must-haves in order to satisfy the more demanding consumers.

Today, a delighter for some may eventually become a must-have for others, once the details are all understood and worked out. Thus, after some time, what's basically happened is that fundamental needs have moved from being delighters to must-haves. Truth be told, the market adjustment to the cell phone means that phones that are not smartphones are no longer on sale.

Comprehending the Kano Model as an activity in an organization can add to the creativity when the staff know that the fundamental services and products offered by the organization might not be adequate or commercially appealing. An organization's creative department that makes this model the center of its development will go a long way in implementing creativity in their products and services.

Organizational Visual Identity*

Visual identity:
Branding guidelines

Logo treatments
This may include stacked, horizontal, small and large versions. It may also cover different color amounts.

What not to do
Treatments such as logo rotation, embossing, color variation and glow effects are examples of what you may want to avoid.

The logo spacing
Giving a space around the logo is imperative to getting maximum impact. Supply a scalable unit that can be used in many scenarios.

The brand colors
Supply PANTONE, CMYK, RGB and hexadecimals of the intended house colors. Consider what their associative colors are too.

House typefaces
You may give examples of header fonts, secondary fonts along with possible leading and tracking properties.

Types of grid/layouts
Any graphic and linear elements that are associated with the brand may require certain margins in order to maintain consistency.

The brand image
Giving examples of styles of imagery is crucial to maintaining brand consistency too. Remember to allow flexability for brand evolution.

Organizational Synectics†

There are three main assumptions with synectics. The first assumption states that the creative procedure can be taught or described. The second assumption states that art and scientific inventions exhibit analogous

---

* Source: https://www.interact-intranet.com/4-creative-internal-comms-ideas-you-need-to-try/.

† When it comes to organizational creativity, synectics is very well known. In the 1950s, the strategy originated from the Arthur Little organization. As a corporate creativity technique, it is an approach to strategies of solving problems creatively. With synectics, a creative activity in any type of process can be analyzed.

features and are driven by similar psychic procedures. The third assumption is that collective and individual creativity are similar. In all organizations, as soon as an organization and its staff understand creativity as the way toward grasping total productivity, notwithstanding that knowledgeable processes and instinct play key parts, the faster the improvement of the company.

For people knowledgeable in the science business, this idea can be especially troublesome. An engineer naturally won't want to implement this concept and be playful while working, which is typical depending on the work being carried out. Applying synthetic standards in an organization conflicts with everything that is judicious, adequate, and typical of individuals who have historically been prepared to operate these organizations and associated procedures. Indeed, even in creative companies like IDEO and Apple, it is perceived dimly, and facilitative and creative management is important to the innovative procedure. In this way, understanding the innovation process is basic for these individuals to comprehend what is happening in their environment.

Brainstorming

In innovative processes, brainstorming is one of the techniques that is usually examined. Brainstorming has been implemented to facilitate group creativity using several approaches not commonly known or understood. Brainstorming, according to Alex Osborne in 1939, involves two essential standards:

1. Reach for quantity
2. Defer judgment

These prompt the all-inclusive aims of lessening the social restraints between a group and individuals, generally improving the group's creativity by the constant creation of ideas.

Osborne's four main standards of brainstorming are

1. *Facilitate quantity*: As a starting point, and using his numerous techniques as one can envision, brainstorming's first task is to create the greatest number of conceivable thoughts possible within a limited time. The goal is that individuals will not hesitate to express their thoughts, regardless of how unacceptable they may appear at first. It

has been indicated on numerous occasions that a portion of the best thoughts originate from sessions that were not overly controlled but rather more freestyle.

2. *Do not permit negative feedback*: Some of the time constraint must be suspended to facilitate quality. Early criticism of ideas hinders the easy flow of the concept by the group. If a person's idea has been condemned, derided, or generally rejected, you can't expect that person to talk about such ideas again. Human instinct in the brainstorming exercise is to ignore criticism or negative feedback.

3. *Unusual ideas should be celebrated*: We have previously discussed cell phones in this chapter. When we work with an organization, once in a while they make use of an approach called the switch time case. In the turn-around time container, workers are requested to take the most bizarre thing that exists today and send it back 25 years. Envision the reception one may have got in the 1980s when faced with advanced music, electric autos, certain apparel and hairdos, or unscripted television. Had those thoughts been presented in a meeting to generate new ideas 25 years back, they may have appeared interesting but outside the domain of plausibility; however, in the current setting, these are the main things that are happening. Innovation that didn't exist 25 years prior is the impetus of the progression we see today. A sci-fi of yesterday has come to life in our present day.

4. *Combine thoughts*: Maybe the piece of conceptualizing that is most enjoyable to individuals is the mixture of thoughts. Utilizing the cell phone illustration once more, can you envision somebody holding a CD player in one hand and a cell phone in the other and asking people a valid reason why they can't be consolidated into one unit. This is exactly what happened when Apple took their iPod music player and joined it with the telephone.

Six Thinking Hats

Six thinking hats, also simply known as the parallel thinking system, challenges companies to use a direct, one-track method for moving toward critical thinking and basic leadership. This technique helps to educate the brain to take a gander at an issue from various points of view with the specific end goal to implement receptiveness, consider creativeness, draw people into the discussion, and deflect closing down the conversation because of criticism. The technique includes:

- Analyzing data and facts, known as the white cap technique.
- Positive emotions and confidence, known as the yellow cap technique.
- Managing and controlling processes, known as the blue cap technique.
- Intuition and sentiments involving the inclination to hear yourself out, known as the red cap technique.
- Exploration and creative interest, known as the green cap technique.
- Danger spotting involving the need to remain cautious, known as the dark cap technique.

In Dan Pink's written work, he talks about the need to stay relevant in the current incredible change in globalization. He doesn't recommend that we dispose of the white caps, blue caps, and dark caps, but rather that we find and support others in an idea, including the ability to identify examples and openings, to make masterful and passionate ideas, to make a fantastic account, and consolidate apparently irrelevant thoughts into something new. This new quality concept includes the capacity to feel for others, to comprehend the nuances of human communication, to discover happiness in oneself, and to inspire it in others. It is the quest for reason and importance past quotidian.

Attribute Listing

Individuals and organizations have preconceived notions that sometimes lead them to think in unplanned ways. Generally, we refer to this as standard desires and attributes. Imagine that a friend invites you to see the local professional baseball team. Without asking more questions, you assume that this is a visit to the local major league baseball team. When your friend picks you up, and takes you to the local AAA baseball field, you find out that your expectations were wrong. Without knowing better, you did attend a professional baseball, although these players are paid significantly less than the Yankees.

In innovation, we are constantly fighting against preconceived notions of what is normal. Often, when we're asked to solve new problems, we start with preconceived notions. Many times when we discuss business with large companies, especially around innovation, the question arises as to what it is that they do. It's amazing how often organizations dismiss or even fail to recognize lines of business that are new or different from what they traditionally do. If an oil company were to write software programs that significantly improved the productivity of the wellhead to the point where those productivity gains are nearly equal to the income from the standard well, does this put the oil company in the software business? If you were to ask the oil company, this is probably not the case. By your organization limiting itself to being in a certain industry or business, what other industries or businesses are you missing out on or what solutions are not being considered?

Along these lines, listing attributes is an innovative method that is used to discover new thoughts, take care of issues, and find creative services and products. Listing attributes includes separating an issue into smaller segments and taking a gander at elective solutions to the issue. It can be valuable to consolidate with other innovative procedures, for example, conceptualizing to create new thoughts.

Attribute listing involves analyzing the major features (traits) of an item, process, or issue and then considering all other conceivable options to these segments. A classic attribute listing example is the pencil. If we consider the traditional pencil, there is the shaft material (lead) that can be described by type, hardness, and width. One could also consider quality lead. With respect to what we think of as the wooden part of the pencil, what color would it be and what kind of wood would be used? We would consider price and other attributes as they came up.

So, when finally laying out the attribute analysis for a pencil, it might look something like this:

Features	Current Attributes	Potential Attributes
Material	Wood	Plastic, metal
Writing material	Gray lead	Colored lead, erasable ink, chalk
Color	Yellow	Matching writing material, multicolor, company color
Shape	Pentagon	Round, oval, curved
Other features	Eraser on top	Eraser on side – swappable in plastic pencil Magnetic Velcro

Storyboarding: Storyboarding is definitely not an easy task and not meant for the feeble at heart – it requires a lot of time, and can be frustrating. The good part about it, however, is that, when you think about it, nearly everyone doodles. In most creative spaces, you will find whiteboard walls and rolling whiteboards all over the place. Most people do not really think of this as storyboarding, but consider that having the ability to quickly put an idea on a wall or a whiteboard makes it easy for people to illustrate their ideas on the fly and you can understand why this particular tool is first choice in so many organizations.

Absence thinking: Absence thinking is relatively easy to conceptualize, but sometimes difficult to do. The problem is that you have to think hard about the situation, product, problem, or whatever, and try to then go to what you are not thinking about. It's difficult for the same reason as trying to get a song out of your head can sometimes be next to impossible. Imagine that song, and then think about the song you aren't thinking about. Artists can state that art exists in the spaces in-between lines and not what's not present within the lines.

Tree diagrams: You probably use tree diagrams each day when you examine your organization chart. Breaking things down into their simplest parts is as old as history; which just goes to show that not everything about innovation is brand new.

Lotus blossom: The lotus blossom is far more technical, but another tool that a manager should be familiar with when dealing with innovation. A problem with opening yourself up to creativity is that we are, in fact, as they say, "standing right on top of the giant's shoulders." Typically, this phrase is applied to academics and the evolution of ideas, but could it not apply in the same way as a wheel on a car. Does a car have to have wheels? In other words, sometimes it is very difficult to change the way you think when you are so wedded to the way things are.

As absence thinking asks you to put aside current thinking and consider what you are not thinking, in lotus blossom, you will need to consider all the preconceived notions that have been drilled into your head as "challengeable." An easy example might be space travel. Originally, the only way up was strapped to a rocket, and the only way down was in a capsule with shielding and a parachute. We spent time returning in a glider (the space shuttle), and companies like Virgin Galactic question whether a rocket is necessary at all.*

When one speaks of creative geniuses thinking differently, such as in the classic "Think Differently" commercial by Apple computers in the 1990s, what they were identifying was the fact that creative people look at a problem in a different way than most. Most, in fact, would actually see many ways to approach a single problem, while their counterparts might only see one. From studies, it was noted that Einstein was asked at a particular time what made him different from other individuals. He disclosed that if a request were made for people to discover a needle in a pile, a great number of people would stop when the needle was found, but he would keep on looking through the whole sheaf to discover all the needles conceivable.

In fact, the geniuses in most endeavors have similar answers. No doubt, the reader has heard the great Wayne Gretzky quote about scoring goals so often as skating to where the puck will be and not where it is. People who are creative naturally see the angles and options that most people never look for. But why can't we teach people to see more than the obvious? Is this not the root of teaching someone to be creative?

When Darwin explored his theories of evolution, he did not jump to a single theory, but ordered everything in themes, or ways of ordering things into many possible scenarios. In the case of the lotus blossom, this means solving a problem by classifying it into many themes and then looking at alternative solutions that you may have never considered outside the exercise.

To perform the exercise:

1. Create a diagram and write the central problem at the center.
2. From there, start to expand with a number of themes related to your problem. Generally speaking, six to eight is about all you want to capture here – if there are more than eight reasonable themes,

---

* A classic experiment that leads you to lotus blossom is one done by a psychologist named Peter Watson. In his experiments, he asked subjects to interpret the following: 2, 4, 6,… . The subjects were then asked to explain the rule and ask as many questions as they liked. Inevitably, they would explain that 4, 6, 8 fit the rule and he would reply in the affirmative. Then 48, 50, 52, for example, and he would respond with a yes. It is very interesting to note that normally the rules were "*three numbers increasing in size*" so the respondents would have answered correctly had they said 1, 2, 3, or 112, 183, 824. The respondents, when given an example of 2, 4, 6, were nearly incapable of interpreting the numbers as anything other than series of numbers increasing by 2 at a time.

then you are probably not defining your problem well. Think about objective, common constants, etc.

3. Take each of the themes and expand them to six or eight new themes and see where it takes you.

4. Continue the process until you feel like the blossom is complete.

When your team applies this to your organization, you might start with the question of increasing the customer's way of evaluating the values provided. Let's say that our product is a calendaring app. Themes could be "time zone," "synchronization," "linking to other apps," "transferability," "management," and "visibility." Let's say that we then expand the visibility theme to "family," "friends," "work associates," "people with whom I would make an appointment," etc. Perhaps we decide that this theme leads us to classifying people instead of appointments.

Our primary view of the world of appointments is now focused not on the event, but on the people who need to know about the event. So, people become the focal point of the calendar transaction and not the appointment itself. Now, groups of designates could see your appointments instead of only your assistant being able to see your work calendar; your family being able to see your home calendar and you being able to see your personal calendar. Imagine, you can book a flight, put it in your calendar, and assign it to all groups so that your family and assistant can see it without entering it into multiple calendaring systems, or giving your significant other, friends, or assistant your user name and password to each calendar.

Of course, the most important component of this approach to a problem is that it shifts you from a relatively static view of the problem to one that is more organic and active. At times when you finish drawing out a chart with ideas for a particular project and you highlight applications for each subject, you might suddenly see a property or highlight that you did not plan for. Normally, expensive properties are viewed as a new car, for instance, interconnected parts of a property during development. As soon as a high-priced car is dismantled and every one of the parts is tossed onto a stack, the property vanishes.

On the off chance that you set the parts in heaps with respect to their features, you start to see an example and make associations between the heaps that may motivate you to envision the new car to be designed, which you would then be able to assemble. Thus, when you pen down your ideas specifically with varying applications and thoughts, it improves your chances to clearly see your expected result. New property or highlight not earlier considered will start to emerge as soon as you begin to connect the ideas and their applications.

TRIZ

The general concept of the Theory of Inventive Problem-Solving (TRIZ)* was developed as Altshuller and his team examined thousands of inventions and the processes of invention. Finally, a hypothesis was built that characterizes generalizable examples in the idea of creative arrangements and the recognizing attributes of the issues that these creative actions help to solve.

There are three primary findings of this research: (1) solutions to problems are repetitive crosswise over ventures and sciences, (2) examples of specialized innovation are additionally similarities crosswise over businesses and sciences, and (3) innovations make use of scientific practices outside of the field of science. The implementation of TRIZ shows that every one of these discoveries is connected to make and enhance the frameworks, products, and services provided.

SUMMARY

At each organization we considered, we met individuals who felt that their company's potential for inventiveness was far greater than it was currently displaying. They are correct. We trust this circumstance won't change until the point that the genuine idea of creativity turns out to be part of the organization's DNA. The main aspects of an organization's creative acts is, for all intents and purposes, inaccessible using the standard "command and control" style of management. The reason is that it lies in those imaginative processes that can't be conjured up on demand, and that no amount of preplanning can bring it into being. Corporate creativity lies in

---

* TRIZ is another one of those tools that relatively few people use, but can be extremely effective in solving problems. (Never mind the actual acronym, it wouldn't actually matter.) It was developed around 1946 by Genrich Altshuller and his colleagues and is known in English as the Theory of Inventive Problem-Solving and is occasionally called TIPS.

these unforeseen inventive acts, and our six components offer an approach to understanding the huge potential they speak to.

> *Too many organizations, management theorist Peter Drucker observed, devote resources to "preserving the past" when they should be allocated to "creating tomorrow."*

5

Innovation Theory for Entrepreneurs*

Everything is determined, the beginning as well as the end, by forces over which we have no control. It is determined for insects as well as for the stars. Human beings, vegetables or cosmic dust, we all dance to a mysterious tune, intoned in the distance.

Albert Einstein

In search for an answer, one would grope his way through a dark labyrinth – he may either find something useful, or hurt himself when bumping into a wall. Another would take a small flashlight along to guide him on his way. And that would shine brighter and brighter, turning into an enormous light source, which would leave not a spot unlighted or unexplained. I am asking you: WHERE IS YOUR FLASHLIGHT?

Dmitri I. Mendeleev
Russian chemist and inventor

> **In a nutshell:** The nature of success in business is almost self-obvious. The company that creates more excellent value for its respective market will prosper while competitors will only get what is left for them by the leader. Repeat this difference

---

* We are indebted to Doblin Consulting and Professor Greg Yezersky for their valuable contributions to the theory of innovation for entrepreneurs. Despite all their operational achievements, Yezersky argues, there is still one stage in the value proposition life cycle that lacks any control. It is the first stage of the process, which forms the content of a future value proposition – the value proposition conceptualization stage. Value creation is possible through both innovation and optimization. While both are valid approaches, innovation is the one that creates new features and provides significant competitive advantage. Source: *The TRIZ Journal*, April 7, 2008.

in value year after year, and success will be permanently associated with that initially leading organization. It seems so simple, but is it? Many innovation theory experts argue that there is only one reliable method to control any kind of activity known to mankind – through the creation and use of science. Science in innovation theory allows for significantly improving problem-solving capabilities, forecasting capabilities, and objective judgment capabilities regardless of the area of application. Also, it enables better control of risk, more effective management, and more consistent results. In this chapter, we will focus on innovation theory by first describing the Ten Types of Innovation in theory, and then describing the main key points of innovation theory. In his research, Peter Drucker found that those entrepreneurs who tried to add value by innovating in several ways were consistently more successful than their counterparts, a fact confirmed by the Doblin consultancy research reports cited in this chapter.

INTRODUCTION

The Ten Types of Innovation is a framework for evaluating the various types of innovations your company is currently trying out. Based on research into more than 2000 innovation projects by innovation consultancy Doblin,* what they found was that overall there are 10 distinct ways that a company can innovate:

1. *Profit model*: How entrepreneurs make money
2. *Network*: How entrepreneurs connect with others to create value
3. *Structure*: How entrepreneurs organize and align talent and assets

---

* See https://www.doblin.com/ten-types. According to Doblin, for many years executives equated innovation with the development of new products. But, creating new products is only one way to innovate, and on its own, it provides the lowest return on investment and the least competitive advantage. The Ten Types of Innovation framework was discovered by Doblin Consultancy in 1988, and provides a unique way to identify new opportunities beyond products and develop viable innovations.

 4. *Process*: How entrepreneurs use signature or superior methods to do their work
 5. *Product performance*: How entrepreneurs develop distinguishing features and functionality
 6. *Product system*: How entrepreneurs create complementary products and services
 7. *Service*: How entrepreneurs support and amplify the value of their offerings
 8. *Channel*: How entrepreneurs deliver your offerings to customers and users
 9. *Brand*: How entrepreneurs represent your offerings and business
10. *Customer experience*: How entrepreneurs foster compelling interactions

What is fascinating is that the research also clearly showed the impact of entrepreneurial companies trying more than one type of innovation. While most entrepreneurs innovate by improving the performance of their product (Type 5), those companies that tried to add value by innovating in several ways were consistently more successful; their innovations were more likely to make a return on investment.

At the heart of the framework is our discovery: throughout history, all great innovations comprise some combination of these 10 basic types. This is the Doblin periodic table. You can use the 10 types to help your innovation efforts in many ways. It can be a diagnostic tool to assess how you're approaching innovation internally, it can help you analyze your competitive environment, and it can reveal gaps and potential opportunities for doing something different and upending the market. Furthermore, Doblin accurately claims that there are over 100 innovation tactics – specific, known ways that entrepreneurs can use the Ten Types of Innovation, combining two or three with the Innovation Profit Model to help entrepreneurs make a profit.* These are like the elements that bond together to form molecules, as shown in the Doblin model; you can use them to construct the breakthroughs that will help you make a real impact on your industry.

---

* According to Doblin, innovative profit models find a fresh way to convert a firm's offerings and other sources of value into cash. Great ones reflect a deep understanding of what customers and users actually cherish and where new revenue or pricing opportunities might lie. Innovative profit models often challenge an industry's tired old assumptions about what to offer, what to charge, or how to collect revenues. This is a big part of their power: in most industries, the dominant profit model often goes unquestioned for decades.

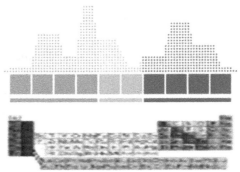

The Doblin periodic table, like the chemical periodic table, is an astonishing achievement. There is no one single or best structure for the periodic table, but by whatever consensus there is, the form used here is very useful and the most common. The periodic table is a masterpiece of organized chemical information and the evolution of chemistry's periodic table into its current form is a triumph.

To see the full impact of trying out more than one type of innovation, check out the following graph in which Doblin analyzes the number of different types of innovations the companies were attempting and how they performed against the stock market.

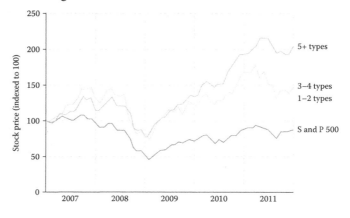

INNOVATION THEORY KEY POINTS

Innovation theory states that standardization and cooperation are the future. We must all become more efficient in today's tough international competition. Consequently, innovation certification standards and recommendations are exactly what are called for. In essence, both the mission and the strategic focus of the business plan are the same.

What will change is the way in which we work together with new technology and what issues are pivotal for collaborating together. We are currently focusing on improved productivity and sustainability along with how we can harness new technology to achieve this.

When it comes to technology, we are facing an exciting evolutionary step including the Internet of Things and big data that are providing unprecedented opportunities.

Also, some of the best sources of both incremental and disruptive innovation will be derived from beyond the regular spheres of company contact and even from beyond its own industry. Cross-industry innovation, beyond incorporating external knowledge into the company itself, may also be deployed as a tool for transferring company-owned technology and patents to industries on an international scale.

Various empirical research projects are expected to confirm that face-to-face contacts and geographic proximity will be key factors in spreading innovation. Additionally, specific forms of exchanging knowledge in cross-industry activity will include: (1) dominant suppliers; (2) intensive-scale companies; (3) science-based companies; and (4) specialist equipment suppliers.

When seeking to identify the ways in which service innovations will take place in the next 10 years, the following types should be taken into consideration: (1) product innovations deriving from innovation processes and very often corresponding to demand-side requests; (2) process innovations, especially those stimulated through new technologies; and (3) delivering innovation through the application of new resources and methods, such as support structures for interactions between service companies and their clients.

The distinction between product innovation and process innovation will make little sense in theory, to the extent that the different forms of innovation are inherently interrelated and, in the majority of cases, the innovation emerging will often be characterized by the existence of strongly varying and different facets.

The cooperation and sharing of experiences between industries in certain non-competitive areas will contribute to achieving your goals more effectively in a cheaper, safer, and more resource-efficient manner, as well as avoiding repeated unnecessary mistakes. Committees and working groups will often come up with a solution to a problem that the industry has highlighted. We will then adapt and package the solution proposal prior to launching it in the market as a new or updated service, such as a guideline, a standard, an IT service, or a training course.

This is where innovation theory gets interesting. We will live on our own income, just as any company does, but the resource base will then come from the companies that participate in the committees. They will provide us with development potential in terms of expertise that we develop and refine into a commercial format. At the same time, companies will benefit from a value network in which they can accelerate their own development by utilizing the knowledge and experience of others.

In a value network, it is about the links between companies, particularly in the form of enhanced cooperation, which will be the key factor. The ability to orchestrate a large amount of external partnerships is a crucial knowledge advantage in this respect, and combining specialized external expertise allows individual companies to create a resource that is very difficult for competitors to mimic.

The competitiveness of the companies will depend on how well they manage to develop partnerships in which they can utilize their expertise as specialists or integrators. The company's capacity for innovation will also grow the external relationships that the company will have with other organizations. In fast-changing industries, it will be increasingly crucial to combine the internal and external knowledge.

Cooperation between the company, its suppliers, and competitors will become a prerequisite for success. Because cooperation implies some form of transparency, a clear business plan framework for a neutral forum where information can be exchanged in a safe and secure manner will be of primary value for collaborations to truly succeed.

Finally, innovation theory shows that cross-industry collaborations (CICs) can be structured to meet multiple objectives, such as reaching the digital consumer or mastering mobile commerce, and can span multiple industries, as illustrated in Table 5.1.

TABLE 5.1

Mobile commerce

Mobile commerce	Digital consumer	Retail	New energy	Commodity trading
Banking	Retail	Retail	Agribusiness	Capital markets
Retail	Consumer	Consumer	Energy	Energy
Communications	Electronics and high tech	Banking	Automotive	Utilities
Electronics and high tech	Communications	Postal		
	Banking	Communications		
		Energy		
		Electronics and high tech		

Source: Accenture Outlook | Cross-industry ecosystems: Growth outside the box (February 2013).

Innovation theory tells us that common standards in the industry will lead to enhanced resource efficiency, greater personal security, higher availability, greater reliability, and consequently greater sustainable levels of innovation. These standards will facilitate both innovation benchmarking for continued efficiency measures, as well as the choice of the best possible sustainable solutions in terms of purchasing and procurement.

Innovation tools and standards will raise demand and develop partnerships with suppliers. In other words, they will be a vital stop on the road to achieving greater sustainability. In order to achieve the optimum organization that best supports the company's strategic business objectives, innovation theory tells us that there must be a greater balance between the structure and the company's internal culture.

Likewise, in theory, the biggest threat to the structural change of a company is its corporate culture. We are endeavoring to create an organization that is as homogeneous as possible, with a common vision and set of values, which will provide the best support for the company's various business processes.

WHAT THE RESEARCH SHOWS

According to a study conducted by Royal Dutch Shell, the average life expectancy of Fortune 500 firms is 40–50 years.* The time as a market leader is even shorter. Leaders thus continue rising and falling. Examples of failures abound; they are so overwhelming that after studying the history of business, Professors W. Chan Kim and Renee Mauborgne wrote in *Blue Ocean Strategy* that "… permanently excellent industries and companies do not exist."

Two aspects of this situation are compelling:

1. The entities, unlike human beings, are at least theoretically immortal.
2. The loss of leadership is universal; entities die too often.

Why is this compelling? There must be a fundamental cause behind this phenomenon, and it must be understood to find a practical solution to this problem. Without identifying the root cause, the risk of failure is high: no enterprise is immune, and no executive is safe. A strong understanding of the theory of innovation is essential to any company wanting to develop an innovative organization. Innovation can be thought of in so many different things, and in fact, one of the most common discussions we have with our clients is how innovation should be defined.

What is clear is that it is much like the description of pornography by Supreme Court Justice Potter Stewart: "I know it when I see it." In fact, too many people get so hung up on trying to define innovation and tend to get so bogged down in the perfect definition that they never actually get to innovate. Two years ago, the International Association of Innovation Professionals (IAOIP) held a retreat in Palo Alto, California, and essentially fell into the trap. The group deliberated the definition of innovation for a full day before "settling" on one that did not quite satisfy any one. Experts write entire books on the definition of innovation, and countless debates try to come up with something better.

The fact remains that, if your employees and customers believe that you are innovative, then does it matter how innovation is defined. Like pornography, whether someone describes a company as innovative depends on their customers. For example, we have seen Samsung come out

---

* Arie de Geus, *The Living Company*, published by Harvard Business School Press, April 1997, ISBN-10: 087584782X. Ref 1 below

with countless "innovations" in their products over the years. They came out with a watch a couple of years before Apple, but Apple continues to be seen as a more innovative company by the majority of people.

While innovation theory may remain an inexact science, there are many things that we are learning about what makes an organization successful. Adopting Lean or a Six Sigma program is relatively straightforward when compared to creating an innovation program, or better yet, an innovative organization. The research into what makes an individual or an organization innovative is still in its infancy.

In fact, there is a lot known and the *International Journal of Innovation Science* (http://www.innovationscience.org) is a start in the effort to better understand how to do innovation. Admittedly, however, even this journal has a long way to go in the development of innovation as a science. Over time, some of the published papers could prove to be a cornerstone of innovation, but many are grasping at anything that might help us to make better sense of the science. That said, let's talk about what we do know about the theory of innovation.

ABOUT PROBLEM ANALYSIS

Since products and services are purchased to solve consumers' problems, the competition between entities can be presented as a competition between the value propositions that the entities offer to their customers. Every value proposition goes through the life cycle process presented in Figure 5.1, which consists of a sequence of stages. This universal process ends up with the market's judgment of the value proposition, which leads to its acceptance or rejection, resulting in financial gain or loss, which is then perceived as a success or failure.

The goal of sustaining success can only be achieved if a company continually comes up with value propositions that are accepted by the market, and the process of fulfillment must be controlled in its entirety.

FIGURE 5.1
Life cycle of a value proposition.

Despite all their operational achievements, however, there is still one stage in the value proposition life cycle that lacks any control. It is the first stage of the process, which forms the content of a future value proposition – the value proposition conceptualization stage. Value creation is possible through both innovation and optimization. While both are valid approaches, innovation is the one that creates new features and provides a significant competitive advantage. The first stage of the value proposition life cycle can thus be considered as the stage of innovation. This early stage is a complex process consisting of a number of procedures depicted in Figure 5.2: identification of market requirements for a future product (service); formulation of problems that need to be solved to meet the criteria; analysis and solution of the issues; solution evaluations that also include identification of potential consequences (both positive and negative) resulting from a planned change; and, finally, formulation of the future value proposition concept, which is the foundation for the rest of the production cycle. Depending on how sound the foundation is, the cycle results will vary greatly.

There is one important observation that needs to be emphasized. Since the period from the inception of a value proposition until its presentation to the market in the form of a product or a service takes time (often years), controlling innovation means to know not what the market's present needs are, but what they will be in the future. It is analogous to shooting a moving target; nobody tries to shoot at the location where the target is now but where the target will be. Currently, companies do not have reliable methods to accurately identify the future of the market's needs, which makes control of the process of innovation impossible in principle.

Since the entire chain is as strong as its weakest link, an inability to control the first stage, innovation, automatically leads to the situation where no company can control the results of the competition, which, in turn, results in a company's inability to continuously succeed and, ultimately,

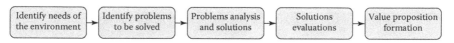

FIGURE 5.2
The process of innovation.

control its destiny. The failure to control the process of innovation is the root cause behind the cessation of growth, market losses, and the eventual mortality of the business enterprises.

INNOVATION ISN'T A CHOICE

Contrary to what you may believe and even to statements we have already made in this book, you have no choice but to innovate if you have plans for your organization to last very long. In fact, the average life of an established company is decreasing with regularity. Companies that one would never imagine going away 50 years ago are gone and new companies (20–30 years) are now some of the biggest and most profitable in the world. In 1990, who would have even imagined that a company like Google would become such a prominent global player? Companies from emerging economies such as China seem poised to become the next wave of global competitors as economies of scale and location are quickly disappearing. Companies that didn't exist 10 years ago are being acquired at tremendous multiples of revenue, and unlike the dotcom era, the companies today seem to have real staying power – built on models of real revenue and mature business models.

This means that your company is not in a position to decide whether it wants to pursue innovation or not. You can name almost any business or industry and find dozens of possibilities for disruption in the model. US automobile manufacturers seemed safe in 1960 because of scale and geography. Japanese competitors saw an opportunity for fuel efficiency, price, and reliability long before Detroit recognized the threat. They felt that they knew the customer better than anyone else and that manufacturing and shipping automobiles from Japan wasn't a logistical strategy.

Today, we have Tesla, which it turns out, may not be an automobile manufacturer as previously defined by the industry. They may be a battery manufacturer, which if you consider for a moment, could be the biggest and most disruptive technology to the automotive industry. Imagine when Google or Apple creates the software for your car to drive itself, and Tesla manufactures the batteries that allow this car to function.

At that tipping point, the manufacture and sale of the car is the step with the least value added, and perhaps people can simply buy a cheap kit, a Tesla motor and battery, and a small onboard computer and just manufacture their vehicle. To add insult to injury, this unit may not even be considered an automobile any longer – only a transportation pod that allows you to get to work more efficiently, faster, and more productively than ever before.

As someone who has lived in cities with mass transportation, I have always been amazed at the amount of work I can get done on a train, the reading in a subway, and the money that could be saved by doing away with a car. While the majority of American cities still don't have anything that can seriously be called mass transit, there are some indications that the automobile may be losing its appeal to Americans. In the suburbs where both authors live, Uber is changing the landscape. We have unscientifically interviewed dozens of friends and acquaintances, and a monumental shift seems to be taking place, enabled by Uber.

The consistent new paradigm is that Uber is better to take to sporting events, concerts, and even out to dinner. With the increasing severity of penalties from driving while intoxicated, many of the people who we have talked to find that calling an Uber car is a much better option than driving. Having a car available to you when going to or from an event allows you to relax instead of worrying about the traffic and the parking, and when looking at the economics of the situation, it is not too expensive. Another added benefit is in the price.

Recently, one of the authors flew to Austin airport and commuted downtown. As an experiment, a cab was taken from the airport to downtown and an Uber X (their lowest level of cars – still cleaner than the average cab), at approximately the same time. The cab was nearly $50, and the Uber ride was about $12.50. The Uber driver was a professional musician and drove his car to supplement his income. He was thrilled with his job, and unlike taking a cab, there were no hard feelings when paying by credit card (the only way to pay for an Uber ride). If enough people take Uber, we will push the cab companies out of existence and potentially take a big bite out of automobile manufacturing since we can now keep a car productive nearly all day instead of having parking lots full of cars just sitting all day long. Will this happen? Perhaps not, but what if the demand for automobiles decreases by just 10% worldwide, enabled by more efficient use of existing vehicles. Now imagine the possibilities that electric cars need no driver and mass transit goes to shared publicly available cars and the numbers for automotive companies become truly frightening.

This is just one example. We can walk almost any company through the possible scenarios they face – it isn't difficult to do.

REQUIREMENTS FOR A SCIENTIFIC THEORY OF INNOVATION*

There is only one reliable method to control any activity known to mankind; namely, through the creation and use of science. Science allows for significantly improving problem-solving capabilities, forecasting capabilities, and objective judgment capabilities regardless of the area of application. It enables better control of risk, more effective management, and more consistent results. Also, it is necessary to define innovation and establish the criteria for judging such a theory, based on the logic previously introduced.

> *Definition 1*: Innovation is a process of value creation, which consists of changing the composition of a set of variables describing a system.
> *Definition 2*: Innovation is an outcome of the process that fits Definition 1.

While the second definition enables alignment with a "typical" understanding of what innovation is, the first (the primary) definition provides most of the benefits.

1. The definition breaks down the process of innovation into a rigid set of stages, each having its own unique goal, input, and output. Further work can (and should) be undertaken in the direction of defining the stages, and identifying the most effective tools, processes, and best practices for each of the stages.
2. Acceptance of innovation as a process points at the need to control each separate stage of the process to avoid inconsistency (variability) of results, as prescribed by the operation management theory and various quality methodologies.
3. Defining innovation as a process and identifying the sequence of stages that constitute the method also enable the assigning of importance to each of the steps; the earlier a stage is, the more critical it is because it predetermines the direction of the subsequent process.

---

* General Theory of Innovation Overview, by Greg Yezersky, *The TRIZ Journal*, April 7, 2008.

4. One of the benefits of defining innovation as a process is the potential to define a set of requirements that any theory of innovation must satisfy. In this case, a theory must
   - Have the capability to address identified issues – analyze and solve existing problems
   - Have predictive capabilities and identify the future needs (challenges) of a respective system's environment
   - Provide objective criteria for judging novel concepts – notably, the theory must provide the means to evaluate an upcoming innovation's potential for future success or failure in the marketplace
   - Be objective – maximally independent from its user
   - Be universal – work for a system of any nature

YOUR BUSINESS IS BEING DISRUPTED RIGHT NOW

As we have either mentioned or eluded to at many points in this book, you ARE being disrupted now. It is the way of the world. It is the way of survival. Life is unusual in that direction. All organisms and organizations are just trying to survive and, at the lowest level, are not really in the game of destroying any other organism or organization – instead everyone is just doing what they have to do to survive and thrive. In this environment, Apple didn't set out to destroy the record companies when it created the iTunes store. After all, the record companies could have created digital outlets long before Apple did – they had the content and contracts with the artists.

They knew that people were digitizing their CDs and distributing them for free on Napster and other nefarious sites. Instead of accepting that the world was changing, they made an example of a small number of people by using them by threatening them with 'piracy' and lawsuits. Had they not resisted them, they might have been in a much more dominant position when Apple came calling and making demands to significantly lower their prices. Amazon is disrupting publishing and Airbnb and other companies are disrupting hotel and flight bookings. Yes, these are all information-based companies, so how can someone disrupt fishing guides in Alaska? What about a fish broker in Seattle? What about a drywalling company in Texas? What about a cattle rancher in Wyoming? Consider these situations for a moment before reading the next paragraph.

The fishing guide is now being graded and rated on social media. If people don't catch fish, bookings decrease and everyone knows that the fishing is unpredictable. What about a local with a small fleet of matching boats, who is savvy at social media and getting clients to rate them very highly. This competitor uses science and computers and algorithms to truly understand where the fish are and when. Since salmon fishermen are required to report their catch, this small-fleet owner is lobbying the state to require the electronic tagging of the fish. They can do this and start to track their small group of boats in real time, for catch information, water conditions, bait, and dozens of other variables that eventually allow them to be the most successful guides and devastating the crusty old guide who still relies on experience and word of mouth.

The fish broker buys fish from the dock, stores them in a warehouse, and distributes them to restaurants and food processors throughout the country. The reality is that the best fish is the most profitable and the majority of the catch is just a requirement of doing business. Let's say that someone creates an app that allows the fisherman to report a significant catch (a very nice salmon, a large tuna, etc.). I go to this app and auction the fish to restaurants throughout the world. The winner of the auction has the fish shipped directly to them as soon as I hit the dock. I receive more money by cutting out the broker on the most profitable part of his business.

The majority of a client's drywalling business is related to the construction business in the local market. His employees are Hispanic males, and he does not pay them very well; after all, the contractor deals with my company for its drywalling. He has noticed an increasing number of employees carrying smartphones. Someone in Silicon Valley creates an app that allows contractors to post their drywalling needs directly to a site that his employees can access. The site manages the location and allows a bidding process to take place directly between client and employees, and he is now left out of the process, or at least forced to find a way to deliver value that can't be provided directly by the employee.

The cattle rancher in Wyoming has been doing business in much the same way for generations. The quality of the meat from the grass in your region combined with feedlot practices produces some of the best meat in the world. The flavor is excellent, and the demand is strong. Now, while some might find it disturbing, a new competitor emerges from China. The meat isn't actually from a cow, it's grown in a lab. The inputs to the production process are significantly cheaper; it is better for the environment and it is indistinguishable from yours in taste. Initially, customers find the concept of manufactured meat disgusting and refuse to purchase the meat, even though it tastes the same – something about the "frankenmeat" is just disturbing. Your fine until the drought catches up to you and the production processes become way more expensive to you. Additionally, environmentalists decide that maybe "frankenmeat" is better than the destruction of the environment that cattle cause (methane, polluted water, etc.). A gradual shift takes place, and soon you are producing a niche market product.

So, you can't be disrupted? Maybe not, but we bet that if you challenged us, you might find out that we can come up with more than one way to do it.

THE GENERAL THEORY OF INNOVATION

Guided by the foregoing requirements, the author proceeded to create a theory satisfying them, resulting in the theory now known as the general theory of innovation (GTI). From the start, three crucial choices were made:

1. The process of creating GTI was based on an historical analysis of the evolutionary processes of real-world systems: products, processes, services, companies, markets.
2. The systems – technology based and not technology based – were deliberately chosen.
3. The investigation focused on both the systems themselves and (mostly) on the relationships the systems had with their respective environments.

The investigation wanted to uncover the driving forces behind the process of evolution, including identifying those factors that caused the need for innovations/solutions as well as those conditions that caused the emergence of the problems and determined the subsequent success or failure of the proposed solutions. The following are a few examples of the investigated systems:

- Sound storage has evolved from Thomas Edison's phonograph to wax cylinders, to discs with lateral grooves, two double-sided discs, to reel-to-reel magnetic tapes, to 4- and 8-track tape cartridges, to compact cassettes, to CDs, to DVDs, to MP3s.

- The use of currency evolved from the barter of goods (cattle, grain, etc.) to silver ingots guaranteed by Cappadocian rulers (2200 BC), to the first crude coins made from a naturally occurring amalgam of gold and silver (640 BC), to Chinese paper money (800 AD), to bank-backed notes (1633–1660 AD), to the first credit card (1950s), to electronic payment.
- Message delivery evolved from sending a messenger on foot, to a messenger on horseback, to the creation of a regular mail service, to mail service supported by cars, trains, and planes, to faxes, to next-day delivery, to email.

Despite being very different, all three examples have some things in common:

- Any product or service (process) is a system. Every product or service represents the union of parts or procedures connected to each other to deliver value to customers. No individual element of a system can provide the same amount on its own.
- Systems (products, services, industries) evolve. Systems evolve to adapt to changes in customers' needs and desires.
- Systems evolve in the predominant direction. The course of a system's evolution coincides with the delivery of ever-increasing performance while requiring fewer resources to provide that performance.

The predominant direction of evolution can be expressed as the ratio of the sum of the functions delivered by a system (an embodiment of performance) to the sum of connections the system needs to establish to obtain the required resources for achieving the functionality.

While "functioning" (consider the term "functions") is easily understood, the term "connections" requires greater explanation. Without getting into great detail, for this chapter, we may perceive connections as the totality of expenditures (sacrifices) required from the system's environment that ensures the delivery of a service provided by the system. The first major group of connections to be considered is the "customers' expenditures" list. For example, the effort needed to use a solution, time involvement, overall cost of ownership, space for storage, the need to learn something new, consequences of use, etc. This is followed by the second group of connections (production expenditures), such as required materials, energy, number of manufacturing processes and suppliers, production time, space needed for production, as well as subcategories and consequences such as scrap, waste, pollution, etc. Through the relationship between function and connection, this ratio, the coefficient of freedom (any function empowers a system and makes it freer while any connection increases its dependency and decreases its freedom), embodies the business world concept of value. The higher the coefficient, the higher the value delivered by a product or a service.

$$C_{Freedom} = S \text{ Functions}/S \text{ Connections}$$

Historical analyses of the evolutionary process of various systems (those previously mentioned as well as bicycles, glass making, baking equipment, welding, shopping, banking, cars, etc.) show the validity of the coefficient of freedom. It is universal, applied to products, processes, and services, or various entities such as organizations (both for-profit and not-for-profit), industries, markets, regions, etc. Moreover, these analyses lead firmly to the conclusion that systems do not evolve randomly. Moreover, the evolutionary cycle of all systems, regardless of their specific nature, is governed by the same set of natural laws that are completely independent of human will and desire, which is the major postulate of GTI (first defined in 1988).

The natural law governing the process of evolution (growth, expansion) of various systems states that a system's evolutionary direction matches ever-increasing degrees of freedom of the system's environment and is thus titled the law of an increasing degree of freedom.

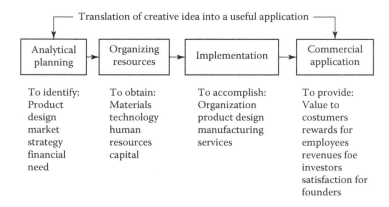

THEORY OF FOUR ZONES OF INNOVATION

The capabilities discussed in the previous section have enabled the creation of various applications and tools. Depending on the nature of an environment and its value system that is of interest to innovation practitioners, the Ten Types of Innovation are divided into four major innovation zones presented in Table 5.2.

The first group of applications relates to the situation when the value for its respective market is known, but an entity has not yet addressed it to the market's satisfaction, and a change in a system state (innovation) is required. Since the need for change is demanded by the market, an entity must react to it – reactive innovation. The second group of applications relates to the situation when the market does not complain about the specifics of an offering. The entity itself pursues a change in its offerings so that a prosperous future is ensured. In this case, the entity proactively seeks change, thus this group of applications (primarily driven by future business goals such as the discovery of strategic opportunities and threats; the discovery of growth avenues; etc.) is proactive innovation. The third group of applications relates to the need for the entities to innovate at each stage of the system life cycle and to do it on-demand, i.e., when the need arises. They are aimed at the creation of the sustainable entity's capability for on-demand innovation. (While the majority of the applications [and all the tools] from the first two groups were tested and proven, the applications of the third group were only partially tested and remain mostly theoretical.)

1. *A performance-based challenge (analysis and solution of system-related problems)*: The essence of any problem is the fundamental conflict between the choices made while pursuing goals and the natural laws of evolution. The process essentially is in identifying the opportunities that lead to the conflict and correcting them. To accomplish these goals, the following tools were created: RelEvent™ diagram; Problem–Solution Templates™; the algorithm for conflict elimination (ACE); generic strategies for conflict elimination; and so on.
2. *Carrying out complex projects*: Cost reduction, quality/reliability improvement, etc. When addressing a system-related problem, it is assumed that the nature of the dissatisfaction is associated with a specific aspect of the system performance: noise, strength, etc. Complex

TABLE 5.2

Innovation Zones Applications and Tools

	Applications	Major Tools
1. Process innovation 2. Delivery innovation (defensive): value is usually known	1. A performance-based challenge 2. Cost reduction 3. Quality/reliability improvement 4. Innovation assessment 5. Failure prevention 6. Patent circumvention/patent protection against circumvention	1. Relevant diagram (systems mapping) 2. Problem–solution templates 3. Conflict strategies 4. Algorithm for a conflict elimination (ACE) 5. Failure prevention analysis
3. Delivery (proactive) innovation (offensive): value is often unknown	1. System evolution forecasting 2. Strategic innovation portfolio creation 3. Business applications, for example: • Growth opportunities • Corporate turnaround • Business strategy/business model • Increasing ROI, including R&D • Investment, including mergers and acquisitions (M&A)	1. Evolutionary templates 2. Generic growth Strategies 3. Value growth templates 4. Value matrix
4. Finance on-demand innovation capability	1. Creation of the capability of an entity (a unit) to innovate on-demand 2. Creation of the innovation management system for an entity	1. All of the above 2. The program template

projects, as GTI defines them, relate these aspects of every organization's activities as cost reduction, quality, reliability, performance, and productivity improvement as well as failure prevention. The reason for being called complex is that any of the foregoing activities can be reduced to an identification of those multiple (hence, complex) problems, the presence of which causes the emergence of high cost (or low quality, reliability, etc.), and the subsequent solution of the issues identified. All the tools, techniques, and principles, which were used for the analysis and solution of a single or stand-alone problem, will also be effective and valid for the efficient achievement of the goals of a complex project.

3. *Innovation assessment and tools for decision-making*: The existence of natural laws of the evolutionary cycle has enabled the creation of objective criteria for evaluating proposed innovations, the importance of such criteria being self-evident. Compliance with the evolutionary laws (or deviation from the laws) constitutes the foundation for evaluating an innovation.

4. *Patent circumvention or patent protection against circumvention*: At the heart of any patent, there is a solution to a problem. Patent circumvention is finding an alternative solution for the same problem; or finding and solving an alternative problem for the same goal; or finding an alternative goal, followed by the identification of a problem that needs to be solved to reach the goal and the subsequent solution of this problem, for which tools are available. The patent protection against circumvention is the opposite procedure and is carried out similarly.

5. *Forecasting the future of the evolution of a system*: Knowledge of a system's location on the evolutionary curve combined with knowledge of the evolutionary laws allows any organization to forecast a system's (product or service) future with great precision. The entire procedure of forecasting the future of a system consists of two major stages: (1) by using the business rules, problems that will cross the path of your system are identified and (2) they are solved by using the problem-solving tools previously discussed.

6. *Strategic management (business applications)*: GTI states that innovation in the area of strategic management (identification of change required for repositioning an organization with the purpose of obtaining competitive advantage) is immeasurably more important than innovation in any other area of corporate activities such as product or process innovation. The reasoning behind this position is simple: the history of business shows that companies

with inferior products but superior strategies beat their technically superior competitors. Examples abound: Microsoft vs. Apple; Dell vs. IBM and Compaq; Big 3 vs. Tucker Corporation.

a. Knowledge of the evolutionary laws is applicable not only to such systems as technology-based products, services, and processes, but also to any business process within an organization, the organizations themselves (both for-profit and not-for-profit), industries, and markets, which are also systems. Moreover, application of GTI to strategic management was enabled by the creation of specialized tools, such as generic growth strategies, value matrix, value growth templates, and others. If an organization can precisely forecast the future of its products and processes as well as foresee where the market will go, this company can use this knowledge at any time to create new powerful strategies, find new markets for products and services, find new sources of revenue, and generate and control growth. This company will have a substantial advantage compared to its uninformed rivals, which is a solid foundation for continuous advantage and success.

7. *Strategic innovation*: Not all innovations are born equal! Out of the minority that are financially successful, only a few are capable of moving markets and increasing the market share for their creators. The deliberate (on-demand) creation of these innovations is the essence of this application, which involves analysis of such systems as the market, a respective company with the focus on its strategy, and products that the company delivers to the marketplace. The GTI-based process of creating strategic innovations is shown in Table 5.3.

8. *On-demand innovation corporate capability*: The beauty of any scientific theory is in the effectiveness of knowledge transfer. It would be difficult to correctly build functioning ships and airplanes without knowing the laws of physics. Knowledge of the laws of the evolutionary cycle combined with GTI capabilities to forecast the future of both a system of interest and its respective market (environment) enables any entity to develop its capability of continually producing commercially successful innovations and thus become the "invincible" enterprise.

9. *Investment opportunities, including mergers and acquisitions (M&A)*: The above-described strategic capabilities of GTI enable accurate identification of those entities that have a strategic advantage over their competitors, which leads to an exciting opportunity to establish

additional (objective) criteria for investment decisions, including M&As. (GTI cannot predict the timing of the change, which is important for short-term investment activities.) (Figure 5.3)

You Have Strategies to be Innovative, Even if You Aren't

In the previous section, we ran through a quick exercise to challenge the possibility that you don't need to innovate, by demonstrating a few random businesses (trust us, they were random) that could be disrupted and how that might happen. Will each of these scenarios play out? Probably not, because we don't know the businesses, but there is someone who does, or maybe someone who doesn't, and those are even more dangerous.

When you consider Airbnb as an example, can you just imagine the discussion around his parent's table when he told them what he and his friends were going to build? "Mom, Dad, you know how I moved out of the house a couple of years ago, and now you just have this empty bedroom upstairs? Well, what we are going to do is build a business where you will be able to rent my old bedroom to strangers for real money. Will I buy spare bedrooms around the world. No, I will just enable people to rent your spare bedroom and make sure that you get paid for doing it. They can rate you and rank you, and it will be easier to do it if you keep the room clean and keep quiet in your own house.

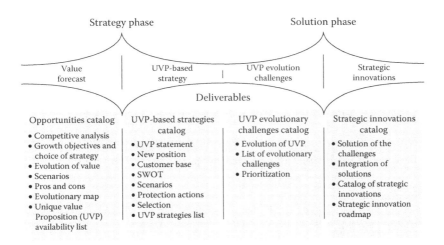

FIGURE 5.3
The process of creating strategic innovations. (See Greg Yezersky, *The TRIZ Journal*.)

The best part is that all I have to do is connect people together and never actually have to own a building, a bedroom, or a vacation house. I just rent yours to other people. Brilliant huh?"

We guess that the entire process takes some socialization. People first need to understand the business, and then they need to accept it. The real beauty of the business is in its simplicity and relatively low price. If we were to compare starting a hotel chain with Airbnb, let's compare the differences. To add a little real-world reality, let's talk about ownership, franchise, and Airbnb.

	Owned	Franchised	Airbnb
Assets	20–50 hotels throughout the world – cost $50 billion in the mortgage	20–50 franchisees throughout the world – cost millions in legal fees	Thousands of locations – cost is millions in technology investment
Start-up period	Perhaps a lifetime	5–15 years	As quickly as you can convince people it is a good idea – initially in select cities
Commitment	Keep the building occupied, pay thousands of people a salary, risk of failure significant	Commitment to franchisees, hundreds of employees who could be laid off	Commitment to renters and rentees, hundreds of employees who could be laid off
Cost of failure	Corporate or personal bankruptcy, the sale of assets	Corporate or personal bankruptcy. Possible long-term commitment to loyalty program members and franchisees	Lay off employees, shut off the server, chalk the entire experience up to another successful start-up failure

SUMMARY OF YEZERSKY'S FIVE CONDITIONS*

Acceptance of major axioms, the existence of the natural laws governing the process of evolution, automatically leads to the following capabilities

---

* According to Professor Greg Yezersky, the goal of sustaining success can only be achieved if a company continually comes up with value propositions that are accepted by the market. To avoid variability of results (failures), as operation management, the process of competition must be controlled in its entirety. That is why the best-run enterprises use all the methods that have been proven over time to reduce variability in the results produced by such diverse corporate activities as procurement, manufacturing, distribution, marketing, design, and sales.

that are direct corollaries, which are natural consequences of that acceptance.

1. *The nature of a challenge (problem, failure)*: The nature of any challenge/problem/failure experienced by a system is in deviating from the direction prescribed by the natural laws of evolution. Consider an analogy of disobeying the natural laws of traffic on a freeway (driving against the traffic, changing lanes continually, driving with a speed that significantly differs from that of the flow, etc.), which always elevates risk and creates problems. Being able to efficiently identify the origins of problems, which are always a result of our choices, greatly improves the ability to effectively address them by going to the cause and restoring "lawful" behavior.

2. *The nature of success*: On the other hand, the nature of success is in obeying "laws." There is no exception to this rule. Just as people must follow the laws of physical science when designing products or services if these products or services are expected to work well, the laws of evolution must be followed if business success is expected. Today's executives, whether they know it or not, follow these laws when they succeed. They do so intuitively, but not consistently or methodically, producing very mixed results. GTI articulates evolutionary laws and introduces a set of tools for working consciously and strategically within the laws.

3. *The capability to forecast the future of evolution*: Knowledge of a system's location on the evolutionary curve combined with knowledge of the evolutionary laws allows any organization to forecast the system's (product, process, service) future with great precision.

4. *The capability to objectively judge upcoming innovations*: The existence of natural laws of the evolutionary cycle has enabled the creation of objective criteria for evaluating proposed innovations, the importance of such criteria being self-evident. At the time of working on a direct-current motor, Thomas Edison completely dismissed the efforts by George Westinghouse, stating that alternating current was nonsense and had no future. Every innovation improves a system, moving it along the evolutionary curve. Whether this move complies with the laws or deviates from the laws, it constitutes a criterion for evaluating the innovation.

5. *The capability to control the process of innovation*: With these capabilities, one can control the entire process of innovation, thereby greatly reducing the risk and variability of results, and increasing the manageability of the process and return on investment of R&D. Finally, while understanding that GTI (just as any other scientific theory) can be endlessly perfected, it, in principle, meets the criteria set at the beginning.

BIBLIOGRAPHY

Alexander A. Bogdanov (Malinovsky), *Tektologia*, Economika Publishing House, Moscow, 1989, in Russian, ISBN 5-282-00538-7.

Alexander A. Malinovsky (Bogdanov), the late father of tectology (1920) whose work prophetically preceded many of the results by Altshuller, Bertalanffy, and Wiener. See Refs 10,11, and 12.

Arie de Geus, *The Living Company*, Harvard Business School Press, Boston, 1997, ISBN-10: 087584782X.

W. Chan Kim, Renee Mauborgne, *Blue Ocean Strategy*, Harvard Business School Press, Boston, 2005, ISBN 1-59139-619-0.

Dr. Ellen Domb, whose wisdom, patience, and perseverance brought the author (and GTI) back to the TRIZ community.

Dr. Gaetano Cascini (Italy), a close friend and colleague, whose advice and opinions are always relevant and thoughtful.

Genrich Altshuller, *And Suddenly the Inventor Appears: TRIZ, the Theory of Inventive Problem Solving*, Technical Innovation Center, ISBN 0964074028.

Genrich Altshuller, *Creativity as an Exact Science: The Theory of the Solution of Inventive Problems*, Gordon and Breach, New York, 1984, ISBN 0-677-21230-5.

Genrich Altshuller, *The Innovation Algorithm: TRIZ, Systematic Innovation and Technical Creativity*, Technical Innovation Center, Worcester, MA, 2000, ISBN 0964074044.

Glyn Davies, *A History of Money*, University of Wales Press, Cardiff, 1996, ISBN 0708317170.

Greg Frenklach (Israel), with whom the original research was conducted.

Dr. John Terninko, a close friend and an intellectual sparring partner, whose challenges of every bit of the GTI content (including axioms and assumptions) made GTI stronger.

Dr. Lev L. Velikovich (Belarus), a close friend and mentor, who was the first to recognize the importance of GTI and wholeheartedly encouraged the author and supported his activities.

Ludwig von Bertalanffy, *General System Theory*, George Braziler, New York, 1968, ISBN: 0-8076-0453-4.

Dr. Noel Leon (Mexico), who created the name, the General Theory of Innovation, and generously presented it to the author.

Norbert Wiener, *Cybernetics*, The Technology Press, New York, 1948.

Praveen Gupta and Brett Trusko, McGraw-Hill, New York, NY, 2014. ISBN-13: 978-0071792707

6

Business Essentials for Innovative Entrepreneurs

In a nutshell: Since innovation is a complex endeavor, especially for startups, it requires a set of business essentials – crosscutting practices and processes to structure, organize, and encourage it. Taken together, the essentials described in this chapter constitute just such an operating system for entrepreneurs. These often overlapping, iterative, and non-sequential practices resist systematic categorization but can nonetheless be stratified into two groupings: (1) the first four essentials, which are strategic and creative in nature, help set and prioritize the terms and conditions under which innovation is more likely to thrive; and (2) the next four business essentials deal with how to deliver and organize for innovation repeatedly over time, and with enough value to contribute meaningfully to overall performance growth and ideation. This chapter explains why innovation is increasingly important to driving corporate startup growth, and brings to life the eight essentials of innovation performance.

Peter Drucker says *"there are three business conditions that must be met for innovation to be successful including**:

1. *Innovation is work. It requires knowledge, ingenuity, creativity, etc. Plus, innovators rarely work in more than one area, be it finance,*

---

* Reading the thoughts of Peter Drucker helps us "connect the dots" for the key concepts of innovation. If you want the perspective of one of Drucker's PhD students at Claremont University, we recommend William Cohen's very insightful book, *A Class with Drucker*. Cohen shares his experience during classes as well as his personal relationship with Peter Drucker over the years following Cohen's graduation. Through the stories of Drucker's interaction with his students, you see the depth of his personality and his mental acuity and reach.

healthcare, retail, or whatever. This work requires diligence, persever-
ance, and commitment.

2. *To succeed, innovators must build on their own strengths. They*
   must look at opportunities over a wide range, then ask which of the
   opportunities fits me, fits this company. There must be a temperamental
   fit with the practitioner and a link to business strategy.

3. *Innovation is an effect in economy and society, a change in the behavior*
   of customers, of teachers, of farmers, of doctors, of people in general. Or,
   it is a change in a process, in how people work and produce something.
   Innovation must always be close to the market, focused on the market,
   and market driven."

INTRODUCTION

The hierarchy of business needs consists of five layers, starting with the foundation of strong business fundamentals.* For your organization to earn the right to be innovative year after year, you need to build the foundation and maintain it. Skip a layer and you'll find your house-of-innovation crumbling, and you'll find yourself scrambling to stay relevant. Build strength at each layer and you'll enjoy the rewards and the customers' love that every entrepreneur hungers for. There should be regular reporting, alignment to relevant regulations and external controls, and periodic external reviews to ensure that those processes and controls are effective. Active measurement and monitoring provide a solid foundation for the business, as shown in the following figure.

---

* Source: Build a strong foundation for Innovation, by SucceedSooner. They provide "strategic innovation services" and have a simple framework and guided approach to implementing a successful innovation program in your company that will drive growth through innovation and build a culture of innovation in your organization. See http://succeedsooner.ca/2016/07/18/foundation-for-innovation/.

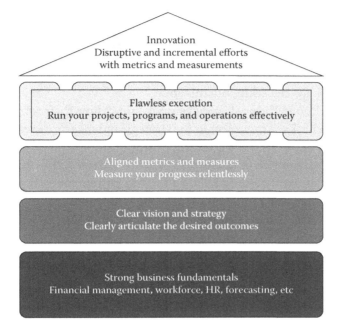

Hierarchy of Organization Needs. In entrepreneurial companies, building a strong foundation for innovation falls to the founder or entrepreneur early in the development of the company. Vision and strategy are where the entrepreneur or chief executive officer (CEO) is likely to focus much of their time. Every business needs to have a clear purpose (WHY?), a clear articulation of how they will achieve it (HOW?), and a customer base that will be used to reach these goals (WHAT?). A well-articulated vision and strategy become the playbook for the entire organization. Everyone knows the goal, and everyone knows how their work connects to that goal. Link every action in a way that is relevant to the goal.

After building a foundation of strong business fundamentals, vision and strategy are where the entrepreneur or CEO is likely to focus much of their time. Every business needs to have a clear purpose (WHY?), a clear articulation of how they will achieve it (HOW?), and an articulation of the core business and customer base that will be used to reach these goals

(WHAT?).* Your vision and strategy should link from the broad vision of the organization down through the elements of the business organization, all the way to the individual supporting strategies and strategic priorities for each area of the business. A well-articulated vision and strategy become the playbook for the entire organization.

Everyone knows the goal, and everyone knows how their work connects to that goal. Link every project to the strategy and measure every action in a way that is relevant to the goal.†

Both input metrics and output metrics are essential for ensuring measures that drive resource allocation and entrepreneurship capability building, as well as a return on investment assessment.

The following three categories contain the metrics portfolio that all entrepreneurs need to care about:

- Return on investment (ROI) metrics.
- ROI metrics address two measures: resource investments and financial returns. ROI metrics give innovation management fiscal discipline and help justify and recognize the value of strategic initiatives, programs, and the overall investment in innovation.
- Organizational capability metrics.

Organizational capability metrics focus on the infrastructure and the process of innovation. Capability measures provide focus for initiatives geared toward building repeatable and sustainable approaches to invention and reinvention. After relying on cost and operational efficiencies to grow the bottom line during the past 20 years, many entrepreneurs are emerging from an innovation slump post-recession. Since 2015, there has been an

---

* See Simon Sinek's TED talk "'Getting to Why': How Great Leaders Inspire Action" for more details on the importance of getting to WHY and the order of operations. Sinek has a simple but powerful model for inspirational leadership – starting with a golden circle and the question "Why?" His examples include Apple, Martin Luther King, and the Wright brothers; and the reflection of the world we live in is created within us. We do have the choice.

† As a founder of a small, successful, high-tech consulting firm in the early 1990s, I appear to have unknowingly followed Simon Sinek's advice, which basically boils down to: "Put the others first!" Fifteen or so years ago, I even indebted myself, not to mention not drawing any salary, so that my bills could be paid, and I could grow the business. So I concur: quite often, the approach of everyone knowing the goal does elicit a strong loyalty. But beware: there are always exceptions. A few of my most talented employees just wouldn't give a hoot, always following the simple "code of silence" or "I just WORK here, why should I care!" No amount of care and selflessness appears to be able to make these types abandon their own personal agenda of "Getting the most money with the smallest possible effort."

imperative to refocus on organic growth. The importance of innovation in driving this growth is resurfacing to the top of the agenda. For many organizations, there are some radically new behavioral, structural, and operational business essentials and models for meeting this challenge.*

For entrepreneurship to prosper, innovation benchmarking is not just another business essential exercise, but primarily another approach to benchmarking. In innovation benchmarking, we want to identify the business essentials behind the benchmark's success. These are business essentials that are not always measurable, so we need to go by some other variables first. Afterward, we want to try to adapt and apply these factors to our own company.

There is overlapping research between benchmarking and related business essentials, such as knowledge management (KM), asserting the notion that the knowledge-based perspective is the main source of competitive advantage. Organizational learning (OL), especially in knowledge-intensive industries (KII), not only leads to organizational innovation, but it is the only sustainable competitive advantage in the long run.

Most startup companies start by benchmarking inside their own company (internal benchmarking) and then move on to their competitors (external benchmarking).

Three types of business essentials involved in benchmarking:

1. *Process benchmarking*: Involves identification of best practices
2. *Strategic benchmarking*: Involves identifying emerging trends
3. *Comparative benchmarking*: More result oriented

There is a difference between *innovation benchmarking* and *benchmarking innovations*. Benchmarking innovation can be seen as a form of contradiction. If we are doing something completely new – applying an invention in a new way – it means that others are not doing the same thing. Thus, there is nothing to benchmark. Innovation benchmarking, on the other hand, can be understood as how to become or stay "innovative."

---

* Corporate accelerators are all about enabling more agility to achieve faster and more radical innovation by temporarily importing a whole startup to be entrepreneurial for you. Large organizations such as Airbus, T-Mobile, and Google are using this unique approach to drive growth through breakthrough innovation. Source: http://innovationexcellence.com/blog/2017/11/28/have-you-tried-new-ways-to-innovate/.

The challenge is to find the right metrics. These metrics should fulfill the following criteria:

- They must be understood by the user
- They must be (easily) available
- They must be the best measures we can find for a given variable we want to measure
- They must be comparable and preferably quantifiable

One-third of all Fortune 1000 companies began by having a set of formal innovation metrics in place. The most prevalent metrics include:

- Annual research and development (R&D) budget as a percentage of annual sales
- Number of patents filed in the past year
- Total R&D headcount or budget as a percentage of sales
- Number of active projects
- Number of ideas submitted by employees
- Percentage of sales from products introduced in the past X year(s)

Leadership metrics: Leadership metrics address the behaviors that senior managers and leaders must exhibit to support a culture of innovation. There are three steps to successful benchmarking:

- Selecting key performance drivers or KPIs
- Selecting companies to benchmark
- Allocating resources to the best value-added areas identified

OVERVIEW

The engineer comes into the office of the general manager with a great new idea. We can build a better (faster, smaller, more beautiful) widget; all we need to do is make them solid gold. Interesting idea, but as an accountant, marketing manager, sales person, or whatever, you immediately recognize that while the product may in fact be better when produced from solid gold rather than plastic, the improvement will never justify the vastly increased cost. The engineer, being an engineer, walks away disgusted that the better widget is within our grasp, but the businesspeople just don't understand.

Alternatively, you are a venture capitalist who is interested in finding a new and interesting project in which to invest. During the show, "Shark Tank," inventors are given a few minutes to try to convince a group of investors that their widget is the greatest thing since sliced bread. While it is definitely entertaining, the reality of the real world is that a complete business plan is generally necessary at all points of the investment life cycle.

To be sure, there's no proven formula for success, particularly when it comes to innovation.* While our years of client-service experience provide strong indicators for the existence of a causal relationship between the attributes that survey respondents reported and the innovations of the companies we studied, the statistics described here can only *prove* correlation. Yet, we firmly believe that if companies assimilate and apply these essentials – in their own way, in accordance with their particular context, capabilities, organizational culture, and appetite for risk – they will improve the likelihood that they, too, can rekindle the lost spark of innovation.

In the digital age, the pace of change has gone into hyper-speed, so companies must get these strategic, creative, executional, and organizational factors right to innovate successfully.

Aspire	Do you regard innovation-led growth as critical, and do you have cascaded targets that reflect this?
Choose	Do you invest in a coherent, time- and risk-balanced portfolio of initiatives with sufficient resources to win?
Discover	Do you have differentiated business, market, and technology insights that translate into winning value propositions?
Evolve	Do you create new business models that provide defensible and scalable profit sources?
Accelerate	Do you beat the competition by developing and launching innovations quickly and effectively?
Scale	Do you launch innovations at the right scale in the relevant markets and segments?
Extend	Do you win by creating and capitalizing on external networks?
Mobilize	Are your people motivated, rewarded, and organized to innovate repeatedly?

---

* Source: McKinsey Study on Innovation, 2015. http://www.mckinsey.com/business-functions/ strategy-and-corporate-finance/our-insights/the-eight-essentials-of-innovation.

BUSINESS ESSENTIAL #1: ASPIRE

President John F. Kennedy's bold aspiration, in 1962, to "go to the moon in this decade" motivated a nation to unprecedented levels of innovation. A far-reaching vision can be a compelling catalyst, provided it's realistic enough to stimulate action today. But in a corporate setting, as many CEOs have discovered, even the most inspiring words often are insufficient, no matter how many times they are repeated. It helps to combine high-level aspirations with estimates of the value that innovation should generate to meet financial growth objectives.

Quantifying an "innovation target for growth" and making it an explicit part of future strategic plans help solidify the importance of and accountability for innovation. The target itself must be large enough to force managers to include innovation investments in their business plans. If they can make their numbers using other, less risky tactics, our experience suggests that they (quite rationally) will.

Establishing a quantitative innovation aspiration is not enough, however. The target value needs to be apportioned to relevant business "owners" and cascaded down to their organizations in the form of performance targets and timelines. Anything less risks encouraging inaction or the belief that innovation is someone else's job. For example, Lantmännen, a big Nordic agricultural cooperative, was challenged by flat organic growth and directionless innovation. Top executives created an aspirational vision and strategic plan linked to financial targets: 6% growth in the core business and 2% growth in new organic ventures. To encourage innovation projects, these quantitative targets were cascaded down to business units and, ultimately, to product groups.

During the development of each innovation project, it had to show how it was helping to achieve the growth targets for its category and markets. As a result, Lantmännen went from 4% to 13% annual growth, underpinned by the successful launch of several new brands. Indeed, it became the market leader in premade food only four years after entry and created a new premium segment in this market.

Such performance parameters can seem painful to managers more accustomed to the traditional approach. In our experience, though, CEOs are likely just going through the motions if they don't use evaluations and remuneration to assess and recognize the contribution that all top managers make to innovation.

BUSINESS ESSENTIAL #2: CHOOSE

Fresh, creative insights are invaluable, but in our experience many companies run into difficulty less from a scarcity of new ideas than from the struggle to determine *which* ideas to support and scale. At bigger companies, this can be particularly problematic during market discontinuities, when supporting the next wave of growth may seem too risky, at least until competitive dynamics force painful changes.

Innovation *is* inherently risky, to be sure, and getting the most from a portfolio of innovation initiatives is more about managing risk than eliminating it. Since no one knows exactly where valuable innovations will emerge, and searching everywhere is impractical, executives must create some boundary conditions for the opportunity spaces they want to explore. The process of identifying and bounding these spaces can run the gamut from intuitive visions of the future to carefully scrutinized strategic analyses. Thoughtfully prioritizing these spaces also allows companies to assess whether they have enough investment behind their most valuable opportunities.

During this process, companies should set in motion more projects than they will ultimately be able to finance, which makes it easier to kill those that prove less promising. RELX Group, for example, runs 10–15 experiments per major customer segment, each funded with a preliminary budget of around $200,000 through its innovation pipeline every year, choosing subsequently to invest more significant funds in one or two of them, and dropping the rest. "One of the hardest things to figure out is when to kill something," says Kumsal Bayazit, RELX Group's chief strategy officer. "It's a heck of a lot easier if you have a portfolio of ideas."

Once the opportunities are defined, companies need transparency about what people are working on and a governance process that constantly assesses not only the expected value, timing, and risk of the initiatives in the portfolio, but also its overall composition. There's no single mix that's universally right. Most established companies err on the side of overloading their innovation pipelines with relatively safe, short-term, and incremental projects that have little chance of realizing their growth targets or staying within their risk parameters. Some spread themselves thinly across too many projects instead of focusing on those with the highest potential for success and resourcing them to win.

These tendencies get reinforced by a sluggish resource reallocation process. Our research shows that a company typically reallocates only a tiny fraction of its resources from year to year, thereby sentencing innovation to a stagnating march of incrementalism.*

BUSINESS ESSENTIAL #3: DISCOVER

Innovation also requires actionable and differentiated insights – the kind that excite customers and bring new categories and markets into being. How do companies develop them? Genius is always an appealing approach, if you have it or can get it. Fortunately, innovation yields to other approaches besides exceptional creativity.

The rest of us can look for insights by methodically and systematically scrutinizing three areas: a valuable problem to solve, a technology that enables a solution, and a business model that generates money from it. You could argue that nearly every successful innovation occurs at the intersection of these three elements. Companies that effectively collect, synthesize, and "collide" the three elements stand the highest probability of success. "If you get the sweet spot of what the customer is struggling with, and at the same time get a deeper knowledge of the new technologies coming along and find a mechanism for how these two things can come together, then you are going to get good returns," says Alcoa chairman and chief executive Klaus Kleinfeld.

The insight discovery process, which extends beyond a company's boundaries to include insight generating partnerships, is the lifeblood of innovation. We won't belabor the matter here, though, because it's already the subject of countless articles and books.† One thing we can add is that discovery is iterative, and the active use of prototypes can help companies continue to learn as they develop, test, validate, and refine their innovations. Moreover, we firmly believe that without a fully developed innovation *system* encompassing the other elements described in this

---

* See Stephen Hall, Dan Lovallo, and Reinier Musters, "How to put your money where your strategy is," *McKinsey Quarterly*, March 2012; Vanessa Chan, Marc de Jong, and Vidyadhar Ranade, "Finding the sweet spot for allocating innovation resources," *McKinsey Quarterly*, May 2014.
† See, for example, Marla M. Capozzi, Reneé Dye, and Amy Howe, "Sparking creativity in teams: An executive's guide," *McKinsey Quarterly*, April 2011; Marla M. Capozzi, John Horn, and Ari Kellen, "Battle-test your innovation strategy," *McKinsey Quarterly*, December 2012.

chapter, large organizations probably won't innovate successfully, no matter how effective their insight generation process is.

BUSINESS ESSENTIAL #4: EVOLVE

Business model innovations – which change the economics of the value chain, diversify profit streams, and/or modify delivery models – have always been a vital part of a strong innovation portfolio. As smartphones and mobile apps threaten to upend old-line industries, business model innovation has become all the more urgent: established companies must reinvent their businesses before technology-driven upstarts do. Why, then, do most innovation systems so squarely emphasize new products? The reason, of course, is that most big companies are reluctant to risk tampering with their core business model until it's visibly under threat. At that point, they can only hope it's not too late.

Leading companies combat this troubling tendency in a number of ways. They up their game in market intelligence, the better to separate signal from noise. They establish funding vehicles for new businesses that don't fit into the current structure. They constantly reevaluate their position in the value chain, carefully considering business models that might deliver value to priority groups of new customers. They sponsor pilot projects and experiments away from the core business to help combat narrow conceptions of what they are and do. And, they stress test newly emerging value propositions and operating models against countermoves by competitors.

Amazon does a particularly strong job extending itself into new business models by addressing the emerging needs of its customers and suppliers. In fact, it has included many of its suppliers in its customer base by offering them an increasingly wide range of services, from hosted computing to warehouse management. Another strong performer, the *Financial Times*, was already experimenting with its business model in response to the increasing digitalization of media when, in 2007, it launched an innovative subscription model, upending its relationship with advertisers and readers. "We went against the received wisdom of popular strategies at the time," says Caspar de Bono, *FT* board member and managing director of B2B. "We were very deliberate in getting ahead of the emerging structural change, and the decisions turned out to be very successful." In print's heyday, 80% of the *FT*'s revenue came from print advertising. Now, more than half of it comes from content, and two-thirds of circulation comes from digital subscriptions.

BUSINESS ESSENTIAL #5: ACCELERATE

Virulent antibodies undermine innovation in many small and large companies. Cautious governance processes make it easy to stifle innovation in many small businesses and create bureaucracies in marketing, legal, information technology (IT), and other functions to find reasons to halt or slow approvals. Too often, entrepreneurs simply get in the way of their own attempts to innovate. A surprising number of impressive innovations from startup companies were actually the fruits of their mavericks, who succeeded in bypassing their early approval processes. Clearly, there's a balance to be maintained: bureaucracy must be held in check, yet the rush to market should not undermine the cross-functional collaboration, continuous learning cycles, and clear decision pathways that help enable innovation. Are managers with the right knowledge, skills, and experience making the crucial decisions in a timely manner, so that innovation continually moves through an organization in a way that creates and maintains competitive advantage, without exposing a company to unnecessary risk?

Small businesses also thrive by testing their promising ideas with customers early in the process, before internal forces impose modifications that blur the original value proposition. To end up with the innovation initially envisioned, it's necessary to knock down the barriers that stand between a great idea and the end user. Startups need a well-connected manager to take charge of a project and be responsible for the budget, time to market, and key specifications – a person who can say yes rather than no. In addition, the project team needs to be cross-functional in reality, not just on paper. This means locating its members in a single place and ensuring that they give the project a significant amount of their time (at least half) to support a culture that puts the innovation project's success above the success of each function.

Cross-functional collaboration can help ensure end-user involvement throughout the development process. In many entreneurships/companies, marketing's role is to champion the interests of end users as development teams evolve products and to help ensure that the final result is what everyone first envisioned. But this responsibility is honored more often in the breach than in the observance. Other companies, meanwhile, rationalize that consumers don't necessarily know what they want until it becomes available. This may be true, but customers can certainly say what they *don't* like. And the more quickly and frequently a project team gets – and uses – feedback, the more quickly it gets a great end result.

BUSINESS ESSENTIAL #6: SCALABILITY

Some ideas, such as luxury goods and many smartphone apps, are destined for niche markets. Others, like social networks, work at a global scale. Explicitly considering the appropriate magnitude and reach of a given idea is important to ensuring that the right resources and risks are involved in pursuing it. The seemingly safer option of scaling up over time can be a death sentence. Resources and capabilities must be marshaled to make sure that a new product or service can be delivered quickly at the desired volume and quality. Manufacturing facilities, suppliers, distributors, and others must be prepared to execute a rapid and full rollout.

For example, in 2004, when TomTom launched its first touchscreen navigational device, the product flew off the shelves. By 2006, TomTom's line of portable navigation devices reached sales of about 5 million units a year, and by 2008, yearly volume had jumped to more than 12 million. "That's faster market penetration than mobile phones had," says Harold Goddijn, TomTom's CEO and cofounder. While TomTom's initial accomplishment lay in combining a well-defined consumer problem with widely available technology components, rapid scaling was vital to the product's continuing success. "We doubled down on managing our cash, our operations, maintaining quality, all the parts of the iceberg no one sees," Goddijn adds. "We were hugely well organized."

BUSINESS ESSENTIAL #7: EXTEND

In the space of only a few years, companies in nearly every sector have conceded that innovation requires external collaborators. Flows of talent and knowledge increasingly transcend company and geographic boundaries. Successful innovators achieve significant multiples for every dollar invested in innovation by accessing the skills and talents of others. In this way, they speed up innovation and uncover new ways to create value for their customers and ecosystem partners.

Smart collaboration with external partners, though, goes beyond merely sourcing new ideas and insights; it can involve sharing costs and finding faster routes to market. Famously, the components of Apple's first iPod were developed almost entirely outside the company; by efficiently managing these external partnerships, Apple was able to move from initial concept to marketable product in only nine months. NASA's Ames Research Center teams up not just with international partners – launching joint satellites with nations as diverse as Lithuania, Saudi Arabia, and Sweden – but also with emerging companies, such as SpaceX.

High-performing innovators work hard to develop the ecosystems that help deliver these benefits. Indeed, they strive to become partners of choice, increasing the likelihood that the best ideas and people will come their way. That requires a systematic approach. First, these companies find out which partners they are already working with; surprisingly few companies know this. Then they decide which networks – say, four or five of them – they ideally need to support their innovation strategies. This step helps them to narrow and focus their collaboration efforts and to manage the flow of possibilities from outside the company. Strong innovators also regularly review their networks, extending and pruning them as appropriate, and using sophisticated incentives and contractual structures to motivate high-performing business partners. Becoming a true partner of choice is, among other things, about clarifying what a partnership can offer the junior member: brand, reach, or access, perhaps. It is also about behavior. Partners of choice are fair and transparent in their dealings.

Moreover, companies that make the most of external networks have a good idea of what's most useful at which stages of the innovation process. In general, they cast a relatively wide net in the early going. But, as they come closer to commercializing a new product or service, they become narrower and more specific in their sourcing, since by then the new offering's design is relatively set.

BUSINESS ESSENTIAL #8: MOBILIZE

How do leading companies stimulate, encourage, support, and reward innovative behavior and thinking among the right groups of people? The best companies find ways to embed innovation into the fibers of their culture, from the core to the periphery.

They start back where we began: with aspirations that forge tight connections among innovation, strategy, and performance. When a company sets financial targets for innovation and defines market spaces, minds become far more focused. As those aspirations come to life through individual projects across the company, innovation leaders clarify responsibilities using the appropriate incentives and rewards.

The Discovery Group, for example, is upending the medical and life insurance industries in its native South Africa and also has operations in the United Kingdom, the United States, and China, among other locations. Innovation is a standard measure in the company's semiannual divisional scorecards – a process that helps mobilize the organization and affects roughly 1000 of the company's business leaders. "They are all required to innovate every year," Discovery founder and CEO Adrian Gore says of the company's business leaders. "They have no choice."

Organizational changes may be necessary, not because structural silver bullets exist – we've looked hard for them and don't think they do – but rather to promote collaboration, learning, and experimentation. Companies must help people to share ideas and knowledge freely, perhaps by locating teams working on different types of innovation in the same place, reviewing the structure of project teams to make sure that they always have new blood, ensuring that lessons learned from success and failure are captured and assimilated, and recognizing innovation efforts even when they fall short of success.

USE MATRIX THINKING TO "THINK OUTSIDE THE BOX"

> If we remain imprisoned in the linear thinking so congenial to bureaucrats, capitalists, commissars, and aspiring gauleiters, the 1980s will be a period of unemployment, alienation, and unprecedented social crises.
>
> **Barry Jones**
> *"Sleepers Wake!," 1981*

In modern times came the development of the "scientific method." This method embraced logic, and added to it further techniques such as experiment and observation, and the requirement for repeatability of results. A very important new facet was that of prediction ("If A applies, therefore B should happen – we'll try it and see").

These methods have served us well. Nevertheless, they can all be classed as examples of linear thinking. With linear thinking, there is a starting point from which all the rest proceeds – perhaps an assumption, an observation to be explained, or even a goal. Even Edward de Bono's *Lateral*

Thinking, of which I am a considerable admirer, is still linear thinking. It is linear thinking that proceeds from an unexpected viewpoint.

Matrix thinking is rather different. It tries to look at a situation from multiple viewpoints, as a complex and not necessarily analyzable matrix. Often, there will be no starting point, no clearly defined logic path "through" the matrix.

USE CONSTRAINTS TO "THINK INSIDE THE BOX"

When it comes to innovation, the single most common piece of advice may be to "think outside the box." Constraints, according to this view, are the enemy of creativity because they sap intrinsic motivation and limit possibilities.

Sophisticated innovators, however, have long recognized that constraints spur and guide innovation. Attempting to innovate without boundaries overwhelms people with options and ignores established practices, such as agile programming, which have been shown to enhance innovation. Without guidelines to structure the interactions, members of a complex organization or ecosystem struggle to coordinate their innovative activities.

Internal collaboration and experimentation can take years to establish, particularly in large, mature companies with strong cultures and ways of working that, in other respects, may have served them well. Some companies set up "innovation garages" where small groups can work on important projects unconstrained by the normal working environment while building new ways of working that can be scaled up and absorbed into the larger organization. NASA, for example, has 10 field centers. But the space agency relies on the Ames Research Center in Silicon Valley to maintain what its former director, Dr. Pete Worden, calls "the character of rebels" to function as "a laboratory that's part of a much larger organization."

Big companies do not easily reinvent themselves as leading innovators. Too many fixed routines and cultural factors can get in the way. For those that do make the attempt, innovation excellence is often built in a multiyear effort that touches most, if not all, parts of the organization. Our experience and research suggest that any company looking to make this journey will maximize its probability of success by closely studying and appropriately assimilating the leading practices of high-performing innovators. Taken together, these form an essential operating system for innovation within a company's organizational structure and culture.

How, then, can organizations embrace a more disciplined approach to innovation? One productive approach is to apply a few simple rules to key steps in the innovation process. Simple rules add just enough structure to help organizations avoid the stifling bureaucracy of too many rules and the chaos of none at all. By imposing constraints on themselves, individuals, teams, and organizations can spark creativity and channel it along the desired trajectory. Instead of trying to think outside the wrong box, you can use simple rules to draw the right box and innovate within it.

Simple rules cannot, of course, guarantee successful innovation – no tool can. Innovation creates novel products, processes, or business models that generate economic value. Trying anything new inevitably entails experimentation and failure. Simple rules, however, add discipline to the process to boost efficiency and increase the odds that the resulting innovations will create value.

Simple rules are most commonly applied to the sustaining kind of innovation, often viewed as less important than major breakthroughs. The current fascination with disruption obscures an important reality. For many established companies, incremental product improvements, advances in existing business models, and moves into adjacent markets remain critical sources of value-creating innovation. The turnaround of Danish toymaker LEGO over the past decade, for example, has depended at least as much on rejuvenating the core business through the injection of discipline into the company's new-product development engine as it has on radical innovation.

THE MATRIX AND RUNNING AN ENTERPRISE*

Let's consider, for example, the operation of running and growing a business organization. There must be thousands of books written about how to run a company. Some of these by nature are very good, very detailed, explaining how best to manage staff, how to control cash flow and monitor productivity, and perhaps, on a more philosophical level, how

---

* http://www.aoi.com.au/matrix/Mat01.html.

to encourage innovation within a company and promote a good public image according to the ideals of the time.

And yet – look again. As far as I know, not one of these books even hints at the situations that matrix thinking would encourage and deal with, one that is close to the real-world situation. That is, one in which there is a complex mix or matrix of companies of every sort. Not only companies that are entrepreneurial, innovative, and progressive, with good labor relations, but also ones that are archconservative and backward. Ones that are founded on brilliant ideas but hopelessly managed, ones that are willing to act as test cases in clarifying legislation (read: "somewhat crooked"), ones that are grossly undercapitalized, and so on, through every permutation found in the real world and a few not yet tried. Even, and this strikes right against our instincts, companies that are very likely to fail, sure to fail, or even designed to fail. We never want the company we are involved with to fail, even though this may be of great benefit somewhere else in the matrix.

The matrix background to all of this will be developed in another tools book on innovation and the entrepreneur. For the moment, it is sufficient to repeat that linear thinking implies not only a starting point but also a goal, a result, an optimum position. In matrix thinking, there may be no such defined points.

Matrix Thinking and Creativity

The testing and resultant refinement of many well-known scientific models is subject to the same linear logic as the rest of science. But the creation of these models is not; in almost every case, the origin of a startling and powerful new scientific model is the product of an "inspiration," almost a religious "vision," which "pops into someone's mind." Hence, Archimedes leaping from his bath, shouting "I have found it" to passersby in the street, and Newton being literally struck with the idea of gravity, in the form of an apple falling on his head.

The creation of such models provides an example of matrix thinking in science. There is nothing logical or linear about it, it is almost as if a mind subconsciously squeezes and massages a bag of facts, and somehow, out of the whole bag, an answer pops out.

In fact, most of the activities we think of as "creative" are matrix oriented. This is an area of human thought about which very little is known or discussed, in that creativity is tied up in some way with the ability to tap into the matrix, rather than purely a linear and somewhat individually owned talent.

The first task in this book will be to formulate some structure and develop some tools for the use of matrix thinking. Then, we will apply the structure and the tools to an examination of human society, with the aim of deriving new viewpoints. These may possibly lead to "improvements" in human society.

Whether a particular change suggested is an "improvement" or not will be left for the reader to judge. Throughout this book, I have tried hard to avoid prejudging the issue, and saying what should be done in a particular situation. Instead, I have limited myself to pointing out what the matrix thinking apparatus suggests will be the outcome of the application of various conditions. That said, I will not hesitate to put up propositions suggesting that a certain course of action is desirable. What I will not say is that any of these propositions are unassailable.

From what has been said, it will be apparent that matrix thinking is not a replacement for, or a competitor with, the linear thinking that Barry Jones warns us about. Nor is it a complementary or alternative approach. Instead, it is a generalization that subsumes and includes the thinking with which we are most familiar.

The following matrix table can be used to map the organizational needs to the business essentials.

Business Essentials	Hierarchy of Organization Needs				
	Strong Business Fundamentals	Clear Vision and Strategy	Aligned Measures	Flawless Execution	Innovation
1. Aspire					
2. Choose					
3. Discover					
4. Evolve					
5. Accelerate					
6. Scalability					
7. Extend					
8. Mobilize					

SUMMARY

First, successful companies apply business essentials to act and behave differently. Secondly, they learn to seek out and always look for opportunities. They always listen to their customers, suppliers, and value chain partners. They ask distributors for ideas and have a means to track those ideas as they evolve. They have cultivated a robust network of advisors who help fill the gaps between ideas and execution and refine the ideas from their earliest versions to something the market wants. They are just as concerned with what their customers will want in 10–20 years as what their customers want today and yesteryear.

To execute your business innovation success plan more effectively, here are five essentials that innovators must know to ensure a long-term, healthy, and prosperous innovative business, which should answer the question: "How Can You Improve Business in the Next 12 Months?" Apply the five essentials for business innovation*:

1. *Strive for the unbelievable*: The goal is to have customers say; "WOW, how do they do that?" – with Service? Speed? How do they Out Care everyone? – with Price? Convenience? Free support? Knowledge? Make them scratch their head in wonder about something every day, week, month, year.
2. *Use an innovation invitation*: Each invitation must be unique and personal each and every time. The more unique and personal your invitation is, the better chance of receiving a response. Don't blast, don't treat everyone the same. Automation is helpful in getting more done but can also send the message of "you are not important."
3. *Be a leader:* A leader must have the highest skill and will. Without a leader in place who can, and will, drag the business behind them versus the other way around, any business will flounder. If a business is being managed by someone who struggles to keep up with the current business volume and flow, how will that same person have the ability to innovate and double business over the next two to three years?
4. *Involve high tech*: Innovators need to include the latest and greatest high tech to leave the competition behind. Technology keeps a small

---

* Source: http://www.michaelhartzell.com/Blog/bid/33019/5-Essentials-to-Business-Success.

business ahead of a large business. In larger businesses, barriers from logistics and lack of capital may exist. Changing systems and processes can be slow. Keeping the latest technology integrated in the business ensures better data, improves decisions, and overcomes service barriers to WOW the customer and improve efficiencies. Technology can make a business look like a winner and people love to be a part of winning, successful teams.

5. *Adopt the mind-set "good" today is not good enough tomorrow*: Even as you execute today, someone is becoming unimpressed or bored, or another business is preparing to improve on what you offer and leap frog, which will pull attention away from you. Seth Godin offers this: "'Good' is not good enough. 'Good' is boring. Where is your purple cow?"

7

Innovation Readiness and Deployment

The Practice of Innovation – Innovation is the specific tool of entrepreneurship, the means by which they exploit change as an opportunity for a different business or a different service. It is capable of being presented as a discipline, capable of being learned, capable of being practiced. Entrepreneurs need to search purposefully for the sources of innovation, the changes and their symptoms that indicate opportunities for successful innovation. And they need to know and to apply the principles of successful innovation.

Peter Drucker, 1985

In a nutshell: Now that you have an understanding of what it takes to create an innovation-based organization, how do you deploy it? For anyone involved in a company takeover (either the acquiring or the acquired), you know that integrating two companies almost never happens successfully – and is one of the most difficult things a company can ever do. The fact is that there is almost always massive turnover and a loss of productivity for some period. The deployment of innovation initiatives can take several forms similar to a merger, and deployment success depends on the degree of readiness. Innovation initiatives in the context of organizational operations and processes are the focus of this chapter. Are you innovation ready to begin plotting your journey on the Innovation Readiness Model?* If not, this means that you are lacking in many of the key elements required to create a successful platform for innovation. Companies may not reap the full benefits of their investments due to low levels of readiness to deploy their innovation initiatives. It is necessary to perform an assessment at the initial stage of implementing an innovation initiative with the purpose of identifying weaknesses or problems that may lead to failure. Questions such as how to deploy and when to deploy should be formally asked and answered prior to management committing to deploying an innovation initiative. This is somewhat like trying to change an organization from an old model to a new one. Let's just say it's like changing the wing of an airplane while in flight. The challenge is to keep the plane flying and the company productive while changing everything you do. Unlike changing a wing in flight, deploying innovation in a company can be a refreshing and enjoyable thing to do.

INTRODUCTION

When electricity was discovered, corporations employed a chief electricity officer. I suppose whenever a new focus is needed, new officers are appointed. Currently, profitable growth and innovation are considered necessary to

---

* The Innovation Readiness Model includes statistical process control (SPC): Lim, S. A. H., & Antony, J. (2013, December). A conceptual readiness framework for statistical process control (SPC) deployment. In *2013 IEEE International Conference on Industrial Engineering and Engineering Management* (pp. 300–304). Bangkok, Thailand: IEEE. 10.1109/IEEM.2013.6962422; Parast, M. M. (2011) The effect of Six Sigma projects on innovation and firm performance. *International Journal of Project Management, 29*, 45–55. 10.1016/j; Ahmadi, S., Yeh, C. H., Martin, R., & Papageorgiou, E. (2015a) Optimizing ERP readiness improvements under budgetary constraints. *International Journal of Production Economics, 161*, 105–115. 10.1016/j.ijpe.2014.11.020; and RFID integration into shop floor operations: Chuang, M., & Shaw, W. H. (2008) An empirical study of enterprise resource management systems implementation. From ERP to RFID. *Business Process Management Journal, 14*, 675–693. 10.1108/14637150810903057. Companies are handicapped by low levels of "innovation readiness": Dutta, S., Lanvin, B., Singh, T. R., Green, A., Berthelon, V., & Bingra, G. B. S. (2009) Are you innovation ready? Plotting your journey on the Innovation Readiness Model. *Insead Report*.

succeed; we are seeing people appointed to lead growth and innovation. Some innovation leaders are called chief innovation officers (CIOs) and others are named innovation managers. According to our research, we believe that the CIO requires skills in managing intellectual and human capital, needs technology experience that comes from the chief technology officer (CTO), and expects to deal with information and idea management, which comes from information technology (IT) professionals. Thus, the CIO requires a combination of expertise in human resources (HR), IT, and technology. It is still an evolving role, and as business models are changing it will take time for the appointment of a new CIO to be recognized and institutionalized. Leaders in any one of the fields with knowledge of the other two could become a CIO.*

Corporate innovation and areas of process deployment provide the ability to choose and implement innovative concepts that can improve the company's capacity to meet its quality and targeted process performance. (The glossary provides a meaning for "value and process execution targets.") The expression "change," which is utilized as part of this procedure zone, alludes to the majority of the ideas, both certain and uncertain, that would change the processes and advancements of the company to better meet the organization's quality and process execution goals.

Attempts to deploy innovation initiatives, especially in manufacturing, fail because managers do not establish sufficient readiness for change, according to our research on this subject covering a 50 year period.†

The readiness qualities and process performance targets that any company can consider are

- Improve the quality of products (e.g., usefulness, execution)
- Increase profitability

* Source: Praveen Gupta.
† According to Jacobson, E. H. (1957) The Effect of Changing Industrial Methods and Automation on Personnel. Symposium on Preventive and Social Psychology, Washington, DC, seminal work on the concepts of readiness. Note: the concepts have been developed further including: Ahmadi, S., Yeh, C. H., Martin, R., & Papageorgiou, E. (2015) Optimizing ERP readiness improvements under budgetary constraints. *International Journal of Production Economics, 161*, 105–115. 10.1016/j.ijpe.2014.11.020; Kwahk, K. Y., & Lee, J. N. (2008) The role of readiness for change in ERP implementation: Theoretical bases and empirical validation. *Information & Management, 45*, 474–481; Lim, S. A. H., & Antony, J. (2013, December) A conceptual readiness framework for statistical process control (SPC) deployment. In *2013 IEEE International Conference on Industrial Engineering and Engineering Management* (pp. 300–304). Bangkok, Thailand: IEEE. 10.1109/IEEM.2013.6962422.

- Decrease process duration
- Satisfy clients and end users better
- Decrease time for production processes to change; implement and analyze new highlights, innovations, and features
- Reduce time to delivery
- Reduce time to adjust to the unique needs of the business and innovation

Accomplishing the desired result relies on the fruitful foundation of a framework that empowers and supports all individuals in the organization to propose potential changes to the organization's procedures and advancements. The accomplishment of these goals likewise relies upon having the capacity to viably assess and send proposed changes to the organization's systems and advancements. All individuals in the organization can take an interest in the organization's procedure and innovation change exercises. Their recommendations are collected and analyzed.

Pilots are directed to assess critical changes, including untried, high-risk, or creative upgrades previously contemplated, providing that they are comprehensively analyzed and conveyed.

Process and innovation upgrades conveyed to the organization are chosen from a process and innovation change proposition given the accompanying criteria:

- A quantitative comprehension of the organization's present quality and process execution
- The organization's quality and process execution targets
- Estimates of the change in quality and process execution coming about because of conveying the procedure and innovation enhancements
- Estimated expense of conveying the procedure and innovation enhancements, and the assets and financing accessible for such organization

The natural advantages included in the procedure and innovation changes are weighed against the cost to and impact on the association. Difference and soundness must be adjusted precisely. Differences and structural soundness must be adjusted precisely. Change that is excessively far-reaching and/or excessively fast can overpower the organizational relationship, wrecking interest in hierarchical learning. Inflexible steadiness can bring about stagnation, enabling the changing business conditions to disintegrate the businesses competitive position. Innovations are conveyed, as suitable, to new and existing ventures. In this procedure, the expression "process and innovation upgrades" alludes to incremental and imaginative changes to procedures and to process or item advances (counting venture workplaces).

There are many different definitions of readiness that cover several constructs such as organizational readiness and technology readiness. Organizational readiness generally refers to "the extent to which organizational members are psychologically and behaviorally prepared to implement organizational change."* Perceptions of organizational readiness for change: Contain factors related to employees' reactions to the implementation of team-based selling.† High levels of organizational readiness are likely to result in more effective implementation of a proposed innovation due to the inclination of members of the organization to be team oriented and cooperative, and also to exhibit greater effort and persistence toward implementing the intended change. On the other hand, low levels of organizational readiness present problems, with members of the organization likely to exhibit uncooperative behavior and avoid or even resist actions that would result in more effective implementation of the proposed change.‡

The particular practices in this procedure zone supplement and expand those found in the organizational process focus sector. The focus of this procedure area is process change, which depends on the quantitative information of the organization's arrangement of standard procedures and innovation and their usual quality and execution in normal circumstances.

---

* See Eby, L. T., Adams, D. M., Russell, J. E., & Gaby, S. H. (2000) Perceptions of organizational readiness for change: Factors related to employees' reactions to the implementation of team-based selling. *Human Relations*, 53, 419–442.
† Eby et al. (2000).
‡ Parasuraman, A. (2000) Technology readiness index (TRI) a multiple-item scale to measure readiness to embrace new technologies. *Journal of Service Research*, 2, 307–320. 10.1177/109467050024001. He referred to technology-readiness constructs as "people's propensity to embrace and use new technologies for accomplishing goals in home life and work." These highlighted constructs bring out the challenges in deploying innovation in manufacturing, principally the complexity and uncertainty associated with the target organization, the technology, and processes.

In the organizational process focus territory, no assumptions are made about the quantitative premise of change.

━━━━━━━━━━

THE CIO'S ROLE

Is there a need for a CIO? In answer, we have to backpedal to our underlying foundations in Six Sigma, and to those of many of our customers today. Back "in the day," nobody was involved with Six Sigma, yet there were (and still are today) many fruitful deployments. Leaders of these organizations regularly have no involvement – and numerous chief executive officers (CEOs) prefer it that way. They tend to be more receptive and figure out how to do things the way their organizations need things done. When you bring excessive understanding to the table, you are potentially blind-sided by your past experiences. A positive response to this situation is, not surprisingly, solid initiative concerning new aptitudes and the capacity to want to learn.

There's a familiar adage: "We should enlist individuals for their insight and experience, and afterward we fire them for their style and identity." In plain talk, that implies that occasionally we place a heavy emphasis on incentive experience and certifications and not enough on identity and authority style.

Leaders have an obligation regarding driving development. Development can't happen on its own; advancement needs persistent help, structure, and direction. Administrators are in charge of determining everyday issues. On one hand, bosses tell their staffs "no" all the time with regards to understanding new various ways to deal with critical thinking. The new has often been routinely been dismissed to retain the standard approach, and the fallout has routinely been severe.

The administrators of organizations need to acquire knowledge about innovation skills and techniques. Everyone needs training to implement a process of conscious innovation in an organization. Managers should know how to lead processes of innovation; they need to know the strategies and methods that help to ease processes of innovation, involving practices that are repeatable, reliable, and unsurprising.

Implementing an innovation typically consists of three phases: pre-implementation, implementation, and post-implementation. The readiness of an organization to deploy innovation is an important issue in the pre-implementation phase. Pre-implementation is the time period prior to physical implementation and can invariably shape the attitudes of those charged with the implementation.*

Opportunities for learning innovative prospects are necessary. However, there are key areas where learning must happen. The path to development isn't about the apparatus or the procedure, it is about adjusting. From studies, we know that innovation can be successful if the approach between an intelligent individual and processes is balanced, authoritative, and contains human components. At the point when there is an irregularity we tend to come up empty or short. This is a reality, whether we survey new ideas, plans of action, methodologies, new business interests, or creative ideas.

"Why" we do it is the human component; "What" we do is the scholarly component; and "How" we do it is the authoritative component. Each of these three components reinforces each other. If one component is deficient with regard to the innovative plans in place, then there is a tendency for the plans to fall flat. This theory is supported by numerous cases across multiple enterprises. Optimizing enterprise resource planning (ERP) readiness, improvements under budgetary constraints entail four main steps: (1) constructing a model for assessing readiness; (2) overall readiness-level estimation of the organization, (3) analyzing the level of readiness; and (4) improving the readiness level of the organization providing a set of effective plans. Central to the methodology is knowing how to measure the degree of readiness, which is fundamental to the other key issue of how to optimize the degree of readiness in order to achieve the best possible implementation.

---

* See Herold, D. M., Farmer, S. M., & Mobley, M. I. (1995) Pre-implementation attitudes toward the introduction of robots in a unionized environment. *Journal of Engineering and Technology Management*, *12*, 155–173. It is during the pre-implementation phase that the organization prepares itself and develops the plans for deploying its innovation initiative. Extensive preparation before implementation is key to the success of implementing innovation initiatives because without proper readiness the implementation is likely to end in failure. Situating the concept of readiness in the pre-implementation phase allows for a more methodological approach to preparing for implementing innovation. A methodological approach suggested by Ahmadi et al. entails four main steps: (1) constructing a model for assessing readiness; (2) overall readiness-level estimation of the organization; (3) analyzing the level of readiness; and (4) improving the readiness level of the organization by providing a set of effective plans. Central to the methodology is knowing how to measure the degree of readiness, which is fundamental to the other key issue of how to optimize the degree of readiness in order to achieve the best possible implementation outcomes.

CULTURAL LEADERSHIP FOR INNOVATION

Entrepreneurship rests on a theory of economy and society. The theory sees change as normal and indeed as healthy. And it sees the major task in society – and especially in the economy – as doing something different rather than doing better what is already being done. That is basically what Say, two hundred years ago, meant when he coined the term entrepreneur. It was intended as a manifesto and as a declaration of dissent: the entrepreneur upsets and disorganizes. As Joseph Schumpeter formulated it, his task is "creative destruction."

Peter F. Drucker
Innovation and Entrepreneurship: Practice and Principles

The cultural environment of an organization sets the tone for innovation deployment. If the organization is resistant to change and hesitant to move away from what has always worked in the past, then there will be considerable anti-innovation inertia and deployment will fail. It is, therefore, critical to understand the organization's state of mind regarding this undertaking. Leaders define an organization's cultural constraints. These same leaders must be willing to lead a culture change so that innovation can thrive and prosper. Some of the elements required for this change are

- Willingness to accept change
- Budget for innovation (time, money, priority)
- Welcome innovation mavericks
- New is welcome
- Fear of failure is no longer a barrier
- Future is equally as vital as the present
- Innovation can be learned
- Innovation is everyone's responsibility

This list is an excellent place to start and can lead to significant improvements in a company's cultural foundation for innovation deployment.

Innovation Infrastructure and Metrics

An organization needs to be disciplined in the way that it deploys innovation and in the way that results are produced and managed. Leaders will be the sponsors of innovation projects; therefore, must be trained in (1) what tools are available, (2) the outputs for each tool, and (3) the expected time intervals for the process. Outcomes must be realistic; idea implementation and completion must be methodically pursued. Metrics must be used to identify progress and performance.

Key metrics may include:*

- Macro
  - Speed to change cultural bias
  - Amount of innovation budget
  - *Ambidextrous index*: Balance of resource allocation between preservation and evolution (capital, human, technology)
  - Time to transition from preservation activity to evolution activity
  - Ratio of innovation projects sponsored by executives (disruptive technologies cannot occur without senior management sponsorship)
- Volume
  - Number of innovations achieved
  - Number of disclosed inventions
  - Number of applied-for patents
  - Number of trademarks obtained
  - Number of people involved in systematic problem-solving
  - Number of systematic innovation projects completed
  - Variance of all of the above
- Speed
  - Time to predict customer/market evolution
  - Amount of time per innovation

---

* Measuring innovation and deployment readiness is important to ensure a successful innovation outcome. Theoretically, a higher level of readiness to innovate will lower the risk of innovation failure, which leads to a more successful innovation outcome. The degree of readiness can be measured in an interval [0, 1] or in percentage points as [0, 100%]. A readiness measure close to 100% implies that there is an outstanding level of readiness to implement the innovation, meaning that the implementation should run smoothly and problem free. The problem of how to achieve the highest degree of readiness to implement an innovation initiative is starting to be addressed. For example, regarding ERP systems, an organization's readiness to implement an ERP system is reported to be influenced by a variety of factors such as a clear project structure, clear implementation goals, the availability of appropriate systems and procedures in the organization, appropriate culture and structures associated with the ERP initiative, and an adequate level of support from human resources.

- Research cycle time
- Product development cycle time
- Average time taken to provide a solution for an innovation task
- Mean time to implement an innovation solution
- Variance of all of the above
- Quality
  - Ratio of innovations attempted to innovations made
  - Time to abandon a poor idea
  - Degree of discontinuity (level)
  - Costs avoided
  - New revenue generated
  - Costs reduced
  - Mean ideality of innovation solutions

The most energetic and open-minded entrepreneurs should be trained in innovation methods and tools. They must be fully committed to the success of the program and willing to relearn everything they thought they knew about innovation.* The training program must take place at both the leadership level and the problem-solver level – the two sessions must overlap so that there is synergy between them. Certification must include project completion and the implementation of hard cost savings. The returns on innovative investment (ROI) should be acknowledged. Program successes must be communicated effectively, including all those who are interested. Innovation must become everyone's responsibility.

Innovation Methodology (Tactical Innovation)

Problem-solving innovation is tactical innovation. The selected innovation methods must work in concert to formulate the problem statement, constrain the problem space effectively, and generate ideas for problem resolution.† The algorithm may be divided into main sections and methods as follows:

---

* "Entrepreneurship is 'risky' mainly because so few of the so-called entrepreneurs know what they are doing."

Peter F. Drucker
Innovation and Entrepreneurship

† "The companies that refused to make hard choices, or refused to admit that anything much was happening, fared badly. If they survive, it is only because their respective governments will not let them go under."

Peter F. Drucker
Innovation and Entrepreneurship: Practice and Principles

- Problem formulation
- Problem statement and problem-solving charter
- Heuristic redefinition process (HRP)
- Ideal solution characterization
- TILMAG – formation of ideal solution elements (ISEs)
- Ideal final result (IFR) – intersection of TILMAG ISEs
- Model the system
- System approach
- Utilization of resources
- Function modeling/FAST modeling
- Solution generation
- TILMAG association matrix
- Forced analogy
- Brainstorming (BST) and brainwriting (BWR)
- The Theory of Inventive Problem-Solving (TRIZ)
- Morphological modeling and hybridization
- Solution selection
- Pugh potential solution selection matrix

The intersection of these methods forms a powerful problem-solving approach that is convergent and divergent as well as open and closed. It creates the approach that should be used for problem-solving, and an understanding of its uses, operations, and results must be integrated into the culture and the infrastructure.

Innovation Proficiency

These innovative methods must be enforced so that proficiency is achieved. It is only with guided application that proficiency is achievable. This has to be an integral component of any innovation deployment. The algorithm must be used in support of actual projects with the results implemented and the effects measured. At least two learning cycles are needed as part of the educational program (training). This must be repeated across the organization so that every department and functional group are trained in the methods. Then, the organization's ability to innovate will be dramatically increased.

Implementing a systematic innovation program is not about the number of people trained or the number of hours spent on coaching. The proficiency's speed matters a lot. How fast can the organization's innovative quotient be increased and by how much? These questions and metrics matter most.

Managers must be involved in each step of the deployment, and they must be trained to foster, promote, and practice innovation. Their skill-sets must expand to include those necessary for cultural transformation, infrastructure development, methodology application, and speed of proficiency. Only in this way can innovation be reduced to science – as have productivity and quality.

When creating advancements, multinational enterprises (MNCs) are faced with two dangerous potential failpoints: (1) make worldwide offerings that can't satisfy the greater part of the distinctive geographical area's needs or (2) make certain offerings that meet the assortment of requirements, but often exceed the cost requirements. As indicated by Sihem Ben Mahmoud-Jouini and Florence Charge-Duboc (CNRS-Ecole Polytechnique), be that as it may, a third way exists. They distinguish key factors that adjust the worldwide mix and neighborhood adjustment and along these lines improve the arrangement of the development of the subsidiaries.

The globalization of business sectors has propelled MNCs into increasing production and setting up operations in progressively different nations. Considering the variety involved with innovation in this market sector, the usual approach of transferring innovations created at the headquarters research facilities to auxiliaries sections has highlighted some possible problem areas (innovations transferred generally might not fit the immediate market setting of the auxiliary organization, thereby gradually moving out of the market). Another approach used by a few organizations has been the on-line Innovation Lab approach. Creative innovations are created particularly for select markets closer, particularly rising ones. At that point, attempts to transfer the process that is already known for the organization's noteworthy markets seems to make some sense. Regardless of the innovation, whether it is implemented locally or corporately, there is always a need to critically consider the transfer of innovative process and products to multinationals.*

---

* "The people who work within these industries or public services know that there are basic flaws. But they are almost forced to ignore them and to concentrate instead on patching here, improving there, fighting the fire, or caulking that crack. They are thus unable to take the innovation seriously, let alone to try to compete with it. They do not, as a rule, even notice it until it has grown so big as to encroach on their industry or service, by which time it has become irreversible. In the meantime, the innovators have the field to themselves."

Peter F. Drucker
Innovation and Entrepreneurship: Practice and Principles

Issues of Deployment

Deployment isn't closely associated with the transfer of innovation, but instead, it is associated with adjusting them while they are being popularized and, all the while, looking for shared advantages between innovation partners. This type of arrangement, set forward by Ben Mahmoud-Jouini and Charge-Duboc, features the progression of the innovation, as they are progressively introduced and marketed in various geographical settings, requiring some unique-type adjustment from time to time. Such an arrangement can be moderate and topographically confined; for instance, a few developments take 12–15 years to achieve just four or five backups. The test is extensive. In what way can innovative processes be faster in multinationals to a greater degree? In answer, the specialists featured four primary achievement factors.

The champion of deploying innovation is a basic player in the organization: he acts well beyond the underlying business sector role for which he was appointed. Part of his task is as improvement pioneer. Amid progressive dispatches, he logically builds up an understanding of the advantages valued by clients and the specialized adjustments needed in the market.* He directs innovators who receive the innovation by giving them business, technical, and commercial guides for successful deployment of the innovation. Another factor to consider in the deployment process is setting up local experts already familiar with the market. Another factor to consider in the deployment process is setting up local experts already familiar with the market, which is systematically built up and implemented by the deployment champion of the innovation process. This ensures the keeping in mind of the end goal of balancing the innovation process, products and services to the local market, while executing the required changes. The champion builds up a group of practices among the auxiliaries in both specialized and business measures related to the innovative process.

The system can include other experts not within the MNC who already have an established relationship with the MNC clients. These are correlative players, for example, the makers of hardware who use the item provided

---

* "And it is change that always provides the opportunity for the new and different. Systematic innovation therefore consists in the purposeful and organized search for changes, and in the systematic analysis of the opportunities such changes might offer for economic or social innovation."
Peter F. Drucker
Innovation and Entrepreneurship: Practice and Principles

by the MNC. Co-improvement associations with these nearby players advance the balance of the innovation to various local market settings.

Integrating Innovation as a Deployment Strategy

Can quality function deployment (QFD), voice of the customer (VOC), TRIZ, Six Sigma, etc., work together? Is it a question of plug-and-play experimentation or are there specific paths to follow? The short answer to this question is YES – these tools have natural interfaces and don't require "messing around" on your part. For example, VOC is the front end of QFD. But if a contradiction arises when you try to design a product or service that satisfies the customer, that's the front end of a TRIZ problem-solving process (removing contradictions.)

SUMMARY

A best-practice method to assessing deployment readiness for innovation has been explored in this chapter, with assessments done oftentimes through simulation within a sequential decision process framework. Simulation offers advantages that include the ability to model complex systems efficiently and effectively to obtain realistic assessments that takes into account uncertainties and dynamics inherent in the system. Given a system with innovation initiatives, a deployment plan, and deployment readiness goal(s), the approach first identifies the deployment states in the sequential decision process and calculates from simulation results a boundary on the probability that the deployment plan will result in smooth and problem-free deployment, as specified by the deployment readiness goal(s).

The simulation experiments show that deployment readiness can vary between deployment states and overall readiness can be improved by revising the deployment plan particularly in states where deployment readiness is relatively low. Future work study programs should include a study of how deployment plan revisions can be best achieved.

BIBLIOGRAPHY

Abdinnour-Helm, S., Lengnick-Hall, M. L., & Lengnick-Hall, C. A. (2003). Pre-implementation attitudes and organizational readiness for implementing an Enterprise Resource Planning system. *European Journal of Operational Research*, 146, 258–273. 10.1016/S0377-2217(02)00548-9

Ahmadi, S., Yeh, C. H., Martin, R., & Papageorgiou, E. (2015a). Optimizing ERP readiness improvements under budgetary constraints. *International Journal of Production Economics*, 161, 105–115. 10.1016/j.ijpe.2014.11.020

Ahmadi, S., Yeh, C. H., Papageorgiou, E. I., & Martin, R. (2015b). An FCM–FAHP approach for managing readiness-relevant activities for ERP implementation. *Computers & Industrial Engineering*, 88, 501–517. 10.1016/j.cie.2015.07.006

Bergamaschi, D., Cigolini, R., Perona, M., & Portioli, A. (1997). Order review and release strategies in a job shop environment. A review and a classification. *International Journal of Production Research*, 35, 399–420. 10.1080/002075497195821

Blackstone, J. H., Phillips, D. T., & Hogg, G. L. (1982). A state-of-the-art survey of dispatching rules for manufacturing job shop operations. *International Journal of Production Research*, 20, 27–45. 10.1080/00207548208947745

Chuang, M., & Shaw, W. H. (2008). An empirical study of enterprise resource management systems implementation. From ERP to RFID. *Business Process Management Journal*, 14, 675–693. 10.1108/14637150810903057

Davison, G., & Hyland, P. (2006). Continuous innovation in a complex and dynamic environment: The case of the Australian health service. *International Journal of Technology Management and Sustainable Development*, 5, 41–59. 10.1386/ijtm.5.1.41/1

Dutta, S., Lanvin, B., Singh, T. R., Green, A., Berthelon, V., & Bingra, G. B. S. (2009). Are you innovation ready? Plotting your journey on the Innovation Readiness Model. *Insead report* 2017 report, pages 81–89. Received 19 Mar 2016, Accepted 15 Oct 2016, Published online: 02 Jun 2017.

Eby, L. T., Adams, D. M., Russell, J. E., & Gaby, S. H. (2000). Perceptions of organizational readiness for change: Factors related to employees' reactions to the implementation of team-based selling. *Human Relations*, 53, 419–442. 10.1177/0018726700533006

Herold, D. M., Farmer, S. M., & Mobley, M. I. (1995). Pre-implementation attitudes toward the introduction of robots in a unionized environment. *Journal of Engineering and Technology Management*, 12, 155–173. 10.1016/0923-4748(95)00008-7

Jacobson, E. H. (1957). The Effect of Changing Industrial Methods and Automation on Personnel. Symposium on Preventive and Social Psychology, Washington, DC.

Kastalli, I. V., & Van Looy, B. (2013). Servitization: Disentangling the impact of service business model innovation on manufacturing firm performance. *Journal of Operations Management*, 31, 169–180. 10.1016/j.jom.2013.02.001

Kwahk, K. Y., & Lee, J. N. (2008). The role of readiness for change in ERP implementation: Theoretical bases and empirical validation. *Information & Management*, 45, 474–481. 10.1016/j.im.2008.07.002

Lim, S. A. H., & Antony, J. (2013, December). A conceptual readiness framework for statistical process control (SPC) deployment. In *2013 IEEE International Conference on Industrial Engineering and Engineering Management* (pp. 300–304). Bangkok, Thailand: IEEE. 10.1109/IEEM.2013.6962422

Maier, P., Jain, D., Waldherr, S., & Sachenbacher, M. (2010). Plan assessment for autonomous manufacturing as Bayesian inference. In *KI 2010: Advances in Artificial Intelligence* (Vol. 6359, pp. 263–271). Berlin, Heidelberg: Springer. 10.1007/978-3-642-16111-7

Mourtzis, D., Doukas, M., & Bernidaki, D. (2014). Simulation in manufacturing: Review and challenges. *Procedia CIRP*, 25, 213–229. 10.1016/j.procir.2014.10.032

Parast, M. M. (2011). The effect of Six Sigma projects on innovation and firm performance. *International Journal of Project Management*, 29, 45–55. 10.1016/j.ijproman.2010.01.006

Parasuraman, A. (2000). Technology readiness index (TRI) a multiple-item scale to measure readiness to embrace new technologies. *Journal of Service Research*, 2, 307–320. 10.1177/109467050024001

Qu, Y. (2014). *Modeling the dynamic decision of a contractual adoption of a continuous innovation in B2B market* (Dissertation). Georgia State University, Atlanta, GA, USA. Retrieved from http://scholarworks.gsu.edu/marketing_diss/29

Razmi, J., Sangari, M. S., & Ghodsi, R. (2009). Developing a practical framework for ERP readiness assessment using fuzzy analytic network process. *Advances in Engineering Software*, 40, 1168–1178. 10.1016/j.advengsoft.2009.05.002

Steiber, A., & Ange, S. (2013). A corporate system for continuous innovation: The case of Google Inc. *European Journal of Innovation Management*, 16, 243–264.

Wang, B., & Moon, Y. B. (2013). Hybrid modeling and simulation for innovation deployment strategies. *Industrial Management & Data Systems*, 113, 136–154. 10.1108/02635571311289719

Wright, T. P. (1936). Factors affecting the cost of airplanes. *Journal of the Aeronautical Sciences*, 3, 122–128. 10.2514/8.155

Yamamoto, Y., & Bellgran, M. (2013). Four types of manufacturing process innovation and their managerial concerns. *Procedia CIRP*, 7, 479–484. 10.1016/j.procir.2013.06.019

8

The Innovation Process Model

In a nutshell: The innovation process model is a strategic collaboration that ensures that the innovation team idealizes an innovation and is more than able to run with it to the point of it being successfully implemented. However, *the way you understand the innovation process will greatly influence the way you establish it.* In this chapter, we discuss why it is good to use a structured, collaborative innovation process. We shall also demystify the innovation process by explaining each sub-step component that needs to be followed until the innovation is implemented. More than ever, corporate executives consider product integrated with process innovation to be a critical aggressive need – and a key factor in improving business development.

This can be achieved if done through the innovation triple effect: expanded income, lower costs, and reduced time to market. What is shown is the fact that even during times of economic crisis, R&D spending has held up well. This chapter describes a unique approach to managing innovation processes and the people involved in those processes; we call it the HOW collaborative/strategic innovation process, and it is based upon the six generations of innovation process concept coupled with the four-stage strategic innovation model, popularized by Productivity, Inc.* and Strategyn. Governing innovation involves an arrangement of interwoven processes dealing with making decisions that characterize, adjust, and oversee innovative

---

* Productivity Inc. is a leading consulting and training firm that helps organizations build new capabilities, save money, and grow. Their focus is on three progressive and interrelated strategies: operational excellence, strategic innovation, and leadership and culture. Working together, these strategies provide the means to continually refresh a company's IP value proposition, while making the organizational changes needed for daily improvement and sustainable growth.

exercises covering the whole lifespan of services and products, guaranteeing the accomplishment of key development objectives. The HOW innovation process model incorporates business choices that affect each period of the lifespan of the intellectual property (IP).

LET'S GET STARTED ...

Now is the time to establish a common understanding of the key terms we use throughout this chapter and in the book.

- *Innovation is people creating value through the implementation of new and unique ideas.*
- *Innovation is how an organization adds value to its creative ideas. To be innovative, a unique and creative idea needs to be developed, funded, produced, and distributed to external customers and result in creating value to both the organization and the consumer/customer.*
- *Note:* Innovation can take many forms. It can be an idea, an insight, or a rearrangement of present ideas and/or hardware, as long as it is new or unique, implemented, and creates significant value to the stakeholders and consumers. Innovation applies to most activities including personal and organization related.
- *Innovator:* A person who develops an original idea/concept and the knowledge and is capable of managing it through the entire innovation cycle.
- *Process:* To take one or more inputs, perform specified operations or routines on those inputs, and produce outputs.
- *Process innovation* results in improved processes within the organization – for example, in operations, human resources, management, or finance.
- *Marketing innovation* is related to the marketing functions of promoting, pricing, and distributing, as well as to product functions other than product development (e.g., packaging).
- *Management innovation* improves the way the organization is managed. Bell Laboratories uses unique management innovations, such as programs aimed at improving researchers' productivity to create new products.

- *Activity*: An activity is second order in a process hierarchy (separation of a major process into its major work elements). It is sometimes called the sub-process. A number of activities that are interrelated and work together often form a major process. The condition in which things are happening or are being done, a thing that a person or group does or has done. An example is putting a motor into an auto housing.
- *Task*: A task is the third level in a process hierarchy. It is the separation of an activity into its subdivisions. The smallest identifiable and essential element of a job that serves as a unit of work, and as a means of differentiating between the various components of a project. An example is tightening the four bolts that hold a motor in place.
- *Creative*: Using the ability to make or think of new things involving the process by which new ideas, stories, products, etc., are created.
- *Create*: Make something: To bring something into existence, create the original.
- *Entrepreneur*: An entrepreneur is a person who organizes and manages any enterprise, especially a business, usually with considerable initiative and risk.
- *Innovator versus entrepreneur*: The entrepreneur does not have to originate the idea/concept. To be considered successful, they both have to produce an output that is value added to someone other than themselves.
- *Innovation versus invention*: Innovation differs from invention in that innovation refers to the use of a better and, as a result, novel idea or method, whereas invention refers more directly to the creation of the idea or method itself.
- *Innovation versus improvement*: Innovation differs from improvement in that innovation refers to the notion of doing something different rather than doing the same thing better.
- *Organization*: Company, corporation, firm, enterprise, association, or any part thereof, whether it is incorporated or not, public or private, that has its own function and administration (Source: ISO 8402 – 1994). It can be as small as a first-line department and as large as the US government.
- *Organizational culture*: The values and behaviors that contribute to the unique social and psychological environment of an organization. Organizational culture includes an organization's expectations, experiences, philosophy, and values that hold it together, and

is expressed in its self-image, inner workings, interactions with the outside world, and future expectations. It is based on shared attitudes, beliefs, customs, and written and unwritten rules that have been developed over time and are considered valid. Also called corporate culture, it's shown in

a. The ways the organization conducts its business and treats its employees, customers, and the wider community.

b. The extent to which freedom is allowed in decision-making, developing new ideas, and personal expression.

c. How power and information flow through its hierarchy.

d. How committed employees are toward collective objectives. (Business Dictionary)

- *S curve*: The S curve is a mathematical model, also known as the logistic curve. It describes the growth of one variable in terms of another variable over time. S curves are found in fields from biology and physics to business and technology. In business, the S curve is used to describe, and sometimes predict, the performance of a company or a product over a period of time.
- *Structure*: The arrangement of and relations between the parts or elements of something complex. "The company's weakness is the inflexibility of its management structure."
- *Organizational structure*: Is a system used to define a hierarchy within an organization. It identifies each job, its function, and where it reports to within the organization. This structure is developed to establish how an organization operates, and assists an organization in obtaining its goals to allow for future growth. The structure is illustrated using an organizational chart.

INTRODUCTION

We have found that every person has a drive for innovation, be it in small things or big ones. As previously discussed, we cannot assume that innovations are a modern-day process. It began long ago, but it wasn't until the 1960s that individuals started coming up with innovation models. So far, six models are relied on for innovations, as shown in Table 8.1. Technology, research and development, and market trends have

TABLE 8.1

Comparison of Linear and Non-Linear Approaches to the Innovation Process.

	Approach to the Innovation Process	
	Linear	**Nonlinear**
Advantages	• Relative ease of constructing the models, the ability to use a highly generalized description of the relationship between basic science and industrial innovation. • A broad statistical material, since it is fixed in a single methodological approach for collecting statistics. • Dominates in the allocation of funds for research activities and in the evaluation of scientific, technological, and innovation potential of the regions.	• Closer to the real-life innovation processes that are rarely linear nor ordered, often chaotic and have gaps. • Includes a feedback loop, alternative ways to innovate. • Takes into account the social value of innovation and the consumer as a co-producer of value. • Reflects the embeddedness of innovation processes in the region and its systemic nature. • Focuses on the processes (interaction) rather than on the structure (individual actors). • Effective in decision-making and managing the innovation process.
Disadvantages	• Distortion of the real innovation process and its formalization. • It is impossible to transmit high-quality communication between the components of the innovation process. • Distract attention from the economic and social determinants of research activities; ignores the role of technology in the choice of goals and methods of research, productivity, and growth of science. • Insufficient attention to the stage of engineering design and re-engineering as a source of innovation. • Does not take into account the features of innovation processes in different industries, regions.	• Not yet formed a statistical base for research and has no agile methodological approach for the collection of information. • Models are mostly descriptive rather than evaluative in nature due to the high complexity of construction. • It is impossible to develop a universal model for all variety of real innovation processes.

contributed to the evolution of the models over time. We will look at the various models to see the innovation processes that the model should follow, as shown in Figure 8.1.

The financial investments made in each stage of the developmental procedure increase along the line. The open innovation model is also known as the sixth-generation model. The model is a network model.* It focuses on internal and external ideas, along with external and internal paths to market. The open innovation model looks at how a combination of the two concepts can lead to technological advancements. Chesbrough came up with the term "open innovation." This model presents less risks when organizations that use this model enjoy a large pool of ideas to start with. They then narrow down the ideas to the most ideal one. The beginning procedure of this innovative development is often referred to as the funneling stage, as shown in the HOW innovation process model, outlined in Figure 8.1.

BRIEF HISTORY OF INNOVATION PROCESS MODELS

If the innovation process is viewed as a process in which only specialists participate, then there will be very little involvement from the employees. Some employees will keep away as they do not feel that they are specialists. Historically, *small companies view innovation as a process for the big companies only.* This is because they conceptualized the innovation process as a complicated process that they lacked the capacity to handle. Innovation can involve small and big changes, so small businesses missed out on market and technical opportunities that they could have enjoyed had they involved themselves in innovation. *Another misunderstanding was looking at the innovation process as a linear process*, relying on either technology or market trends as the sources. As a result, a lot of money was spent on research and development, and other sources of innovation were often ignored, such as customers, suppliers, the public, and employees. Besides, some organizations looked at the process of

---

* Galanakis developed an innovation model that borrows a lot from the fifth-generation model. His model uses the thinking approach, which he refers to the "creative factory concept." The firm is at the center of the model. Its position signifies its role in generating and promoting innovations to the nation, industrial sector, and the market.

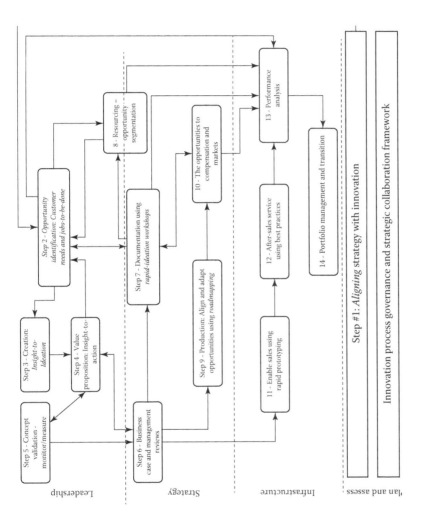

FIGURE 8.1

The innovation process model. This model depicts the components that our suggested innovation process flow consists of: a foundation and 14 steps or activities, which our strategic and collaborative process model outlines in detail.

innovation differently from the products being produced. This is always a mistake as the process and product are related to each other. In the past 20 years, innovation in business models has forced existing businesses to adapt to the new rules of the game or their market share has been reduced. In our experience working with Global 1000 companies for more than 30 years, we have found that most organizations set specific targets for growth, but fall short on detailed, substantive strategies to achieve them.

Platforms for growth can range across several types of opportunities, aimed at different levels of innovation, from

- Capturing all the potential of current value propositions in order to sustain and extend the performance of your present business, to
- Building new value propositions that can generate earnings in the context of existing business models, to
- Sowing the seeds of new businesses by implementing game-changing ideas that require new business models

Technology, research and development, and market trends have contributed to the evolution of the models over the past half century or so. Table 8.1 looks at the seven major generations of models since the 1960s to see the processes that these models proposed, which have led to a collaborative innovation process that modern organizations and their value chains are encouraged to take advantage of.

The development of representations about the innovation process in science led to the identification of two main approaches: linear and nonlinear, which for the past several decades are being refined in parallel. The author highlights the strengths and weaknesses of each approach in Table 8.2. Thus, there is no replacement of one approach by another. The large variety of models proposed in the framework of each approach points to a failure to develop a universal model of the innovation process that meets all the requirements of a particular company and time. However, nonlinear models are closer to the real innovation process at the present stage and are therefore better able to transmit qualitative changes that occur in the economy. So the idea of a rooted innovation process is reflected, in particular, in the nonlinear models. The main features of nonlinear models regarding the localization of the innovation process are that they (1) take into account the nature of the networked relations between regional actors; (2) reflect models of triple, quadruple, and

TABLE 8.2

No Caption

Innovation Model Gen	Name	Era	Description	Assumptions
First generation	Technology push	1960s	NASA developed as a management tool and referred to the process as the phase-review-processes or the technology push. The process was broken down to help in systematizing the work and for controlling contractors and suppliers who were working on space projects	Model assumes that technological advances from scientific discovery and research and development come before "pushed" technological innovation through engineering, marketing, applied research, and manufacturing toward successful inventions or products as outputs
Second Generation	Market pull	1970s	The second generation models are similar to their predecessor except that the model draws its innovation ideas from the market place	The first-generation model draws its idea from research and development and science, which are different from the second model. Also, they are both linear structures
Third Generation	Coupling models	1970s–1980s	The model uses the stage-gate approach in developing an innovation. Every stage has a purpose that must be completed before moving to the next stage. If one stage is reviewed negatively, then the team does not move on to the next stage. As a result, they continue working on the present stage until it is positively reviewed, ensuring it meets the specified standard stated in gate three. During the validation stage, customer field trials, in-house product tests, trial productions	An idea originates from creativity, customer feedback, or basic research. Evaluation of the ideas takes place in the first gate. Consequently, if the idea is accepted, the process of developing the product begins in stage three. In addition, the team develops a marketing concept. Gate three produces a prototype of the product. The prototype is evaluated to make and tests in the market take place. After the product is verified, then you can plan for market launch and production startups. The third-generation model allows for not only linear processes but also parallel ones in order to speed up the process

(Continued)

TABLE 8.2 (CONTINUED)

No Caption

Innovation Model Gen	Name	Era	Description	Assumptions
Fourth Generation	Interactive models	1980s–1990s	The model looks at the innovation process as a set of parallel activities across the organizational functions. The Minnesota Innovation Research program (MIRP) has three distinct stages that companies follow to develop an innovative idea. There is the initiation period, then the development period, and finally, the implementation period. The model does not include the adoption, continued improvement, or introduction to the market place processes	Greater emphasis on cross-functional and parallel integration development within firms. The purpose for the interaction and collaboration is to gain greater potential from real-time information processing. There are specific processes that take place during each stage of the process. However, there are no boundaries between the periods. In fact, the characteristics between periods seem to overlap
Fifth Generation	Network models	1990s–2005	Is a closed innovation model that explains the intricacy of the innovation process. Its main focus is the involvement of the external environment. Besides, the model also focuses on effective communication with the external environment. Since innovation relies on both external and internal networks, the model emphasizes the need for establishing links between the two networks	The firm is at the center of the model. Its position signifies its role in generating and promoting innovations in the nation, industrial sector, and the market. Hence, the model relies on three main innovation processes: (1) the first process involves creating knowledge from industrial or public research; (2) the product development process where the knowledge is transformed into a product; (3) product success in the market

(Continued)

TABLE 8.2 (CONTINUED)

No Caption

Innovation Model Gen	Name	Era	Description	Assumptions
Sixth Generation	Open innovation	2005–2015	The model is a network model. It focuses on internal and external ideas, along with external and internal paths to markets. It looks at how a combination of the two concepts can lead to technological advancements. The central idea behind open innovation is that, in a world of widely distributed knowledge, companies cannot afford to rely entirely on their own research, but should instead buy or license processes or inventions (i.e., patents) from other companies. In addition, internal inventions not being used in a firm's business should be taken outside the company	These are distributed innovation processes based on purposively managed knowledge flows across organizational boundaries, using pecuniary and non-pecuniary mechanisms in line with the organization's business model. It is based on the systematic encouragement and exploration of a wide range of internal and external sources for innovative opportunities, the integration of this exploration with firm capabilities and resources, and the exploitation of these opportunities through multiple channels

(Continued)

TABLE 8.2 (CONTINUED)

No Caption

Innovation Model Gen	Name	Era	Description	Assumptions
Seventh Generation	Collaborative/ Strategic Innovation *(HOW)*	2015 and beyond	Organizations will explore strategic ways to devise new and innovative forms of value – not in sporadic "aha!" moments, but as an evolving cross-enterprise capability. Long-term success demands that we work systematically to conceptualize, develop, and deliver new value. A true innovation system relies on the ability to capture and interpret the articulated and unarticulated needs of your current and future customers. This type of process innovation model thrives in organizational cultures that create space for new ideas and foster collaboration among employees and enterprise networks. And, most important, it requires the leadership behavior, infrastructure, and processes to execute effectively on key insights	An organizational value chain incorporates their contributors into the development of the product. This differs from platforming in the sense that, in addition to the provision of the framework on which contributors develop, the hosting organization still controls and maintains the eventual products developed in collaboration with their contributors This model gives organizations in the value chain more control by ensuring that the correct product is developed as fast as possible, while reducing the overall cost of development. Collaborative/strategic innovation covers all areas of the business model – customer experiences, distribution channels, modes of delivery, partner networks, and market spaces

Appendix to the above Table: Summary of the linear and nonlinear approach to the innovation process.

quintuple helices in the structure of the innovation network; (3) reflect the multiple changes of types of knowledge in the innovation process; and (4) reflect the ambiguity and variability of the source of innovation.* Over the past 50 years or so, the effect of trends in the localization of the innovation process in the current models has been studied, but the outcomes have been mixed and confusing, at best. The modeling of the innovation process at the present stage is considered a complex, interactive, nonlinear, localized learning process. The traditional model of the innovation process is a linear model of innovation, which has proliferated since the era of Henry Ford. It assumes great significance of codified scientific knowledge, the dominance of basic research as a source of innovation, consistency in the innovation process, and the technocratic nature of innovation.

The linear model can be regarded in three aspects[†]:

1. Streams from a methodological basis for the allocation of certain categories of the process of creating knowledge, such as basic research, applied research, and oftentimes new developments.
2. As a theory of knowledge production, in which each subsequent level is connected with the previous via direct one-way links (i.e., the knowledge obtained in the output of the first stage is the input to the second stage, etc.).

---

* Source: Alekseevna, M. A. "Evolution of the innovation process models," *Science and Education Publishing (SciEP)*, 2(14), 2013. Science and Education Publishing is one of largest open access journal publishers. It is currently publishing many open access, online, peer-reviewed journals covering a wide range of academic disciplines. SciEP serves the worldwide academic communities and contributes to the progress and application of sciences with its publication. The article provides a review of the evolution of scientific concepts on the innovation process. Two main approaches to the innovation process are presented: linear and nonlinear, and their distinctive features are defined. Within each approach, the main types of models of the innovation process are considered. The stages of the formation and development of a linear model of the innovation process are also reviewed, along with the influence of various factors on the occurrence of nonlinear models of the innovation process. The author discusses the advantages and disadvantages of linear and nonlinear approaches to the development of models of the innovation process, along with the effect of trends in the localization of the innovation process. The modeling of the innovation process at the present stage is proposed to be considered as a *complex, interactive, nonlinear localized learning process*.

† Mahdjoubi, D., The linear model of technological innovation: background and taxonomy. 1997. [Online Available: https://www.ischool.utexas.edu/~darius/04-Linear%20Model.pdf.]

3. As epistemology, that characterizes the process of knowledge transfer from the universal principles and a comprehensive theory to particular cases.

The result of a great deal of scientific debate has been the formulation of two types of linear models of the innovation process: The first type is a technology push model, and the other is the market pull model. The "push" model appeared in the 1950s and gained wide popularity among manufacturing companies in the 1960s and 1970s. The main features of this model lie in the fact that innovation is seen as the final result of sequential processes, which are based on the free pursuit of science not being limited by strategic objectives; there is no common control of the entire chain of innovation and market impact is minimized, i.e., "buy what is sold."

Since the 1960s, resulting from increased competition and the diversification of production, the second type of linear model of the innovation process was developed. It suggests that innovations are driven by the market and its needs (i.e., the market pull model). In comparison with the first type, this model does not rely on the results of scientific research, but on information obtained from the diagnosis of market preferences. This approach was consistent with the ideas of J. Schumpeter, who noted that innovation is possible without inventions and inventions do not necessarily lead to innovation.*

The process of the diffusion of tacit knowledge reveals yet another special feature – "stickiness," characterized by the increased complexity of their transmission.†

Mikhaylova Anna Alekseevna writes: *"In response to the challenges of globalization unfolds the process of regionalization that acts as a counterbalance to the overall integration through the disclosure of local competences and ability to be creative. Creativity is a key factor of production in the innovation economy, no less important than the knowledge in the knowledge economy. It is a creative approach, according to some scholars,*

---

* Schumpeter, J., *Business Cycles: A Theoretical, Historical, and Statistical Analysis of the Capitalist Process*. McGraw-Hill, New York, 1939; revised 1965–1967.

† See Janzen, F. *The Age of Innovation*, Financial Times Prentice Hall, London, 2000. Exchange of accumulated tacit knowledge between actors occurs through a process of collective learning, which tends to be localized, and can be submitted through the "learning loop" of David Kolb: "Actions" – "Reflections" – "Connections" – "Decisions" – "Actions."

that allows to improve the quality of innovation processes and decisions, and is a major catalyst for economic growth. The essence of the innovation economy can be expressed in the effective connection of knowledge, creativity and entrepreneurial skills."*

INTRODUCTION TO HOW™: A COLLABORATIVE/ STRATEGIC INNOVATION PROCESS† (FIGURE 8.2)

Building the Knowledge, Practices, and Behaviors (KPB) to Foster and Sustain Innovation

Current research and experience show that effective leadership is the most important capability for high-performance strategic innovation … and one of the most elusive.

- *Checklist of key questions to address include:*
  - What innovation and creativity skills and behaviors are important at all levels, and how can we foster them?
  - How can we create alignment toward strategic innovation objectives throughout our organization?
  - How will we effectively measure, govern, and manage a portfolio of innovation initiatives?

---

* See Alekseevna, M. A. "Evolution of the innovation process models," *Science and Education Publishing (SciEP)*, 2(14), 2013; also see Berkhout, A. J., Hartmann, D., van der Duin, P., Ortt, R. "Innovating the innovation process", *International Journal of Technology Management*, 34(3/4), 390–404, 2006.

† The HOW Innovation Process Model™ was developed by Frank Voehl, in collaboration with Jim Harrington and Rick Fernandez, along with the IAOIP Academy; it is based upon the evolution of the previous generations of innovation models (see Table 8.1). The acronym HOW stands for *heuristic outcome workflows (how)*. Historically, it had its origins as a usability inspection method for computer software that helped to identify usability problems in the user interface (UI) design. It specifically involved evaluators examining the interface and judging its compliance with recognized usability principles (the "heuristics"). These evaluation methods are now widely taught and practiced in the new media sector, where UIs are often designed in a short space of time on a budget that may restrict the amount of money available to provide for other types of interface testing.

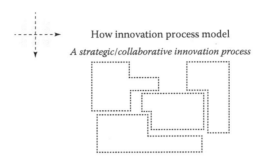

FIGURE 8.2

The Four Blocks of the HOW™ Innovation Process Model. HOW Innovate™ is built on four foundational elements that are essential to developing and sustaining a holistic approach to innovation and new value creation. But, the scope and approach to implementation is flexible, ensuring that you develop the optimal system and skill-sets to fit your organization and its environment, business situation, and culture.

- *Opportunity development and innovation measurement*
  - Instill the processes and knowledge to develop a common understanding of how an innovation system works and can be measured for leaders and all appropriate levels of your organization.
  - Define, develop, and practice innovation leadership roles, skills, and the rules of engagement.
- *Culture and change management*
  - Refine and communicate the top-level vision for new value creation, and how it will transform the organization.
  - Manage and monitor the structural and behavioral changes needed to move the needle on your cultural compass.
  - Create and manage performance measures that drive innovation.
- *Governance and oversight*
  - Define the parameters and scope of your innovation portfolio.
  - Determine policies and processes for managing the portfolio and pipeline, and for making critical decisions.
  - Develop behaviors, processes, and skills to foster "ambidexterity" – the ability to balance resources needed for growth with those needed to run the core business.

Repeat of the revised HOW Swimlane Flowchart goes here

THE 12 STEP ACTIVITIES THAT MAKE UP THE INNOVATION PROCESS

The four phases that make up the innovation process are subdivided into the following 12 step activities and two foundations as follows:

Phase I: Planning and Readiness
- Foundation: Aligning Strategy with Innovation
- Foundation 2: Create Strategic Objectives
- Step-Activity 1: Opportunity Identification: Customer Needs & Jobs-to-be-Done (JTBD)

Phase II: Leadership and Creation
- Step-Activity 2: Creation Activity = Insight-to-Ideation
- Step-Activity 3: Value Propositions = Insight-to-Action
- Step-Activity 4: Concept Validation = Action-to-Monitor/ Measure

Phase III: Strategy for Production
- Step-Activity 5: Business Case Analysis and Management Reviews
- Step-Activity 6: Resourcing = Opportunity Segmentation
- Step-Activity 7: Documentation = Visual Rapid Ideation Workshops
- Step-Activity 8: Production to Align/Adapt Using Roadmapping
- Step-Activity 9: Tie to Compensation and Markets

Phase IV: Infrastructure for Delivery
- Step-Activity 10: Enable Sales Using Rapid Prototyping
- Step-Activity 11: After-Sales Services & Performance Analysis Using Best-Practice Methods
- Step-Activity 12: Portfolio Management and Transition

The next section will explain the HOW innovation process architecture, its tools and methods, and how the model works. However, the first order of business is to align the strategic objectives with innovation, as shown in Figure 8.3.

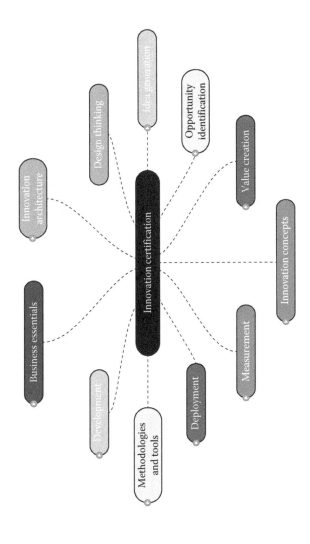

FIGURE 8.3

The Innovation Body of Knowledge (IBoK) for Certification. The IBoK is the sum of the knowledge within the profession of innovation and innovation management. As we have found with other professions such as Lean, Six Sigma, medicine, and accounting, the body of knowledge rests with the practitioners and academics who apply and advance it. The complete IBoK includes proven practices that are widely applied, as well as practices that are emerging in the profession, including published and unpublished materials. As a result, the IBoK is constantly evolving.

Foundation: Innovation Process Governance and Strategic Collaboration Framework*

CIO Mission:
– Promotion of innovate agenda
– Animation of a network of 'coaches'
– Innovation process development and measurement
– Innovation technology strategies and new ventures

Innovate® process governance and strategic collaboration

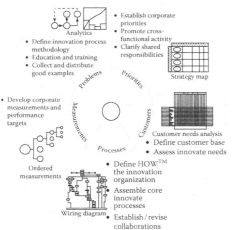

- Define innovation process methodology
- Education and training
- Collect and distribute good examples

- Establish corporate priorities
- Promote cross-functional activity
- Clarify shared responsibilities

Analytics

Strategy map

Problems

Priorities

- Develop corporate measurements and performance targets

Measurements

Customers

Processes

Ordered measurements

Customer needs analysis
- Define customer base
- Assess innovate needs

Wiring diagram

- Define HOW™ the innovation organization
- Assemble core innovate processes
- Establish / revise collaborations

Sample governance check points

Plan, Do, Check, Act (PDCA)

Information used in reviews

Alignment

Customer requirements

Focus on strategic intent, operations, and budget

Management decision-making and constancy of purpose

Communication of management review decisions

Accountability

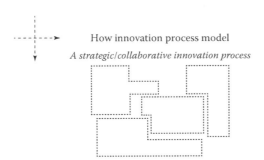

How innovation process model

A strategic/collaborative innovation process

---

* The *collaborative/strategic innovation framework* consists of four phases: (1) planning and readiness, (2) leadership, (3) strategy, and (4) infrastructure. Before launching a strategic innovation effort, it is deemed essential to understand in detail where you are starting from and what your aim or purpose is to accomplish. Current research and experience show that effective leadership is the most important capability for high-performance strategic innovation, and one of the most elusive. Creating a meaningful, manageable, and sustainable strategy for fulfilling your innovation vision is critical to high performance and consistent top-line growth. Best practices should guide the design of your innovation system's processes for capturing, developing, and evaluating promising new concepts, and implementing them quickly and effectively. But these processes must be geared to work in your company and business environment.

The HOW innovation process framework starts with good governance. Although it is not specifically mentioned in this section, the
chances are that the more satisfactory models in this category belong
to the most empowered ones, i.e., that the high-level chief innovation
officer (CIO) model is more likely to ensure effective innovation governance than the lower-level innovation manager model.

Good governance is about the processes for making and implementing
decisions. It's not about making "correct" decisions, but about the best
possible process for making those decisions.* Good decision-making
processes, and therefore good governance, share several characteristics.
All have a positive effect on various aspects of local innovation, "including
consultation policies and practices, meeting procedures, service quality
protocols, councilor and officer conduct, role clarification and good
working relationships."

The seven attributes of good innovation governance are *accountable,
transparent, follows the rule-of-law, responsive, equitable & inclusive,
efficient & effective*, and *participatory.*

Governing innovations involves that, while item advancement includes
the activities of innovative people inside the organization, key business
choices should be bolstered by proficient, organized procedures from the
idea of the product to dispatch and afterward. Such procedures create the
skill and knowledge that frame the premise of quality basic leadership,
guaranteeing an innovative process arrangement, and how to idealize and
execute these procedures.†

---

* Source: http://www.goodgovernance.org.au/about-good-governance/what-is-good-governance/.
Governance is "the process of decision-making and the process by which decisions are implemented (or not implemented)." The term "governance" can apply to corporate, international,
national, local governance or to the interactions between other sectors of society. The concept of
"good governance" often emerges as a model to compare ineffective economies or political bodies
or innovations with viable economies and political bodies and innovations. The concept centers
on the responsibility of "quality councils" and governing bodies to meet the needs of the masses as
opposed to certain select groups in society.
† Crozier, M. "Rethinking systems: Configurations of politics and policy in contemporary governance," *Administration and Society*, 42(5), 504–525, 2010, is another work analyzing good governance. Crozier's article discusses the different dynamics of changes that occur throughout
communication systems and the effect they have on governance. The idea of various perspectives
is presented throughout the article. This allows the reader to see what contemporary governance
is like through different pairs of eyes. Crozier's motive was to also create an innovative and open
mind-set when referring to how governance and policy within society operates, especially with
the constant changes occurring day to day.

An innovation culture is a strategy toward becoming a market leader. A company that has an innovation culture enjoys larger profit margins and is an authority in its area of industry. Though there are risks involved with the innovation process, there are more benefits. You should ensure you keep close contact with the trends in the market to avoid creating a product that will be rejected.

Again, involve all stakeholders in the innovation process; they all have different knowledge and experience that will positively influence the process. The success of any innovation is when the product or service is accepted in the market. Such arrangement empowers those associated with product innovation to choose and organize the best, to advise other to abstain from squandering valuable resources on product ideas that are not innovative, and to take to participate in development forumns productively.

The area of governance and the implementation of first-class procedures laid out in this chapter are subsequently of key significance to enhancing the model used by the business development and management of innovations in the organization. It is based on the innovation body of knowledge (IBoK), along with an innovation process model.* There are 76 primary innovation methods and tools, which are outlined in the three volume set, *The Innovation Tools Handbook.*†

The primary purpose of the IBoK is to identify that subset of the IBoK tools and methods that is generally recognized as good practice. "Good practice" means that there is general agreement that the correct application of these skills, tools, and techniques can enhance the chances of success over a wide range of different innovation initiatives. Good practice does not mean that the knowledge described should always be applied uniformly

---

* A professional membership organization, the International Association of Innovation Professionals (IAOIP) is the world's only innovation certification body, providing members with the knowledge, skills, and opportunities to deliver real change in their industry or field. The Innovation Body of Knowledge (IBoK) is developed and maintained by members through a transparent and democratic process that ensures that everyone has the opportunity to contribute. The IAOIP is a US 501(c), not-for profit, and its chapters are equivalent not-for-profits in their respective countries. The IAOIP acts as an expert third party to certify individuals as knowledgeable professionals in the science of innovation. As a non profit organization, the IAOIP's goals are to grow the formal recognition of the profession, enrich the knowledge and practice of the science of innovation, and to support career development for professional innovators throughout world.

† The three volumes of *The Innovation Tools Handbook*, edited by H James Harrington and Frank Voehl, and published by CRC Press/Taylor & Francis, cover 76 top-rated tools and methods, from the hundreds available, which every innovator must master to be successful. Volume I covers 24 creative tools/methodologies most frequently used to change an organization's structure and operations; Volume 2 presents 23 tools/methodologies related to innovative evolutionary products, processes, and services, or the improvement of existing one; Volume 3 provides the creative tools and methods that every innovator should know.

on all projects; the innovation project team is responsible for determining what is appropriate for any given project. Also, as a foundational reference, this standard is neither comprehensive nor all-inclusive, and this reference book does not address all details of every topic.*

The IBoK for Certification also provides and promotes a common language for discussing, writing, and applying innovation and innovation management. Such a standard language is an essential element of a profession.† The management of portfolio choices fills in as an interface between plans that are strategic and innovative project execution, as shown in Figure 8.3. The most customary type of product that is innovative is the product project, described by the process of "jobs-to-be-done."‡ However, there are other processes where effective execution is paramount, including idea development, concept-development, post-launch processes, and sub-processes – such as technology development and range and/or variant management.

Step #1: Aligning Strategy with Innovation

Strategy is about achieving objectives, innovation is about solving problems. As shown in Figure 8.4, we need to develop frameworks for innovation that are separate from, although compatible with strategy. Although this seems like a no-brainer, companies continue to struggle

---

* Polidoro (2013) states that "Certifications are relevant social cues that assist decision-making under uncertainty." When an employer wants to know if a potential candidate has the necessary competencies and knowledge to perform a set of tasks, they often look to education, experience, certificates, and/or certifications. When the experience and education of two or more candidates are similar, the presence or absence of a certificate or certification can make a difference about who will be hired. Certification in the science of innovation will assist employers in reducing uncertainty in the hiring process and in the professional development of those who focus on the tasks, goals, and processes of innovation. Finally, topics that are not mentioned should not be considered unimportant. The organization or the innovation project team must decide how those activities are going to be addressed in the context and the circumstances of the project.

† The IAOIP certifying body has developed these concepts in a comprehensive way so that aspiring innovation professionals, existing experts, and other interested parties can understand and apply these tools to become more effective and better in generating big bold ideas for their companies.

‡ *Jobs-to-be-done* is a collaborative innovation tool that proposes the following solution to the low innovation success rates that plague companies around the world: to gain insight into the customer's needs, companies should stop focusing on the product or the customer and instead focus on the underlying process or "job" the customer is trying to get done. According to Strategyn, who has popularized this tool, its use has a game-changing implication: When using jobs-to-be-done to examine product successes and failures, they observed the same phenomenon time and time again: *new products and services win in the marketplace if they help customers get a job done better-faster-cheaper.* Customers use a comprehensive list of metrics to evaluate success when getting a job done. These metrics, a special type of need statement called "desired outcomes, form the basis for the collaborative innovation process.

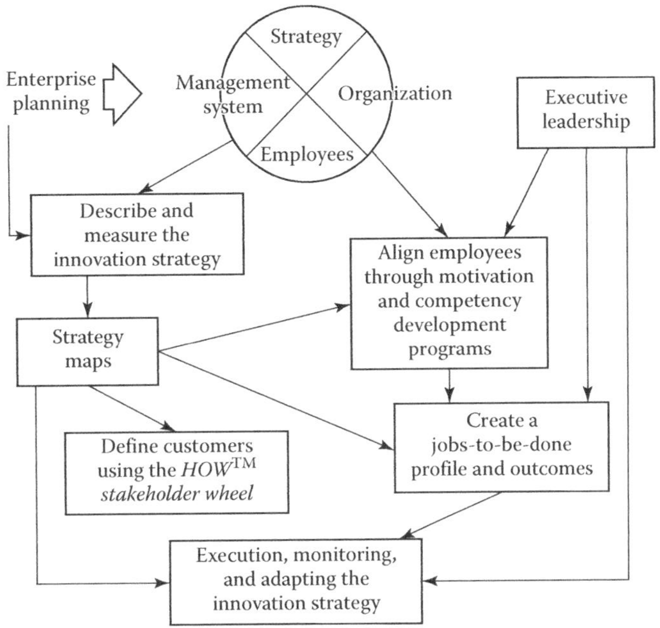

Aligning Strategy with Innovation

Strategy is about achieving objectives, innovation is about solving problems. As shown in Figure 4 on the left, we need to develop frameworks for innovation that are separate from, although compatible with strategy. Although this seems like such a no-brainer, companies continue to struggle with the practicalities of maximizing their programs to meet their strategic objectives. What type of innovation does this apply to?

FIGURE 8.4

Aligning strategy with innovation. Before launching a strategic (collaborative) innovation process, it's essential to understand in detail where you are starting from and what you aim is – a baseline and a target.

with the practicalities of maximizing their programs to meet their strategic objectives. What type of innovation does this apply to?

This building block will discuss what that actually entails from focused idea generation, through designing the evaluation criteria designed to emphasize strategic concerns and to measuring idea viability according to strategic decisions based on an accepted vision and shared datasets. We will outline how highly innovative companies insist on buy-in from senior management, how to estimate the value that innovation should generate to meet financial growth targets, then how they quantify it and make it part of future strategic plans that are cascaded down in the form of growth targets and performance targets.

The pros and cons of designating an individual or to be responsible for the design and construction of the innovation engine should ensure that:

- All the pieces come together in one coherent system so that employees are being trained
- Everyone has access to resources they need
- Customers and suppliers are plugged in
- Projects are funded and monitored
- Innovation is being measured
- All of the above are aligned to support the corporate goals

How do you implement *in step with the context and culture of the organization?* To answer this question, you need to answer the following:

- What are the strategic design elements of our collaborative innovation systems?
- What are our current strategic collaboration capabilities and processes?
- How does our current *business model strategy align* and work in the context of our competitive environment?
- How will we define collaborative innovation and begin to develop our strategic system?

At this stage, it can be helpful to engage innovation counselors and coaches with your organization to provide essential information, diagnostics, and a rollout "JTBD roadmap" specific to your organization.

Innovation primer kit. The primer is an informative toolkit that serves as a quick-start guide to the fundamentals of an effective innovation process model. The primer kit includes a simple self-assessment instrument to illuminate the dynamics of your current organization/structures, along with capabilities for new portfolios of value creation.

Comprehensive diagnostics. A flexible approach to diagnose your organization's innovation quotient (IQ), clarify your business models, identify known and latent high-level business issues, and determine the likely scope of your collaborative strategic innovation efforts.

Customized roadmap and rollout plan for JTBD. Customers use a comprehensive list of metrics to evaluate success when getting a job done. These metrics, a special type of need statement called "desired outcomes," form the basis for the collaborative innovation process. A tailored plan that configures the sequence and timeline needed to develop the right leadership, strategy, and infrastructure elements for your organization.*

Step #2: Opportunity Identification: Determine Customer Needs and Jobs-to-be-Done

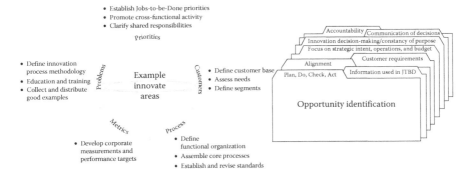

This is where an individual or group views the same old situation but sees it in a different light than had been reviewed before. It's where an

---

* In Clayton Christensen's September 2016 HBR article, he states, "Innovation can be far more predictable—and far more profitable—if you start by identifying the jobs that customers are struggling to get done."

individual or group states, "We should be able to do it differently bringing additional value to the organization." At this point, the individual or group usually does not know how to make the improvement but has committed themselves to come up with an innovative/creative solution. Frequently, this ends up with a mission statement being approved.

What is Jobs-to-be-Done

JTBD is a collaborative innovation tool that proposes the following solution to the low innovation success rates that plague companies around the world: to gain insight into the customer's needs, companies should stop focusing on the product or the customer and instead focus on the underlying process or "job" the customer is trying to get done.

According to Strategyn, who has popularized this tool, its use has a game-changing implication: When using jobs-to-be-done to examine product successes and failures, they observed the same phenomenon time and time again: *new products and services win in the marketplace if they help customers get a job done better-faster-cheaper.* Customers use a comprehensive list of metrics to evaluate success when getting a job done. These metrics, a special type of need statement called "desired outcomes," form the basis for the collaborative innovation process.

The collaborative strategic innovation process solution enables effective management of, and alignment across, all aspects of the processes encompassed within the scope of innovation. This is outlined in the four-milestone approach of a collaborative/strategic innovation process model described in this chapter. There are two kinds of opportunity identification:

1. *We can do this opportunity*: An individual or group sees something going on and thinks that they could find a way to do it better. In this case, they know that what they want to accomplish is to determine if the process will be changed to make it better. In this case, they know what needs to be improved but they don't know how to improve it.
2. *This can be used opportunity*: An individual or group observe something could be applying to other applications, but they don't know which applications to apply it to. In this case, they have a potential fix to a problem but they don't know if they have that problem.

In today's world, this is the effective part of the innovation process for the majority of people. Everyone identifies many improvement opportunities every day; some may not be related to the work environment but many of them are. Just sitting here, one can look around and identify 12–13 improvement opportunities that we can start working on right now. For example, I could get a smaller monitor so that it would not block my view of Silicon Valley. I could put up a 10-foot fence around the house so that the deers can't eat my flowers. We all have a long list of things we have an opportunity to improve but do nothing about it. For innovation, you need to make a similar list, only in this case it must be limited to items that will add value to the organization.

Now that we have identified the improvement opportunity, we're ready to move on to Activity 2: Create–Creation–Activity. No, not so fast, we still have a little more work to do before we have a legitimate improvement opportunity. We need to estimate what the *improvement potential* is for the opportunities we want to move on to Activity 2. An improvement potential estimate is a very rough estimate of what the value added is for the customer and the organization. Typically, this is prepared by the individual or group proposing an improvement opportunity and as someone who represents the customer (or product) it is usually marketing. It typically takes hours not days to prepare. After the group that is proposing the improvement opportunity explains to the internal customer's representative what the opportunity is and what the output could look like, the internal customer's representative will give a rough estimate of what they believe are the potential output requirements. For products, marketing will estimate what the potential sales price would be.

The group that is proposing the improvement opportunity will provide estimates related to costs to develop, install, and produce the required quantities. From this information, the improvement potential can be calculated. This calculation will essentially provide the organization with an estimated return on investment (ROI). Based upon this calculation, the decision will be made to discontinue work on the improvement opportunity or to move it into the creation activity. It is accepted that this estimate would be a very rough estimate, typical activities are ±25%. As a result, I personally look for a 5 to 1 ROI minimum to continue pursuing the improvement opportunity. Typically, the cost to define the actions necessary to produce the output is estimated low and the quantity of outputs needed in the value of the output is high. As a result, most of the improvement potential estimates are much greater than the actual realized ROI. This estimate will be refined during Activity 3 (preparing value proposition).

The individual or group identifying the improvement opportunity/ problem will prepare an *opportunity charter**. Although the opportunity charter may undergo a number of changes during Activities 2 and 3, we suggest that you keep a copy of the original improvement charter to use when preparing and presenting the value proposition in Activity 3.

Step #3: Creation Using Insight-to-Ideation†

Creation insight = business success

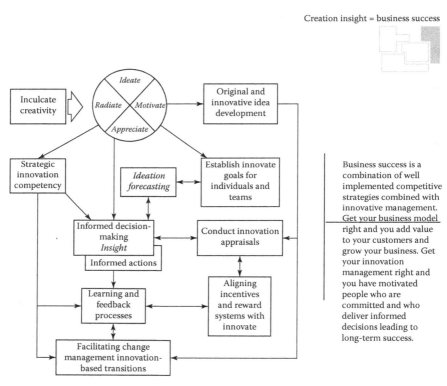

Business success is a combination of well implemented competitive strategies combined with innovative management. Get your business model right and you add value to your customers and grow your business. Get your innovation management right and you have motivated people who are committed and who deliver informed decisions leading to long-term success.

---

* Typical items that would be included in the opportunity charter are (a) description of the opportunity/problem; (b) approach or plan to be use in addressing the opportunity/problem; (c) people and resources required to complete Activities 2 and 3; (d) any other resources required to complete Activities 2 and 3; and (d) the improvement potential along with any other value activity that is included in the improvement potential. (Example, improved employee morale, decreased cycle time.)

† Insight-to-ideation is the concept currently being popularized in China, which has joined the top 25 most innovative countries in the WIPO global innovation index. This is because they no longer rely on cost-effective manufacturing alone. They also applied for more patents than the next two countries, the United States and Japan, combined! This clearly shows that China is improving ideation as well as their innovation. But, they know they must do even more. To become a truly competitive nation, they have to better understand their customers, especially their growing middle- and higher-income residents, who continue to prefer primarily imported Western brands.

Many companies create great new products and services – from their perspective – but then, low and behold, they fail! They then ask if we can help them to identify the opportunity and to whom they should be selling. Even though we help them, we also suggest that next time it would be better if they called us before they started innovating! Why? They tell us that their market research is a great source of information, but for insight, you have to integrate multiple sources of information. It is rare for a single project to provide that deep an insight. This comes from truly understanding the customer and that takes time. It takes data and information, turned into knowledge and then understanding. We call this insight-to-ideation.*

Why? In a failure situation, it is almost always due to an outdated innovation process in which the customer has not been involved. Knowing why your customers do what they do, buy what they buy, and consume what they consume, and then watching and listening to them, will put you in the best possible position for improving ideation and innovation. But, there's still more you can do, more than tossing bright ideas into the following invention machine.

During this activity, a number of potential problem solutions and or opportunity improvement approaches will be identified, analyzed, and prioritized. Also during this activity, steps are actually taken to protect intellectual capital – patents, along with new and unique concepts – to ensure that there are no patent infringements.

---

* Our recommendation, therefore, if you are struggling to develop insight, is to analyze your competitors or the brands targeting a similar audience. If you can identify on what human truth and insight their message is based, you may be able to use it too.

Insight and Strategic Product Innovation

This results from the innovative development of improved or new products, including substantial services and goods; management bodies know that this is vital to the survival and productivity of the cutting-edge company. In a current McKinsey study, innovation is one of the main factors driving development, according to about 70% of CEOs included in the survey.

It was observed that the majority viewed innovation as imperative and fundamental to the strategy execution and performance of a company. The extent of development is in no way, shape, or form constrained to just innovations in a product. Instead, it covers numerous parts of an organization's business. The IAOIP Academy,* for instance, records the accompanying central meanings of innovation as

- *Operational*: Innovation that enhances the viability and productivity of central procedures and capacities
- *Business model*: Innovation in the structure or the potential money-related model of the business
- *Products/markets/services*: Innovation connected to services or products, or activities involving marketing and sales

While each of these three forms of innovation is viewed as vital, respondents to a worldwide review of CEOs, carried out by IBM, noted that the potential market and product are the beginning stages and principal drivers of innovations in plans of action and business operational exercises.† Did recovering from the recession change the states of mind of innovative practices amid the financial downturn of 2008–2009? It was noticed that even in turbulent circumstances there is a small logjam in R&D spending among worldwide pioneers of innovation. Almost 75% of

---

* The IAOIP Academy provides access to organized, curated training from IAOIP and other organizations in diverse areas of innovation and related topics, with levels ranging from introductory to advanced, to be used by aspiring, new, or established learners from various fields. Several courses will be offered in languages other than English. Each course offers a certificate of completion. Some courses require you to pass a quiz, while other courses simply require you to watch a course video.

† A perception that market and product innovation empowers over time is shown in the solid relationship between effective innovative strategy and general business achievement. A current worldwide review of practices of innovation directed by Boston Consulting Group in association with *Business Week* demonstrated how innovative organizations ordinarily produce prevalent returns for investors: a premium of 12% contrasted with industry peers over a three-year time span.

the organizations analyzed by Booz and Company during the recession were keeping up or growing the portfolios of their R&D areas.

Also, solving improvement opportunities is one of the most effective ways to move up within an organization. With all of these advantages, what keeps us from being an enthusiastic problem-solver? Some of the reasons follow:

1. I don't have enough time to get involved with problem-solving. Let somebody else waste their time I got real work to do.
2. That job is not part of my job description. Let the person that is responsible for sell their own problems. It is not my problem why should I take my time to solve it.
3. I serve on opportunity/problem-solving teams before the team leader get all the visibility and credit.
4. I get to work Saturday because I cannot get all my work done through the first 5 days.
5. Errors as a way of life. So I made an error you have to expect a few of them. There's nothing you can do about them so him let's just forget it and go on.

Management needs to provide six items to transform couch potatoes into dynamic problem-solvers:

1. *Awareness*: People need to be aware of why problems need to be solved now and why those solutions need to be applied to new products. It's important to develop a sense of urgency in order to keep up with your competition.
2. *Desire*: People need to have the desire to make things better. To do things faster. To get out the new design.
3. *Error analysis*: People need to be taught how to define the root cause of problems and not try to sell the eye treating the symptoms.
4. *Follow-up system*: There needs to be a follow-up system that highlights the most important activities and measures the effectiveness of any improvement effort.
5. *Liberal credit*: The people who come up with the creative ideas need to give credit to their teams of people as they need to be recognized for their accomplishments.
6. *Training*: People need to be trained in effective problem-solving methods and the use of statistical analysis tools to analyze complex problems and make accurate projections.

Step #4: Value Propositions = Insight-to-Action

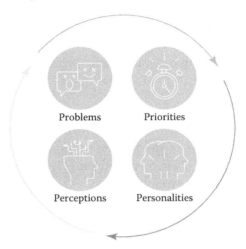

To kick-start the value proposition, intensive stakeholder analysis is required. Understanding the problems, priorities, perceptions, and personalities (the four P's) of each stakeholder or interest group becomes critical in determining the most effective way of communicating with them. The problem can be classified by difficulty and size; for example, is it easily reversible as in a pricing change, or strategically committed as in an acquisition? The priorities need to be mapped as they could potentially raise awareness, revenue, profit, or the personal standing of the decision-maker. Perceptions, both past and present, matter – and must be anticipated by the storyteller. The stakeholder's personality must also be mapped.

Overview

Some of the highest performing and most agile companies in the world work with uncertainty to develop creative solutions to emergent issues. In the context of high-speed complex change, an over abundance of data is not only normal, but it is not always in the form you need. And how do you blend it with your "gut feel" or instinct? Getting to know your personal blueprint for seeing and sensing the best decision in the context of innovation needs and complexity starts with greater self-awareness and self-knowledge. Otherwise, the focus is too narrow, options either too many or too few, and key information in the working environment very likely gets missed. Learning from high-stakes mistakes strengthens your decision-making toolkit.

Today, uncertainty and unpredictability are the new norm. With complexity, most of the information you need is outside of your immediate view. And, since the days of engineering, controllable outcomes are over, you need more tools to see subtle influences. We call these tools for aggregating your customer data *insight-to-action.**

- Identify your intuitive strengths that blend social data with factual data giving you insight.
- Apply listening and sensing to detect what isn't in clear view.
- See how focus on decision-making can intentionally stimulate innovation and achieve cost savings.
- Observe the conditions in your workplace that steer decisions away from growth.
- Identify patterns that companies fall into when making decisions.
- Learn why making mistakes builds decision-making strength.
- Understand and learn why setting an environment for making mistakes is key for leadership and business growth.
- Install checkpoints to mitigate the risk of error caused by complacency.
- Use diversity of perspectives and storytelling to make better decisions.

By applying the age-old principles of storytelling and the new tenets of data journalism, organizations can evolve their analytics practices from gut-wrenching exercises of "guesstimation," to a fact-based art of storytelling that not only informs and inspires meaningful decision-making but keeps key stakeholders aligned and engaged.†

The last step in bridging the gap between insights and action and creating a pervasive data-driven decision-making culture is analytical storytelling,

---

* The process of aggregating your customer data into more actionable insights can seem like an overwhelming endeavor. The key to moving forward starts with a clean slate of consolidated customer data. From there, prioritize finding an interface and team strategy for the marketing team to easily access those insights, integrate them into different channels, and measure real-time results.
† See Cognizant (NASDAQ-100: CTSH), one of the world's leading professional services companies, transforming clients' business, operating, and technology models for the digital era. They have a unique industry-based, consultative approach that helps clients envision, build, and run more innovative and efficient businesses. Headquartered in the United States, Cognizant is ranked 230 on the Fortune 500 and is consistently listed among the most-admired companies in the world. Learn how Cognizant helps clients lead with digital at www.cognizant.com or see https://www. cognizant.com/whitepapers/analytical-storytelling-from-insight-to-action-codex2475.pdf.

says Cognizant. Simply stated, this is the process of bringing data to life to tell a well-constructed narrative – one that ultimately connects with the hopes, fears, and motivations of each stakeholder to encourage and guide a change in behavior. Such storytelling enables companies to shift from being instinct driven to being insight driven in their decisions. Navigating the needed change in corporate culture is inseparable from the quality of the corporate decisions themselves; both halves need to progress in support of each other, and analytical storytelling links them together.

In excess of 90% of managers viewed innovation as essential in preparing for an upturn after the recession. This pattern was additionally obviously unmistakable in the Boston Consulting Group's examination: 84% of organizations analyzed considered innovation as a necessity for profiting from the monetary recovery. Considering all factors, innovation has evolved into a centerpiece of corporate technique and strategy, tied down in long-running improvement cycles and concerning suppliers and consumers.

Before a decision can be made, the facts and situation should be documented and clarified. Only then can organizations apply "analytical storytelling" to bring the recommended action forward to the key stakeholders. This preparatory process is often called "data journalism." According to author and data journalism trainer Henk van Ess, "Data journalism can be based on any data that has to be processed first with tools before a relevant story is possible."*

Innovations on decision support products include an entire arrangement of choices, connecting strategic methodology to execution. The Booz and Company study mentioned previously discovered that reasonable basic leadership rights and a satisfactory data flow were the two most vital prerequisites for the effective execution of a strategy. Decision support and flow of data are additionally at the center of the IAOIP way to deal with the innovative administration process. In this way, it takes the more viable and productive basic leadership and converts it into more viable innovative development.

> "To start with, a value proposition should evaluate a proposal separating the bad from the good, the winners from the losers, and the moneymaker from the money losers."
>
> **H. J. Harrington**

---

* Data journalism can be likened to investigative reporting. The goal is to ultimately "expose" the real story and to uncover a single version of the truth. According to industry experts, professional data journalists are encouraged to not share their work until there is evidence to support their findings. Data journalism assists in finding and developing the true narrative.

Definition: A value proposition is a document that defines the benefits that will result from the implementation of a change or the use of output as viewed by one or more of the organization's stakeholders. A value proposition can apply to an entire organization or part thereof: sponsor customer accounts, products, services, and internal processes.

During this activity, the ROI for the high-priority changes will be calculated and it is important that both the positive and negative impacts that an individual change would have on the organization are defined and analyzed. Communicate, to develop, refine, and implement is divided into the value-added content that the changes will bring about. Based upon this analysis, the changes that have the biggest impact both real and imaginary on the organization will be prioritized. The following is a typical table of contents for a value proposition:

- Executive overview.
- List of key people associated with the value proposition.
- Financial calculations.
- Details related to other value-added results (e.g., reduced cycle time, increased customer satisfaction, reduce stock, and less floor space).
- List of risks and exposures.
- List of assumptions.
- Other solutions that were evaluated.
- Implementation plans.
- Connect three-year projections of output requirements.
- The next value added when the cost (money and other resources) related to developing, installing, and operating the change are considered.
- Estimated selling price.
- Validation strategy.
- Recommended time schedule.
- Detailed recommendations.
- References.

It is realized that the error in the estimates could be as much as plus or minus 50%. By the time the project is completed the business case analysis, the error rate will be greatly reduced.

At a minimum, the value proposition should be prepared by the individual or team that is proposing the project. It should be from the point of view of the individual or group that will be getting and using the output. Approval of the value proposition helps the project to be classified as active in the organization's project portfolio. The output from the value proposition with the executive team or the executives that will be funding the additional analysis will bury their agreement that the project has additional potential and may only be funded up to the business case analysis.

Step #5: Concept Validation = Monitor/Measure

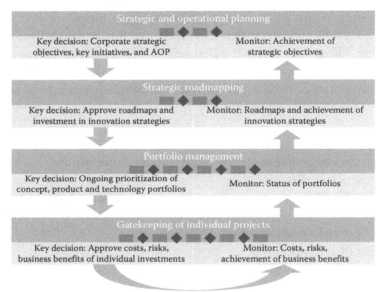

The figure shows that key choices are made and conveyed down through the organization. Business process execution is persistently observed at different levels of product development and changed over into an upward stream of data that empowers administration at each level to check whether choices are being taken afterward, keeping them informed of the aftereffects of any activities.

During this activity, the proposed change is modeled, allowing new performance data to be collected. Modeling can be accomplished by building an engineering model of the change and submitting it to a number of conditions (e.g., temperature, humidity, vibration, and electronic delays); the results can be used to protect failure rates and/or reliability. Simulation models are also frequently used to validate the engineering and financial estimates.

For process-type changes, a model of the future state flowchart and floor layout plan can be set up and operated. Typically, extensive IT programs are not put in place at this point in time but behind the scenes mock activities provide equivalent results. A controlled experiment is then run using the as-is (current) process in the mock future state process to compare results.

The results of concept evaluation are very important as they provide a performance specification that will be presented to the customer, analysis of manufacturability, and much more accurate production costs than estimates. It is recommended that the concept validation team is made up of people from product engineering, manufacturing engineering, test engineering, quality engineering, industrial engineering, and manufacturing.

Monitor: Innovation Measurement and Management

We always take into account the industry, the competitor, the market, and the organization's capabilities—all the good stuff that classic strategy teaches us how to do—but that is all in service of the big idea, the breakthrough experience, and we use it after we've discovered the space and the opportunity where we are going to play. Big breakthroughs in experience, value creation, and growth come when you take this creative approach rather than the more traditional, analytical approach.

Timothy Morey, VP, Innovation Strategy, Frog Design*

Goal: Developing comprehensive metrics to allow your organization to set specific innovation goals, proactively rebalance innovation spending, and measure results

Innovation is notoriously difficult to measure but any activity that significantly impacts investment, staffing, resources, and competitiveness needs to be measured. In this section, we will look at what metrics are proving useful in organizations when pure financial metrics don't work.

What techniques are being used to quantify and score innovation to push forward winners?

---

* Frog uses a wide range of strategic tools and methods to help organizations take advantage of untapped opportunities in the market, including research, ideation, market strategy, forecasting, technology planning, and business modeling. But, we start with the bigger creative question that can transform businesses: How should people experience a product or brand, and what impact can it have on their lives? Their motto is: We transform businesses at scale by creating systems of brand, product, and service that deliver distinctly better experiences for consumers, customers, citizens, and employees.

What types of dashboards are out there and what are they tracking?

How best should investment dollars and staff time, leadership and mentoring time be quantified?

What is coming from internal sources and what is from customers and partners?

How much time does it take to move projects forward?

How are people quantifying the number of projects that move from concept to reality in different risk categories, revenues derived, efficiencies, and improvements to output?

The $64,000,000 Question: How Do You Measure Innovation?

One of the reasons that only about one-third of all Fortune 1000 companies have formal innovation metrics is because this simple question does not have a simple answer. Metrics can be important levers of innovation – for driving behavior, as well as evaluating the results of specific initiatives. Companies like 3M and Google have had innovation metrics for years – the most noteworthy that 10% of employees' time is dedicated to experimentation with new opportunities. Some companies like 3M have tried to mandate that 35% of the corporations' revenues should come from products introduced within the past four years. Defining the right metrics for your business can be tricky.

The best solutions create simplicity from complexity. Assuming that successful innovation results from the synergies between complementary success factors, it is important to address these by

- Creating a "family of metrics" for ensuring a well-rounded portfolio of measures
- Including both "input metrics" and "output metrics" to ensure measures that drive resource allocation and capability building, as well as ROI

A "family of metrics" ensures a portfolio of measures that covers the most important innovation drivers. The following are the three categories to consider for any metrics portfolio:

Return on investment metrics: ROI metrics address two measures: resource investments and financial returns. ROI metrics give innovation management fiscal discipline and help justify and recognize the value of strategic initiatives, programs, and the overall investment in innovation.

Organizational capability metrics: Organizational capability metrics focus on the infrastructure and process of innovation. Capability measures provide focus for initiatives geared toward building repeatable and sustainable approaches to invention and re-invention.

Leadership metrics: Leadership metrics address the behaviors that senior managers and leaders must exhibit to support a culture of innovation within the organization, including the support of specific growth initiatives. Within each of these categories, there are "input metrics" and "output metrics." Input metrics are the investments, resources, and behaviors that are necessary to drive results. Output metrics represent the desired results for the metric category. There's generally no one right answer and agreeing on what to measure can feel more like art than science.*

Innovation measurement example

Establishing innovation metrics, deployment flow, planning control

Linkage occurs when one level's means becomes the next level's measures
each level develops measures and means to achieve them

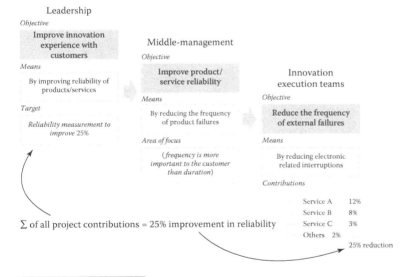

* Soren Kaplan, founder of InnovationPoint; writer for Fast Company; author of the award-winning and best-selling books *Leapfrogging* and *The Invisible Advantage*; and a contributing writer for FastCompany and Inc. Magazine. As the founder of InnovationPoint and upBOARD, he works with organizations including Disney, Kimberly-Clark, Colgate-Palmolive, Medtronic, Philips, Red Bull, and numerous other global firms. Soren previously led the internal strategy and innovation group at Hewlett-Packard (HP) during the roaring 1990s in Silicon Valley and was a co founder of iCohere, one of the first web collaboration platforms for online learning and communities of practice. He is an adjunct professor within the Imagineering Academy at NHTV Breda University of Applied Sciences in The Netherlands and sits on the advisory boards of several startups.

HOW Software

IAOIP is one of the select few providers who offers an integrated end2end innovation management process, from environmental scanning to innovation portfolio management and roadmapping, ensuring that the return on innovation increases sustainably. This type of modular software suite will ideally combine strategy and innovation on a web-based collaboration platform, as shown in Figure 8.5. The advantage of linking trend management, technology management, idea management, and strategic foresight: all innovation management activities are connected to the *HOW™ Innovation Process Roadmap* that serves as a strategic planning platform for the division-spanning product, technology, and resource management.

Step #6: Business Case and Management Reviews

Establishing organizational objectives, business case analysis, management reviews

- Important innovation activites appear in the deployment flow providing leadership with a road map.
- Business units develop Innovation Strategy Maps (ISMs) and balanced scorecards to help them gain consensus for the strategy planning process among the executive leadership team and commmunicate the innovation strategy to the employees.
- Resources consistent with the innovation strategy must be allocated and the strategy plan monitored and the strategy's performance guided in order to enable the enterprise to create value from its customer relationships.

During this activity, the proposed change is analyzed to determine if it should be included as part of the organization's portfolio of active projects. Once the change becomes part of the organization's portfolio of projects, resources are set aside to support the change process; to create the necessary engineering and manufacturing documentation; to validate the

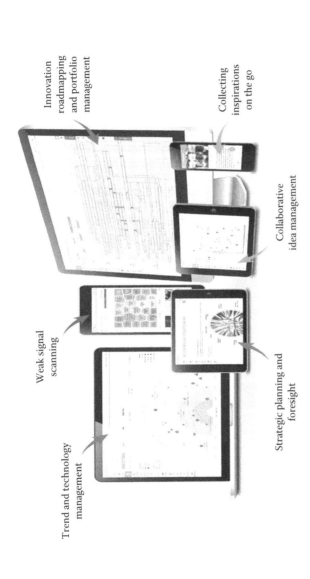

Innovation roadmapping and portfolio management

Collecting inspirations on the go

Collaborative idea management

Weak signal scanning

Strategic planning and foresight

Trend and technology management

FIGURE 8.5

The HOW Innovation Process Software Suite. This software suite is loosely based upon the Itonics* software package. It provides one holistic approach for IT-supported integrated innovation management – from environmental scanning to innovation portfolio management through to innovation roadmapping.

---

* We provide one holistic approach for IT-supported integrated innovation management - from environmental scanning to innovation portfolio management through to innovation roadmapping.

acceptability of the production outputs through a series of manufacturing process model evaluations, product announcement, upgrading of data systems, training and manufacturing personal; and start shipping to an external customer/consumer.

It is during this phase that the effectiveness of our *project management and change management* plans are evaluated. If both are carried out in just an average way, Phase 2 will run very smoothly. Unfortunately, in most organizations both project management and change management activities do not meet even minimum requirements. You need to make it a point to excel and to manage the change necessary to successfully implement the new process.

Definition: A business case analysis is an evaluation of the potential impact a problem or opportunity has on the organization to determine if it is worthwhile investing resources to correct the problem or take advantage of the opportunity. An example of the results of a business case analysis for a software upgrade could be

1. That it would improve the software's performance as stated in the value proposition but
   a. It would decrease overall customer satisfaction by essentially three percentage points
   b. It would result in increasing profit time by 5% and
   c. It would reduce systems maintenance costs by only $800 per year.

As a result of the business case analysis, it is not recommended that the project be included in the portfolio of active programs. Often, the business case is prepared by an independent group, thus giving a fresh unbiased analysis of the benefits and costs related to completing the project or program. During this activity, an independent analysis is conducted to estimate the value-added content that the project would have and compares it to other active and proposed opportunities to determine how the organization's resources can best be utilized. Approved projects have detailed project management packages prepared for them that the project team starts to implement. To obtain a better understanding of the business case analysis activity, read *Effective Portfolio Management Systems*, published by CRC Press, 2016. Projects that successfully complete this analysis are funded through first customer ship and become part of the organization's portfolio of active projects.

Step #7: Documentation using Visual Rapid Ideation Workshops

HOW™ innovation process results

Innovation management, informed
decision-making/action, rapid ideation

- HOW innovation process creates informed decisions and actions
- Results are the natural outcome of effective rapid ideation, utilizing data and structured analysis techniques.
- Once the system architecture has evolved, disparate datasets can be correlated to deliver better rapid ideation and decision-making information.

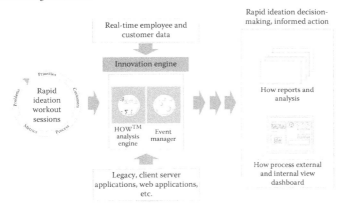

Overview

During this activity, the engineering documentation, maintenance manuals, production routings, and job instructions are prepared. Assembly personnel and operators are trained on how to use them. Packaging and shipping containers are evaluated to ensure that they provide adequate protection for the product. The information collection system is defined and put in place. The project management data system generates frequent status reports to keep the management team aware of the status and point out activities where they need to be involved. The typical documents prepared and put into use are

Product engineering: Product specifications, blueprints, operating instructions, material specifications, bills of material, etc.

Manufacturing engineering: Process routings, job instructions, training programs, assembly diagrams, operating plans, etc.

Test engineering: Test procedures, equipment drawings, operating plans, requests for corrective action, etc.

Quality engineering: Inspection plan, visual criteria, operating plans, non-conforming materials status, field failure rate status, quality cost status, failure analysis status, problem resolution status, etc.

Industrial engineering: Poor instructions, equipment operating procedures, facility requirements, approved suppliers.

Production control: Work breakdown structures, stacking requirements, production schedules, etc.

Marketing and sales: Advertising specifications, supplier lists, forecast sales projections, sales orders, book entry status take all of the items related to, etc. In marketing, a paperless organization still has a huge amount of documents being transferred, updated, and used to sell, order, and deliver the output. In addition, the documentation system provides a measurement of how good each of the individual parts of the organization is performing.

The following will give innovators a feel for the complexity of the measurements that are being used in marketing and sales and other areas for suggested quality documentation requirements:

- Success in reducing defects through suggestion submittal
- Success in capturing new business versus quotations
- Responsiveness to customer inquiries
- Accuracy of marketing forecasts
- Response from news releases and advertisements
- Effectiveness of cost and price negotiations
- Success in response to customer inquiries (customer identification)
- Customer liaison
- Effectiveness of market intelligence
- Attainment of new order targets
- Operation within budgets
- Effectiveness of proposals
- Exercise of selectivity
- Control of cost of sales
- Meeting proposal submittal dates
- Timely preparation of priced spare parts lists
- Aggressiveness
- Effectiveness of G-2
- Utilization of field marketing services
- Dissemination of customer information

- Bookings budget met
- Accuracy of predictions, planning, and selections
- Accurate and well-managed contracts
- Exploitation of business potential
- Effectiveness of proposals
- Control of printing costs
- Application of standard proposal material
- Standardization of proposals
- Reduction of reproduction expense
- Contract errors
- Order description error
- Sales order errors

Rapid Ideation and Front-End Management

Ideas can often grow exponentially – especially if the participants are encouraged to think quickly without fear of judgment. Rapid ideation uses the power of groups to create a volume of new ideas/solutions to evaluate shortly thereafter. To get started, assemble a group of at least three to four people who may be directly, or even indirectly, involved in your project.* Then, find a space that is conducive to your session (warning: these sessions can sometimes get loud – so be considerate of your neighbors) and get ready to write/sketch fast using a Post-it® Super Sticky Dry Erase Surface or a Post-it® Big Pad sheet.

1. Before inviting participants to generate ideas, take 10 minutes to discuss your audience. Who are they? What do they want? What do they need? Briefly role-play as a group to put yourself in their shoes and start addressing the realities of the situation. Generate ideas.
2. Next, spend 20 minutes discussing the scope of the project. What are the budget and time parameters your project is dealing with? How can these parameters potentially shift? Think of best- and worse-case scenarios to set the framework for your discussion.
3. Now it's go time! Use the next 40 minutes to brainstorm ideas/ concepts that address your project's needs. Have everyone in your

---

* This process outline is provided by Post-it at https://www.post-it.com/3M/en_US/post-it/ideas/ articles/rapid-ideation/. For over 35 years, the Post-it® brand has helped people be more productive, communicate better, and express themselves in a number of creative ways. Yet, as universal as these products have become, their beginnings were far from certain. Looking back, the birth of the canary-yellow phenomenon reminds us of what Edison once said: perspiration can be just as important as inspiration when it comes to bringing an idea to life.

group participate and encourage them to write/sketch their idea to help articulate their points.

4. The final step in this process is testing. Spend 20 minutes examining the ideas and filter out the ones that don't necessarily address your project. Then, act out the best ones from the viewpoint of your audience – how would your audience interact with your idea? What are its strengths and weaknesses? Sketch out a user-flow to refer to as necessary.

5. Finally, record the session by taking photos/documenting your rapid ideation session. *This will serve as a resource/framework to keep your ideas focused and action oriented.* Innovation governance is an important achievement factor for basic leadership in product improvement. It centers expressly around the front end of the operational period of managing innovation, to specifically generate concept and idea improvement.*

Web-empowered idea generators that anybody can have are incapable of producing great innovations. That is because they just go about accumulating ideas, with no specific roadmap for recognizing and building those ideas with genuine potential. The best ideation system is supported by idea events and innovative development, while likewise guaranteeing that strategy is connected to the ideation procedure. Effective development of ideas is certainty required, as often as possible, to be focused on a particularly vital point and for a specific, important group of people.

A viable solution for the development of an idea depends on an arrangement of prescribed procedures. In our view, adherence to the accompanying standards will show the contrast between an arrangement of normal ideas and an arrangement of incredible ideas that can end up as extraordinary products. These standards are

- Supporting the development of ideas using viable campaigns that mirror your corporate values.
- Strategically interface submissions to other information sources and use those associations with creative ideas through organized exchanges and connections to ideas that have been used before.
- Participation of society and culture to take part in the innovative process (being able to envision and structure these features).

---

* In rapid idea development, a shortage of ideas isn't the fundamental issue that numerous organizations encounter; despite what might be expected, they have an excessive number of them, with no reasonable method for implementing and sustaining the possibly incredible thoughts that will drive genuine innovative market achievement.

- Enable a suitable work process of ideas and not the customary stage-based procedures, which will be connected later amid the development process of the product.

An innovation administration solution empowers the evaluation of ideas by different individuals inside the organization, encourages the investigation of a few prospective ideas, and consolidates benchmarking correlations and contributions from outsider industrial specialists.

Step #8: Resourcing for Opportunity Segmentation and Methods and Tool Selection

Introduction

Nothing can be accomplished without resources. Resources are at the heart of everything we do. If you have too few, you fail. Too many is waste, which can erode the organization's competitive ability. Too many organizations limit their thinking about resources to people and money. These two are important, but they are only a small part of the resources that the organization must manage.

Resource management in the broadest sense includes all the resources and assets that are available to an organization. This includes stockholders, management, partnerships, real estate, knowledge, customers, patents, investment, goodwill, and brick-and-mortar. When all of these are considered, it becomes apparent that effective resource management is one of the most critical, complex activity within an organization.

"The essence of competitiveness is liberated when we make people believe that what they think and do it is important – and then get out of their way while they do it." Jack Welch former CEO of GE.

During this activity, the resources required for the approved project are put in place. In small and startup companies, financing usually becomes a major problem. Initially, personal funding is used, then family funding, angel funding, and borrowing from banks, which are all legitimate sources. The primary reason most startup companies fail is due to lack of financial support.

Viable portfolio and gate management choices are reliant on knowledgeable judgments, which must be made based on solid and constant information. Effective process execution, together with a framework that empowers the social impact of this information with at least time and exertion events, add extraordinarily to the opportunity segmentation business effect involving process innovation.

Some Innovation Methods and Tools*

There is no innovation without having something to deliver to the customer and this always requires some form of practice generally referred to as a tool or methodology. There are many tools that can be applied to the general cases of innovation activity and the list seems endless when we consider special cases. The following list shows the common names for 60 of the 150 tools that are most used by professional innovators around the globe.

1. 5 Why questions
2. 76 standard solutions
3. Absence thinking (GISH tool 9)
4. Affinity diagram
5. Attribute listing
6. Biomimicry
7. Brain-writing 6-3-5-
8. Business case development
9. Combination methods
10. Competitive analysis
11. Comparative analysis
12. Concept tree (concept map)
13. Consumer co-creation
14. Consumer journey mapping
15. Contingency planning
16. Costs analysis
17. Creative problem-solving model
18. Jobs-to-be-done (JTBD)
19. Ethnography
20. Focus groups
21. Force field analysis (GISH tool 16)
22. Generic creativity tools
23. Imaginary brainstorming
24. Kano Analysis (GISH tool 2)
25. Knowledge management systems
26. Lead user analysis

---

* Many of these tools are discussed in this study guide or other specialized references. Scan the list for any tools that you feel you do not have a basic understanding of, go first to the *Global Innovation Science Handbook* (GISH) and look up the general information or a specialized reference. Also see the *Innovation Tools Handbooks* (Vols 1– 3) for specific information on each tool shown, plus others.

27. Lotus blossom (GISH tool 11)
28. Market research
29. Matrix diagram
30. Mind mapping
31. Nominal group technique (GISH tool 3)
32. Online idea platforms/innovation platforms
33. Open innovative platforms act (GISH tool)
34. Outcome-driven innovation
35. Patent analysis
36. Plan-Do-Check-Act (GISH tool)
37. Potential investor presentations
38. Project Management Act (GISH tool)
39. Quickscore creativity test (GISH tool 1)
40. Reengineering/redesign
41. Robust design
42. S-curve model
43. Scamper
44. Scenario analysis
45. Simulations
46. Six thinking hats
47. Social networks
48. Solution analysis diagrams
49. Stakeholder analysis
50. Statistical analysis
51. Storyboarding (GISH tool 8)
52. Surveys
53. Systems thinking
54. Synectics (GISH tool 4)
55. Tree diagram (GISH tool 10)
56. Value analysis
57. Value propositions
58. Visioning
59. Hoshin planning
60. Creative thinking

The HOW Funnel™ must have the ability to deal with different process models. It should bolster and mechanize the definition and execution of models. The best devices in this classification can take a procedure model idea that has been used once and use it as a layout to create better project designs, point-by-point venture timetables, and part prerequisites for team members each time you start another project using the HOW Funnel.*

HOW funnel™

- Collect, organize, and engage ideas with less effort
- Spend more time innovating and growing your business with idea management.

Top features:
- Automatic linking on conversion
- Linking Emails
- Convert leads to contacts/opportunities
- Advanced permissions
- Simple permissions
- Mobile business card scanning
- Web to lead forms
- Lead assignment rules/lead routing
- Ideas are great, but winning opportunities are what pays the bills. The *HOW funnel* offers a painless way to convert ideas into opportunities.
- Just click "convert idea," and software takes it from there. The idea record is instantly converted into an opportunity, contact, and organization – each one linked to the other.
- At any point, you can click back into the original idea record for a 360 degree overview.

People resources also present a problem for both small and large companies. Although there are sufficient people out of work today to fill all the available jobs, there's big shortages in fields like product engineering, programming, industrial engineering, and manufacturing engineering. Finding the right suppliers at the right price that can produce the correct item, and can do it on schedule in small lots is another problem faced during this activity. The last major item addressed in this activity is facilities. Not having the right equipment and/or the floor space required to support the output is a problem that is stressed during this activity.

Different cases of process productivity web-based devices incorporate email notice instruments (that keep colleagues up-to-date without their entering the framework), "helpful hints" on layouts that take team

---

* We also need a workstation-style interface that can help knowledge workers survive the information flood of modern society. And that's where the authors think we really need revolutionary designs that go beyond the Mac. For example, ways of managing tens of thousands of documents using a rich set of attributes and content-oriented navigation. Simply showing files as icons in folders doesn't cut it beyond a few hundred. We also know from many studies that the average user is very bad at hierarchical filing and typically never moves a file once it gets to live in some directory – even if the file would be better off elsewhere. This problem is magnified several hundred times when it comes to managing email. We are beginning to think that the solution is to treat information objects as members of a group, and manage them by attributes rather than by hierarchy and name.

members straight to required data assets, and status cautions or cautioning symbols that quickly feature those activities or assignments that need consideration.*

Doing Projects Right: Getting New Products to Market More Efficiently

Poor execution of a process is a huge issue in product innovation management. Execution deficit is one of the greatest single reasons for new product disappointments. Then again, several studies show that sound execution can have a significantly beneficial outcome on the product innovation's business effect. Strong usage of major specialized modeling exercises† would be able to perform more than twofold product improvement innovation rate; and create items that corner above 18% piece of the overall industry.

Communication: Poor correspondence is one of the greatest hindrances to process productivity and the clever utilization of assets. Poor communication frequently happens in areas such as

- Gathering data about business sectors, contenders, or advancements
- Project task and activities status tracking
- Defining what to incorporate into gate expectations
- Reporting fundamental task data, status, and measurements to pertinent groups
- Recreating work effectively finished somewhere else
- Creating and sorting out new tasks from the beginning
- Synthesizing and arranging data for gate gatherings
- Traveling to attend meeting and gate activities
- Searching for inside information and ability
- Training and updating new colleagues

---

* In the software world, the audience is predictable and targeted, making learning styles more predictable. On a website, it's anybody's guess who might be using the site. The website visitor might be a particle physicist, a teen, or a grandparent. Learning styles, comfort levels, and expectations differ greatly. This is perhaps why you hear a lot of reference to progressive disclosure in conversations and interviews, but rarely any ideas about how to apply it effectively.

† According to Jakob Neilsen, "Good usability includes ideas like progressive disclosure where you show a small number of features to the less experienced user to lower the hurdle of getting started and yet have a larger number of features available for the expert to call up; Progressive Disclosure is the best tool so far: show people the basics first, and once they understand that, allow them to get to the expert features. But don't show everything all at once or you will only confuse people and they will waste endless time messing with features that they don't need yet."

Step #9: Production: Align and Adapt Opportunities Using Roadmapping

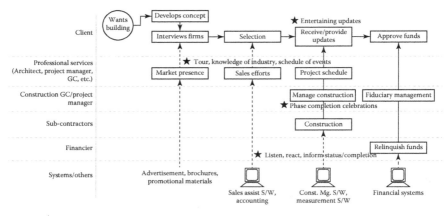

★ Example of roadmapping service opportunities to deliver the unexpected

Overview

Whether your innovation challenge is product, process, or business model oriented, business problems all benefit from a methodological analysis to separate experiential bias from business need. Continuous improvement methodologies such as Lean and Six Sigma (many more exist) enable

practitioners to refine their existing solutions, but do not offer an effective map for the management of novel and unconventional thinking.

As soon as the product is approved for shipment to the customer/consumer, the manufacturing floodgate is open. The documentation and estimates are put under stress to net the initial demands that occur at start-up. The information collection system is initialized and status reports are generated. We like the analogy of a horse race with eight people on horseback lined up in a paddock, full of energy and vigor, dancing, prancing, and jumping, much like Santa's reindeers – eager to get started. Horse No. 3 is so eager, it jumps forward and has to be pushed back into the paddock. Horse No. 2 is equally eager, and in an effort to constrain the horse, the jockey backs it up too far and it has to be led back into position. With the crack of the pistol, the doors are open wide and eight horses jump out, each trying to get ahead of the others. This is exactly the feeling you get when the floodgates are open to start shipping to external customers/consumers.

To manage an innovation process, the following must be defined and agreed upon:

- An output requirement statement between process owners and customers
- An input requirement statement between process owners and suppliers
- A process that can transform suppliers input into output that meets customers' performance and quality requirements
- Feedback measurement system between process and customer and between process and supplier
- The method by which people are trained to understand the process
- A measurement system within the process

You should address these key factors when designing a new innovation product/process; however, the problems facing most organizations are that many of their support processes were never well designed in the first place. They were created in response to a need without understanding what the process was. Also, the execution of business forms is persistently observed at different levels of item advancement, and changed over into an upward stream of data that empowers administration at each level to check whether choices are being taken afterward, keeping them informed of the aftereffects of any activities.

For most associations, this includes arranging over various timelines and clarifies why the arranging expectations are in some cases alluded to as timeline designs. The action may center around making arrangements for now or an operational arrangement for the coming year or a three-year mid-term plan. Nevertheless, governance of innovation is an all-encompassing procedure. You likewise need to extend your reasoning crosswise over more far off timelines to characterize transformational objectives that last for a long time.

Targets that keep going forward for a long time will change from one organization to another – for some clients it can be 3 years, and for others it can be 20 years. Yet, for the most part, it means asking what market openings they would like to address, what systems would address those issues, and what innovative processes should resources be placed on productivity. Innovative designs using JTBD can enable you to distinguish top-down, key methodologies and goals identifying with advertise openings and guarantee they target future benefits. The Strategyn's Universal Job Map* can be useful as shown next.

The universal job map

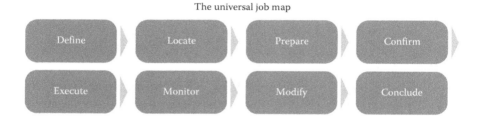

Cross-Functional *Roadmapping*

While many still feel that a systematic approach to innovation is impossible, innovation practitioners know how repeatable processes can be applied to achieve innovation objectives. A rapid innovation cycle provides a process for leading teams through the front end of the innovation journey.

The objective of the front end of innovation is to precisely identify the unmet customers' needs, identify the right ideas, and test them quickly and cheaply. On the other hand, the back end of innovation focuses on

---

* The *Strategyn Universal Job Map* uses the JTBD framework to deconstruct the job a customer is trying to get done. By working through the questions here, we can map a customer job in a handful of interviews with customers and internal experts. We start by understanding the execution step, to establish context and a frame of reference. Next, we examine each step before execution and then uncover the role each plays in getting the job done. To ensure that we are mapping job steps (what the customer is trying to accomplish) rather than process solutions (what is currently being done), we ask ourselves the validating questions in the map at each step. For more information: https://strategyn.com/customer-centered-innovation-map/.

perfecting the right idea identified through the front-end process. The key task during the back-end process is "design for X," where "X" stands for parameters such as performability, durability, reliability, manufacturability, robustness, environment, cost, serviceability, and maintainability. To be the best, an innovation roadmap is required at various layers of the business:

- Market guides that can help distinguish potential long-term breakthrough opportunities
- Roadmaps that separate you from others
- Roadmaps that are technical and assist you to get ready for long-haul opportunities

Progressive Disclosure Roadmapping

This is an interaction design technique that emerges from the insights gained during task analysis (user observation of tasks). Observing users in the field allows one to understand their workflow outside of specific technologies. This insight provides the necessary data required to prioritize and sequence content and functionality. Progressive disclosure can be validated by conducting task analysis (behavioral observation) with a user base. Observing users in their native problem-solving environment provides data about how they interact with the information.

Step #10: Tie Opportunities to Compensation and Markets

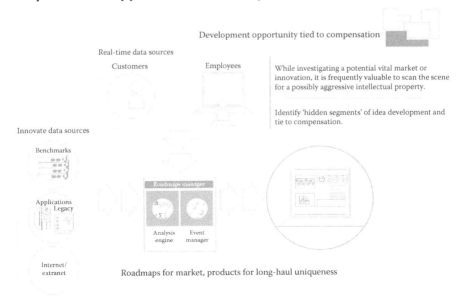

Development opportunity tied to compensation

Real-time data sources

Customers   Employees

While investigating a potential vital market or innovation, it is frequently valuable to scan the scene for a possibly aggressive intellectual property.

Innovate data sources

Identify 'hidden segments' of idea development and tie to compensation.

Benchmarks

Applications
Legacy

Roadmaps manager

Analysis   Event
engine   manager

Internet/
extranet   Roadmaps for market, products for long-haul uniqueness

Horizontal perspectives can assist business pioneers with stretching their reasoning past the present and spotlight on those market needs that speak to the best development chances without bounds, using the concepts of progressive disclosure* to tie to compensation and markets. Horizontal designs are best seen in roadmaps. To be the best, the arranging procedure requires that a roadmap is made at various layers of the business:

- Roadmap for market that can help distinguish potential future opportunities
- Roadmap concerning product that guarantees long-haul uniqueness
- Roadmap concerning technology that assists you to get ready for future innovation developments[†]

While investigating a potential vital market or innovation, it is valuable to scan the scene for a possibly aggressive IP. This enables an organization to decide if it is allowed to work specifically recognized territories of chance. Inquiries that ought to be thought about include:

1. What is the relative quality of our IP position against existing and potential rivals in this field?
2. What new patent filings, assuming any, have our rivals put out as of late? What is the substance of those licenses? Do they encroach on any territories our organization has been examining?
3. Are there fleixbility-to-work accommodations, that could be of an incentive to our company as well as ought to be explored further? Are there territories that we ought to put resources into now to ensure our opportunity to work against future rivalry?

---

* Progressive disclosure is the best tool so far: show people the basics first, and once they understand that, allow them to get to the expert features. But don't show everything all at once or you will only confuse people and they will waste endless time messing with features that they don't need yet.

† Nielsen, Jakob (2002-11-06). "Interview – Jakob Nielsen, PhD" Sitepoint. Retrieved 2006-11-24. "Jakob Nielsen Answers Usability Questions," Slashdot. Archived from the original on 2013-04-16. Retrieved 2006-11-24.

Step #11: Enable Sales Success Using Rapid Prototyping*

Sales success management, informed
decision-making, rapid prototyping

· HOW innovate™ process creates informed decisions and actions using rapid prototyping

· Results are the natural outcome of effective rapid ideation, utilizing data and structured analysis techniques.

· Once the system architecture has evolved, disparate datasets can be correlated to deliver better rapid prototyping and decision-making information.

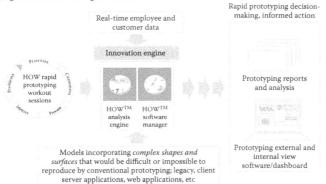

Real-time employee and customer data

Rapid prototyping decision-making, informed action

Innovation engine

HOW rapid prototyping workout sessions

Priorities

Customers

Problems

Metrics

Process

Prototyping reports and analysis

HOW™ analysis engine   HOW™ software manager

Models incorporating *complex shapes and surfaces* that would be difficult or impossible to reproduce by conventional prototyping; legacy, client server applications, web applications, etc

Prototyping external and internal view software/dashboard

We have entered a different world. Somehow the sales and marketing activities are a counterculture all of their own. In many cases, the personnel in sales and marketing are mostly motivated based on commissions rather than on their salaries or organizational stature.

During this activity, promotional and advertising campaigns are put in place with the accounting documentation. Sales strategy and two approaches are prepared and the motivational compensation packages are designed. This work started early in the project as the first checkpoint in the business case analysis. The sales and marketing groups are forced to be very innovative to survive. Usually, there is more innovation going on in sales and marketing than there is in product engineering.

There are many different types of sales channels that the sales organization needs to consider. Usually, as the organization increases its sales channel, this increases the total quantity of sales. The more sales channels involved usually means more sales. The following is a list of typical sales channels:

---

* Rapid prototyping is a modeling technique that can speed up and improve new product development. Manufacturers, component suppliers, and product designers use computer-aided design tools and rapid prototyping techniques such as three-dimensional printing or stereolithography to create physical scale models of products for analysis and production tooling. It helps create models incorporating complex shapes and surfaces that would be difficult or impossible to reproduce by conventional prototyping.

- *Personal selling*: Using a sales team to establish a network of customers to sell to.
- *Sales outsourcing*: Using a third party as a sales force.
- *Retail*: Selling through physical locations such as a shops, outlets, or showrooms.
- *Automated retail*: Automated retail such as self-service kiosks.
- *Ecommerce*: Selling through digital channels such as a website, app, or game.
- *Resellers*: Firms that purchase your products and services to resell them such as sellers on an ecommerce platform.
- *White label*: Another organization puts its name on your products or services.
- *Direct marketing*: Directly contacting prospective customers by telephone, mail, door-to-door, or digital communication tools such as email. This is the primary and past channel for startup companies.
- *Value-added resellers*: Firms that add something to your products and services to increase their value.
- *Original equipment manufacturer*: Parts suppliers selling to manufacturers of a finished product.
- *Wholesale*: Distributors that sell to retailers.
- *Import and export*: Distributors in a foreign market that import products to local distributors.
- *Agents*: Agents are intermediaries who are authorized to represent you in a transaction.

The innovator has to understand the differences between marketing* channels and sales channels in order to have a successful product at a reduced cost, which is another advantage of using rapid programming.[†] Rapid prototyping is an iterative process, so it is easy to incorporate individual customers' requirements and create customized products cost-effectively. Development teams do not have to design each customized

---

* In midsize to large organizations, marketing is one of the few places where professional innovators reside. The total responsibilities of an innovator come into play in developing an advertising or promotional campaign.

† Rapid prototyping helps to reduce the costs of product development and cost-of-sales. There is no need to develop special tools for each new product. Rapid prototyping uses the same CAD and printing equipment each time. The automated prototyping process also reduces staff costs. The costs of waste are lower, because the prototyping technique only adds modeling material where needed. Conventional prototyping techniques create waste through cut-off material or chippings as the tools create the finished model and sales prototypes.

product from scratch. Customization can provide a strong competitive advantage by offering customers greater choice and flexibility.

Disadvantages. Some people are of the opinion that rapid prototyping is not effective because it fails in the replication of the real product or system. It could happen that some important developmental steps could be omitted to get a quick and cheap working model. This can be one of the greatest disadvantages of rapid prototyping. Another disadvantage of rapid prototyping is one in which many problems are overlooked resulting in endless rectifications and revisions. One more disadvantage of rapid prototyping is that it may not be suitable for large-sized applications.

Step #12: After-Sales Service Using Best Practices

The following is a partial service diagram for the construction industry illustrating the relationship between the client and all areas responsible for delivering value. More detailed activity flows are developed as needed with the addition of management metrics and other data germane to efficiency and client value.

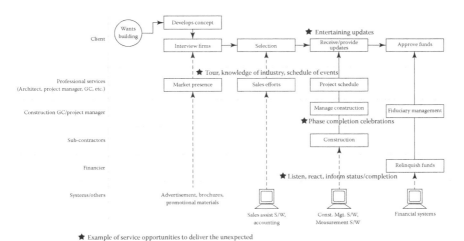

★ Example of service opportunities to deliver the unexpected

After-sales service can include free maintenance and repairs, a telephone *service* for dealing with customers' queries, and an express parts delivery *service*. An *after-sales service* is an important part of the marketing mix, serving to enhance customer loyalty and provide valuable feedback about its goods and *services*. During this activity, individuals are making repairs to the product, annexing consumers' questions, defining fields' stocking levels, defining potential customers, and determining which sales opportunity (conferences and or exhibits) sales should attend.

The call center responsiveness and knowledge level has a large impact upon customer's level of satisfaction with after-sales service. The dis-satisfaction level of the individual who is having problems with products and services as he contacts the call center personal increases one hundred fold each time they have to speak to a different individual. Empowerment in the control center personnel is one of the best investments an organization can make in order to promote customer loyalty.

After-sales service is an important part of the design criteria.

Step #13: Performance Analysis Using Best-Practice Methods

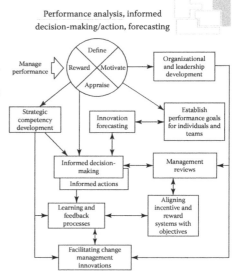

- HOW innovate uses proven success principles and powerful implementation tools that you can immediately apply to bring out the best in yourself, your team, and your organization.

- Managing innovation performance every day is the key to an effective innovation management system

- Good decisions are informed decisions, and along with effective and economical forecasting, are the building blocks of great business performance excellence.

Overview

During this activity, data is collected to determine if the actual results meet or exceed the commitments made at the business plan analysis stage. It is important that the measurement system used in the business plan analysis stage is the same as the equipment used for the performance analysis.

For processes, it is recommended that a pilot program be used to compare the before and after results. We have seen occasions where the improvement in the current process as a result of being part of the analysis was greater than the improvement that was proposed for the process.

It is not unusual for the current process to perform better than it had in the past if the employees realize it is part of a controlled experiment. The McKinsey Report on The Eight Essentials of Innovation Performance was based upon ongoing research and a current database of more than 300 companies containing survey results from over 2500 executives. This represented a full range of industry sectors, and demonstrated the measureable innovation performance improvement that can result when the Eight Essentials are rigorously put in place.*

- *Aspire*: Do you accept innovation-led growth as absolutely critical, and do you have cascaded targets that reflect this?
- *Choose*: Do you invest in a coherent, time–risk balanced portfolio of initiatives that are resourced to win?
- *Discover*: Do you have actionable and differentiated business, market, and technology insights that translate into winning value propositions?
- *Evolve*: Do you create new business models that provide defensible, robust, and scalable profit sources?
- *Accelerate*: Do you beat the competition with fast and effective development and launch of innovations?
- *Scale*: Do you launch innovations in the relevant markets and segments at the right magnitude?
- *Extend*: Do you win by creating and capitalizing on external networks?
- *Mobilize*: Are your people motivated, rewarded, and organized to repeatedly innovate?

---

* On page 1 of the report, the following statement was made: "When we set out several years ago to determine whether there really was a set of enhancements that all companies could make to dramatically improve one of the most notoriously difficult management activities, we were skeptical. To our surprise, both our experience working with companies and our quantitative research uncovered a set of practices that really do matter."

Also, a compelling solution for portfolio management enables organizations to expand on known prescribed best practices in measurements and the management of the portfolio while tweaking those measurements and reports to their own values and needs. The solution ought to contain the core details of best-practices measurements usually utilized as a part of apropos sectors. This thus lessens the measure of the time required to organize projects since significant, objective, and institutionalized factors are promptly accessible.

Portfolio management and resource planning are vital to take note of in this specific situation; solutions for product portfolio management enhance basic leadership for teams working on a project address task and asset planning, and not the definite administration timetables and conditions for the project.

- From the viewpoint of resource management, they guarantee that asset necessities are plainly imparted and enhance estimating by permitting better comprehension of expected resources requests.
- They help avoid bottlenecks before they emerge.
- From the viewpoint of reporting abilities, they give the allocation of resources required for the product portfolio – lastly, wanting to quantify limit and usage while recognizing trends in resources requirements that assist with addressing designated needs is crucial to innovation management.

Customary undertaking and asset administration instruments are likewise fundamental to the development procedure.* For more than 20 years, execution "structured and structure" (ESS) processes of product development – and most remarkably the stage-gate process – have been in use. On the off chance that they are suitably used, they enable organizations to take great steps toward enhancing the business effect of product improvement. One reason is that these procedures accentuate the significance of finishing the work required at the fluffy front end

---

* Nevertheless, they commonly work at a more granular level that is helpful to the necessities of the members of the team. A high state of focus is required for project undertakings, expectations, and assets asked for, so that groups can focus on the vital components of their working together as team members without losing all sense of direction in the points of interest.

with the goal that the correct items are supported using interaction design.*

The management of product portfolio and governance of innovative solutions ought to guarantee that front-end best practices are methodically connected. Particular examples of best practices include:

- Facilitating adherence to an association's organized improvement process
- Controlling the predictable utilization of process and deliverable formats
- Training group pioneers and individuals in compelling procedure execution
- Helping to update new team members as fast as possible under the circumstances

Best-practice process solutions suitable to look into the business effect of product development empowers organizations to more viable use of best practices by utilizing innovation to make it simpler to embrace an organized procedure. There are forms of stage-gate or potentially phase-gate that are appropriate for specific businesses. A reasonable solution guarantees process adherence by utilizing predefined models to set up every new undertaking and design of a new project. The procedures should be noticeable in a quick manner to see the projects that are in the pipeline and the progress they have made.†

---

* Interaction design, often abbreviated as IxD, is the practice of designing interactive digital products, environments, systems, and services. Beyond the digital aspect, interaction design is also useful when creating physical (non-digital) products, exploring how a user might interact with it. Common topics of interaction design include design, human–computer interaction, and software development. While interaction design has an interest in form (similar to other design fields), its main area of focus rests on behavior. Rather than analyzing how things are, interaction design synthesizes and imagines things as they could be. This element of interaction design is what characterizes IxD as a design field as opposed to a science or engineering field. See Cooper, A., Reimann, R., Cronin, D., *About Face 3: The Essentials of Interaction Design*, Wiley, Indianapolis, IN, p. 610, 2007. ISBN 978-0-470-08411-3.

† On page 12 of the McKinsey Report, the emphasis is put on needed resources. Dedicated innovation resources can act as a catalyst to mobilize the wider organization. Such dedicated resources might take the form of an innovation team at the business-unit level, tasked with framing opportunities and developing new value propositions based on market and customer insights. Alternatively, they might take the form of a corporate-level team responsible for driving innovations that span business units and assessing and building innovation-driven sourcing relationships.

Best-Practice Deliverables, Templates, and Metrics

The following are the top five ways that each of the stakeholders might measure:

- Management
  - Return on assets.
  - Value added per employee.
  - Stock prices.
  - Market share.
  - Reduced operating expenses.
- Investors
  - ROI.
  - Stock prices.
  - Return on assets.
  - Market share.
  - Successful new product.
- Customer
  - Reduce costs.
  - New or expanded capabilities.
  - Improved performance.
  - Ease of use.
  - Improvement responsiveness.
- Suppliers
  - Increase ROI for the supplier.
  - Improved communications/fewer interfaces.
  - Simple selling requirements/fewer changes.
  - Longer contracts.
  - Longer cycle times.
- Employees
  - Increased job security.
  - Increased compensation.
  - Improved growth potential.
  - Improved job satisfaction.
  - Improved morale.
- Employee's families
  - Less time at work.
  - Increased job security.
  - Increased salary.

- Improved benefits.
  - Improved working conditions (safety).
- Community/mankind
  - Employment of more people.
  - Increased tax base.
  - Reduced pollution.
  - Support of community activities.

In evaluating the value added, you need to look at each of the stakeholders five most important factors in determining if the proposed change will have a negative or positive impact upon each stakeholder. A good innovative solution will have a positive impact on a minimum of two or more stakeholders than it has a negative impact on. What's more, the governance of innovative solutions improves the nature of the execution of projects by giving best-practices formats and substance, for example, how to use a layout as the best method to execute a specific task concerning a project. These formats identify the contribution of the diverse sectors (R&D, production network, marketing, procurement, IP, security, environment, health, and so on).

They might be straightforward Microsoft Word archives, spreadsheets, or scorecards. The learning of the front office, for example, ought to be spoken to in the structure of the money-related examples and context. The planners of this record must guarantee that the proper measurements are being entered and computed. Since knowledge is acquired amid the development procedure and made accessible electronically (as opposed to recorded in a three-ring folio), the solution helps to reduce the time and to prepare costs by making learning instruments accessible on a "just-in-time" basis. This enables users to rapidly comprehend information about an emerging task.

About Progressive Disclosure

Progressive disclosure is a technique for managing information complexity. When you use progressive disclosure, you show only the information necessary at that point in the interaction. And you display more advanced functionalities of the app interface, as the user interacts with it.

It is a simple, yet powerful design pattern where the designer (a) initially shows users only a few of the most important options and (b) discloses a larger set of specialized options only if a user asks for them.

To design a good progressive disclosure, you need to learn about your users, involve them in the design process, and interact with them. Progressive disclosure means that everything in the user interface should progress naturally, from simple to complex. This mimics the natural way the brain processes information, successively; we build upon each subsequent step of experience and learning, adding to what we know. In terms of the app, site, or system we're designing, this means only the *necessary or requested information* is displayed at any given time.

Put another way, we only want what we need *right now*. We only need enough to take the very next action; we only need what we've asked for. Information presented to someone who isn't interested in it – or isn't ready to process it – is *noise; it's background stuff; it's not what we want; it's in the way, and it's distracting to us.*

For example, take your Facebook Feed: Your Facebook feed is filled with a potentially overwhelming amount of content – and it's multiplying every few seconds! But Facebook is designed specifically with progressive disclosure in mind, using multiple methods to help you manage the volume of stuff you see.

1. Facebook automatically truncates long posts with a "see more" link after a few paragraphs. This allows you to read a quick snippet and decide if you're interested enough to read more.
2. When you post a link to an article, Facebook includes a "preview" of the content to come, consisting of a headline and image. Again, this allows for quick evaluation as to whether it's worth your time or not. So, if the end result is a blog post, you get a quick look before you click or tap.
3. As you scroll, Facebook loads more posts – essentially obeying your request for more. Nothing loads until you ask for it, which, incidentally, also makes pages load a LOT faster, which, in turn, improves the user experience. In addition, when you search, it loads the first 10 matches, and gives you the option to see more, if you so choose.

Or your Bank ATM: The first screen shows only the most important options, in the order a user is most likely to need them. Notice that the first three options are the most commonly used: withdrawal, deposit, and balance inquiry. And while there are a number of other, less commonly used options, they're all tucked away behind the "additional options" button.

All of these examples demonstrate three core principles of progressive disclosure that can (and *should*) be applied to any kind of digital product:

1. Show only the *most important options* up front.
2. *Prioritize* those options according to user needs and expectations.
3. Offer a larger set of specialized options *on request*; disclose additional features/info *only* if the user *asks* for them or *needs* them.

Consciously applying these principles when you design is what delivers the simplicity and ease of use we all crave. When you help people prioritize content and interaction in this way, you're also helping them use their cognitive abilities more efficiently. Focus is maintained, distractions are removed.

Step #14: Portfolio Management and Transition

Data plays an integral part of portfolio management and needs to be available, presented logically, and flexible to accommodate changes in internal and external conditions.

Value is realized by building/buying the system for portfolio management and incorporating analysis tools for general use.

The data schema presented implies a functional understanding of the types of data, rudimentary analysis techniques, and management commitment to use data for decision-making.

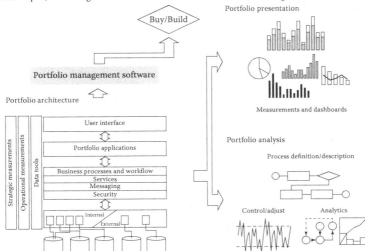

Portfolio management is at the core of the governance of product innovation development, and remains central to doing the correct innovation ventures and initiatives. In particular, the monitoring part of portfolio administration enables an organization to see whether it is doing the JTBD right. Typical portfolio management challenges include the following: legitimately estimating exercises, successfully overseeing ventures with accessible assets, and growing all-around characterized portfolio choice criteria, giving access to exact target data upon which to base choices.

Usually, the project team is disbanded after Step 11 is complete but that's only the beginning of the project story. The real test of the project occurs over the next year or two. With time and experience, the following three conditions can occur:

1. The pearl approach was successful and became part of the organization's culture and habit patterns.
2. The approach needs to be modified to make it usable.
3. The approach is not accepted by the employees as it reverts back to their old process and habit patterns.

People perform better when they are getting special attention. The Innovation Process reverts back to every-day rhythms unless the new process is significantly better and easier to perform. Thus, employees tend to drift back to the original process. This is one of the reasons you want to have a good process measurement system in place before the project management team turns the responsibility for the process over to the manufacturing manager.

An ideas development management process should make it simple to drive high-value ideas to the execution phases of the development of products, and quickly abandon those that are losers.*

---

* Boo.com is one good anecdote. They wasted millions of dollars on a fancy design that they had to retract shortly after the launch because nobody could use it. Even on a fashion site, people care more about the products than about the bleeding edge design. Also, the web itself is one big anecdote. *What all the big sites have in common is minimalist design.* We made a very simple analysis of the *usability of the 10 sites with the most traffic* compared to the sites from the 10 biggest companies (which would have had an inherent advantage if they had been more usable). The result was very clear: The 10 biggest sites had much better usability scores than the sites built by huge corporations. For example, the download time for the home page was eight seconds for the big sites and 19 seconds for the big companies. What happens is very simple: the good sites win. If the pages download fast, people return. If they can find the products, then they can buy the products. If people understand the site, they use it.

Top-Down Portfolio Management

The Aberdeen Group has recognized various key systems for enhancing the management of a product portfolio:

- Aligning portfolio to corporate procedure
- Establishing a repeatable item development process
- Formalizing system appraisal process
- Defining a reasonable proprietor of procedures and portfolio audits

With regard to guaranteeing strategies among procedures and portfolios, the management of a portfolio can be of great help. For instance, they can pull vital guide and task information into a solitary database store. Officials would then be able to utilize this incorporated information to create a variety of reports that take into account complex investigations on changing levels of detail.

Such best-known perspectives empower executives to adjust spending to key targets and to amplify the estimation of portfolios by guaranteeing early identification of good and bad innovative ideas.*

Bottom-Up Portfolio Monitoring

To have access to credible, progressive information on developmental product projects, an organization should first set up a repeatable development process. Figure 8.3 demonstrates the business process that produces the data required for the production of better perspectives on portfolios. These perspectives empower administrators to screen the status of numerous tasks. They additionally encourage more knowledgeable and better portfolio choices.

The greater part of the business process with respect to innovation governance requires cross-utilitarian information (e.g., promoting data and administrative information). A practical process for portfolio

---

* According to Jakob Neilsen, he believes in an alternative interpretation of the data, which is that the various approaches to designing better Unix interfaces were doomed because they always kept reinventing the same thing again and again. They never did the two things that are necessary for great user interface: (1) Don't just reimplement something that had a different design center (the Mac that was designed for a small black-and-white screen, 1MB RAM, and a puny 68000 processor); and (2) iterate. Your first design will be a flop (say, Xerox Star or Apple Lisa). "You gotta keep improving rather than giving up as the Unix vendors have done." Source: https://slashdot.org/story/00/03/03/096223/jakob-nielsen-answers-usability-questions.

management gives instant best-practice formats that bolster the analysis of both the task and value of the portfolio. A viable portfolio management framework additionally imparts venture status continuously, enabling officials to track risky projects, comprehend plan delays, recognize basic choices, and make strategic moves to advance results.*

Best-Practice Portfolio Reports

As previously mentioned in the governance of innovation solutions, there needs to be a proper arrangement of reports that reflects best-practice data prerequisites:

- Pipeline reports should demonstrate the status of all activities.
- Portfolio investigation reports should demonstrate whether ventures are lined up with procedure, convey adequate system support with incremental and breakout advancement and are an adjustment of here and now and long haul, expansive, and little, incremental and breakout advancement.
- Process execution graphs should demonstrate whether there is an adequate volume of ideas, regardless of whether the ideas and ventures in each stage give a palatable return on investment.

By and large, item development apparatuses should consolidate a suitable master file of procedures, expectations, information and measurements, and portfolio reports, as seen in Figure 8.3. Arranging and collaborating effective basic leadership is additionally basic in the strategic procedures of venture arranging, asset arranging, and coordinated effort. In this specific situation, great decisions result in doing the project

---

* We do need more attention to the productivity of expert users. All the same methods apply for how to study and measure interfaces, no matter what their interaction style, but I admit that there is not much work these days on keyboard interfaces. How to smooth the curve from novice to expert? Nobody has found the way yet. Cue cards, boot-up tips, and the little annoying paper clip are all attempts, but nothing works really well. *Progressive disclosure* is the best tool so far: it shows people the basics first, and once they understand them, it allows them to get to the expert features. But don't show everything all at once or you will only confuse people, and they will waste endless time messing with features that they don't need yet. Interestingly, research by Jack Carroll at IBM in the 1980s proved that a "training wheels" approach to computers makes people better at understanding the expert features once they get to them; the reason being that users learn the conceptual structure of the system better when they are presented with the smaller set of features first. In other words, not seeing something during initial use of the system would result in better use of the hidden features later.

right. Product innovation management should in this way offer the accompanying abilities:

- Tracking of the project using simple access to status and detailed data. This maintains a strategic distance from "surprises," for example, ventures coming in late or over spending on the plan.
- Clear task of expectations and undertakings by methods for a typical "team profile" that permits team members to see obligations, and also open and finished activities.
- Easy area of current records; data ought not to be arranged on different detached, floppy drives, but rather shared inside the task. Ability to work together adequately crosswise over departments and locations.
- Simple sharing and correspondence with other innovation development experts.
- Integrate business modeling and interaction design.
- Use *progressive disclosure* methods to help maintain user's attention.*

Epilogue

The new material is no longer in a blue-collar worker, a financer, or a manager, but the innovator who combines imagination and knowledge into action. In addition to the health of the organization, the health, development, and self-actuation of people are promoted immeasurably by the creativity and the innovation process.

Alvin Toffler
page 168 creative toolkit

Most business leaders are recognizing the value of innovation. In a recent study from consulting firm Accenture,[†] 96% of executives surveyed said that their organization's long-term success depends on developing new ideas to

---

* Progressive disclosure is an interaction design technique that sequences information and actions across several scenarios in order to reduce feelings of being overwhelmed for the user. By disclosing information progressively, you reveal only the essentials and help the user manage the complexity of feature-rich sites or applications. Progressive disclosure follows the typical notion of moving from "abstract to specific"; only it may mean sequencing interactions and not necessarily level of detail (information). In other words, progressive disclosure is not just about displaying abstract then specific information, but rather about "ramping up" the user from simple to more complex actions.

† https://www.accenture.com/us-en/insight-innovation-survey-clear-vision-cloudy-execution.

open new windows. In addition, 87% of leaders believed their companies' innovation resulted in a good ROI; however, 82% of respondents didn't make a meaningful distinction between significant innovation and achieving incremental performance gains.

Why are businesses unsuccessful with innovation? Accenture notes that 72% of companies allow innovations to languish because there is no formalized process or organizational home for such initiatives. And, according to an exploratory study of more than 30 companies in the United States and Europe, researchers found that companies generally lack a process to guide innovation. Innovation is a process and as such can be managed to improve its efficiency, effectiveness, and adaptability. Too often, innovation and creativity are assumed to be the same thing. Creating a new and unique idea, product, or process is a small part of the innovative process. If you limit your innovation concepts to developing a solution to a problem or a means to take advantage of an opportunity, then you're only looking at less than 10% of the total innovation process.

The belief among US executives that innovation is a critical tool for growth and market differentiation is stronger than ever. Accenture research carried out in 2015–2017 – the third in a series of surveys first conducted in 2009 and again in 2012 – confirms that today's companies are increasingly embracing innovation as a tool to drive their businesses forward over the long term. According to the latest Accenture survey, they need to focus on the complex challenge of making it successful. The discipline of innovation is maturing and key principles – such as two-speed innovation and collaborative innovation described in this chapter – are emerging to help companies achieve a competitive edge.

Innovation and its governance is all about innovative product development that relies upon the activities of inventive people within an organization. Enhancing the business advantages of innovation is linked to expanding the ability of an organization to settle on successful choices throughout the innovative product and/or service development process. Compelling decision-making offers various advantages:

- Process execution is lined up with systems to develop worth and expand individual share of the market.
- Those engaged with innovative product can choose and prioritize the best.

- Management can abstain from squandering valuable, innovative assets on product ideas that are bound to disappoint.
- Innovators can follow development forms effectively, which enhance marketing capacity.

Knowing the end goal to accomplish these advantages, decision-making should be bolstered by effective, organized procedures that create the vital information without frustrating the creativity of those occupied with the development of the product innovation.* Also, processes of innovation management must enhance the data flow on which indispensable business choices are based, while at the same time empowering and implementing innovations that are beneficial. Our guiding principle for innovation is the experience gained from over 100 clients that executing and enhancing innovation governance can bring about substantial and quantifiable benefits to the business†:

- 75%–85% achievement rate of new product development contrasted with 50% verifiably
- Higher innovation throughput of 15%–30%
- Higher estimation of product portfolios of 75%–100%

Above all, an innovation process governance system that is viable will position your products and services for long-term success, which will then lead to the development of new offerings with a beneficial revenue generation increase. *However, most companies do not have the execution capabilities and processes they need to achieve their innovation goals.* Why are companies' stated intentions to pursue big innovations not materializing? It's not due to a lack of enthusiasm, confidence, or investments in formalized programs. *It is due, rather, to how they innovate.*

---

* Some experts like Nielsen feel that there are two big paradigm shifts coming: *Augmented Reality* and *Content-and Time-based Computing*. Augmented Reality is the ability to project a user interface onto the physical world. For example, when repairing an airplane engine, a trainee mechanic can see an animated hand grab exactly in the right spot. And read-outs from various diagnostics will display in the context of the thing they are diagnosing rather than on a separate device. Lots of other ideas in this realm, including wearable computing, smart clothes, etc. Source: https://slashdot.org/story/00/03/03/096223/jakob-nielsen-answers-usability-questions.

† According to Jakob Neilsen, it is pretty standard for big computer companies to get as many patents as they can for basic reasons of self-defense: if somebody tries to come after you then you can fight back with your own patents. That usually does not mean that the company wants to go after smaller companies unless they attack first. See https://slashdot.org/story/00/03/03/096223/jakob-nielsen-answers-usability-questions.

Our studies found that over 80% of respondents do not distinguish how they innovate from how they go about achieving incremental performance gains.

   Successful innovation requires new thinking, new collaboration models, and new approaches to execution. While many companies are creating the building blocks of successful innovation, few have assembled those foundational elements in a way that drives the change – and generates the investment returns. To get more from their innovation programs, *companies need to fundamentally change how they approach innovation* and *HOW they execute* their innovation initiatives.

BIBLIOGRAPHY

Bolter, J. D., & Gromala, D. (2008). *Windows and Mirrors: Interaction Design, Digital Art, and the Myth of Transparency*. Cambridge, MA: MIT Press. ISBN 0-262-02545-0.

Buchenau, M., & Suri, J. F. *Experience Prototyping*. DIS 2000. ISBN 1-58113-219-0.

Buxton, B. (2005). *Sketching the User Experience*. San Francisco, CA: New Riders Press. ISBN 0-321-34475-8.

Cooper, A. (1999). *The Inmates are Running the Asylum*. Indianapolis, IN: Sams. ISBN 0672316498.

Cooper, A., Reimann, R., Cronin, D., & Noessel, C. (2014). *About Face* (4th ed.). Indianapolis, IN: Wiley. ISBN 9781118766576.

Dawes, B. (2007). *Analog In, Digital Out*. Berkeley, CA: New Riders Press.

Dix, A., Finlay, J., Abowd, G. D., & Beale, R. (2004). *Human–Computer Interaction* (3rd ed.). Harlow: Pearson Education Limited. p. 324.

Gerhardt-Powals, J. (1996). Cognitive engineering principles for enhancing human-computer performance. *International Journal of Human-Computer Interaction*, 8(2), 189–221.

Hvannberg, E., Law, E., & Lárusdóttir, M. (2007). Heuristic evaluation: Comparing ways of finding and reporting usability problems. *Interacting with Computers*, 19(2), 225–240.

Nielsen, J., & Mack, R. L. (eds) (1994). *Usability Inspection Methods*. New York: John Wiley & Sons Inc.

Goodwin, K. (2009). *Designing for the Digital Age: How to Create Human-Centered Products and Services*. Indianapolis, IN: Wiley. ISBN 978-0-470-22910-1.

Houde, S., & Hill, C. (1997). What do prototypes prototype?. In Helander, M., Landauer, T., & Prabhu, P. *Handbook of Human–Computer Interaction* (2nd ed.). Amesterdam, Holland: Elsevier Science.

Jones, M., & Marsden, G. (2006). *Mobile Interaction Design*. Chichester: John Wiley & Sons. ISBN 0-470-09089-8.

Kolko, J. (2009). *Thoughts on Interaction Design*. New York, NY: Morgan Kauffman. ISBN 978-0-12-378624-1.

Laurel, B., & Lunenfeld, P. (2003). *Design Research: Methods and Perspectives*. Cambridge: MIT Press. ISBN 0-262-12263-4.

Tinauli, M., & Pillan, M. (2008). Interaction design and experiential factors: A novel case study on digital pen and paper. In *Mobility '08: Proceedings of the International Conference on Mobile Technology, Applications, and Systems*. New York: ACM. doi:10.1145/1506270.1506400, ISBN 978-1-60558-089-0.

Norman, D. (1988). *The Design of Everyday Things*. New York: Basic Books. ISBN 978-0-465-06710-7.

Raskin, J. (2000). *The Humane Interface*. New York: ACM Press. ISBN 0-201-37937-6.

Saffer, D. (2006). *Designing for Interaction*. Berkeley, CA: New Riders Press. ISBN 0-321-43206-1.

Anthony, R. N., & Day, J. S. (1952). *Management Controls in Industrial Research Organizations*. Harvard University, Boston.

Berkhout, A. J., Hartmann, D., van der Duin, P., & Ortt, R. (2006). Innovating the innovation process. *International Journal of Technology Management*, 34(3/4), 390–404.

Bernal, J. D. (1973). *The Social Function of Science*. Reprint. MIT Press, Cambridge, MA.

Brokel, T., & Binder, M. (2007). The regional dimension of knowledge transfers – A behavioral approach. *Industry and Innovation*. 14(2), 151–175.

Chesbrough, H. (2006). *Open Innovation: The New Imperative for Creating and Profiting from Technology*. Harvard Business Press, Boston, MA.

Cooper, R. G. (1990). Stage-gate systems: A new tool for managing new products. *Business Horizons*, (5/6), 44–54.

Drucker, P. F. (2008). *Management Revised*. Harper Business, New York.

Dyatlov, S. A. (2012). Global innovation hypercompetition as a factor of transformation and development of economic systems. *Theoretical Economy*, 6, 39–54.

Florida, R. (2003). *The Rise of the Creative Class*. Basic Books, New York.

Godin, B. (2006). The linear model of innovation. The historical construction of an analytical framework. *Science, Technology, & Human Values*, 31(6), 639–667.

Gomory, R. (1989). From the ladder of science to the product development cycle. *Harvard Business Review*.

Graves, A. (1987). Comparative trends in automotive research and development, DRC Discussion Paper No. 54, Sussex University, Brighton, Sussex.

Hein, L., & Andreasen, M. (2000). *Integrated Product Development*. IPU, Lyngby.

Huxley, J. S. (1934). *Scientific Research and Social Needs*. Watts and Co., London.

Imai, K., Nonaka, I., & Fakeuchi, H. (1985). Managing the new product development. In Clark, K. and Hayes, F. (Eds), *The Uneasy Alliance*. Harvard Business School Press, Boston, MA.

Isaksen, A. Building regional innovation systems: Is endogenous industrial development possible in the global economy? *Canadian Journal of Regional Science*. 24.

Janszen, F. (2000). *The Age of Innovation*. Financial Times Prentice Hall.

Kline, S., & Rosenberg, N. (1986). An overview of innovation. In Landau, R. and Rosenberg, N. (Eds). *The Positive Sum Strategy: Harnessing Technology for Economic Growth*. National Academy of Sciences, Washington, DC. 275–306.

Kodama, F. Technology Fusion and the New R&D. [Online]. Available: http://hbr.org/1992/07/technology-fusion-and-the-new-rd/ar/1

Kodama, F. (1995). *Emerging Patterns of Innovation: Source of Japan Technological Edge*. Harvard Business School Press, Boston, MA.

Lall, S. (2001). *Competitiveness, Technology and Skills*. Edward Elgar, Cheltenham.

Mahdjoubi, D. (1997). The linear model of technological innovation: background and taxonomy. [Online]. Available: https://www.ischool.utexas.edu/~darius/04-Linear

Murray, A., & Hanlon, P. (2010). An investigation into the stickiness of tacit knowledge transfer. In *13th Annual Conference of the Irish Academy of Management*, Cork Institute of Technology, 1–3 September, 2010.

Rothwell, R. (1994). Towards the fifth-generation innovation process. *International Marketing Review*, 11(7), 7–31.

Schumpeter, J. (1939). *Business Cycles: A Theoretical, Historical, and Statistical Analysis of the Capitalist Process*. McGraw-Hill, New York.

Szulanski, G. (1996). Exploring internal stickiness: Impediments to the transfer of best practice within the firm. *Strategic Management Journal*, 17, 27–43.

Tidd. J., Bessant, J., & Pavitt, K. (2005). *Managing Innovation: Integrating Technological, Market and Organizational Change*. Wiley, London.

Van De Ven, A. H., Polley, D. E., Garud, R., & Venkataraman, S., (1999). *The Innovation Journey*. Administrative Science Quarterly. Oxford University Press, Buckingham.

Wheelwright, S. C., & Clark K. B. (1992). *Revolutionizing Product Development: Quantum Leaps in Speed, Efficiency and Quality*. The Free Press, New York.

Ziman, H. (1991). A neural model of innovation. *Science and Public Policy*, 18(1), 65–75.

Žižlavsky, O. (2013). Past, present and future of the innovation process. *International Journal of Engineering Business Management*, 5(47), 1–8. [Online]. Available: http://cdn.intechopen.com/pdfs-wm/45701.pdf.

9

Innovation and Consumer/Customer Insight

The practice of innovation is the specific tool of entrepreneurship, the means by which they exploit change as an opportunity for different business or a different service. It is capable of being presented as a discipline, capable of being learned, capable of being practiced. Entrepreneurs need to search insightfully (with customers) for the sources of innovation, the changes and their symptoms that indicate opportunities for successful innovation. And they need to know and to apply the principles of successful innovation

Drucker
1985 (p. 19)

In a nutshell: Most organizations that are creating an Innovation Infrastructure would like to see themselves as consumer-driven and aspire to create products, services, and solutions that are grounded in consumer needs. In reality, organizations often have scant understanding of consumers' deep-seated behaviors, perceptions, and needs. Companies that are product inclined, could profit significantly from taking a more customer-based approach; however, this is frequently inconsistent with the association's social standards, particularly if the technologists hold the energy of the association's development foundation.

KEY LEARNINGS FROM DRUCKER

The strategies in this chapter will help you

1. Upgrade your current Innovation Infrastructure to accommodate the needs of the digital world
2. Reduce cost and time associated with delivery of insights
3. Increase data quality without adding cost
4. Build the relevance of innovation-based market research within your organization
5. Connect insights data to other areas of your business

OVERVIEW

Customer Insight is a subjective, "base up" approach that implements experiences into practices, observations, and requirements of present and potential buyers/clients by including them as obvious accomplices in the innovative procedure. Customer Insight calls for a non-customary, creative way to deal with requirements that looks for a profound comprehension of customer needs and wants, along with active researchers operating at a level well past what the buyers/clients could hope to express themselves.

While it is important to include traditional consumer data in the innovation process, many organizations are uncomfortable experimenting with approaches they see as less black and white. Customer contributions to the improvement of products regularly involves conventions and gatherings, boards, or online studies. These often are limited to requesting a client reaction to the company's products that are internally produced, including inclinations, bundling or promotions.

While validating ideas with consumers is essential, limiting consumer interactions to feedback gathering is a missed opportunity. The Strategic Innovation approach uses conventional consumer forums (focus groups, interviews, panels, etc.) in far more imaginative ways. The goal of this "exploratory" consumer work is to spark fresh thinking about future possibilities that then translate into a growth strategy and new product categories, and so on. Exploring different avenues regarding non-traditional strategies new to industry contenders will help increase further knowledge and recognize creative ideas that have a more noteworthy level of "complete reverberation" with buyers.*

Similarly, numerous purchaser inquiries about projects are content with hearing what clients really say, yet don't investigate the prolific ground of their unstated (inactive) needs. The "Voice of the Consumer" has turned into a standard piece in the toolbox of advertisers and scientists in most enterprises; however, innovation tools capturing the voice of the customer are widespread and generally clear. Furthermore, since competitors are doing this as well, it provides very little in the way of a competitive edge. Furthermore, since competitors are doing it too, this provides little in the way of a competitive edge.

Ethnographic research practices are increasingly prominent – more so in some industries than in others – but they have been slow to gain acceptance. If conducted poorly, the output may be highly ambiguous, and the implications may not be very clear. Despite the opportunity ethnographic research offers for breakthrough insights, many enterprises are reluctant to consider it as a viable approach. Customers' investment in corporate technique improvements is for all intents and purposes incomprehensible. There is enormous potential in including clients (and providers and other outside partners.) as obvious partners in development procedures by integrating Consumer Insights into an innovative approach.

There are many challenges and inefficiencies in the market research industry that affect many businesses and compromise the sector's reputation.

The Relevance of Market Research

In the United States, $20bn is spent per year on market research. Much of this spending comes from brands that want to understand how they are perceived, what makes customers tick, and what products customers likely want and want to buy, as they create their innovation infrastructure. Market research safeguards the $206bn that brands subsequently spend on advertising.

---

* Customer data is usually fragmented across systems. Use an integrated customer relationship management (CRM)-type system data to unify these fragments into complete identities, so you can communicate seamlessly with your customers across various channels. Entrepreneurs need to transform data fragments into customer intelligence by turning any email, phone number, Twitter handle or domain into a full person or company profile.

The figure for US advertising spending in 2017 is $206bn (Source: eMarketer), for US market research spending in 2016 it is $206 bn (Source: eMarketer).

However, with very public mishaps like the failure to predict the US election and Brexit, data quality has been called into question. It is important that we tackle the elephant in the room and address the fact that traditional ways of conducting research are no longer adequate. The 20–30-minute survey is a perfect example.

Respondents may be representative of an age, gender, and location perspective, but are they really representative of the feelings, attitudes, and lifestyles of the audience we'd like to engage? If you had to make an important decision, such as which bank you should take out a loan with, would you trust the opinion of someone that did desktop surveys all day? Probably not!!

The Hyper-Connected Consumer*

Today's consumer is hyper-connected, time-poor, and overstimulated.

The average American spends 10 hours per day looking at a screen*, this makes engaging with them incredibly complex. The *Salesforce State of the Connected Consumer Report 2017*, which studied 7000+ consumers and business buyers, states, "today's customers expect companies to quickly innovate in accordance with their changing preferences – otherwise they'll simply switch brands." Millennials and Gen Z add a further layer of complexity; they completely disrupt how media and products are normally consumed and bought, leaving marketers unsure of how to engage with them.

---

* Consumer Respondents may be representative from an age, gender and location perspective.

SPEED OF DELIVERY IS IMPORTANT (AND SLOW)

Define problem with stakeholder — 1 day	Establish research objectives — 1 day	Brief research agency/ies — 1 day	Agency research design and proposal preparation — 4 days
Evaluate research designs and approve proposal — 1 day	Questionnaire design — 1 day	Survey programming — 2 days	Fieldwork — 3 days
Data processing — 1 day	Data analysis — 1 day	Report writing — 3 days	Presentation — 1 day

A typical project could take one month to conduct, may involve many parties, and it usually takes even more time before any insight is acted on by your organization's relevant team. If that insight happens to be that your brand sentiment decreased by 10%, you will need to obtain that data as close to real time as possible in order to take action.

The *GRIT Report Q1-Q2 2017* states that "insights buyers and research providers are equally pessimistic about the future of sample quality, with far more believing that quality will erode in the next three years*."

The search for higher quality data can often result in higher costs. The good news is that the *GRIT Report* also showed that 45% of North American research budgets have increased. Even so, it can still be difficult to shift from the traditional way of doing something when a higher cost needs to be justified.

We have identified some of the industry's weak spots and can now start to look at solutions to overcome them. To upgrade your Innovation Infrastructure/program, here are some key implementable strategies:

Optimize the Respondent Experience and Connect with Engaged Consumers

The consumer now engages across many different devices throughout different times of the day. Consider how you can engage with them in the right environment at the right time. Optimize the Respondent Experience and Connect with Engaged Consumers "Almost 41 million US web clients went online exclusively by means of mobile phones in 2017. As web clients move toward depending on such gadgets, there will be an increase to about 53.2 million by 2021, of mobile online customers."

Ask yourself

A Kiss Metrics study revealed that "*47% of consumers expect a web page to load in 2 seconds or less.*" Think of the sample you are losing out on by not addressing these items.

Automate Your Repetitive Data-Gathering Work

Look for repeatable areas in your data-gathering processes. What processes follow the same or similar formats each time?

Ask yourself

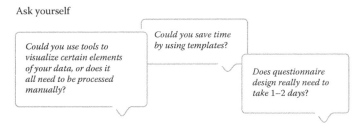

Build First-Party Data

Consider survey- and online-based data as your first-party data. Would you discard email addresses or other information from customers? Of course not, because this data is highly valuable. If your survey data does not get fed into a centralized data warehouse, you are throwing money away.

Often, researchers run a campaign to solve a particular problem. They solve that problem and then move on, leaving the data behind, while not creating longitudinal insights and not making an asset of the data. Companies with offices in numerous locations without a central data repository that can be accessed by all users are particularly prone to inefficiency. Properly stored and visualized, survey data can be revisited for additional questions, synced to customer records and online-based cookie data, and easily shared across the organization.

Each time an individual is surveyed or more data is synced to their profile, you will be able to watch for a shift in their behavior and gain very detailed insights on that user. Taking a look at the subsequent example, you can dive deep to find more information on why an individual's brand preference or purchase behavior has shifted over time.

Link Data and Insights to Other Areas of Your Business

Now that you have built your first-party data set, start linking this to other areas of your business, like advertising. If you have captured a cookie or device ID and matched that to a survey respondent, your marketing or media team can then target that individual with digital advertising. Upon serving them an advertising campaign, your marketing team can track further behaviors of that prospect and see if they convert into a customer. In addition, the insights team can survey that person a few days after they have seen your advertisements and ask them whether, as per the subsequent example, they went on to purchase your product, closing the loop between insights and marketing return on investment (ROI). Let's consider the following consumer for instance.

We know that this person's behavior has changed, and that they have not shopped for pet food in some time, nor do they have a brand preference. By feeding that information to our marketing team, we have a new prospect for them to target.

Step #1: Take a survey respondent and target them with digital advertising.

Step #2: After they see your advertisement, further profile that respondent with follow-up questions.

Forget insights being something that take a month to generate. Data can be in real time and you can start seeing customer and brand metrics alongside sales and market-share data immediately.

Append Other Data Sets

Now that you have a first-party data asset, you are going to store a lot of information on respondents, but you are also going to have gaps in your data sets. These gaps can be mitigated by looking at other data sets available to you that can be appended to your data. If we use the same sample customer as previously mentioned, you may already have data coming in from other areas of your organization that you can append, or you can partner with other providers who will allow you to syndicate their profile data.

Appending this additional data increases your understanding of the individual and helps you to reduce the number of questions you need to ask them as you already have data on their preferences. This can lead to a much higher percentage of your sample data set being eligible for individual studies (incidence rate), lower length of an interview (LOI), and lower cost per interview (CPI).

> Useful data sets to seek out and append include:
>
> 1. Profile data syndicated from a panel provider
>
> 2. Online behavioral data in the form of cookies and device IDs
>
> 3. Interactions with your websites
>
> 4. Customer data syndicated from non-competing businesses

Remove Operational Silos

Living in a data-driven world affords many benefits to an organization; however, the thing that many businesses get wrong is that they look at data in silos. It is very likely that you already have some great data flowing into your business that could be leveraged by the insights team.

Some examples include

- Your media agency could be sending through competitive reporting
- Your search agency could be sending through online customer journey and sales attribution data
- Your social agency could be sending insights on what people are saying about you

A Forbes study showed that data-driven marketing* produces the following forms of data. Assess which of these data sets would benefit

---

* Customer Insights Marketing is more meaningful, effective, and rewarding for all parties – entrepreneurs, marketers, customers, and prospects – when it's backed by data-driven insights. Data-driven marketing capabilities from Equifax deliver powerfully precise insights about your top-performing customers, their household economics, and ultimately, their needs and preferences. When you understand these things, you can speak their language, get their attention, and engage them with a more personalized experience that helps you win their business and deepen the relationship; grow customer value for clients through unique data, actionable insights and marketing precision.

you and find out where they live in your organization. Automatically send them to your team, centralize the data, or sync them into your own reporting dashboards wherever possible.

Type of data being collected for data-driven marketing initiatives being

Source: Forbes information and insights: Data driven and digitaly savvy: The rise of the new marketing organization,January 2015

*Some key takeaways to upgrade your insights program for the digital world:**

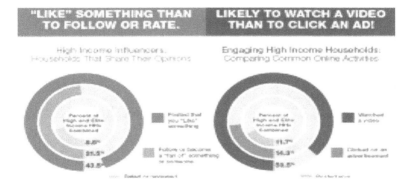

Social Networking
Behaviors for High
Income Households

---

* Entrepreneurs need to see the bigger picture by transforming data into actionable insights. Between customer data and prospecting data, you likely have a lot of data. But, are you able to use it to grow your business? Does it help you better understand your customers, their lifestyle and preferences, or their financial trajectory?

1. *Create a data asset*: Build a sub-panel of consumers you can survey at will. Ensure that any data built off other panels is syndicated so that you can have continuous access to it. Sync in your own customer data so that you can conduct voice of the customer, voice of the market, and brand saliency in one place. Make sure that all studies conducted in your organization flow from and add to this data set.*

2. *Data sharing*: Look at other divisions within your business that can feed into your data asset, helping you to overlay additional data points. Syncing online behavioral data is a quick win. See if your media team uses a data management platform that can directly feed information into your insights platform.

3. *Data syndication*: Secure partnerships with panel providers to allow you to append their profile data or look for non-competing companies that will be open to a data swap. This is a faster and lower cost route to growing your data sets than trying to do it yourself.

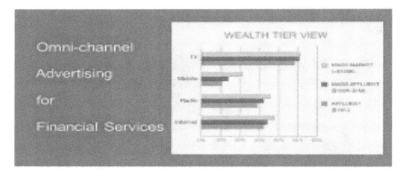

Omni-Channel Advertising: Channels for Financial Services

4. *Insights audit*: Talk to peers on the marketing team and see what reports and insights they have access to. Since you know that a lot of this "new data" is coming from online sources, speak to your Digital Marketing team, as they will likely have some great data for you to work with.

---

* See the example on the right of the Equifax Customer Insights Model database category: *Social Networking behaviors for High Income Households; and Omni-Channel Advertising.*

5. *Invest in research technology to automate the grunt work*: Look at providers who have templates, access to groups, user-friendly layouts, good visualization tools, ability to warehouse past knowledge from studies,* and good search functionality to find them.
6. *Rethink your research supply chain*: Ask yourself if your agency needs to process all of the data, or whether you can visualize some of the data in a dashboard in real time so that you can take action on it more quickly. Consider where the agency can add value and where inhibitors lie, then get them to work on the parts that add the most value.
7. *Take action*†: Most importantly, insights should inform every aspect of a business. Become better after stepping up from conventional processes. Bring your organization up to speed, succeed in the digital world and put market research back on top (Figure 9.1).

AT THE CENTER OF CUSTOMER INSIGHTS

At the center is implementing Customer Insights that help grow, win, and keep customers.

The *Equifax Customer Insights Model* helps entrepreneurs see the bigger picture by transforming data into actionable insights.

---

* Drucker on Knowledge-Based Innovation: Knowledge-based innovation is the superstar of entrepreneurship! Characteristics include the long lead times between emergence and the application of knowledge to knowledge-based innovations; this could be shortened by an external crisis (e.g., World War II). The also include the convergence of different types of scientific and non-scientific knowledge (e.g., computers, universal banking, airplanes). What does knowledge-based innovation require? (1) Careful analysis of missing social, economic, and perceptual factors (e.g., Britain's failure to commercialize penicillin and the jet engine). (2) Often, such an analysis is led by layperson, rather than scientists. (3) A clear focus on strategic position and the market. (4) The practice of entrepreneurial management to reduce risk. Note that there are unique risks due to uncertainty and windows of opportunity, followed by shake-outs and shaped by receptivity.
† Drucker on the principles of customer insights – The dos (1) begin with an analysis of opportunities. (2) Go out to look, ask, and listen to customers. (3) Innovation is effective, simple, and focused. (4) effective innovations start small. (5) Customer Insights are aimed at leadership. The Don'ts, (1) anything too clever, fails. (2) Don't diversify or do too many things at once.(3) Don't innovate for the future. There are three conditions to remember: (1) innovation is work; (2) to succeed, innovators must build on their strengths; and (3) innovation is an effect on the economy and society. The conservative innovator lacks Customer Insight. Innovators are successful to the extent that they define and confine risks.

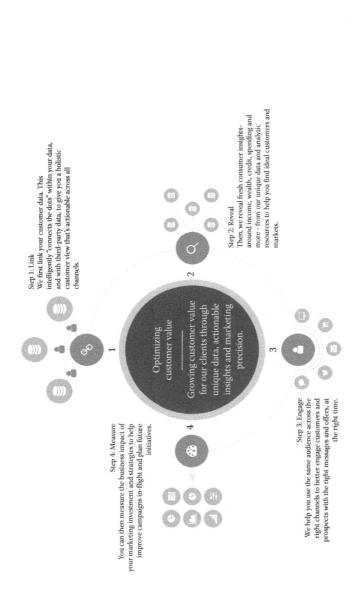

Step 1: Link
We first link your customer data. This intelligently "connects the dots" within your data, and with third-party data, to give you a holistic customer view that's actionable across all channels.

Step 2: Reveal
Then, we reveal fresh consumer insights– around income, wealth, credit, spending and more - from our unique data and analytic resources to help you find ideal customers and markets.

Step 4: Measure
You can then measure the business impact of your marketing investment and strategies to help improve campaigns in-flight and plan future initiatives.

Step 3: Engage
We help you use the same audience across the right channels to better engage customers and prospects with the right messages and offers, at the right time.

Optimizing customer value

Growing customer value for our clients through unique data, actionable insights and marketing precision.

FIGURE 9.1

Example: The Equifax Customer Insights Model (*Source:* https://datadrivenmarketing.equifax.com/insights/. Leading businesses of all sizes use data-driven marketing capabilities from Equifax to help maximize the return on their marketing and sales efforts. Equifax's depth and breadth of high-quality, unique data means better marketing insights. By leveraging these insights, marketers can inform intelligent marketing decisions at a consumer, household, or market level and better measure marketing ROI. We offer thought leadership based on our data through our monthly Insights that Drive Marketing series, Best Practices, and other thought leadership, as well as case studies and use cases. The "Did You Know?" series from Equifax provides monthly insights on the likely financial and economic position of US households and geographies.)

Between your customer data and prospecting data, you likely have
a lot of data.

But, are you able to use it to grow your business? Does it help you
better understand your customers, their lifestyle and preferences, or
their financial trajectory?

This model will help you to leverage unique data, innovative analytics, technology, and expertise to power decision-making and drive
better business outcomes. Data-driven marketing solutions will help
emerging organizations drive profitable growth.

You will have access to new and unique data sets, powerful and predictive data analytics, and game-changing technology that helps you:

1	2	3	4
Enhance, synthesize and activate customer data	Turn complex insights into a solid understanding of customer needs	Personalize the customer experience with the right messages in the right channels	Meaningfully measure performance to optimize marketing spend and customer value

Step 1: Link
We first link your customer data. This
intelligently "connects the dots" within your data,
and with third-party data, to give you a holistic
customer view that's actionable across all
channels.

Step 2: Reveal
Then, we reveal fresh consumer insights-
around income, wealth, credit, spending and
more - from our unique data and analytic
resources to help you find ideal customers and
markets.

Step 4: Measure
You can then measure the business impact of
your marketing investment and strategies to help
improve campaigns in-flight and plan future
initiatives.

4

Step 3: Engage
We help you use the same audience across the
right channels to better engage customers and
prospects with the right messages and offers, at
the right time.

SUMMARY

Providing a good product and service is simply not enough for today's businesses. Customers demand a personalized, seamless experience throughout their buying journey – no matter the channel. Teradata helps companies utilize advanced analytics and past customer behaviors to uncover real-time insights and unlock specifically what makes a sale stick at an individual level. Digitalization is making the problem worse. Unhappy customers will often leverage social media and other communication channels to communicate their unhappiness, and this can have a material impact on a business's ability to compete. And furthermore, many clients engage over multiple channels in rapid succession (e.g., web, stores/branches, call centers), expecting businesses to know each interaction in real time. This new-age complexity is incredibly difficult to manage at almost any scale. As a result, significant investments in information and digital capabilities are being required by entrepreneurs to allow their organizations to optimize and automate many parts of the client experience, while significantly reducing day-to-day operational costs.

The real leaders will be the companies that have the ability to respond to customers with personalized, contextually relevant offers and communications in real time, using insights not only based upon customers' in-the-moment activity, but also past behaviors. They will reinvent and reimagine customer journeys to increase client delight, sales, and service productivity, while automating processes to reduce operational costs and drive standardization. They will identify suboptimal channel/cross-channel processes that lead to complaints/attrition and increased costs, while fixing them quickly. They will drive enhanced loyalty and customer engagement through improved focus on managing and measuring customer satisfaction and retention. Finally, they will drive increased sales through smarter marketing, presented at the right time and within the right channel based on current context and past interaction history.*

---

* *Source*: http://assets.teradata.com/resourceCenter/downloads/Brochures/EB9592.pdf. Teradata believes that Customer Experience focuses on analytics and solutions to create a holistic yet highly personalized omni-channel customer experience. Teradata enables companies to make the most of customer experience, and to be the real leaders that thrive in today's environment. Teradata Customer Experience is a unique solution that integrates and collects customer and product data from all touchpoints to provide a holistic view of the customer experience.

10

Building a Strong Organizational Foundation for Innovation

One of the foundations for innovation is Purposeful Innovation. Purchasing power is the creation of an innovating entrepreneur • Innovation is economic or social rather than technical, and is best defined in demand terms than supply terms • The last century has witnessed the "invention of invention" as a foundation. Entrepreneurs must learn to practice systematic innovation, which involves the purposeful and organized search for changes, and in the systematic analysis of the opportunities such changes might offer for economic or social innovations.

Peter Drucker
1985

In a nutshell: Entrepreneurs always need to be constantly pushing their companies forward. You need to focus on reinventing what you do and how you do it as often as possible to drive new value for your customers and your organization. To succeed, you need to build a strong foundation for innovation. Companies like GE or IBM who have consistently changed their business, sold off core components, reinvented their primary revenue base, and evolved how they execute based on the demands of an evolving market. These are great examples of companies that innovate very well. But their innovative success isn't based solely on a mindset, fancy frameworks, or crazy wild innovators although that often helps. To earn the right to be innovative they first had to be exceptional companies.*

INTRODUCTION

For your organization to earn the right to be Innovative, you need to build the foundation. Skip a layer, and you'll find your house crumbling, and you'll be scrambling to stay relevant. Build strength at each layer, and you'll enjoy the rewards that IBM and GE have. You will develop the ability to shift and adapt to the market and customer demand.

Hierarchy of Organizational Needs. In entrepreneurial companies, building a strong foundation for innovation falls to the founder or entrepreneur early in the development of the company. Vision and strategy are where the entrepreneur or CEO is likely going to focus much of their time. Every business needs to have a clear purpose (WHY?), a clear articulation of how they will achieve it (HOW?),

---

* Build a Strong Foundation for Innovation, by SucceedSooner. They provide "strategic innovation services" and have a simple framework and guided approach to implementing a successful innovation program at your company that will drive growth through innovation and build a culture of innovation in your organization. See http://succeedsooner.ca/2016/07/18/foundation-for-innovation/

and an articulation of the core business and customer base that will be used to reach these goals (WHAT?). A well-articulated vision and strategy become the playbook for the entire organization. Everyone knows the goal, and everyone knows how their work connects to that goal. Link every project to the strategy and measure every action in a way that is relevant to the goal.

CONDUCT AN INNOVATION CULTURE AUDIT

Culture is like a glue that holds people and things together. Every organization has a culture. It may be written or hung on a wall. Or it may be *just the way we work here* and never written down – just passed on informally in new employee training or by hand-holding by senior people in the organization. How can you know where you are going to go with innovation if you don't first know where you already are? For this reason, I created a *50-question innovation audit* and linked it to an Innovation Maturity Model from Karl T. Ulrich and Christian Terwiesch of Wharton Business School.

Innovation maturity model

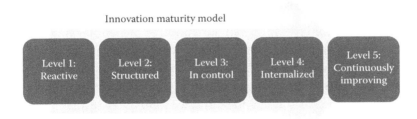

A culture can have characteristics including, but not limited to

- Creating and nurturing collaborative teams
- Providing rewards and recognition that focus on a specific area such as innovation
- Allowing for and supporting a self-managing culture
- Displaying curiosity, courage, and level of risk allowed

An organization that realizes it needs to change its culture cannot simply fire everybody one day and instantly replace everyone with the right people the next day, even if it knows exactly what kind of people it needs. Culture change and adjustment takes time and patience. The last thing an organization should do is to make a speech discussing the need for new behaviors and then expect the culture to change overnight.

This chapter focuses on how to successfully align the accountable organization's attitudes, feelings, values, and behaviors with the needs of an innovation project. Whenever you have the idea that you want to convert to a successfully commercialized innovation, you need to evaluate your culture against the alignment of your people (skills), processes, tools, metrics, stakeholders and sponsors, management model, organizational structure, and reward and recognition mechanisms.

Four key categories of activities in culture change are Vision, Motivation, Skills Development, and Implementation. The four key categories can be made into a matrix by coordinating with the phases of technology delivery known as initiate, customize, fan-out, and institutionalize.

DEFINE AND BENCHMARK WHAT INNOVATION MEANS FOR YOUR ORGANIZATION

Innovation benchmarking is not just another benchmarking exercise, but primarily another approach to benchmarking. In innovation benchmarking, we want to identify the factors behind the benchmark's success. These are factors that are not always measurable, so we need to go by some other variables first. Afterward, we want to try to adapt and apply these factors to our own company. There is overlapping research between benchmarking and related areas such as knowledge management (KM), asserting the notion that the knowledge-based perspective is the main source of competitive advantage. Organizational learning (OL), especially in knowledge-intensive industries (KII), not only leads to organizational innovation but is the only sustainable competitive advantage in the long run.

Most companies start by benchmarking inside their own company (internal benchmarking) and then move on to their competitors (external benchmarking). Three types of benchmarking are

- Process benchmarking: Which involves identification of best practices
- Strategic benchmarking: Which involves identifying emerging trends
- Comparative benchmarking: Which is more result oriented

There is a difference between *innovation benchmarking* and *benchmarking innovations*. Benchmarking innovation can be seen as a form of contradiction. If we are doing something completely new – applying an invention in a new way – it means that others are not doing the same thing. Thus, there is nothing to benchmark. Innovation benchmarking, on the other hand, can be understood as how to become or stay "innovative."

The challenge in benchmarking is to find the right metrics. These metrics should fulfill the following criteria:

- They must be understood by the user.
- They must be (easily) available.
- They must be the best measures we can find for a given variable we want to measure.
- They must be comparable and preferably quantifiable.

One-third of all Fortune 1000 companies have a set of formal innovation metrics in place. The most prevalent metrics include

- Annual R&D budget as a percentage of annual sales
- Number of patents filed in the past year
- Total R&D headcount or budget as a percentage of sales
- Number of active projects
- Number of ideas submitted by employees
- Percentage of sales from products introduced in the past x year(s)

Both input metrics and output metrics are essential for ensuring measures that drive resource allocation and capability building as well as return on investment (ROI) assessment. The three categories contain the following metrics portfolio:

a. ROI metrics
   i. ROI metrics address two measures, resource investments and financial returns. ROI metrics give innovation management

fiscal discipline and help justify and recognize the value of strategic initiatives, programs, and the overall investment in innovation.

b. Organizational capability metrics

   i. Organizational capability metrics focus on the infrastructure and process of innovation. Capability measures provide focus for initiatives geared toward building repeatable and sustainable approaches to invention and reinvention.

c. Leadership metrics

   i. Leadership metrics address the behaviors that senior managers and leaders must exhibit to support a culture of innovation.

There are three steps to successful benchmarking:

- Selecting key performance drivers or KPIs
- Selecting companies to benchmark
- Allocating resources to the best value-added areas identified

CREATE A COMMON LANGUAGE AND FRAMEWORK FOR INNOVATION

Creating a definition of innovation is the first step in creating a common language of innovation. The importance of creating a common language of innovation is that language is one of the most important components of culture. If people in your organization don't talk about innovation in a consistent way and see communications reinforcing the common language, how can you possibly hope to embed innovation in the culture of the organization? Ensuring consistent language in presentations, emails, and so on and having people read the same book on innovation or taking the same training courses are just some ways to help create and reinforce a common language of innovation. A number of frameworks have been used to look at types of innovation. Generally, these approaches for categorizing innovation consider the sources of innovation from past successes or attempt to identify where to look for new innovation in the future. The variety of innovation types demonstrates that the benefits of innovation are not limited to new product development. Categorization also helps in the measurement of innovation, allowing for performance comparison and evidence-based choices that can guide where improvements or advances might generate the most return.

Terms and Definitions

Process innovation: is the innovation of internal processes. New or improved delivery methods may occur in all aspects of the supply chain in an organization.

Functional innovation: involves identifying the functional components of a problem or challenge and then addressing the processes underlying those functions that are in need of improvement. Through this process, overlaps, gaps, discontinuities, and other inefficiencies can be identified.

Design innovation: focuses on the functional dimension of the job-to-be-done, as well as the social and emotional dimensions, which are sometimes more important than functional aspects.

Product innovation: is a multidisciplinary process usually involving many different functions within an organization and, in large organizations, often in coordination across continents.

Service innovation: is not substantially different than product innovation in that the goal is to satisfy customers' jobs-to-be-done, wow and retain customers, and ultimately optimize profit.

Business model innovation: changes the method by which an organization creates and delivers value to its customers and how, in turn, it will generate revenue (capture value).

Co-creation innovation: is a way to introduce external catalysts, unfamiliar partners, and disruptive thinking into an organization in order to ignite innovation. The term co-creation innovation can be used in two ways: co-development and the delivery of products and services by two or more enterprises; and co-creation of products and services with customers.

Open innovation: makes use of external ideas and technologies to enhance the enterprise's internal technology base, reduce the cost of R&D and time to market, and achieve superior product, service, or process innovations. At the same time, unused intellectual property and technology – latent internal intellectual capital – is made available for other firms to license.

Most organizations rely on their traditional attempts at innovation – improvements to business-as-usual – to provide security, and hope they might stumble upon a disruptive innovation, if they are lucky. This is not a formula for longevity. Successful companies incorporate processes for generating both sustaining and disruptive initiatives for their innovation pipeline. The majority of organizations may never achieve a radical innovation, yet they are able to remain viable and profitable. This is because they have adopted change as a fact of life and are engaged in more than one type of innovation.

DEFINE YOUR INNOVATION VISION AND MEASURES

A startup begins life as a single-minded entity focused on innovating for one set of customers with a single product or service. Often as a company grows to create a range of products and/or services, the organization can start to lose track of what it is trying to achieve, which customers it is trying to serve, and the kind of solutions that are most relevant and desired by them.

Jack Welch, CEO of GE once said, "Good business leaders create a vision, articulate the vision, passionately own the vision, and relentlessly drive it to completion."

Innovation, is a complex and unknown process, proves to be a challenge when defining clear and correlating measurements. Experience shows that measurements do not correlate to the innovation activity; financial and count-type measurements include product- or service-specific sales or revenue growth, and count-type measurements include items like the number of patents, trademarks, articles, and product or service versions produced; therefore, they should not be used as a business measure of performance.

Corporations implement innovation through network-centric, pipeline-fed, and opportunity-driven approaches:

- The network-centric approach is taught in colleges and based on collaborative brainstorming. The concept is that more minds are better than one at a given time.
- The pipeline model as driven by chance or innate genius is a somewhat common perception of the innovation process. Inventors who work

in research drive the pipeline model and development environment on a specific topic, explore new ideas, and develop new products and services.

- The opportunity-driven model is more representative of street-smart individuals who take an idea at the right time and the right place, devise a solution, know how to market it, and capitalize on their breakthrough. They also appear to be lucky, which is defined as an intersection of continual preparation and opportunity.

Peter Drucker's process, detailed in his book *Innovation and Entrepreneurship*, identifies various phases of innovation, including the phases of opportunity identification, analysis, acceptability, focusing on a core idea, and leadership. The act of innovation, though, is still not clearly explained. Measuring innovation effectively is contingent on understanding the details of the innovation process, its inputs and outputs, and its controls.

State of Measures of Innovation

- *The creative problem-solving group*: Data shows that innovative companies outperform in the areas of risk-taking, play or humor, challenge or motivation, and idea support. The most significant factor that differentiated an organization for innovation is risk-taking. Innovative companies that encourage risk-taking by their employees included the following nine criteria to evaluate the link between climate and organizational innovation:

Many of the previously mentioned criteria have a core set of questions:

- What data to collect
- How to collect data
- How to analyze the data
- How to interpret the data
- How to drive improvement

Paul H. Jensen and Elizabeth Webster of the Melbourne Institute of Applied Economic and Social Research (MIAESR) identified four specific dimensions to the problem of measuring innovation. They are as follows:

- The innovation process may take years from concept to commercialization.
- In the narrow sense of innovation, the novelty of products or services is difficult to benchmark, and the process measurements are difficult to adjust.
- Time carries an important economic value for the innovation process. Therefore, innovation measures must have some way to adjust for value over time.
- Much of the innovation activity is categorized as unobservable and is not reported in conventional methods.

The authors, Jensen and Webster, identified three main characteristics of innovation measures: type of innovation, stage of pathway, and firm characteristics. The measures of innovation in their reported research included patent applications, trademark application, design application, expert assessment, journal counts, and survey of managers. A challenge exists in identifying a complete list of innovation measurements.

Mark Rogers of the Melbourne Institute at the University of Melbourne has attempted to establish measurements of innovation at the corporate level. Rogers also identified input and output measures of innovation, along with their descriptions and, more importantly, the source of data collection. Each measure of innovation has some validity, but none can be used as a stand-alone measure of innovation. However, combining various measures to develop an index of indicators must consider tangibles and intangibles, economic and noneconomic measures of innovation-related resources, processes, deliverables, and value.

On Understanding Measures of Innovation

The SIPOC (Supplier, Input, Process, Output, and Customer) model can be used for analyzing the innovation process. The analysis of the innovation process shows many process steps and dozens of measures that can be used for monitoring innovation. Most management people would like to identify some measures, set targets, provide incentives, and start monitoring them.

A Process for Developing Measures of Innovation:

- The goal, question, metric (GQM) approach consists of the following conceptual, operational and quantitative level understandings of processes. In order to identify innovation measures, understanding the purpose of innovation, its environment, and the input, in-process, and output parameters is essential.

- Goal is defined as an intent or conceptual understanding in terms of products or outputs, processes or activities, or resources or inputs.
- Questions provide an operational understanding of measurements that can be used to assess realization of goals and objectives.
- Metrics represent the data that provide a quantitative understanding of the answers to the questions in assessing performance against goals. The data can be objective or subjective, or the object itself along with the viewpoint from which the data is taken.

The following is a list of steps used to establish measures for a process or an activity:

- Define the purpose of innovation in the organization.
- Establish expected deliverables (basic and specific) and their contribution to business performance, including growth and profitability.
- Determine the measures of success of key deliverables.
- Identify challenging opportunities for improvement in the innovation process.

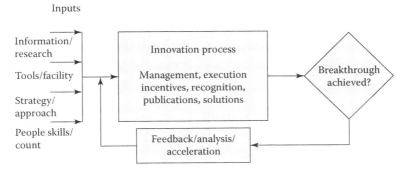

- List activities that must be performed to accelerate innovation.
- Identify input, in-process, and output variables that are critical to the success of innovation in the organization. If these variables are not monitored and managed effectively, the innovation outcomes will be adversely affected.

- Establish an Innovation Index and determine the data collection capability for selected measures of innovation.
- Establish reporting and communication methods, and monitor (levels and trends) critical and practical measures of innovation to drive business growth and profitability.

Measures to Consider for Innovation Index

• Industry innovation	• Indicators innovation index measures	• Process innovation measures
• Innovation funding, including R&D	• Resources: funding, a culture of risk-taking, rewards, tools	• Excellence in research, innovation management, time allocation (%)
• New products, services, or solutions	• Activities: targets for innovation, process of innovation, extent of institutionalization, idea management, internal and external publications, knowledge management, internal and external collaboration, recognition	• New idea deployment; extent of improvement or change; degree of differentiation, disruption, or innovativeness; time to innovate
• Market capitalization	• Outputs: patents; new products, services, or solutions; sales growth; market position or ranking; customer perceptions	• Rate of innovation, savings, opportunities

Vision is about focus and vision is about the "where" and the "why" not the "what" or the "how." A vision gives the business a sense of purpose and acts as a rudder when the way forward appears uncertain. An innovation vision is no less important, and it serves the same basic functions. An innovation vision can help to answer some of the following questions for employees:

- Is innovation important or not?
- Are we focusing on innovation or not?
- What kind of innovation are we pursuing as an organization?
- Is innovation a function of some part of the business?
- Or, is innovation something that we are trying to place at the center of the business?
- Are we pursuing open or closed innovation, or both?
- Why should employees, suppliers, partners, and customers be excited to participate?

When people have questions, they tend not to move forward. For that reason, it is crucial that an organization's leadership both has a clear innovation vision, and clearly and regularly communicates it to key stakeholders. If employees, suppliers, partners, and customers aren't sure what the innovation vision of the organization is, how can they imagine a better way forward?

DEFINE YOUR INNOVATION STRATEGY

Many organizations take the time to create an organizational strategy and a mission statement, only to then neglect the creation of an innovation vision and an innovation strategy. An innovation strategy is not merely a technology roadmap from R&D or an agenda for new product development. Instead, an innovation strategy identifies who will drive a company's profitable revenue growth and what will represent a strong competitive advantage for the firm going forward. Under this umbrella, the innovation goals for the organization can be created.

An innovation strategy sets the innovation direction for an organization toward the achievement of its innovation vision. It gives members of the organization an idea of what new achievements and directions will best benefit the organization when it comes to innovation. As with organizational strategy, innovation strategy must determine WHAT the organization should focus on (and WHAT NOT to) so that tactics can be developed for HOW to get there.

Intersection of innovation vision, strategy, and goals

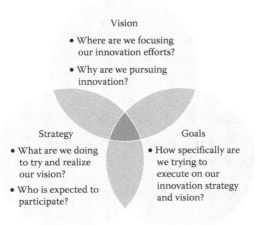

Vision
- Where are we focusing our innovation efforts?
- Why are we pursuing innovation?

Strategy
- What are we doing to try and realize our vision?
- Who is expected to participate?

Goals
- How specifically are we trying to execute on our innovation strategy and vision?

DEFINE YOUR INNOVATION GOALS

Just as managers and employees need goals to know what to focus on and to help them be successful, organizations need innovation goals too. Clear innovation goals, when combined with a clear innovation strategy and a single-minded innovation vision for the organization, will maximize the instinctual innovation that emerges from employees and the intellectual innovation that occurs on directed innovation projects.

While an innovation vision determines the kinds of innovation that an organization will focus on, an innovation strategy determines what the organization will focus on when it comes to innovation; it is the innovation goals that break things down into tangible objectives that employees can work against. Let's look at P&G as an example to see how these three things come together at the highest level:

Innovation Vision
- Reach outside the company's own R&D department for innovation

Innovation Strategy
- Create a formal program (Connect + Develop) to focus on this vision

Innovation Goal
- Source 20%–30% of the company's innovation from outside

The 20%–30% goal gives employees and management something to measure against, and it sets a very visible benchmark that the whole organization can understand, it allows them to visualize how big the commitment and participation must be in order to reach it. It is at this point of communicating the innovation goals that senior management also has to communicate how they intend to support their efforts and how they will help employees reach the innovation goals.

CREATE A POOL OF MONEY TO FUND INNOVATION PROJECTS

This is where "the rubber meets the road." Product managers leading product groups and general managers leading business units typically have revenue numbers they are trying to hit, and they will spend their budgets trying to hit those numbers. As a result, there are often precious little financial resources (and human resources) available for innovation projects that don't generate immediate progress toward this quarter's business goals. As a result, many organizations find themselves setting money aside outside of the product or business-unit silos that can be allocated on the future needs of the business instead of the current needs of the product managers and general managers. This also allows the organization to build an innovation portfolio of projects with different risk profiles and time horizons. But, however you choose to fund innovation projects, the fact remains that you need to have a plan for doing so, or the promising projects that form your future innovation pipeline – will never get funded.

CREATE HUMAN RESOURCE FLEXIBILITY TO STAFF INNOVATION PROJECTS

Some organizations allow employees to spend a certain percentage of their time on whatever they want, but most don't. Some organizations allow employees to pitch to spend a certain percentage of their time on developing a promising idea, but most organizations are running so lean that they feel there is no time or money for innovation. Often this is true and so employees sometimes work on promising ideas on their own time, but they shouldn't have to. And if you make them do so, it will be much more likely that they will develop the promising idea with others outside the company, and the organization will gain nothing from these efforts.

Don't turn your motivated intrapreneurs into entrepreneurs.

You must find a way to create resource flexibility. Organizations that want to continue to grow and thrive must staff the organization in a way that allows managers to invest a portion of their employees' time into promising innovation projects. One model to consider is that of Intuit, which allows employees to form project teams and to accumulate percent time and then schedule time off to work on an innovation project with co-workers in the same way that they schedule a vacation. This allows the manager to plan for the employees' absence from the day-to-day and allows the employee to focus on the innovation project during that scheduled leave from their workgroup. But that's just one possible way to create human resource flexibility.

FOCUS ON VALUE – INNOVATION IS ALL ABOUT VALUE

Value creation is important, but you can't succeed without equal attention being paid to both value access and value translation because innovation is all about value …

Innovation = **Value Creation** (×) **Value Access** (×) **Value Translation** = Success!

Now you will notice that the components are multiplicative, not additive. Do one or two well and one poorly and it doesn't necessarily add up to a positive result. Doing one poorly and two well can still doom your innovation investment to failure. Let's look at the three equation components in brief:

Value Creation is pretty self-explanatory. Your innovation investment must create incremental or completely new value large enough to overcome the switching costs of moving to your new solution from the old solution (including the "Do Nothing Solution"). New value can be created by making something more efficient, more effective, possible that wasn't possible before, or by creating new psychological or emotional benefits.

Value Access could also be thought of as friction reduction. How easy do you make it for customers and consumers to access the value you've created. How well has the product or service been designed to allow people to access the value easily? How easy is it for the solution to be created? How easy is it for people to do business with you?

Value Translation is all about helping people understand the value you've created and how it fits into their lives. Value translation is also about understanding where on a continuum between the need for explanation and education does your solution fall. Incremental innovations can usually just be explained to people because they anchor to something they already understand, but radical or disruptive innovations inevitably require some level of education (often far in advance of the launch). Done really well, value translation also helps to communicate how easy it will be for customers and consumers to exchange their old solution for the new solution.

The key thing to know here is that, even if you do a great job at value creation, if you do a poor job at either value access or value translation, you can still fail miserably.

FOCUS ON LEARNING FAST

There is a lot of chatter out there about the concept of "failing fast" as a way of fostering innovation and reducing risk. Sometimes the concept of "failing fast" is merged with "failing cheap" to form the following refrain – "fail fast, fail cheap, fail often." One of the most important things an organization can do is learn to accept failure as a real possibility in their innovation efforts, and even to plan for it by taking a portfolio approach that balances different risk profiles, time horizons, and so on.

But when it comes to innovation, it is not as important whether you fail fast or fail slow or whether you fail at all, but how fast you learn. And make no mistake, you don't have to fail to innovate (although there are always some obstacles along the way). With the right approach to innovation, you can learn quickly from failures AND successes.

The key is to pursue your innovation efforts as a discrete set of experiments designed to learn certain things, and to instrument each project phase in such a way that the desired learning is achieved.

The central question should always be: "What do we hope to learn from this effort?"

When you start from this question, every project becomes a series of questions you hope to answer, and each answer moves you closer to identifying the key market insight and achieving your expected innovation. The questions you hope to answer can include technical questions, manufacturing questions, process questions, customer preference questions, questions about how to communicate the value to customers, and more. AND, the answers that push you forward can come from positive discrete outcomes OR negative discrete outcomes of the different project phases.

The ultimate goal of a "learning fast" approach to innovation is to embed in your culture the ability to extract the key insights from your pursuits and the ability to quickly recognize how to modify your project plan to take advantage of unexpected learnings, and the flexibility and empowerment to make the necessary course corrections.

The faster you get at learning from unforeseen circumstances and outcomes, the faster you can turn an invention into an innovation by landing smack on what the customer finds truly valuable (and communicating the value in a compelling way). Fail to identify the key value AND a compelling way to communicate it, and you will fail to drive mass adoption.

SUMMARY

When you start with an innovation audit and creating a common language of innovation (including a definition of innovation), it sets you up well to create a coherent innovation vision, strategy, and goals. And then if you build in the financial and human resource flexibility necessary to create a focus on value creation, access, and translation – and support it with a culture that is focused on learning fast – YOU WILL have built a solid foundation for your innovation efforts to grow and mature on top of. Are there more things that go into embedding innovation into your culture and creating sustainable innovation success? Absolutely. But, if you work diligently on these ten items you will get your innovation efforts off to a strong start.

11

Innovation Methods

In a nutshell: There are many innovation methods that an organization can choose. Telling someone that there is only one way to do innovation is like telling someone that pepperoni is the only way to eat pizza (some of you will agree, but the point is that many would not). Even for the die-hard pepperoni fans, sometimes an Italian sausage is in order. This is how it is in innovation. Sometimes, Six Sigma DMADV (Define-Measure-Analyze-Design-Verify) is appropriate, while TRIZ may be a reasonable method for someone else. We also recognize that breakthrough innovation may work for your organization. Maybe crowdsourcing is the solution for you? Of course, there are a number of ways to "do" innovation and our apologies to anyone's methodology that we may not mention in this chapter – We have friends and acquaintances that all have their own spin on the topic, and we really have nothing against any of their approaches – they are generally all very good methodologies. Choosing the one that is right for you is the purpose of this chapter.

Key Points
1. Examples of innovation given by Joseph Schumpeter in the 1930s
   a. The introduction of new goods or qualitative changes in an existing product
   b. Process innovation new to an industry
   c. The opening of a new market
   d. Development of new sources of supply for raw materials or other inputs
   e. Changes in industrial organization

2. The scientific method is one of the keystones to systematic innovation methods. It is based on testing and observations. It is reported to have originated over 1000 years ago and basically involves the following steps:
   a. Formulating a question that needs answering based on experience and available data
   b. Formulating a hypothesis that can explain the behavior and that can be shown to be false
   c. Prediction of the consequences of the hypothesis
   d. Testing that can show the predictions are true or not false and therefore that the hypothesis is not false
   e. Analysis of the results to determine if the hypothesis is verified and determining a modification of the hypothesis if it was not verified.

3. Methods useful to systematic innovation include
   a. *Analogical thinking and mental simulations*: Using past successes applied to similar problems by mental simulations and testing.
   b. *Theory of inventive problem-solving (TRIZ)*.
   c. *Scientific method*: A classical method that uses a hypothesis based on initial observations and validation through testing and revision if needed.
   d. *Edison method*: Consists of five strategies that cover the full spectrum of innovation necessary for success.
   e. *Brainstorming*: Recording many ideas, without initial criticism, that could solve a problem, followed by organization and evaluation. This is one of the most used methods and several versions have been developed.
   f. *Osborn method*: Original brainstorming method developed by Alex F. Osborn by primarily requiring solicitation of unevaluated ideas (divergent thinking), followed by convergent organization and evaluation
   g. *Six Hats*: Structured method of brainstorming through different roles, to control thinking and emotions, that can speed up the process of brainstorming

h. *Problem detection and affinity diagrams*: Focus groups, mall intercepts, mail, and phone surveys that ask customers what problems they have. They are all forms of problem detection. The responses are grouped according to commonality (affinity diagrams) to strengthen the validity of the response. Developing the correct queries and interpreting the responses are critical to the usefulness of the method.

i. *Explore unusual results*: Unusual results can be investigated for how they occurred and what problems they could solve.

j. *Ethnography*: Observing and recording what people do to solve a problem and not what they say the problems are. It is based on anthropology but used on current human activities. It is based on the belief that what people do can be more reliable than what they say.

k. *Function analysis and fast diagrams*: Analyzing a system for the different functions by which it operates is believed to generate more ideas than focusing on the physical part.

l. *Kano method*: Based on the idea that features can be plotted using axes of fulfillment and delight. This defines areas of must-haves, more is better, and delighters. The latter is used to excite the customer and close a sale.

m. *Abundance and redundancy*: Based on the belief (not necessarily factual) that if you want a good invention that solves a problem, you need lots of ideas.

n. *Hitch-hiking*: When a breakthrough occurs, it is a fertile area for innovators. They should hitch-hike on the breakthrough to create new applications and improvements that can be inventions.

o. *Kepner Trego*: This method is very useful for processes that were performing well and then developed a problem. It is a good step-by-step method that is based on finding the cause of the problem by asking what changed since the process was working fine.

p. *Quality function deployment (QFD), aka the house of quality*: This creates a matrix that looks like a house that can mediate the specifications of a product or process. There are subsequent derivative houses that further mediate downstream implementation issues.

q. *Design of experiments*: This method is a statistically based method that can reduce the number of experiments needed to establish a mathematical relationship between a dependent variable and independent variables in a system.

r. *Failure mode effects analysis*: A matrix-based method used to investigate potentially serious problems in a proposed system prior to final design. It creates a risk priority number that can be used to create a ranking of the biggest risks and then ranks the proposed solution.

s. *Fishbone diagrams, aka Ishikawa diagrams*: A mnemonic diagram that looks like the skeleton of a fish and has words for the major spurs that prompt causes for the problem.

t. *Five whys*: A simple but effective method of asking five times why a problem occurred. After each answer, ask why again using the previous response. It is surprising how this may lead to a root cause of the problem, but it does not solve the problem.

u. *Medici effect*: The book by this name describes the intersection of significantly different ideas that can produce cross-pollination of fields and create more breakthroughs.

v. *Technology mapping and recombination*: A matrix-based method that lists the various technologies that can perform a function and then examines combinations that have not been tried to see if there is enhanced performance or features.

w. *Trial and error*: Attempts at successful solutions to a problem with little benefit from failed attempts. This is not a good method.

4. Systematic Innovation can be viewed as occurring in the
   a. Concept stage – it includes problem identification, problem dissection into smaller problems, ideation for potential solutions for the smaller problems, and combinations of these potential solutions into concepts that could solve the larger problem; documentation in the form of a witnessed lab notebook, information disclosure sheet (IDS), and so on.

b. Feasibility stage; prototypes of key subsystems or theoretical validation of a solution to the main problem. They should be adequate to establish a preliminary basis for technical feasibility; assessment of patent potential and patent infringement. The results may indicate the need to submit a provisional patent to establish the date of invention or submit a patent application, an analysis of a preliminary business plan (preliminary versions of market size estimation, capital expenditure plan, resource plan, project schedule, risk abatement recommendations, and financial plan).

c. Development stage = generally the stage with the largest financial commitment.

d. Execution stage, in preparation for production the marketing plan is further developed with a launch strategy; facilities are readied for tooling; reviews are conducted and sought (aesthetics, internal safety, agency approvals, and quality in the form of overall design conformance, vendor part approvals, and reliability); preproduction trials are run; final bills of materials are released; and a production plan is developed.

e. Production stage = the first production of units for sale.

f. Sustainability stage = the maintenance of the product in use via service personnel, customer support (mail, web, and telephone lines), warranty, customer assurance, monitoring of field performance, and recycling.

g. Chesbrough identifies the elements of the business model as

   i. Value proposition to the target audience

   ii. Target audience who will purchase the product

   iii. Value chain that describes where the company resides and what value it brings in the chain that delivers the product to the customer

   iv. How the company will collect money

   v. Cost and margins that are required to make the product or process profitable

   vi. Value network of ancillary suppliers that enhance the product but may not be in the direct chain to the customer

   vii. Competitive strategy that will give the company longevity

INTRODUCTION

There isn't a business that doesn't want to be more creative in its thinking.

According to one study, 75% of CEOs of the fastest growing companies claim their strongest competitive advantage is unique products and services and the distinct business processes that power them to market – innovation by another name. In another survey, the Boston Consulting Group reported that 90% of organizations believe innovation is a strategic priority for 2004 and beyond. The trend was also confirmed by research undertaken by the consulting firm Strategos.

Their conclusion: The importance of innovation in all sectors is growing, and it is growing significantly. In today's ever-changing economic landscape, inventiveness has become a key factor influencing strategic planning. IT guru Kevin Kelly once said, "Wealth flows directly from innovation ... not optimization ... wealth is not gained by perfecting the known." Efficiency, while a necessary condition for business success, is insufficient to sustain growth over decades. While new levels of efficiency and productivity require inventive solutions, the goal of efficiency is not the same as the goal of innovation. In other words, business and technology-driven innovation is different from design-driven innovation, as shown subsequently.

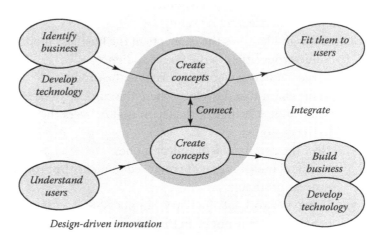

Business and technology-driven innovation

Design-driven innovation

Chip Holt, inventor of the hugely successful Xerox DocuTech publishing systems, initially an obscure skunk-works effort almost killed at birth by the Xerox corporate immune system, is quoted as saying that "I characterize a lot of my efforts as the pursuit of productivity. I'm amazed at how many perspectives can be brought to bear in the pursuit of that one word. In its simplest form, productivity is the measure of the output divided by the input. The output management, which is associated with growing revenue, is an exciting one. But many times, corporations get overly excited about the ease by which investment can be reduced and therefore the productivity equation increased. As an engineer and scientist, I come down squarely and strongly on the side of making investments in innovation that increase the output part of the equation."

Systems thinking, as in systematic innovation, is the process of understanding how those things that may be regarded as systems influence one another within a complete entity or larger system. In nature, systems thinking examples include ecosystems in which various elements such as air, water, movement, plants, and animals work together to survive or perish. In organizations, systems consist of people, structures, and processes that work together to make an organization "healthy" or "unhealthy." Systems thinking has been defined as an approach to problem-solving that attempts to balance holistic thinking and reductionistic thinking. By taking the overall system as well as its parts into account, systems thinking is designed to avoid potentially contributing to further development of unintended consequences or suboptimization of the whole in favor of the parts. Knowledge management is a related discipline that promotes an integrated approach to identifying, capturing, evaluating, retrieving, and sharing all of an enterprise's information assets. These assets may include databases, documents, policies, procedures, and previously uncaptured expertise and experience in individual workers.

Companies Cannot Afford to Rely Upon Flashes of Brilliance by Individual Inventors Working Alone

Hoping that what is cooking in the lab will turn up trumps is not a reasonable approach for a custodian of stockholder value. Very often, innovation results from the planned and deliberate recombination of ideas, people, and objects from the past that spark new technological revolutions, sought-after service concepts, and effective business models. Yet to stand as valuable innovations, new products and services must be sufficiently robust to progress efficiently through the end-to-end commercialization process and into the hands of customers. How does this happen?

Leading companies continuously seek out and institutionalize the insights and tools they will need if they are to stay at the leading edge and be top-rated stars in their sector. Some companies build enduring capacities for breakthrough innovation. They find ways to circumvent the years, if not decades, it can take to move from invention to commercial exploitation of a new technology. They manage the associated risks and continuously enhance their ability to solve the complex engineering and business process design problems that would otherwise place limits on their ability to envisage, and then create sustainable value from, the next generation in their industry. Far from a sporadic creative event, leading organizations, whether product or service-centric, treat innovation as a systemic and systematic process.

Economist and management consultant Peter Drucker once said, "An established company which, in an age demanding innovation, is not capable of innovation, is doomed to decline and extinction."

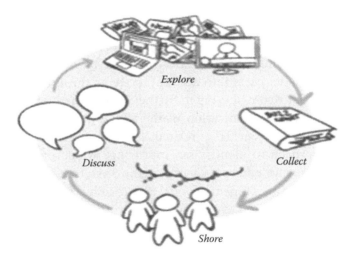

Today, many companies are taking steps to strengthen their ability to innovate – innovating to renovate the innovation process itself. In short, such companies are developing a reliable operating system for innovation, one based upon discussions in group sessions, as a key indicator of corporate sustainability.

Improving the Innovation Operating System

According to innovation theorists, a company should think about improving its operating system for innovation if any of the following apply: You feel you are nearing the end of a long and expensive development race and your competitors are about to pass you by and win a valuable brand name and profitable chunks of the market before you are able to act.

The value in your industry is shifting from perfecting the old, toward inventing the new, in processes, products, and services. Even when you take on significant new contracts, vast amounts of new work, or hundreds of new orders, your share price won't budge. It seems that the innovation efforts in your organization are not systematic enough and are based on chance flashes of genius or ad hoc ideas raised by individuals in skunk-works projects. You sense that your R&D staff members are sated and have settled into complacency, and the flow of ideas is not what it was.

Your company has an excellent product that, "if we could only solve that problem," would conquer the world.

You are certain that reducing development time, production costs, and product price by 15% would make your firm and your product a winner. Despite all the consultants, ISO standards, and best practices you deploy, the cancer of "it'll be okay," and of undirected improvisation, has taken a grip on your firm, and this is something you are unwilling to accept.

A SYSTEMS FRAMEWORK FOR INNOVATION

In his landmark book, *The Fifth Discipline*, Peter Senge taught us that the most successful organizations are those that are learning organizations. Opening that work, he wrote, "From a very early age, we are taught to break apart problems, to segment the world. This apparently makes complex tasks and subjects more manageable, but we pay a hidden price. We can no longer see the consequences of our actions; we lose our intrinsic sense of connection to a larger whole." For Senge, the answer lay in systems thinking, the antidote to reductionism.

Systems thinking helps creative individuals to see wholes, perceive relationships, uncover connections, expose root causes, and master complexity. Systems thinking, Senge argued, integrates what might otherwise be separate management disciplines, preventing them from becoming "gimmicks or the latest organization change fads." Some companies certainly took on that message. Jack Welsh, ex-CEO of most-admired company GE, once said that "An organization's ability to learn, and to translate that learning into action rapidly, is the ultimate competitive business advantage."

Do you believe that innovation and creativity is a learning skill; that it can be developed and improved if only one knew how? In short, does a systems-thinking framework for innovation exist? Edward de Bono thinks so. Inventor of methods to foster lateral thinking and a prolific author of textbooks on creativity, his work has been taught in the boardrooms of some of the world's largest corporations and to four-year-olds in school. There is nothing more wasteful than a roomful of intelligent and highly paid people waiting for inspiration. ABB used to spend 30 days on their multinational project team discussions. Applying De Bono's "Six Thinking Hats," discussion now takes as little as two days. This experience is not unusual.

Using an applied creativity system developed by author and consultant, Min Basadur, snack foods purveyor Frito-Lay involved employees at every level in cost-improvement teams and achieved its goal of reducing costs by $500 million one year ahead of schedule. Some at the firm claim a bigger bonus: A permanent shift to a creative problem-solving culture. Retired president and CEO, Jim O'Neal, is quoted as saying that "Creativity methods provide senior management with a unique tool to tap into a massive organizational resource.

Learning to leverage the creative thinking skills of every individual, regardless of their level, creates the sustainable competitive advantage every corporation is striving for."

Basadur, who honed his methods at P&G and is the creator of the Simplex creativity process, often tells a story about a green-striped soap bar called Irish Spring.

Manufactured by Colgate and one of the most successful new product introductions in history, the soap posed a problem for P&G. After developing several unsuccessful copycat bars, P&G finally used creativity methods to shift focus from competing on market share to competing on experience. The result: P&G's new soap bar, Coast. Using blue swirls, not green stripes, Coast "out-refreshed" Colgate's customers with a new advertising concept that linked its bar design not to Irish spring water, but to the illusion of an invigorating swim in the ocean.

Whatever we feel about such apocryphal marketing stories, psychological methods of enhancing creativity, while effective, are unlikely by themselves to yield inventive companies that dominate markets. Although mankind has tried to understand the human mind for centuries, and questions about "how we get ideas" go back to antiquity, one can hardly imagine the CEO of a major corporation reassuring stockholders about company strategy on the basis of facile instructions, such as "Let your mind roam free." When Peter Senge wrote about systems thinking, we can be sure he was referring to something beyond creativity tools and marketing renovations.

Companies need more than creativity; they need a reliable innovation process, just as they have processes governing all other aspects of their business. Can innovation be codified? And if so, should companies make the effort? Help is at hand, but the buyer must beware.

Caveat Emptor amid Growing Innovation Chic

To those business leaders who are sitting on the innovation fence, Gary Hamel has a dire prediction: "Out there in some garage is an entrepreneur who's forging a bullet with your company's name on it. You've got one option now – to shoot first. You've got to out-innovate the innovators. ... Conventional thinking says get back to basics. Conventional wisdom says to cut costs.

Conventional wisdom is doomed." Caveat Emptor. Writing in 1976, George Downs and Lawrence Mohr, observed that "Innovation has emerged over the last decade as possibly the most fashionable of social science areas." Are we set for another round of innovation chic? Should we view Hamel's pronouncements with caution? Innovation has become a mantra: Innovate or Die. Innovate or Die. Writing in the *Harvard Business Review*, Hamel tells us that "A company can't outgrow its competitors unless it can out-innovate them. ... Innovation is the fuel for growth.

When a company runs out of innovation, it runs out of growth." Surely everyone knows that corporate growth – true growth, not just agglomeration – springs from innovation and that it implies more freedom for the R&D lab? How then did Southwest, Cemex, and Shell Chemicals reap the benefits of innovation without spending lavishly on R&D?

According to marketing expert Sergio Zyman, many companies rely too heavily on expensive product innovation to solve their problems. Whenever a brand or business gets old and tired, the impulse is to scrap it and start over with something fresh. It sounds great, but more often than not innovation simply doesn't work. Zyman, author of *Renovate Before You Innovate*, knows this first hand – he was the chief marketing officer at Coca-Cola during the disastrous launch of New Coke. He reminds us that "many companies mistakenly focus on innovation to drive growth. They look to create new products and lines of business instead of the more promising alternative of marketing renovation."

Renovation May Be a Better Bet

Why? Because it involves doing a drastically better job of leveraging your existing assets and competencies. At Coca-Cola, renovation might have been a better bet than risking the company's heritage with a new drink formula; but surely renovation is not limited to the marketing process only? Isn't there more to marketing soap than green stripes and blue swirls? What about innovations in soap chemistry, such as moisturization for an aging population, built-in deodorants, antibacterial agents, and other ingredients that promote all-over healthy skin?

Companies that wish to move beyond marketing-led renovations quickly discover that there are as many definitions of innovation as there are innovation pundits. A superficial search of the Internet or Amazon. com reveals numerous sources of advice on how to generate new ideas, recognize innovation opportunities, remove mental blocks to creativity, foster creative conflict, create an innovation-friendly culture, and move innovations to market. Has innovation become the new knowledge management? As Thomas Davenport points out in his book *What's the Big Idea?*, "Knowledge management did have problems as a new business idea. One issue was that too many people – particularly IT vendors – conflated the use of knowledge technologies with the successful management of knowledge. Sometimes this was done in rather obvious ways.

One of us, for example, remembers speaking at a KM conference in Florida. At the beginning of the conference, each attendee's seat was graced with a new publication, KM World. How nice, we thought – KM now has its own little newspaper. On examination, however, we discovered that the paper was chock-full of press releases from imaging and document management technology vendors, with only a thin veneer of KM articles on the front page. Only the previous week it had been known as Imaging World." Is innovation suffering a similar fate? If we replaced the word "innovation" with the word "knowledge" in many popular books and articles that offer innovation advice, would it make any difference? In "e-business" we found it was the business that mattered. What's the real beef in innovation?

THE MYTH OF DISRUPTIVE INNOVATIONS

A recurring theme of what some call the "innovation industry," is how business leaders get blindsided by disruptive innovations because they focus too closely on their most profitable customers and businesses. The idea became popular following the publication of Clayton Christensen's influential 1997 book, *The Innovator's Dilemma*. Since then, the work of the Harvard Business School professor and founder of strategy consulting firm Innosight, has spawned a hundred imitations. These beguiling ideas dominate popular thinking about innovation. In the IT industry, they are interpreted as the search for so-called "killer apps," entirely unrealistic expectations for new, holy grail, software solutions.

In IT or any other industrial sector, these ideas appeal to senior managers because they speak of the potential of specific innovations in a market system, and they imply that silver bullets exist to take markets by storm. Yet by reading these theories we learn little about the process of innovation. Even when, as in Christensen's 2003 book *The Innovator's Solution*, things are switched around to show how companies get to the other side of the innovation dilemma, creating disruptions rather than being destroyed by them, we find no solution for the innovator.

Sony releases 5000 new products per year. A laptop's expected life is now only two years. Drug development is down from 10 years to four years. Professional services firms are in a race to find ways to retain valuable customer accounts.

There has never been a time when more products and services are being launched or when new technologies are being introduced to the market ever more rapidly. To cope in this environment, companies need more than big ideas about disruptive market innovations – they need new stuff, the stuff with which they can disrupt markets.

To win the next battle in the unending market wars, companies must be able to spot important trends and deliver compliant products, in soap products or anything else. Only by solving problems inherent in the current generation of a product or service, does innovation progress. Companies achieve this through the talent of their employees and the work environment provided for them by their employers. It is creativity, inventiveness, and the thoughtful application of systematic, scientific, and predictable methods that allows the innovator to move beyond the current state of the art.

When Christensen and like-minded management consultants write about "innovators" they are really referring to the mega-corporations that seek to dominate markets. The individual inventor, scientist, engineer, or problem-solver is never discussed. Their day-to-day, month-to-month, and year-on-year efforts to solve the hard problems in engineering, organizational design, service-concept, or process are never acknowledged. Yet it is precisely these activities that lead to new or improved products, services, processes, and business models.

Management books about innovation are important in so far as they help business leaders determine if an idea has disruptive "market" potential – which competitive situations favor incumbents, which favor new entrants, and which customer segments are ready-primed to embrace new offerings – but they won't help us to be more creative or to solve the problems that innovators will inevitably face as new concepts are commercialized with the objective of bringing in new business. Management books start where innovation leaves off.

They assume innovation has already taken place, and that all problems limiting commercial success, across the value chain and in all business processes, will be solved in the future. Drawn as they are from management theory, as opposed to engineering science, the ideas in such books have no impact on the number of innovations companies are able to generate or commercialize. Neither will reading such works enhance the creative and problem-solving skills of employees. Management frameworks have value in screening out bad ideas before too much time and resource is invested in the wrong place, but they do not describe the sources of innovation, despite the catchy book titles. Whether developing a mass-market product or delivering intimate services one customer at a time, management frameworks won't turn dullards into innovators.

In Christensen's latest book, *Seeing What's Next – Using the Theories of Innovation To Predict Industry Change*, he provides a powerful synthesis of the many management frameworks he has written about over the years, including disruptive innovation theory, resources, processes, and values (RPV) theory, jobs-to-be-done theory, value chain theory, schools of experience theory, emergent strategy theory, and motivational/ability frameworks. Yet the truth is, many of the disruptions he is concerned with do not occur or are the results of normal business logic. Southwest grew in the airline business because they were not unionized. The company bought up cheap slots at airports when the established players were cutting back. They similarly bought cheap aircraft from Boeing when the major players could not afford them. Then they had to develop an online or telesales presence because the airlines owned the booking systems.

Often, it is brutal business logic, not methodology, that drives innovation. The innovator is a problem-solver and uses intelligence and instinct to knock down barriers one by one that, unless overcome, would prevent the growth of their business. Yet problem-solvers, and the methods they use, never even get a mention in the index to Christensen's work. Companies must look deeper to find the source of innovation and of competitive advantage.

At the MIT Emerging Technology Symposium 2003, GE CEO, Jeff Immelt, set out his beliefs about innovation, stating that "We are all just a moment of complacency away from an abyss called commodity hell, where you compete only on price, where share goes to the least common denominator, and where you're working for your customers instead of your investors and you cannot build a business for the future." Immelt identified four factors driving companies to "commodity damnation."

First, lower growth and higher risk. There's more excess capacity today than at any time since the 1970s. There's more volatility in geopolitical risk than at any time in the last 20 years. "The toughest thing that any company has to get today is an order," he said.

Second, we're facing the strongest competitors that we've faced in our lifetime in China, India, and other emerging economies. Thomas Friedman, writing in the *New York Times* in an article entitled "Oops. I Told the Truth," points out that "The Chinese and the Indians are not racing us to the bottom. They are racing us to the top. Young Indian and Chinese entrepreneurs are not content just to build our designs. They aspire to design the next wave of innovations and dominate those markets. Good jobs are being outsourced to them not simply because they'll work for less, but because they are better educated in the math and science skills required for 21st-century work." Have no doubt; these societies have a strong technical foundation and both human and material resources.

Immelt told the MIT audience that "The trick is not low cost labor; it's the fact that we can hire two to three PhDs in India for the same amount we pay one hourly worker in Louisville, and we have to compete in that world."

Third, is the Internet. Restating GE's oft-reported belief in "digitization," Immelt stated that "The Internet has had a profound impact on how the world works. It's primarily profound in terms of the world of perfect information. GE every year does 15 billion dollars of purchasing online via auction, saving 20%–30%. The ability to get value for your product is fleeting and the tendency is to go to the lowest price everywhere in the world."

Lastly, the dominant business models today are distribution-oriented, consolidating channels. Companies like Wal-Mart and Dell tend to dominate the industries they're in. They take value from the manufacturers and more value has gone to distribution. Immelt's conclusion? With utter certainty, he told the assembled business leaders that "The only source of profit, the only reason to invest in companies in the future is their ability to innovate and their ability to differentiate." If innovation is so important, what is innovative about innovation today?

INNOVATION AS DESIGN PROCESS

Tom Kelley, general manager leading design consultancy IDEO, describes how innovative teams immerse themselves in every possible aspect of a proposal for a new product or service. For IDEO, research from the perspective of clients, consumers, and other critical audiences is central to innovation. IDEO has institutionalized a process for innovation – creating hot teams, pioneering ways to see through the customer's eyes, unique brainstorming methods, and rapid prototyping.

For cool and fast IDEO, whose mottos include "one conversation at a time," "stay focused on the topic," "encourage wild ideas," "defer judgment," and "build on the ideas of others," the innovation process is a blend of methodology, work practice, culture, and infrastructure. Shadowing, behavioral mapping, consumer journey, extreme interviews, storytelling, deep dives, and body storming are a few of the terms IDEO use to describe what they do. Sam Hall, vice president for mMode at AT&T Wireless Services Inc., turned to IDEO to redesign its mMode service. He was quoted in *Business Week* as being "Thrilled with the results. We talked to Frog Design, Razorfish, and other design firms, and they thought this was a Web project that needed flashy graphics. IDEO knew it was about making the cell phone experience better."

In the roaring 1990s, IDEO were best known for designing user-friendly computers, PDAs like the Palm V. They also designed the first no-squeeze, stand-up toothpaste tube for Procter & Gamble. Now IDEO are transferring their ability to create consumer products into designing consumer experiences in services, from shopping and banking to healthcare and wireless communication.

Is IDEO's eclectic mix of out-of-the-box thinking, structured exploration of design alternatives and creative flair enough? Not for IDEO.

Domain experience is an essential component of innovation. The members of IDEO's creative team are far from generalists – they are scientists, engineers, artists, and management theorists. Although IDEO is quick to point out they are not experts in any one field and that their core expertise lies in the process of design, the majority of their employees have advanced degrees in many different kinds of engineering: mechanical, electrical, biomedical, software, aerospace, and manufacturing. This background and formal training covers materials science, computer-aided design, robotics, computer science, movie special effect, molding, industrial interaction, graphics, fashion, the automobile business, finance, communications, linguistics, sociology, ergonomics, cognitive psychology, arts, therapy, ethnology, management consulting, statistics, medicine, and zoology.

As a result of these qualifications and experience, the IDEO project portfolio reads like a design encyclopedia. Closer examination of individual projects reveals the power of cross-fertilization from diverse domains. IDEO's clients have carried them far beyond the traditional high-tech product categories that might have defined the firm a decade ago when their reputation was established by association with early successes for Apple and Palm. Today, IDEO projects include an insulin delivery device, eyewear that exploits the design potential of new materials such as cellulosic plastics, the architectural design of a public learning laboratory, a new type of cap for recreational drink bottles, hospital environments and associated processes, office furniture, luminescent bathroom tiles, aircraft interiors, the passenger train experience, novel exhibition concepts, a radio data system, and a communicator for soul-mates.

A quick skim through IDEO – *Masters of Innovation*, a coffee table book that describes the story and features many gorgeous images of their design work, it is easy to forget that IDEO is not just a frothy concept company whose work rarely gets further than a 3D digital mock-up or Photoshop image. Far from it: IDEO construct real prototypes of the products they design and IDEO's engineers design for manufacturability.

Manufacturing specialists are on IDEO's project teams from the earliest phases.

IDEO employ materials specialists for all types of products, whether low-volume or mass-produced consumer devices. IDEO's experience extends to hardcore topics, such as lean manufacturing; supply chain, purchasing strategy; electrical, mechanical and assembly DFM; yield production; factory assessment; injection, transfer, multi-shot, and many other kinds of molding as well as processes for cast, net-shape, finishing, printed-circuit design, and production and packaging.

At IDEO, as in the R&D labs of major corporations, innovation is predicated on current experience and a deep understanding of what worked in the past. And to speed up learning, the design firm often turns to "real" experts, often end users, via an observation methodology they dub "design anthropology," which draws from ethnographic methods. Psychologist Jane Fulton Suri, who leads IDEO's human factors projects, has been called a "bird watcher with attitude," except the birds she specializes in are humans. Nearly all IDEO projects now include an element of "bird watching."

In an exotic setting, one might learn how to build a canoe, weave a hammock, make rain, or deliver a baby. In the industrial workplace, one gets insights into the intricacies of returning customer's phone calls, adjusting a piece of machinery, smelling a vat of chemicals, or negotiating with co-workers about a useful strategy. IDEO anthropologists observe consumers and workers as they use, make, or repair the products, services, or spaces that the firm are brought in to improve. A Ford engineer once noted that "When people look at a car in the showroom, the first thing they do is open and close the doors. They may not realize it, but if they don't like the sound, they'll just walk away from the car."

Knowing this, Ford and its competitors now engineer the sounds a car makes, including doors, latches, and of course engines. Design anthropology is what turns up this type of knowledge. And IDEO is smart about the way it captures design expertise from one project to provide creative design-seeds for others.

One of IDEO's most useful creativity tools is the Tech Box, a combination library, database, website, and organizational memory of parts, mechanisms, and materials. As IDEO's innovators discover new technologies in one industry, the Tech Box allows their knowledge to be distributed throughout the company so that it can be applied to projects in other industries. The Tech Box really is in daily use. It's a creativity amplifier for IDEO and their customers. And IDEO has created specialized Tech Boxes for their clients as they become aware of the central role of knowledge management in innovation.

For many corporations, the experience of working with IDEO is a wake-up call. The usual pattern is this: IDEO are engaged on a specific project, senior managers hear of the results on the grapevine, and a larger problem is revealed – culture. Interviewed for ABC News Nightline as part of a program in which the firm was challenged to design and manufacture a more innovative shopping trolley in just five days, David Kelley, IDEO founder and creative engineer, observed that "If you go into a culture and there are a bunch of steps going around, I guarantee they are not likely to invent anything."

Is IDEO inventing? Sometimes. Whoever came up with the idea for dental floss is an inventor, but the person who created the little plastic box that lets you tear off just the right amount is a designer. It's not so easy to understand the boundary between invention and design innovation, yet a specialist at the patent office can, with due diligence, determine what is genuinely new in a product or process and what is just new spin. Looking across the IDEO portfolio, it is clear that the value they bring is far more than spin and marketing renovations, irrespective of whether or not individual projects create patents. What IDEO do is a significant step up on the innovation ladder, and far more than a room full of creative generalists with no domain knowledge.

Method cards are one tool IDEO use to help explore new approaches in design. They are used to take a new view, enhance creativity, communicate amongst a team, avoid a roadblock, or turn a corner. IDEO have hundreds of techniques they employ during their total immersion "Deep Dives." Here are four:

Card Sort

HOW: On separate cards, name possible features, functions, or design attributes. Ask people to organize the cards spatially, in ways that make sense to them. WHY: This helps to expose people's mental models of a device or system. Their organization reveals expectations and priorities about the intended functions. EXAMPLE: In a project to design a new digital phone service, a card-sorting exercise enabled potential users to influence the final menu structure and naming.

Scenarios

HOW: Illustrate a character-rich story line describing the context of use for a product or service. WHY: This process helps to communicate and test the essence of a design idea within its probable context of use. It is essentially useful for evaluation of service concepts. EXAMPLE: Designing a website, the IDEO team drew up scenarios to highlight the ways particular design ideas served different user needs.

Still-Photo Survey

HOW: Follow a planned shooting script and capture pictures of specific objects, activities, and so on. WHY: The team can use this visual evidence to uncover patterns of behavior and perceptions related to a particular product or context. EXAMPLE: For a faucet design, the team documented all the situations in which people accessed water.

Character Profiles

HOW: Based on observations of a real process, develop character profiles to represent archetypes and the details of their behavior or lifestyles. WHY: This is a useful way to bring a typical customer to life and to communicate the value of different concepts to various target groups. EXAMPLE: In order to understand different types of customers and how to target them, IDEO developed four characters for a pharmacy wanting to reach the male-beauty-product market.

BEYOND DESIGN

Over the past decade, IDEO has steadily risen to the top of the international design consultancy prestige table, picking up over 200 clients including Nike, Amtrak, BMW, Canon, and Pepsi. IDEO may represent the cutting edge of design innovation today, but the problem they are addressing is a century old. In 1867, German chemical giant BASF established the first industrial R&D laboratory to develop dye technology. Soon afterward, Thomas Edison, the founder of GE and an individual who filed an average of 25 patents a year for his entire adult life, created the first organized and systematic corporate-research model for product innovation with a predictable return on investment at his Central Laboratory in Menlo Park in 1876. His work formed the prototype for corporate innovation and development in the industrial era. For example, DuPont created one of the most successful of the first-generation R&D labs, in which a project by chemist Wallace Carothers led to the invention of nylon in 1939. During the next 50 years, nylon earned the company between $20 and $25 billion in profits. These early labs were managed by scientists, but as the complexity of products and services grew by a thousand-fold over the next few decades, other disciplines, such as finance and governance, were added to the mix.

Mastery of the R&D process remains critical to survival today whether in products or services. It involves years of patient (and impatient) investigation, punctuated by moments of inspiration. It requires uncontrollable creativity side-by-side with disciplined business practice. And it is, for most companies, tremendously difficult to achieve. Many top managers acknowledge that their corporations are failing at innovation, and particularly at making the substantial leaps that are required to create products or service concepts that lead to market-changing breakthroughs. Some have lost confidence in the ability of their organizations to innovate effectively. No wonder then that some larger, and no doubt older, corporations are turning to external sources – firms such as Innosight, Strategos, Doblin, and IDEO – for help. What is it that they are seeking? Many managers wish to understand the steps they can take to foster a genuine culture of innovation and, just as importantly, to institutionalize an ability to continuously create and shape new products and services for today's ever-changing global markets. Companies have learned that they need to manage the innovation process so as to serve the business objectives. Today, R&D is an intensely commercial activity, governed by numerous business processes, such as competitive advantage analysis, risk, life cycle aging, timing of technology in the pipeline, fit with core business strategies, and the commitment of resources.

Creativity, invention, design, and innovation are often confused. Innovation is a holistic process involving the entire organization of a commercial enterprise, whereas invention is a discrete event, typically performed by specialist individuals or very small teams. Innovation requires multidisciplinary teams and is a complete life cycle process. Creativity and design are necessary, but insufficient. In this sense, IDEO's design innovations are, like every other element in the operating system for innovation, just a part of the mix. Yet in a world of product abundance, mass-customization and extraordinarily high expectations when consumers interact with public or private services or business people deal with suppliers, IDEO's core competence is no doubt a vital ingredient. Their design process turns genuine inventions into usable, interesting, and beautiful products and services, rendering them fit for commercialization. What IDEO produce must be relevant to the target markets, and the timing of the release of those innovations to those markets is critical, as Christensen has taught us. Yet just as we must move beyond Christensen's management frameworks if we are to understand the sources of innovation and the critical role of problem-solving, so too must we move beyond IDEO's design innovation if we are to understand the full extent of what innovation is.

Senge, De Bono, Basadur, IDEO, Christenson's Strategos, and Hamel's Innosight, each supplies a distinct component of the operating system for innovation. Thinking tools, work practices, culture, market analysis, strategy, education, training, and knowledge management – what's missing? What lies beneath the surface of the innovation iceberg?

HERDING AND HEARING FLOCKS OF BRAINS

According to Jonas Ridderstråle and Kjelle Nordström, researchers at the Institute of International Business at the Stockholm School of Economics, "Business success is a matter of herding flocks of brains." In their book *Funky Business – Talent Makes Capital Dance*, they observe that in a modern company, 70%–80% of what people do is now done by way of their intellects ... and the human brain is overpowering the traditional means of production. Hal Sirkin, leader of Boston Consulting Group's Operations Practice, observes that "Most people think of innovation only in terms of R&D or new product development – but taking an idea and turning it into cash is an effort that involves almost every part of a company. The challenge is thinking about and managing this extremely broad set of interrelated activity as a unified process." To meet the challenge, some companies are turning to a concept called idea management.

If the phrase brings to mind the proverbial company "suggestions box," think again. Idea management focuses the creativity of employees on critical business problems and increases their participation in solving both line-of-business and "big picture," market- and revenue-related issues. Some call it the "Innovation to Cash" process.

In the past, innovation was defined largely by creativity and the development of new ideas. Today, the term encompasses coordinated projects directed toward honing these ideas and converting them into developments that boost the bottom line. A new event, fact, or idea emerges, and is sent for evaluation by those able to make the appropriate judgments and guide the development of the idea.

Does the idea embody the possibility for a new dominant design, service, or platform? Can a project be constituted to manage the development of this initial "seed"? Marsha McArthur, innovation manager at Bristol-Myers Squibb, one of America's largest pharmaceutical companies, used an idea management solution to help the company through a period of industry consolidation and widespread patent expiration on many "blockbuster" drugs.

When a patent expires and an alternative generic drug enters the market, it is possible to lose 80% of revenue in the patented drug line within six months. In 2001, Bristol-Myers Squibb had four such drugs, each with more than US$1 billion in annual sales. Following an audit of innovation activities in late 2000 involving over 400 managers and executives, the company decided it needed to build a pipeline of revenue generating ideas to grow its pharmaceuticals and medical products businesses. Bristol-Myers Squibb deployed an idea management hub from idea innovator Imaginatik. This software application, accessible on the company intranet, captured, structured, assembled, organized, evaluated, and ranked suggestions collected from the field. It provided essential features such as workflow, idea reviews, and security.

Rather than just collecting random ideas through a traditional electronic suggestion box, the system was structured to maintain employee interest levels and participation rates, aligned to corporate innovation objectives. Workflow-based peer review weeded out bad ideas and promoted good ideas to become mature concepts. Related items were grouped and expanded through further input. Project-specific review teams evaluated ideas against weighted scorecards customized to company-significant events.

The idea management application at Bristol-Myers Squibb was first offered to brand teams supporting specific products, and it was subsequently used to manage ideas generated around line extensions, marketing tactics, and direct communications with doctors and consumers. By 2003, more than

5000 ideas had been collected. One project was the "War on Diabetes," in which Bristol-Myers Squibb introduced a range of diabetes management tools that help improve the quality of life for patients, achieving one of the fastest conversion rates for a patented drug in the history of the pharmaceutical industry. Over 3000 individuals from sales and marketing worldwide contributed to the "ideation" process, generating 400 ideas in four weeks. In 2002, sales of Glucophage XR extended-release tablets grew 29% to $297 million.

Sometimes referred to as the "fuzzy front end" to product development, idea management may ultimately provide the knowledge-management industry with the validation it's been seeking, says Jonathan Spira, an analyst with research firm Basex. "People have been waiting for five or six years for a reason to latch onto knowledge management," he says. "Idea management could rescue knowledge management from oblivion."

Bristol-Myers Squibb's marketing research group conducted an extensive post-ideation audit of around 1000 ideas collected in their system to validate the quality of the concepts and the eventual business value. The "Idea-thon" study found that 10% of the ideas had significant business value, 2.5% were truly exceptional, and even a single "small" idea could pay for the entire company-wide implementation effort of the associated software. No wonder that the idea of idea management is growing in popularity. Advocates describe different kinds of "idea-flow" meeting the needs of different kinds of organizations. Some speak of extended "idea-chains," designed to manage the collection and development of ideas from external partners, such as suppliers, customers, and research partners. Such systems include additional features to manage access rights, rewards, and intellectual property (IP) rights. Idea management structures the collaboration process between business partners.

Designed with sensitivity to fit the culture of an organization, idea management can help ensure that the voices of employees are properly heard within, and focused upon, important corporate objectives. The aim is the identification and evaluation of those ideas that present the most substantial benefits, allowing the development of a fruitful idea pipeline aligned to top-down objectives. The byproduct may be increased buy-in to new management initiatives and positive support for the associated organizational and process changes that will inevitably result from the implementation of those ideas. A form of coordinated innovation, idea management solutions supply a starter pack of processes that act as the tipping point for a sustainable innovation program. The approach can generate a long-term corporate memory bank, a central and accessible location to organize, categorize, and harvest the constant influx of ideas.

Idea management processes close the loop between employees with ideas and senior managers who have the authority, budgets, and motivation to make them happen. Senior managers, business-unit heads, product/service development leaders, or process owners establish each campaign, and ideas generated in the field and throughout the business are directed to qualified experts in the business who can evaluate each idea. These ideas might be promoted, demoted, or aggregated with related ideas and further development, often through collaboration with the individual that created the seed. Idea management helps in other ways too. It plays a key role in helping to ensure that time and resources are not wasted on ideas that have been rejected in the past. Conversely, it can be used to revive ideas that were inappropriate before but now have increased relevance. In all these senses, idea management helps focus resources and further thinking on ideas with high potential.

Typical software systems for idea management issue reminders to evaluators of upcoming deadlines and unevaluated inputs. Lacking such features, simpler electronic suggestions boxes tend to fill up with large numbers of low-quality ideas that are not focused on business goals. Without automated support, employees are unable to follow up on what happened to their thoughts and tend to become cynical, no longer sharing their insights with their employer.

Skeptics of idea management point to depressing statistics. The *Economist* reckons that an enterprise has to start with around 3000 bright ideas if it is to come up with 100 worthwhile projects, which, in turn, will be winnowed down to four development programs for new products. William Miller and Langdon Morris, authors of a sweeping and insightful analysis of innovation in the knowledge economy, *Fourth Generation R&D*, observe that "During the 1980s, American corporations wasted billions of dollars on failed attempts to innovate, which demonstrates that just spending more money doesn't help if assumptions are incorrect and the process is flawed. ... Measuring downstream, it seems that, of four projects that enter the development stage, only one becomes commercially successful." Yet such figures should not be used to dismiss idea management so lightly.

Case studies have shown that idea management is a collaboration tool, linking top management with innovative employees with domain expertise via those able to interpret, develop, and guide those ideas to fruition. Perhaps idea management should be renamed solution development. The intelligent user of idea management is doing far more than idea-fishing; they are focusing the talent of employees by challenging them to solve hard problems, in engineering, in development, in operations, and in marketing. Here is where the real value of idea management lies, not only in the trawl for ideas at the outskirts of the organization, but also in the continued and sustained involvement of all employees throughout the commercialization process.

This contribution is necessary because companies often underestimate the costs involved in driving adoption of a new product or service. The *Economist*'s figures refer only to new product development, and this accounts for just 15%, or less, of the innovation activities a company should be doing. Reflecting on the invention of the Alto personal office computer, author, consultant, and ex-director at Xerox PARC labs, John Seely Brown observes that "as much, if not more, creativity goes into the implementation part of the innovation as into the invention itself." In this respect, Xerox, the inventor, failed as an innovator, leaving billions in profits for Apple and Microsoft.

In turbulent times, it is easy to give up on innovation. The uncertainty associated with success rates for new ideas and the difficulty of commercializing any individual new idea leaves many with the sense that innovation – the creation of new value – is mysterious, unpredictable, and apparently, unmanageable.

Searching for breakthroughs is expensive and time-consuming, and many managers fall back on incremental improvements to existing products and services. After all, line extensions help the bottom line immediately. Some companies seek solid ground by eradicating all activities that are not requested by the customer, a focus on the consumption chain. Others make up for innovation gaps and new product failures by pursuing parallel efforts such as increasing volume in existing markets through market share warfare, reducing costs through downsizing, process improvements, quality improvements and outsourcing, using methods and tools to enhance productivity or customer loyalty, making acquisitions or exiting marginal businesses. But as Miller and Langdon observe, "None of these strategies address the fundamental need to increase the value that is provided to customers. Only innovation is competent to do this."

Where does innovation come from? The "Run Loop" helps to answer this question.

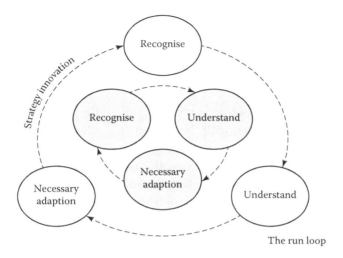

The run loop

AN AGE OF TIME, TALENT AND INTANGIBLES

To keep up with all the new product launches, Procter & Gamble has more scientists on its payroll than Harvard, Berkeley, and MIT combined. Physical assets and means of production, even those upgraded and installed last year, hardly help companies keep pace and compete in the future. Sure, you need plumbing; otherwise things get very messy. But it is no longer enough. In a world of contract manufacturing and outsourcing overcapacity, "Use all the force you want. Bludgeon down walls; threaten and cajole. It won't get you anywhere if you are dealing with someone who is smarter, quicker and hungrier ... the new competitive battlefield is not the engine or the air conditioner – it is the design, the warranty, the service deal, the image and the finance package," claim Ridderstråle and Nordström. In this environment, typified by General Motor's advertising slogan, "a car full of ideas," it is more accurate to talk about "provices" and "serducts" than products and services, as you can hardly separate the two. And this is especially true in service-based businesses.

Companies seeking new wealth need to look toward intelligence, and intangibles; and of course, people. Innovation and competence are locked in an inseparable embrace. According to Ridderstråle and Nordström, "This is the age of time and talent, where we are selling time and talent, exploiting time and talent, organizing time and talent, hiring time and talent and packaging time and talent. The most critical resource wears shoes and walks out the door around five o'clock every day." They mean innovative people. At design firm IDEO, for example, those who have the best ideas define what it means to be more senior.

Stanford Research Institute's Paul Romer, speaking about the 300 largest multinational companies that control 25% of all the productive assets on earth, states that "the ones with the best recipes will win." The individual, team, organization, or economic region that excels in developing innovative concepts and ideas about how to combine and re-combine the ingredients of business will be most successful. The recipe must be unique enough to capture the attention of oversupplied and demanding customers, a recipe that adds real value and a recipe that is extremely difficult to copy. Preferably, it should be protected by law. Over the next decade, dealers in and of atoms alone are in for some pretty tough times. Unfortunately, atoms are easier to count.

"The financial balance sheet is probably the only 500-year-old supermodel still capable of arousing a few people," observe Ridderstråle and Nordström. Yet despite its long-lasting allure, it often only manages to capture around 15%–20% of the real value of many modern companies. Pfizer's $270 billion market cap is supported more by the patents it owns on innovative drugs, such as Zoloft (depression), Zyrtec (allergies), and Norvasc (hypertension) – which have no value on its balance sheet – than by its machinery, land, and buildings, which have a book value of $20 billion.

Douglas Graham and Thomas Bachman, in their book Ideation: *The Birth and Death of Ideas*, point out that recently there has been a sea change in accounting, driven by the Financial Accounting Standards Board (FASB) 141 and 142 Statements, as well as the Securities and Exchange Commission (SEC) S-X ruling. The former requires companies that have acquired other companies to identify and value all the intangible assets in the acquired company. Soon this rule will extend to all intangibles, whether acquired or developed in-house.

"These are not mere arcane accounting rules," claim Graham and Bachman. "The regulatory bodies are recognizing that the world has changed and most of the value of companies is tied up in their intangibles." As Alan Greenspan put it, "We are entering the era of "Ideanomics." Yet the FASB is the first to admit that the CFO is ill-equipped to handle these new requirements. Their view: "Companies' inability to identify and inventory intangible assets may be the most significant obstacle to any comprehensive recognition of intangible assets. Managers cannot measure assets they do not, today, identify and manage as assets."

Is innovation an operating expense or an investment? Cecily Fluke and Lesley Kump, writing in *Forbes*, suggest that accounting bias penalizes earnings of companies with strong R&D efforts. So, they came up with a novel approach to deal with this conundrum: Adjust earning by adding back R&D expenses, arriving at what they call innovation-adjusted earnings. Chris Mallon took the idea one stage further in an article in the *Motley Fool*. Assuming R&D is an investment, why not add it back to operating cash flow, leading to what could be called innovation-adjusted-free-cash-flow. Mallon calculated how this might affect the valuation of some leading technology companies. For the fiscal year 2004, Microsoft generated $14.6 billion in operating cash, had $7.8 billion in R&D expenses, and $1.1 billion in capital expenditures. Under the strict definition, free cash flow was $13.5 billion, or about $1.24 per share. Using the adjusted formula, the answer would be $21.3 billion or $1.95 per share. This may be a good idea for shareholders, but it hardly counts as innovation.

According to the Economist, the new acid test for global firms is whether or not it hurts when you drop your competitive advantage on your toes, leading to the imperative to manage IP and intangibles as never before.

In the real time, globally linked, surplus society, competitors will steal your ideas in two to three weeks. "Knowledge is perishable. Treat it like milk. Date it," urge Ridderstråle and Nordström. Are they right? If so, it is hardly surprising that, alongside tried and tested business strategies, such as continuous product evolution, channel expansion, globalization, and margin growth, leading firms are now placing more emphasis on the management of intangibles.

Research by academics, such as Baruch Lev at the New York Stern School of Management has led some companies to note a correlation between the successful businesses that emerged from the last 100 years; the companies that hold the most patents in the last 100 years are those who have been the most innovative in the last 100 years. No wonder then that IP and other forms of intangible assets have become a major focus of US businesses, with many other nations seeking to follow the US lead. Germany is legislating new IP ownership laws for universities and encouraging public-private research partnerships to more closely follow the US model. Japanese companies are being required by government-led initiatives to improve their IP competitiveness. In the growing IP wars, the process by which companies manage IP is nothing less than a strategic market-led business process.

Bill Gates recently pointed to Microsoft's R&D as a differentiator. For the fiscal year 2004, R&D spending at Microsoft represented about 17.8% of revenue.

Gates noted that, according to some measures (for example, "current impact"), its patent portfolio outpaces those of Oracle, Sun, Apple, and IBM. The company is on something of a patent tear, filing for 2135 patents in the fiscal year 2004 versus 519 in the fiscal year 1998. It's the same story in many other industrial sectors. Aerospace leader BAE Systems places emphasis on IP and educates employees about the danger of allowing IP to leak into the public domain. Once that happens, ideas can't be patented and can't be protected. The company believes it is never too early to start thinking about the patent filing process and they stress that an idea doesn't have to be a major technological change to warrant a patent, it can be a "new, improved" version of an existing technology.

It's a view also held by the majority of CEOs who adopt the general stance that innovation, inventions, and technical know-how are the lifeblood of the company and, that, to leave them unprotected and let IP drain away, is reckless.

Patents are a legal proxy for innovation. A patent excludes others from making, using, offering for sale, or selling inventions. Granting a US patent is a transfer of the competence of an inventor from the realm of ideas into the realm of binding property rights. And it isn't just engineering solutions that can be patented. Utility patents may be granted to anyone who invents or discovers any new and useful process, machine, article of manufacture, composition of matter, or any new useful improvement thereof.

By not patenting, companies risk losing important future technical advances and the revenue that can result from licensing. And the principle extends to process design, although legal practice in this area is far less developed. But not everyone is convinced about a sole and direct link between IP, the size of a company's patent portfolio, and future earnings potential.

Not all companies are avid patent filers, and many believe that the significance of patent ownership can be overstated. It is relatively easy to point to successful firms with reliable returns to stockholders who have rarely sought legal protection for their intangibles: knowledge, competence, methodologies, and processes. While patent filing may be an indirect indicator of innovation activity for high-tech firms, the vast majority of individual patents have little commercial value, and the process of obtaining, and enforcing, patents is complex, expensive, and time-consuming. Plus, there are indicators that the patent system itself is under stress.

Adam Jaffe and Josh Lerner believe that the U.S. patent system has become sand rather than lubricant in the wheels of American progress. Such is the premise behind their new book, *Innovation and Its Discontents: How Our Broken Patent System Is Endangering Innovation and Progress, and What to Do About It*. It tells the story of how recent changes in patenting have wreaked havoc on innovators, businesses, and economic productivity. First, new laws have made it easier for businesses and inventors to secure patents on products of all kinds, and second, the laws have tilted the table to favor patent holders, no matter how tenuous their claims. Jaffe and Lerner, who have spent the past two decades studying the patent system, show how legal changes initiated in the 1980s converted the system from a stimulator of innovation to a creator of litigation and uncertainty that threatens the innovation process itself.

On the other hand, patents do provide one way to demonstrate value to the marketplace. Numerous empirical studies (e.g., Lev and Sougiannis, 1996) have established an economically meaningful and statistically significant relationship between R&D outlays and subsequent benefits, in the form of increased productivity, earnings, and shareholder value. In the United States, knowledge assets account for six of every seven dollars of corporate market value. For high-tech companies this ratio is larger. At the same time, the intangible assets arising from this investment are undervalued on the balance sheet. Obviously, the uncertainty about intangibles (e.g., products, services, and processes under development) in respect of their future value-generating potential is substantially larger for outsiders than for corporate insiders.

Lev Barach has observed that "Investors react to uncertainty by demanding a compensating return premium, which translates to a higher cost of capital to the company. Indeed, research shows that increased investment in knowledge assets increases both the cost of equity capital and debt of corporations." His research points to the methods companies can use to strengthen the way in which their intangibles are presented to the market. Barach believes that "A credible and coherent disclosure strategy can alleviate the undervaluation problem," and he urges companies to "elaborate on the major knowledge-related items relevant to investors – product pipeline, technological and commercialization capabilities – and on the effective means of disclosing them, while minimizing the potential competitive and legal harms of disclosure."

The link between intangibles and the balance sheet leads many companies to envelop innovators with a plethora of legal, compliance, and other structured procedures to maximize the downstream value of their creativity. R&D programs are structured to collect, assess, and foster the development of insight.

Collaborative research is dominated by the language of contracts, subcontracts, patent filing, licensing, insurances, indemnification, acquisition processes, teaming agreements, cooperative research and development agreements, memorandums of understanding, non-disclosure agreements, performance-based contracting, grants, and cost reimbursement. In effect, companies are building balance-sheet amplifiers around their people as they work to think, create, invent, and improve.

Companies are playing a tightrope-balancing act. In fiscally cautious times, where every line item in every budget is under intense scrutiny, organizations are subjecting nascent product and service development to rigorous screening.

R&D personnel and innovators in other business units are being trained to think in business terms. The hope is that companies will be in a better position to decide whether an idea is worth pursuing in the first place. One company reported that "Our biggest barrier to success is balancing rigorous examination of ideas while not eroding our people's motivation to keep coming up with them."

At Rohm and Haas (a company that makes specialty materials that enhance the performance of paints and coatings, computers and electronic devices, household goods, and more) IP strategy is integrated into all technology generation and subsequent commercialization. Patent attorneys sit in development teams as new technologies emerge.

Under the leadership of David Bonner, who until July 2002 was the global director of technology, together with Marc Adler, chief patent counsel, the processes governing research and IP management became a holistic business process, focused on growth markets. At the IP Summit in Japan in July 2002, Bonner explained that as a result of this approach, "Investment by Rohm and Haas in R&D has grown and stayed consistently robust for its industry. Our resolve never wavered because our senior business management had confidence in a holistic, transparent process." A properly constituted R&D program avoids swamping business units with an uncontrolled, and rapid, flow of new ideas into their commercial operations, often with little connection to the existing business strategies.

Resource constraints lead companies to structure the innovation process so as to focus limited resources on the most promising ideas. They seek to increase learning through small, low-risk proof-of-concept projects. Development efforts are funneled through an innovation pipeline, from ideas, to experiments, ventures, and new businesses. At one end of the pipe, projects are many and resources are few. At the other end, projects are few and resources are many.

Idea management focuses creativity on the few ideas that are relevant. Product development identifies viable ideas and expands them to generate the most value. Everyone benefits in the end. By managing resources and projects against the portfolio of relevant initiatives, a company develops a capability for continued renovation. IP flows through the pipeline, from mind to market.

Companies are building their operating systems for innovation, step-by-step and brick-by-brick. They are bonding their R&D process to their commercialization process. Reducing the friction is a major challenge. While it is natural to hide high-potential secrets and protect valuable insights that could be the basis of profitable future products, the widespread distribution of useful knowledge enabled by the Internet and other media can make such controls unfeasible. In the face of pressure to collaborate with partners and customers in the real-time economy, are we worrying unnecessarily?

While the key to successful innovation once lay in the controlled environment of the corporate laboratory, Eric von Hippel, author of the influential book *The Sources of Innovation*, shows us that the manufacturer-as-sole-innovator assumption is wrong. In a global economy, one in which companies focus on core competencies – outsourcing all else and in-sourcing myriad services and competencies from numerous partners – the innovation process is predictably distributed, across users, manufacturers, suppliers, and other collaborators. Yet while external ideas help create value, it takes internal R&D to claim a portion of that value (legally and with legal protection).

No innovation holds value until a viable business model successfully commercializes it. Henry Chesbrough points out that "If you don't unlock this value, someone else will." Companies must recognize that not all the smart people work for you. Others are equally able to innovate or exploit someone else's promising ideas. Chesbrough advises companies to profit from the use of their own IP, but also to buy IP from others whenever it advances their own business model. Companies, he says, should expand the role of R&D to include not only knowledge generation, but also knowledge brokering. Other voices echo similar sentiments.

In his book *Resolving the Innovation Paradox*, George Haour encourages the "mobilization of substantial external inputs into the innovation process, requiring companies to excel as entrepreneurial architects of innovation."

Quoting examples from Generics, Intel, Nokia, and Samsung, his ideas about distributed innovation "help companies to raise revenue by using channels such as licensing and selling innovation projects."

Alph Bingham, former VP of R&D at Eli Lilly, was frustrated that the company was spending billions of dollars on R&D, yet the rate at which it was developing drugs had not changed. In 1999, he proposed using freelancers to supplement internal resources. Lilly decided to test the idea with the creation of an external commercial enterprise, InnoCentive, founded in 2001. Today, InnoCentive is a Web-based community that matches top scientists to relevant R&D challenges facing leading companies around the globe, allowing them to reward scientific innovation through financial incentives. InnoCentive's clients include Procter & Gamble, Dow Chemical, and BASF, and the research brokerage is reported to have saved Lilly millions on R&D expenses.

Fifty-three percent of InnoCentive's best freelance researchers are based in China and India, and North American corporations have created divisions just to create and oversee InnoCentive-hosted projects. One company, Dial Corporation, advertises directly on the site and offers cash prizes for inventions that improve their bottom line. Other companies treat InnoCentive as a source of additional resources that can be targeted at well-defined fragments of internal R&D efforts.

A Shortcut via Experimentation

Business managers who speak only of intangibles management and the protection of IP may have got it wrong. Perhaps the focus should be on managing the innovators, as much as it is on managing the innovations? While it is essential to upgrade product development systems, deploy stage-gate processes, structure judgments about risky projects, bring in collaborators, and add in timely data about real and projected market demand into the commercialization process, a focus on methods is equally important.

"Rather than knowledge management, the key to increasing internal knowledge is knowledgeable management," so say Ridderstråle and Nordström. They describe the process of turning core components into core competencies: Gas is what we have in our minds; fluid knowledge comes about when we discuss things with others, and solid knowledge is the stuff that is embodied in customer's offerings, routines, and systems. "A car, a PC, a software program, an ice-cream, or whatever is, in reality, nothing more and nothing less than frozen creativity. We get an idea (gas), start discussing it with others (fluid), and finally develop a customer offering (solid). We rely on our ability to develop processes that enable us to deep-freeze new pieces of knowledge faster than others – decreasing the duration of the insight–output cycle."

It was competence-based leverage, linked to an insatiable drive to experiment, that let Honda, which originally focused on engines, to nevertheless utilize their knowledge to make cars, motorcycles, watercraft, pumps, snow blowers, and now robots such as POLAR II, the most advanced pedestrian test dummy in the world. The same is true for service-centric firms. It is competency-based knowledge, honed at the customer interface, that ultimately gives rise to enduring service businesses. Competence-transference, coupled to experimentation, seems to have legs in the innovation race.

Stefan Thomke, author of *Experimentation Matters*, believes that every company's ability to innovate depends upon a process of experimentation whereby new products and services are created and existing ones improved.

Citing the availability of computer simulation and modeling that promise to lift the economic barriers to being allowed to fail, Thomke reminds us that "Never before has it been so economically feasible to ask 'what if' questions, generate preliminary answers and guide the innovation process. ... Put concretely, without experimentation, we might all still be living in caves and using rocks as tools."

According to Thomke, all organizations need a system of experimentation and, of course, the more rapid and efficient the system is, the quicker researchers can find solutions. Thomke urges companies to organize for rapid experimentation; fail early and often; anticipate and exploit early information; and combine new and old technologies.

When Edison noted that inventive genius is "99% perspiration and 1% inspiration," he was well aware of the importance of an organization's capability and capacity to experiment. Edison designed his labs, including personnel, equipment, and libraries, to allow for efficient and rapid iteration. As today's digital technologies for product, service, and process modeling and simulation offer more value for less money, they provoke fundamental challenges to the innovation organization, culture, and design.

Michael Schrage, author of *Serious Play: How the World's Best Companies Simulate to Innovate*, argues that the future of modeling, simulation, and prototyping is the future of innovation. Drawing on the experience of companies, including Walt Disney, Boeing, Merrill Lynch, GE, Sony, IBM, IDEO, Microsoft, Royal Dutch Shell, Daimler Chrysler, and American Airlines, Schrage shows us that serious play is not an oxymoron; it is the essence of innovation.

The challenge and thrill of confronting uncertainty requires a healthy dose of improvisation. Whether these uncertainties are obstacles, or allies, depends on how you play. His central message: "Any tools, technologies, techniques, or toys that let people improve how they play seriously with uncertainty is guaranteed to improve the quality of innovation. The ability to align those improvements cost-effectively with the needs of customers, clients, and markets dramatically boosts the odds for competitive success."

Experimentation, simulation, discovering options, evaluating alternatives, and problem-solving, these all lie at the heart of innovation in virtually every discipline. When the IDEO creative team files a new technology in the Tech Box, they are storing knowledge about a past problem and a future creative solution option. The same idea is inherent in every legal patent. All inventions embody solutions to previously unsolved problems. Leibniz once observed: "It pays to study the discoveries of others so that we also find a new source for inventions." Perhaps managing innovators is, in itself, not enough? Should we study the methods used by those we employ to innovate: engineers and scientists? They may be locked in a lab and cloistered by legal processes, but their experimental methods are universally applicable.

AND SUDDENLY THE INVENTOR APPEARED

All significant innovations embody solutions to complex problems. While ideas sometimes take the form of a technical insight with no apparent commercial application, in most cases, a problem or opportunity inspires the insight. As Imaginatik have found through practice, there is always a reason to solve a complex problem otherwise nobody would bother. This is why the most effective idea management campaigns are those where a serious challenge is put to employees. All who innovate are required to eradicate obstacles and find approaches that move them closer to the ideal systems they seek to build.

Opportunity recognition occurs when someone says, "This material we've invented might be of value to customers," or "If we could solve this problem, we could create value for our customers and our shareholders," or "This might produce a huge cost advantage." Every product, service, and process proceed through generations of design and evolution in its market, and, at every stage, the innovator faces formidable barriers for which inventive solutions are required. These solutions may be technological or they may require a business innovation, such as process redesign or market alignment. For example, it's one thing to create an innovative product or service, but it's quite another to create a process capable of manufacturing the product or delivering the service at a price the target market will accept.

SUMMARY

A complex cocktail of problems limits a company's ability to innovate.

Innovation in the product, service, and process realm is connected; some innovative ideas must await process innovation before they can achieve market traction. At every stage – from the conception of a new idea, through development, to commercialization, and eventually to marketing and business coming in – hundreds of problems must be resolved. The innovation process is littered with hurdles, both high and low, from new science, to creative means of delivery, to detailed product architecture, to service-concept, to business model. These problems are what innovation is, and it is up to the individual and the teams they work within to solve them.

Problem-solving lies at the heart of a new methodology for innovation that, at its core, is a study of contradiction. A contradiction exists in a system when, in attempting to improve one parameter of the system, another parameter you care about deteriorates. For example, if we attempt to make a product stronger by making it thicker, it also gets heavier. If we use better materials, the cost goes up, and so on. Stan Kaplan, engineer and applied mathematician, an expert on Quantitative Risk Assessment (QRA), and the founder of Bayesian Systems, points out that "the typical engineering approach to dealing with such contradictions is to trade-off, in other words, to compromise."

While compromise may be useful in some situations, and may itself contribute to minor improvements, compromise cannot be considered to be innovation and is unlikely to help solve further problems down the line that prevent or limit the product, service, or process from being successfully developed, commercialized, and improved in ways that provide value to customers. By contrast, Kaplan believes that "an invention is an idea that surmounts the contradiction, moving both parameters in a favorable direction." If true, the patent literature should be littered with useful solutions, and inventions must be inherent to all commercially successful products, services, and organizations.

Innovators solve problems by focusing upon the useful parameters of a system that, if increased, would enhance it substantially, but also, the harmful aspects that, if left unchecked, would lead to a contradiction. Contradictions are significant, for if eradicated or reduced, directly or indirectly, they contribute to the development of a breakthrough solution. Avoiding compromise is central to innovation. Trade-offs – strength versus weight, reliability versus cost, service quality versus resource, and output versus input – are not the same as an inventive solution that creates new value. Inventive solutions emerge by exploiting useful effects and eliminating harmful effects. The subject can even be taught as a discipline, with the effect of increasing the overall "inventiveness" of employees. Problem-solving is a generic skill and can be applied across many different domains. Make someone more effective in one domain, and they will be more effective in others.

But if you thought you had heard about all the best-practice acronyms and trends out there, think again. To the current plethora of strategies for adaptation and survival is now added something that may be a way of thinking, a set of tools, a methodology, a process, a theory, or even possibly a deep science, but that may be gradually shaping up as "the next big thing." It's called TRIZ, pronounced "trees" and is an acronym for the Russian words that translate as "The Theory of Inventive Problem Solving."

The suggestion that innovation can be taught lies uneasily with those who believe it arises from psychological factors and that great ideas come from a special place in the mind. Yet we happily teach Six Sigma to create black belts who are able, using reliable statistical methods, to substantially improve process reliability, even in fields where they have no domain knowledge. By applying the Six Method discipline, a "black belt" is able to identify process instances that fall outside of the specification, root out the cause of process failure, and suggest avenues for redesign. Is there a reliable innovation algorithm that, simply by being applied, identifies contradictions and finds solutions by avoiding compromise?

Experiments are guided by science. Teams solve problems that lead to valuable innovations using systematic methodologies. Examples include the Theory of Constraints (TOC), Critical Chain, Design for Six Sigma (DFSS), Quality Function Deployment (QFD), and the Taguchi Method.

1. DFSS led GE to deliver record financial results in 1999, with revenue and earnings growth exceeding 25%. In that year, GE introduced seven products using Six Sigma methods, and more than 20 were released in 2000. Jeffrey Immelt said at the time, "These products are different – they capture customer needs better and can be brought to market faster than ever before. We will see more than $2 billion worth of DFSS products by the end of 2000."

2. QFD enabled 3M, AT&T, Boeing, DaimlerChrysler, Ford, GM, Hewlett-Packard, Hughes, Kodak, Lockheed-Martin, Pratt & Whitney, Motorola, NASA, Nokia, Raytheon, Texas Instrument, United Technologies, Visteon, Xerox, and other Fortune 500 companies to reformulate products without sacrificing customer satisfaction. Their objectives were to open the path to foreign markets, to differentiate services where there was customer value, engineer common elements that were invisible to the user, see opportunities in advance of market demand, and develop hybrid products from two or more best-selling lines.

3. The Taguchi Method (robust design) enabled Kodak's copy machine manufacturing division to improve the reliability of its paper feeder from a mean time between failures of 2,500 sheets to 40,000 sheets.

12

Managing an Intellectual Property Portfolio

Hierarchy of Organizational Needs. In entrepreneurial companies, building a strong foundation is part of managing an Intellectual Property (IP) portfolio. Vision and strategy are where the entrepreneur or CEO is likely going to focus much of their time. Every business needs to have an Innovation Portfolio clear purpose (WHY?), a clear articulation of how they will build the portfolio (HOW?), and an articulation of the core business and customer base that will be used to reach portfolio goals (WHAT?). A well-articulated vision and strategy become the playbook for the entire organization. Everyone knows the goal, and everyone knows how their work connects to that goal. Link every project to the strategy and measure every action in a way that is relevant to the goal.

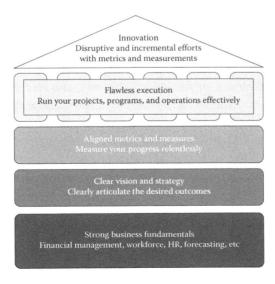

In a nutshell: Once you have a portfolio of ideas in the organization, how do you manage them in a flawless manner so that the truly great projects/ideas rise to the top, while the pet projects of one department or manager are set aside for future consideration? As mentioned earlier in the book, managing the pipeline and portfolio of innovations is a critical component of the process.* Doing so doesn't necessarily require a computer program or expert. It is more likely that the change needs a very organized, motivated, and charismatic leader who is genuinely excited about innovation and always wants to see the best ideas get heard, evaluated well and make it to the top.

INTRODUCTION

Management knows it and so does Wall Street: The year-to-year viability of a company depends on its ability to innovate. Given today's market expectations, global competitive pressures, and the extent and pace of structural change, this is truer than ever. But chief executives struggle to make the case to the Street that their managerial actions can be relied on to yield a stream of successful new offerings. Many admit to being unsure and frustrated. Typically, they are aware of a tremendous amount of innovation going on inside their enterprises but don't feel they have a grasp on all the dispersed initiatives. The pursuit of the new feels haphazard and episodic, and they suspect that the returns on the company's total innovation investment are too low.

Making matters worse, executives tend to respond with dramatic interventions and vacillating strategies. Take the example of a consumer goods company we know. Attuned to the need to keep its brands fresh in retailers' and consumers' minds, it introduced frequent improvements and variations on its core offerings. Most of those earned their keep with respectable uptake by the market and decent margins. Over time, however, it became clear that all this product proliferation, while splitting the revenue pie into ever-smaller slices, wasn't actually growing the pie. Eager to achieve a much higher return,

---

* As mentioned in Chapter 6, Simon Sinek's TED talk on 'Getting to Why': How Great Leaders Inspire Action contains more details on the importance of getting to WHY (as described in the callout box) and the order of operations. Sinek has a simple but powerful model for inspirational leadership—starting with a golden circle and the question "Why?"

management lurched toward a new strategy aimed at breakthrough product development – at transformational rather than incremental innovations.

Unfortunately, this company's structure and processes were not set up to execute on that ambition; although it had the requisite capabilities for envisioning, developing, and market testing innovations close to its core, it neither recognized nor gained the very different capabilities needed to take a bolder path. Its most inventive ideas ended up being diluted beyond recognition, killed outright, or crushed under the weight of the enterprise. Before long, the company retreated to what it knew best. Once again, little was ventured, and little was gained – and the cycle repeated itself.*

We tell this story because it is typical of companies that have not yet learned to manage innovation strategically. It demonstrates an all-too-common contrast to the steady, above-average returns that can be achieved only through a well-balanced portfolio. The companies we've found to have the strongest innovation track records can articulate a clear innovation ambition; have struck the right balance of core, adjacent, and transformational initiatives across the enterprise; and have put in place the tools and capabilities to manage those various initiatives as parts of an integrated whole. Rather than hoping that their future will emerge from a collection of ad hoc, stand-alone efforts that compete with one another for time, money, attention, and prestige, they manage for "total innovation."

Be Clear About your Innovation Ambition

What does it mean to manage an innovation portfolio? First, let's consider how broad a term "innovation" is. Defined as a novel creation that produces value, an innovation can be as slight as a new nail polish color or as vast as the World Wide Web. Most companies invest in initiatives along a broad spectrum of risk and reward. As in financial investing, their goal should be to construct the portfolio that produces the highest overall return that's in keeping with their appetite for risk.

One tool we've developed is the Innovation Ambition Matrix (see the exhibit subsequently). Students of management will recognize it as a

---

* Unlike small businesses, big companies do not easily reinvent themselves as leading innova-tors. Too many fixed routines and cultural factors can get in the way. For those that do make the attempt, innovation excellence is often built in terms of a multiyear effort that touches most, if not all, parts of the organization. Our experience and research suggest that any entrepreneur looking to make this journey will maximize its probability of success by closely studying and appropriately assimilating the leading practices of high-performing innovators.

refinement of a classic diagram devised by the mathematician H. Igor Ansoff to help companies allocate funds among growth initiatives. Ansoff's matrix clarified the notion that tactics should differ according to whether a firm was launching a new product, entering a new market, or both. Our version replaces Ansoff's binary choices of product and market (old versus new) with a range of values.

This acknowledges that the novelty of a company's offerings (on the *x*-axis) and the novelty of its customer markets (on the *y*-axis) are a matter of degree. We have overlaid three levels of distance from the company's current, bottom-left reality.

THE INNOVATION AMBITION MATRIX*

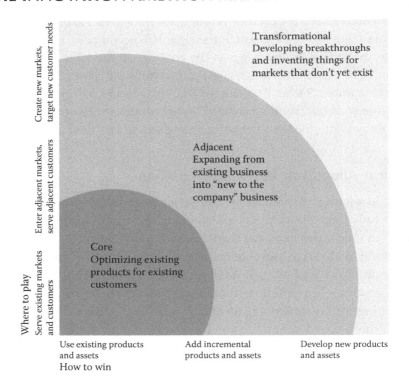

---

* The Innovation Ambition Matrix offers no inherent prescription. Its power lies in the two exercises it facilitates. First, it gives managers a framework for surveying all the initiatives the business has under way: How many are being pursued in each realm, and how much investment is going to each type of innovation? Second, it gives managers a way to discuss the right overall ambition for the company's innovation portfolio.

In the band of activity at the lower left of the matrix are core innovation initiatives – efforts to make incremental changes to existing products and incremental inroads into new markets. Whether in the form of new packaging (such as Nabisco's 100-calorie packets of Oreos for on-the-go snackers), slight reformulations (as when Dow AgroSciences launched one of its herbicides as a liquid suspension rather than a dry powder), or added service convenience (e.g., replacing pallets with shrink-wrapping to reduce shipping charges), such innovations draw on assets the company already has in place.*

At the opposite corner of the matrix are transformational initiatives, designed to create new offers – if not whole new businesses – to serve new markets and customer needs. These are the innovations that, when successful, make headlines: Think of iTunes, the Tata Nano, and the Starbucks in-store experience. These sorts of innovations, also called breakthrough, disruptive, or game-changing, generally require that the company call on unfamiliar assets – for example, building capabilities to gain a deeper understanding of customers, to communicate about products that have no direct antecedents, and to develop markets that aren't yet mature.

In the middle are adjacent innovations, which can share characteristics with core and transformational innovations.

An adjacent innovation involves leveraging something the company does well into a new space. Procter & Gamble's Swiffer is a case in point. It arose from a set of needs Procter & Gamble knew well and built on customers' assumption that the proper tool for cleaning floors is a long-handled mop. But it used a novel technology to take the solution to a new customer set and generate new revenue streams. Adjacent innovations allow a company to draw on existing capabilities but necessitate putting those capabilities to new uses. They require fresh, proprietary insight into customer needs, demand trends, market structure, competitive dynamics, technology trends, and other market variables.

For one company – say, a consumer goods producer – succeeding as a great innovator might mean investing in initiatives that tend toward the lower left of the Matrix, such as small extensions to existing product lines. A high-tech company might move toward the upper right, taking bigger risks on more-audacious innovations for the chance of bigger payoffs. Although this may sound obvious, few organizations think about the best level of innovation to target, and fewer still manage to achieve it.

---

* *Source:* https://hbr.org/2012/05/managing-your-innovation-portfolio

STRIKE AND MAINTAIN THE RIGHT BALANCE

Product	Deployment	Collaboration	Dashboard	Milestone Tracking	Portfolio Management	Project Planning	Resource Management	Status Tracking
Workfront- Project Management Software ★★★☆ (387)	☁	✓	✓	✓	✓	✓	✓	✓
Mavenlink ★★★☆ (182)	☁	✓	✓	✓	✓	✓	✓	✓
Wrike ★★★★ (577)	📱☁	✓	✓	✓	✓	✓	✓	✓
Sciforma 7.0 ★★★★★ (6)	☁	✓	✓	✓	✓	✓	✓	✓
Smartsheet ★★★★☆ (273)	📱☁	✓	✓	✓	✓	✓	✓	✓
LiquidPlanner ★★★★☆ (264)	📱☁	✓	✓	✓	✓	✓	✓	✓
Accelo ★★★★☆ (3)	📱☁	✓	✓	✓	✓	✓	✓	✓
Meisterplan ★★★★★ (32)	🖥📱☁	✓	✓	✓	✓	✓	✓	✓
Asana ★★★★☆ (2397)	🖥📱☁	✓	✓	✓	✓	✓	✓	✓
Clarizen ★★★☆ (120)	📱☁	✓	✓	✓	✓	✓	✓	✓

In contemplating the balance for an innovation portfolio, managers should consider the findings of research we conducted recently as to Project Management features and modules, as shown in the previous Matrix.* In a study of companies in the industrial, technology, and consumer goods sectors, we looked at whether any particular allocation of resources across core, adjacent, and transformational initiatives correlated with significantly better performance as reflected in share price. Indeed, the data revealed a pattern: Companies that allocated about 70% of their innovation activity to core initiatives, 20% to adjacent ones, and 10% to transformational ones outperformed their peers, typically realizing a P/E premium of 10–20% (see the exhibit "Is There a Golden Ratio?"). Google knows this well:

* *Source:* Compare all software products on Capterra's Project Portfolio Management Software Directory. Also see https://www.capterra.com/sem-compare/project-portfolio-management-software?headline=Project%20Portfolio%20Software&gclid=EAIaIQobChMI7b-yopW92AIVAYezCh2zzgoDEAAYAyAAEgIANfD_BwE&gclsrc=aw.ds.

Cofounder Larry Page told *Fortune* magazine that the company strives for a 70-20-10 balance, and he credited the 10% of resources that are dedicated to transformational efforts with all the company's truly new offerings. Our subsequent conversations with buy-side analysts revealed that this allocation is attractive to capital markets because of what it implies about the balance between short-term, predictable growth and longer-term bets.

IS THERE A GOLDEN RATIO?

A second research finding adds more food for thought. In an ongoing study, we're focusing on more-direct returns on innovation.* Of the bottom-line gains companies enjoy as a result of their innovation efforts, what proportions are generated by core, adjacent, and transformational initiatives? We're finding consistently that the return ratio is roughly the inverse of that ideal allocation described previously: Core innovation efforts typically contribute 10% of the long-term, cumulative return on innovation investment; adjacent initiatives contribute 20%; and transformational efforts contribute 70% (see the exhibit "How Innovation Pays the Bills").

How Innovation Pays the Bills

Together these findings underscore the importance of managing total innovation deliberately and closely. Most companies are heavily oriented toward core innovation—and must continue to be, given the risk involved in adjacent and transformational initiatives. But if that natural tendency leads to neglect of more-ambitious forms of innovation, the outcome will be a steady decline in business and relevance to customers. Transformational initiatives are the engines of blockbuster growth.

Let us be clear: We're not suggesting that a 70-20-10 breakdown of innovation investment is a magic formula for all companies; it's simply an average allocation based on a cross-industry and cross-geography

---

* Drucker on the practice of innovation: "Innovation is the specific tool of entrepreneurship, the means by which they exploit change as an opportunity for different business or a different service. It is capable of being presented as a discipline, capable of being learned, capable of being practiced. Entrepreneurs need to search purposefully for the sources of innovation, the changes and their symptoms that indicate opportunities for successful innovation. And they need to know and to apply the principles of successful innovation."—Drucker, 1985 (p. 19)

analysis. The right balance will vary from company to company according to a number of factors (see the exhibit "Different Ambitions, Different Allocations").

Different Ambitions, Different Allocations

One important factor is industry.* The industrial manufacturers we studied have a strong portfolio of core innovations complemented by a few breakouts, and they come closest to the 70-20-10 breakdown. Technology companies spend less time and money on improving core products because their market is eager for the next hot release. Consumer-packaged goods manufacturers have little activity at the transformational level because their main focus is incremental innovation. Of these three sorts of businesses, industrial manufacturers collectively have the highest P/E ratio relative to their peers, perhaps suggesting that they are closest to getting the balance right – for them.

A company's competitive position within its industry also influences the balance. For example, a lagging company might want to pursue more high-risk transformational innovation in the hope of creating a truly disruptive product or service that would dramatically alter its growth curve. A struggling Apple made this decision in the late 1990s, effectively betting its business on several bold initiatives, including the iTunes platform.

A company that wants to retain its leadership position or believes the market for its more ambitious innovations has cooled may decide to do the reverse, removing some risk from its portfolio by shifting its emphasis from transformational to core initiatives.†

A third factor is a company's stage of development. Early-stage enterprises, especially those funded by venture capital, must make a big splash. They may feel that a disproportionate investment in

---

* Drucker, 1985 13 V. Demographics • Sharp demographic changes (migration, policies, baby-booms, baby-busts, labor force participation of women) offer opportunities for entrepreneurs • Most such events have already happened, and the need is to accept the reality and not just see it as an opportunity • Focusing on age distribution • Identification of 'representative' behavior • Income distribution (disposable and discretionary).

† Peter Drucker on Incongruities: Discrepancy or dissonance between what is and what "ought to be" • Symptom of change and are qualitative rather than quantitative • Create an instability in which quite a minor effect can move large masses • Often overlooked by insiders, but visible to those on periphery (yet are part of the industry) • Sources • Economic realities • Between reality and the assumptions about it • Between perceived and actual customer values and expectations • Within the rhythm of logic of a process • Fueled by intellectual arrogance and dogmatism • Opportunities of small, highly focused organizations.

transformational innovation is warranted, both to attract media attention, investors, and customers, and because they don't yet have much of a core business to build on. As they mature and develop a stable customer base, and as protecting and growing the core becomes more important, they may shift their emphasis toward that of a more established company.

The point is that a management team should arrive at a ratio that it believes will deliver a better return on investment (ROI) in the form of revenue growth and market capitalization, should discover how far its current allocation is from that ideal, and should come up with a plan to close the gap.

ORGANIZE AND MANAGE THE TOTAL INNOVATION SYSTEM

Targeting a healthy balance of core, adjacent, and transformational innovation is a vital step toward managing a total innovation portfolio, but it immediately raises an issue: To realize the promise of that balance, a company must be able to execute at all three levels of ambition. Unfortunately, the managerial toolbox required to keep innovation on track varies greatly according to the type of innovation in question. Few companies are good at all three.

Companies typically struggle the most with transformational innovation. A study by the Corporate Strategy Board shows that mature companies attempting to enter new businesses fail as often as 99% of the time. This reflects the hard truth that to achieve transformation – to do different things – an organization usually has to do things differently. It needs different people, different motivational factors, and different support systems. The ones that get it right (GE and IBM are notable examples) have thought carefully about five key areas of management that serve the three levels of innovation ambition.

Talent

The skills needed for core and adjacent innovations are quite different from those needed for transformational innovations. In the first two realms, analytical skills are vital, because such initiatives call for market and customer data to be interpreted and translated into specific offering enhancements. Procter & Gamble, for example, deploy a cadre of 70 senior employees around the world to help identify promising adjacencies. These "technology entrepreneurs," as the company calls them, are responsible for researching a variety of sources, including scientific journals and patent databases, and for physically observing activities in specific markets in order to find new ideas that can build on P&G's core businesses. The company credits its technology entrepreneurs with uncovering more than 10,000 potential offerings for review.

Transformational innovation efforts, by contrast, typically employ a discovery and concept-development process to uncover and analyze the social needs driving business changes (what's desirable from a customer perspective), the underlying market trends (what kinds of offers might be viable), and ongoing technological developments (what is feasible to produce and sell). These activities require skills found among designers, cultural anthropologists, scenario planners, and analysts who are comfortable with ambiguous data. Thus, when Samsung decided to compete on the basis of innovative design, it recognized that it needed new and different skills. The company moved its design center from a small town to Seoul in order to be closer to a valuable pool of young design professionals. It also teamed with a number of outside firms with strong design skills and created an in-house school, led by industrial design experts, to hone the abilities of designers who exhibited potential. The results speak for themselves: In a decade, Samsung has garnered numerous design awards while evolving from a manufacturer of nondescript consumer electronics to one of the most valuable brands in the world.

Rather than hoping that their future will emerge from a collection of ad hoc efforts, smart firms manage for "total innovation."

Integration

Although the right skills are critical, they are not sufficient. They must be organized and managed in the right way, with the right mandate, and under the conditions that will help them succeed. One of the most important decisions will be how closely to connect the skills and associated activities with the day-to-day business.

In most companies, the majority of people engaged in innovation are working on enhancements to core offerings; they're most likely to succeed if they remain integrated with the existing business. Even teams working on adjacent innovations benefit from the efficiencies that come with close ties to the core business, assuming they're given the appropriate tools to take their work further afield.

However, as Samsung's move suggests, transformational innovation tends to benefit when the people involved are separated from the core business – financially, organizationally, and sometimes physically. Without that distance, they can't escape the gravitational pull of the company's norms and expectations, all of which reinforce an emphasis on sustaining the core.

Funding

Most efforts related to core and adjacent innovation are fairly small-scale projects that don't need major infusions of cash. They can and should be funded by the relevant business unit's profit and loss (P&L) through annual budget cycles.

Bold transformational efforts typically require sustained – and sometimes significant—investment. Their funding should come from an entity (perhaps the executive suite, and ideally the CEO) that can rise above the fray of annual budget allocation. But companies should avoid the "innovation tax" approach, whereby the C-suite asks all areas of the business to contribute a percentage of their budgets to transformational initiatives (under the theory that innovation benefits the whole company, so everyone should support it). Business units rarely see their "contribution" as going to a good cause; they simply perceive that the corporate office is siphoning off 5% of their budgets, and they come to regard the innovation team as the bad guys.

Companies might instead create a completely different funding structure for transformational innovation, one that's separate from the regular P&Ls of the business. An example is Merck's Global Health Innovation venture fund, a separate limited liability corporation that invests in interesting health care companies operating at the periphery of Merck's core pharmaceutical, vaccines, and consumer health businesses. The main purpose of the fund is to place bets on components of an evolved future business model for the company. It is also used on occasion to fund organic innovation initiatives, such as Merck Breakthrough Open, a crowdsourcing forum that solicits employee ideas for transformational growth opportunities.

Pipeline Management

Any well-managed innovation process includes mechanisms to track ongoing initiatives and ensure that they are progressing according to plan. Companies typically rely on stage-gate processes to assess projects periodically, recalculate their projected ROI according to any changed conditions, and decide whether they should get a green light. But such projections are only as reliable as the market insight the company can glean. In the case of a core product extension, that insight is usually sufficient: Customers can say whether they would like a proposed product variant and, if so, how much they'd be willing to pay for it. However, if the innovation initiative involves an entirely new solution – one that customers may not even know they need – traditional stage-gate processes are dangerous. It's impossible to predict fifth-year sales for something the world has never seen before.

Moreover, whereas pipeline management for core or near-adjacent innovation involves gradually finding a small set of winners from among a vast number of ideas, the process is very different for transformational innovation. Here the challenge is to take a small number of possibly game-changing ideas and ensure that they emerge from the pipeline stronger. A company must spend sufficient time up front exploring what's possible, constantly expanding the options available in pursuit of the right big idea. In other words, transformational efforts are not generally managed with a funnel approach; they require a nonlinear process in which potential alternatives remain undefined for a long period of time. This is another reason why a stage-gate process is so lethal to transformational innovation: It results in the rejection of promising options before they are properly explored.

Metrics

Finally, there is the question of what measurements should inform management. For core or adjacent initiatives, traditional financial metrics are entirely appropriate. But using such metrics too early in transformational efforts can kill potentially great ideas. For instance, net present value and ROI calculations, commonly used to assess core and near-adjacent initiatives, require assumptions about adoption rates, price points, and other key variables – which in turn require customer input. Such input is impossible to obtain for something the world does not yet know it needs.

Managers should discuss thoughtfully where economic and noneconomic metrics, along with external and internal metrics, are most appropriate. Stage-gate systems operate at the intersection of economic and external metrics – they estimate how much money the company will make when its innovation is launched in the outside world. And, again, this combination is appropriate for evaluating core or near-adjacent initiatives on the basis of information that is obtainable and largely accurate.

Companies should use the polar opposite – a combination of non-economic and internal metrics – to assess transformational efforts in their early stages; this can enhance the team's ability to learn and explore. For example, what if the only hurdle an initiative must clear to receive continued investment is that the company is likely to learn (not earn) from it? That is how Google has assessed transformational innovation from the start.

Eventually, a company must focus on the hard economics of a transformational project. But that can wait until there's something ready to pilot and launch.

SUMMARY

Managing total innovation will require a significant shift for most companies, which are used to a less orderly approach. But the pathway to such discipline is clear. The first step is to develop a shared sense of the role innovation plays in driving the organization's growth and competitiveness. Managers should agree on an appropriate ambition level for innovation and find a common language to describe it.

Next, it makes sense to survey the company's current innovation landscape. A comprehensive audit will reveal how much time, effort, and money are allocated to core, adjacent, and transformational initiatives – and how that allocation differs from the ideal ratio for the company in question. With the difference exposed, managers can identify ways to achieve the desired balance, usually by paring core initiatives down to those focused on the highest-value customers, encouraging more initiatives in the adjacent space, and creating conditions more conducive to breakthroughs in the transformational realm.

Throughout all this activity, leaders must communicate clearly and relentlessly about innovation goals and processes. There's no getting around the fact that to improve the overall return on innovation investments, managers must take a hard look at projects – all of which are attached to people who feel a sense of ownership and pride in them. The imperative is to identify and accelerate the most promising ideas and kill off the rest (some of which may be perfectly viable but don't represent the best use of resources). Open commitments and clear messaging will go a long way toward ensuring that the entire organization knows what is being decided by whom and why, and how those decisions will benefit the business over the short and long terms.

For many companies, innovation will remain a sprawling collection of activities, energetic but uncoordinated. And for many managers, it will remain a source of frustration. For the best managers, however, it represents the most exciting and important challenge of all. By figuring out how to manage innovation as an integrated system within overall portfolio goals, they can harness its energy and make it a reliable driver of growth.

13

TRIZ & STEM Joined at the Hip

THE IMPORTANCE OF STEM AND TRIZ IN AN INNOVATION INFRASTRUCTURE

STEM is based on the application of foundational academic skills, knowledge, and the application of approaches usually based on the Scientific Method. It is process-based where the sequence of project/problem-based activities escalate in complexity as the process is proceeding. It increases in complexity and direct application dependent on the talent and skill requirements and needs required in each critical business sector. It also escalates in interdisciplinary engagement and alignment of the academic content areas and related elective and technical content areas. Innovation is addressed as a primary area of instruction and includes tools for innovation, methods, and assistive technologies such as TRIZ. The primary outcome is talent development through career and college preparation, preparing the student for an "Innovative STEM" career.

TRIZ, as a powerful, direction instrument, extrapolates from the specific to the general and further refines a progression of logical techniques and guidelines of innovation and specialized critical thinking on the investigation of various abnormal state development licenses. TRIZ, which comprises numerous answers for the specific issues of creation and development, is anything but difficult to coordinate with courses and work on strategies to motivate innovative reasoning and the critical thinking capacities of students. Likewise, it is extremely important to apply TRIZ to training to prepare specialists and encourage their accomplishment with the help of their involvement.

Both TRIZ and STEM support the development of Engineering and Technical staff. They are integral to an Innovation Infrastructure.

THE ORIGIN OF TRIZ

The hypothesis of creative, critical thinking (TRIZ), developed by the Soviet designer Geinrich Alshuller, is a well-loved, national "Brilliant Touch" of the Soviet Union. It was formulated based on an investigation of 2.5 million abnormal state innovations in the global patent literature. Following the end of the Cold War in the 1990s, TRIZ became increasingly popular in Europe and the United States. These days, it is broadly perceived as a legitimate and compelling critical thinking technique. Alshuller was curious about how innovation occurs, and he studied the process of innovation itself. He wondered whether it was

- Random – No pattern to it – Lucky
- Person-dependent – It was dependent on the person who was attempting to come up with something new and limited by the personal experience of the inventor.
- Systematic – where the new thought or inventive idea was the consequence of efficient utilization of examples in the advancement of frameworks?

ALTSHULLER'S FIVE TRIZ LEVELS OF INVENTION

As a result of his work studying patent data Altshuller classified the different levels of invention into five categories:

1. Apparent or conventional solutions: 32%
2. Small invention inside paradigm: 45%
   - Improvement of a current framework, more often than not with some bargain
3. Substantial invention of technology platform: 18%
   - Essential change of existing framework
4. Invention outside technology platform: 4%
   - New age of configuration utilizing science, not innovation
5. Discovery: 1%
   - Major discovery, new science, basis for new technology platforms

It is on these five categories that we base the TRIZ–STEM Conundrum™ at the beginning of the chapter. It is important to understand that different levels of invention require a different type of thinking to get to that level. The higher the TRIZ level, the more revolutionary the idea is and the more impact it will have. These higher levels are more easily attained by STEM-educated students or staffs that have enough knowledge of STEM. If there was any initial doubt that such a systematic approach to innovation would not be helpful, it has been proved to be so in many organizations that have implemented TRIZ methods.

INTERDISCIPLINARY APPROACH OF STEM

The interdisciplinary approach can be characterized as an educational approach that takes an informational view that deliberately applies procedures and approaches from more than one discipline to inspect a focal topic, issue, subject, or experience (Jacobs 1989). One run-of-the-mill system utilizes, as a part of the interdisciplinary approach, (Figure 13.1) issue-driven, interface information to explore complex issues (Nikitina 2006).

The real component of the STEM educational module is the fusion of Problem-Based Learning (PBL) and Inquiry-Based Learning (IBL) (see Figure 13.1). Experience Learning (EL – Constructivist Theory) is the

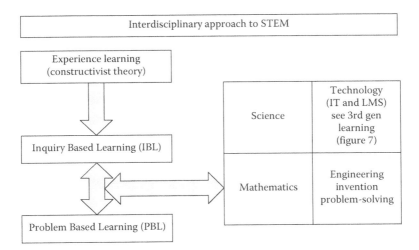

FIGURE 13.1
Interdisciplinary approach of STEM.

backbone of both PBL and IBL. EL is also critical to the success of 3rd Generation Learning™ platforms since they utilize both simulation and gamification to create the experience portion of the training.

Likewise, higher STEM education levels are also based on EL (Sanders 2009). The student needs to integrate both present and earlier understandings while finding new information. Also, the student needs to be persistently absorbing and refining information, while thinking about it and the illuminating encounters that are provided. The IBL process provides students with opportunities to investigate and understand the real world on their own; as a result, they become autonomous and innovative scholars. This has been incorporated into determining the required training and education for the different levels of STEM education, see Figure 13.1.

The core of STEM is science, but with the application of Information Technology (IT) including the advent of electronic tools for team collaboration and communication purposes as well as application tools provided as part of current MS Office software and TRIZ software, the results are multiplied. The successes that can now be achieved are at a much higher level than when this technology did not exist.

THE LEVELS OF STEM EDUCATION

As one examines the teaching methods, curriculum, and knowledge base of STEM, one can agree on a certain set of common areas or levels of STEM education that would progress from an elementary and pre-K level all the way up to a college or university level. You can visualize these levels as a System Diagram. Voehl developed a model that he refers to as the "Breakthrough Equation" that is very appropriate to apply to understand this concept of levels better. Also a very basic tool of the Lean Six Sigma, the SIPOC Model can also be utilized. First the "Breakthrough Equation":

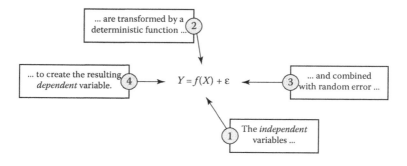

Simply stated, the Breakthrough Equation could be used to explain any system where certain inputs are acted upon by some function or black box to create specific outputs. The outputs are not only dependent on the input and the function but also on the random error for which one should attempt to find solutions that can mitigate the variability they may cause. When applied to STEM education, a student, their knowledge, experiences, applications, and level of understanding are the input. The output is that same student whose characteristics hopefully have changed for the better where they now can perform at a higher level of understanding and of application. The student is made ready to receive the next higher level of instruction and so forth.

Another way to show this is via a SIPOC, which is one of the simpler LEAN Six Sigma tools. As the acronym implies, a SIPOC depicts the relationship between the following levels:

S   Supplier who initiates the process – in the case of education that would be the level that the student is in at the time.

I   Input from the supplier to the customer – also, the outputs from the previous level become inputs to the next level.

P   Process takes the inputs from the supplier and adds value. Examples in education would be instructional media, equipment, technology, curriculum scope, standards, and objectives, as well as student assessments needed at each level.

O   Outputs from the process that now have added value to the customer – in this case, the outputs from the previous level become inputs to the next higher level of STEM. This would encompass the levels of proficiency in each of the skill areas and application of those as required.

C   Customer who uses the outputs to his benefit – in the case of STEM education, that would be the next STEM level.

The SIPOC concept was then used to develop the different levels of STEM education in Table 13.1, shown subsequently. These levels are the ones that were previously discussed as part of the TRIZ-STEM Conundrum™ introduced and explained earlier in this chapter.

INTRODUCTION TO THE TRIZ-STEM CONUNDRUM™

TRIZ and STEM are both important concepts that are integral parts of an Innovation Infrastructure. In the simplest form, TRIZ is a set of method

TABLE 13.1

STEM education levels

Level	Supplier	STEM Curriculum	Outputs
1	Elementary, pre-k–5	• Engagement • Excitement • Foundation in math, science, language arts, technology • Preparation for systems, process, and theoretical studies in middle school level	• Proficiency in grade level math & science • Enthusiasm for STEM content and activities • Teamwork skills • Ability to question • Foundational approach to problem-solving • Basic systems and processes
2	Grades 6–10, middle school	• Theoretical applications • General systems and processes • Problem- and inquiry-based projects • Applied academics • Career exploration	• Prep for technical and practical • Id'd career interest • Proficiency in grade level math and science • Appreciation of value of STEM skills in the workplace • Teamwork skills • Applied basic project management skills • Ability to question • Use of enhanced problem-solving tools and methods • Basic systems and processes

(Continued)

TABLE 13.1 (CONTINUED)

STEM education levels

Level	Supplier	STEM Curriculum	Outputs
3	Grades 11–12, technical education, high school, middle/early, college prep	• Technical education and training • Applied practical STEM applications • Applied academics • Workplace soft skills • Problem-solving based learning • Innovation concepts—TRIZ introduction • Employer-provided instruction	• Career and college ready • Competency in technical skills in identified career interest • Business and industry credentials, • Diploma or certificate, • Use of business tools/technologies for project management, problem-solving, and innovation. • Work experience
4	Community college, technical/apprenticeship	• Technical education and training • Practical STEM applications • Applied academics • Workplace soft skills • Problem-solving/innovation • Innovation Concepts—TRIZ competency • Internships/apprenticeship	• Career and University ready, • Internships • Registered apprenticeships • Certificate • Associates degree • Use of business tools/technologies for project management, problem-solving, and innovation
5	University, undergraduate & graduate	• All of the previous plus proficiency in workplace application of the concepts learned • Higher levels of TRIZ • Professional internships	• Internships • Bachelor degrees • Graduate degrees • Leads others in the use of business tools/technologies for project management, problem-solving, and innovation

and tools that guide the practitioner to prioritize the best alternative solutions or directions of study to more quickly and effectively reach the best outcome. However, STEM as the acronym suggests, is the application of Science, Technology, Engineering, and Mathematics to problems to reach logical conclusions and to prove the viability of such solutions. The association amongst TRIZ and STEM isn't as self-evident. This chapter will help us develop the concept that these two approaches are somewhat interrelated so that the reader can more easily determine when it is most appropriate to use each or the combination of both to create new and viable ideas worth investigating. The idea is to solve complex problems, and then to institutionalize their use so that these can be systematically implemented successfully in the organization. We will refer to this concept as the TRIZ-STEM Conundrum™ and will suggest the best way to utilize these in an integrated and aligned fashion.

In typical fashion, different functional areas in an organization have differing opinions about the level of creativity and cooperation that they have for each other. Some of the largest differences occur between the sales function and either the research and development (R&D) department or the engineering department. The following is a typical interchange that occurs:

A sales manager comes into the chief engineer's office with a great idea. A customer has suggested that if we could just make our widget 50% smaller with a longer battery life, we could corner the widget market and sell billions. The engineer, knowing a little something about current battery technology, suggests that what the sales manager proposes just isn't possible. Of course, the idea is great, but the ability to execute it is pretty much impossible (not to say that the idea shouldn't be taken as a challenge). The sales manager, disappointed, walks away mumbling something about the "rigid" engineer who has "no imagination" and doesn't even want to "try" to improve the product.

If one were to look at the lack of success of well-trained engineers, one could conclude that they are less creative. They are staid in their approaches to problem-solving and have a tough time identifying new and different ways to attack them. Their experience and extensive knowledge base of their industry can sometimes limit their ability to "think outside the box." STEM is known for the rigid processes that provide excellent results when applied to common and even some complex problems. This training ensures that a design will work, but it may also ensure that they stay within the bounds of existing proven processes with known outcomes.

The application of TRIZ methods and software open possibilities for investigation in an efficient manner allowing the knowledge, experience, as well as the approach of the STEM community to be focused on ideas that have a high probability of success.

TRIZ-STEM CONUNDRUM™ EXPLAINED

In Figure 13.2, one can see the relationship that exists between different levels of stem education in different levels of TRIZ. In a subsequent section of this chapter, these levels will be explained. For now, it's important to note that when the level of TRIZ Invention that is being utilized on a problem is high and the level of STEM education that the user has attained is high, then the level of success is HIGH as shown subsequently on the top right of Figure 13.2. On the other hand, when a low level of TRIZ Invention is being utilized on a problem and a high level of STEM education has been attained by the user, then the level of success is MEDIUM.

When a high level of TRIZ Invention is being utilized on a problem, but it is being used by a user who has only attained a low STEM education level, then the level of success is also MEDIUM.

Lastly, when a low level of TRIZ Invention is being utilized on a problem, and it is being used by a user who has only attained a low STEM education level, then the level of success is LOW.

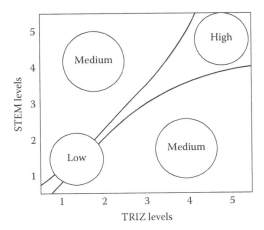

FIGURE 13.2
TRIZ-STEM Conundrum™.

The importance of this relationship has everything to do with the innovation infrastructure. For an organization to have a successful innovation infrastructure, both a high level of STEM Education should be prevalent either through the selection of staff that is adequately prepared with both of these abilities or through training programs that must be developed internally to fill that void.

REALIZATION THAT A SYSTEMATIC APPROACH CAN BE BENEFICIAL FOR INNOVATION AND CREATIVITY

A structured innovation process such as TRIZ integrates well with the disciplines of STEM. It is somewhat contradictory that such structure would allow for the opportunity to innovate when most "creative" individuals claim that "creativity" cannot be structured. A structured approach similar to TRIZ was followed by the late Thomas Alva Edison when he was trying to develop the electric light bulb. He had tried thousands of combinations of materials, attachments, voltages, and environments before he and his team came up with the proper filament that would provide sufficient light and last long enough to be a useful replacement for whale oil lamps. Companies today that used a structured innovation approach such as TRIZ claim huge growth in the number of patents produced and are recognized as innovation leaders by their competitors and investors.

Senior scientists and engineers at some early adopters of the TRIZ methodology were reluctant to believe that it could assist in the resolution of major complex problems they had been working on for years. They were hesitant to accept that the use of TRIZ, in conjunction with subject matter experts, was able to solve problems that they had been working on for years.

Therefore, if TRIZ is a systematic approach to creativity and invention, then it follows that it would also integrate well with STEM since the STEM disciplines are all based on a systematic approach as well, namely the Scientific Method. This chapter will get deeper into this concept as we progress.

APPLICATION OF TRIZ TO INNOVATIVE EDUCATION

The TRIZ system comprises a broad range of answers for advancement, techniques, and devices for specialized innovations, for example, the eight examples of development, the 39 parameters of the logical inconsistency table (Matrix), and the 40 standards of creation. It is possibly connected to specialized businesses, for example, hardware, gadgets, science, science and military design, and afterward reached out to a more extensive application in nonspecialized areas, for example, administration, promoting, and instruction, and brain research. TRIZ, as inventive techniques and theory, is the way to creative instruction. Numerous countries have introduced TRIZ into their educational modules and urged instructors to use TRIZ strategies, to encourage students' innovative reasoning and creativity.

TRIZ: INNOVATION CAN BE SOFTWARE ASSISTED – A NEW USE FOR ARTIFICIAL INTELLIGENCE

Keep in mind how shocked you were when Google discovered the site you required and positioned it at Number 1? Some TRIZ clients encounter a comparable epiphany. Don Masingale, a senior architect at Boeing Corporation, reveals that TRIZ is the answer to pretty much any building issue you can envision. Cited in *PlaneTalk*, a Boeing publication, he stated, "When you see something this great, you can't leave it. I utilize TRIZ consistently in my reasoning and procedures. It's a creative method for taking care of issues and meeting every one of the criteria our clients need us to have, regardless of whether business or military."

Down-to-earth preparation sowed the seeds of TRIZ at Boeing. More than 700 individuals went to Masingale's five-day sessions. The impact was profound. Boeing's official designing division set up a senior specialized group to examine the issues that arose. There have also been suggestions for expanding the feasibility of TRIZ among specific and administrative positions.

TRIZ helped Boeing solve a slow-burn issue that had kept a team of aeronautical engineers scratching their heads for nearly three years. Even given the fact that the participants at one of Masingale's inward instructional courses were not acquainted with it at the time, the arrangement they created under the direction of TRIZ master Zinovy Royzen would bring about US$1.5 billion worth of client orders. As announced in *Business 2.0*, Masingale credits TRIZ-enlivened outlines with pitching Boeing's new 767 aerial refueling plane to the legislatures of Italy and Japan. For engineers like John Higgs, 767 Tanker Transport lead task designer, it was an initial step out of the "mental dormancy" that hampers imagination. The outcomes, as indicated by Higgs, "put us ahead in our race to reconfigure the 767 into a joined tanker and transport for military utilize."

The Tanker Transport program at Boeing displayed what Higgs and Masingale allude to as a "great building struggle." The 767, named the world's most productive plane, is a two-motor airship and, by configuration, has no overabundance water driven power. However, it should be fit for directing fuel at 900 gallons per minute at the blast spout interface—while flying 300 bunches at 15,000 feet elevation. This is no simple accomplishment. Higgs says that "By applying TRIZ standards, the class concocted two finish arrangements and two steady arrangements that my group had never thought of. These arrangements have numerous helpful assistant arrangements." As with numerous leaps forward propelled by TRIZ, "the arrangements must stay under wraps since they are very rivalry touchy," claims Higgs.

Astounding as it might sound, TRIZ pulls rabbits from caps, discover needles in bundles, and produces licensed innovation. Its precise way to deal with development is the direct opposite of problematic, hit and miss, experimentation, mental methods for parallel reasoning. It's logical, repeatable, procedural and algorithmic procedures shock all who first experience them.

APPLY TRIZ TO STEM EDUCATION FOR THINKING TRAINING AND PRACTICES

The pith of TRIZ is looking for answers to development issues through imagination and concentrated strategy. In 2009, the Ministry of Science and Technology of the People's Republic of China began to introduce TRIZ to training. The aim was to improve the innovative capability of China's scientific and technical personnel. The experiences of TRIZ practices in foreign universities and industrial applications indicated that TRIZ had played a catalytic role in shortening the development cycle of new products and original R&D and in improving the efficiency of innovation.

Various articles have been written about the practice of integrating STEM and TRIZ education. STEM education is a foundation for the development of future engineers. It is important to coordinate STEM with TRIZ regarding the general instruction or expert training.

All the STEM courses in Chinese colleges contain 39 general designing parameters and 40 creation standards. Propelling TRIZ instruction early can prepare more superb designers and propel the inventive ability for China's industrial development. Currently, in China's advanced education, STEM involves the greater part the extent of a wide assortment of logical, claims to fame. Most universities devoted to the training of STEM offer four things as part of these essential modules: electronic design, mechanical building, material science, and materials design.

The way toward preparing fantastic specialists appears in Figure 13.3. Through learning and the application of hypotheses to practice, students can become brilliant architects. The training of brilliant architects is demonstrated and deemed effective when a STEM student has graduated, begins his vocation, and soon can demonstrate that he is able to

- Produce multiple invention patents
- Superior innovative accomplishments
- Develop a high-quality thesis or dissertation
- Portray solid critical thinking capacities

The TRIZ system is well on the way to being acknowledged by STEM education. The previous procedure enhances the incredible quality and creativity of architects through learning, gathering information, and practical aptitude. The key is to use the essential information of operation and of expert learning systems in order to distinguish issues. This then will lead to the utilization of particular instruments to take care of the issues in a straightforward manner in order to accomplish imaginative results. In this manner, advancing the application of TRIZ in STEM instruction is a viable method to prepare fantastic architects.

The practice of applying TRIZ to higher engineering education indicates that TRIZ methodology significantly improves the engineering and innovative abilities of students. Due to logical, down to business, and operable properties, TRIZ can be a powerful method to build up the creative capacities, proficient fitness, and designing abilities of students, and furthermore, it is an awesome beginning stage for the use of an association's Innovation Infrastructure.

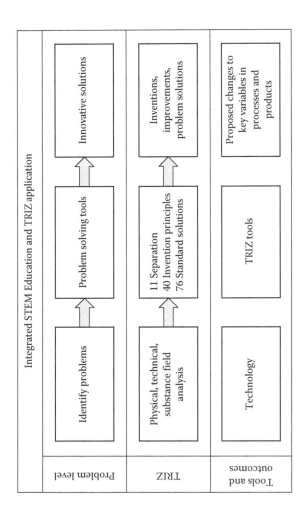

FIGURE 13.3

Integrated STEM education and TRIZ application. (Adapted from Fan, Qiu, & Zhang, *Engineering*, 4, 908–913, 2012.)

China has 194 schools and colleges propelling the TPEE (Training Plan of Excellent Engineers) as the core of instruction innovation.

From the point of view of showing change, here are a few suggestions for the utilization of TRIZ:

- Have colleges and universities cooperate with industry. Interchange ideas on the use of STEM and TRIZ together to create an integrated curriculum.
- Try to understand how companies that are currently using TRIZ in their R&D and new product development activities, and how they utilize their own engineers to guide the TRIZ training platform as part of their Innovation Infrastructure.
- Execute a TRIZ training program by creating distinctive TRIZ educational programs for various students, for example, secondary school, junior school, undergraduate, graduate, and doctoral students.
- These can be used to move the TRIZ-STEM Conundrum™ plot into the upper right quadrant. This training program is also to be used with existing staff. The level that will be provided to the existing staff will be dependent on the STEM level that they are in as well as the TRIZ level of application required. See Figures 13.2 and 13.3.

With the development of 3rd Generation Learning™ platforms, as developed by Voehl and Fernandez (©2016), that not only include the subject matter but also include simulation capabilities. Learning Management Systems, online libraries for content enrichment, and other integrated modules, a student or staff can more efficiently be trained either to move them up the STEM levels or to better understand the need for integration of TRIZ and STEM. See Figure 13.4.

THE INTEGRATION OF THE STEM CURRICULUM WITH TRIZ METHODOLOGY

As found in a study of Chinese female students who were asked to design a boat propeller utilizing TRIZ methods and STEM knowledge, the STEM and TRIZ integrated instruction that they were provided systematically

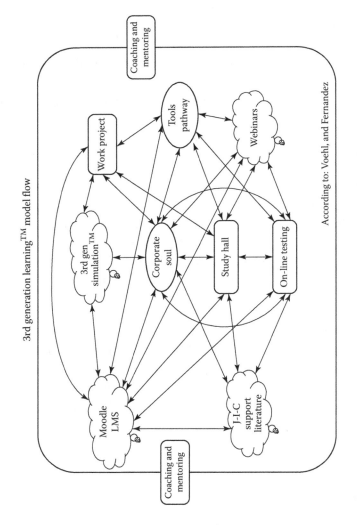

FIGURE 13.4

3rd generation learning™ model flow.

promoted the student's knowledge integration and application of STEM. The results further explained that learning effectiveness showed that the STEM and TRIZ instruction model could systematically guide students to assimilate STEM knowledge more readily than STEM alone.

This improved their level of STEM knowledge individually as well as a part of sharing and collaborating in a team environment. Most of the students were satisfied with the cultivation of problem-solving skills, hands-on practice, data collection, and analytical ability, as well as with the learning effects of engineering and math. STEM and TRIZ training integration not only improved the final product and the retained knowledge of the STEM subject matter but also that of the TRIZ methodology and its application. It also improved students' positive learning attitudes and was shown to increase their interest in learning.

THE NEED FOR STEM EDUCATION: THE WORLD IS WINNING

Leaders in the European Union, India, China, the United States, and other nations are now requesting for more graduates of STEM to drive more innovation. We also know that there continue to be unemployed STEM professionals. This supply/demand function is not working as expected. Simply training more STEM professionals may increase the supply side of the equation but it can't increase the number of STEM professionals unless these are also trained to be better innovators. Is STEM education a necessary and sufficient condition for innovation? Incorporation of casual instruction as a methodology for upgrading and enhancing STEM training won't get the job done.

STEM education needs are supplemented with education in innovation. Innovation training as described in this book can be very helpful to pull the STEM-educated individual into a more creative mode and yet maintain the structured approaches that they were trained in. TRIZ and STEM complement each other. The approach should be to inform federal and state policymakers on the critical role that STEM education plays in US competitiveness and future economic prosperity. For STEM to be an effective component of the Innovation Infrastructure, in business, academia, and the government sector, the following must occur:

- STEM instruction must be hoisted as a national need.
- STEM Innovation Training composed of the integration of TRIZ approaches into the STEM curriculum must be developed and implemented.
- The United States must grow the limit and assorted variety of the STEM workforce pipeline prepared in TRIZ and other Innovation strategies.
- Policymakers at each level must be educated about arrangement issues identified with STEM and TRIZ training.
- Advancement of a thorough instruction base to promote innovation in education through a basic understanding of the use of both STEM and TRIZ.
- Extension of junior colleges and colleges to prepare students for additional STEM and TRIZ instruction.
- Development of 3rd Generation Learning Management Systems that integrate STEM and TRIZ approaches to develop "Creative Engineers."
- A solid emphasis on hands-on, request-based learning exercises, and reenactment of critical thinking and item advancement exercises.
- Complete and vital endeavors to organize, enhanced, or killed.
- Fantastic projects directed by other science and innovation government organizations that have a positive effect on student accomplishments in STEM subjects and other instructive results.
- Integration of STEM-focused activities directed at learning environments outside the K-12 classroom and in alignment with the needs of the community at large.

Experts have noticed that many STEM professionals develop many new concepts and technologies with a PhD level education. Most of these discoveries are for long-term benefits. I also notice many STEM graduates with a BS- and MS-level education doing rote jobs, and they are unable to contribute their intellectual best. There are many PhD graduates who have not discovered a whole lot, and there are many BS- and MS-educated professionals who have innovated very successfully. There are even college dropouts who turned out to be some of the most successful innovators and entrepreneurs. The question arises, "Is STEM education enough and is it driving innovation?" The answer isn't obvious, especially if one can understand the potential integration of STEM and TRIZ into an effective, systematic approach to Innovation with the rigor of a scientific approach.

SUMMARY OF THE TRIZ-STEM CONUNDRUM™

The practice of applying TRIZ to STEM education will produce job candidates with a better success rate in the real world. Instruction shows that TRIZ altogether enhances the designing and imaginative capacities of students. It also:

- Enhances their attainment of success as Engineering or Technical Professionals
- Enhances workplace creativity and cultivates innovative skills
- Improves the ability to apply STEM knowledge more consistently with better outcomes
- Systematically improves the retention of both TRIZ and STEM knowledge
- Improves the application effectiveness of both concepts at the same time

The remainder of this book will go deeper into all aspects of the Innovation Infrastructure. This integration of TRIZ and STEM in both the training and development of staff as well as the application of these in projects in an integrated and systematic fashion will inevitably lead to better performance in the organization's ability to create more unique products and services and to perform better than its competition.

BIBLIOGRAPHY

Ministry of Education of China, Measurable Report of National Education Development Affairs, 2011. http://www.moe.edu.cn/publicfiles/business/htmlfiles/moe/moe_633/201208/141305.html

Zhu, G. F. (2011). Momentum status and prospects of engineering education in China. *Research in Higher Education of Engineering*, 22(6), 1–4.

Li, P. G., Xu, X. D., & Chen, G. S. (2012). On practical teaching of undergraduate engineering education in China: Problems and causes. *Research in Higher Education of Engineering*, 23(3), 1–6.

Busov, B., Mann, D. L., & Jirman, P. (1999, May). TRIZ and invention machine: Methods and systems for creative engineering and education in the 21st century. In *First International Conference on Advanced Engineering Design* (pp. 1–10). Prague.

Minds, W. W., Vaneker, T. H. J., & Souchkov, V. (2010, 3–5 November). Full immersion TRIZ in education. In *Proceedings of the TRIZ Future Conference 2010* (pp. 269–276). Bergamo.

Ogot, M., & Okudan, G. E. (2006). Methodical creativity methods in engineering education: A learning styles perspective. *International Journal of Engineering*, 22(3), 566–576.

Nakagawa, T. (2011). Instruction and training of creative problem solving thinking with TRIZ/USIT. *Procedia Engineering*, 9, 582–595.

Xu, D.-Z., & Xiong, W. (2010). Research and exploration of introducing TRIZ into innovation education of Institutions of Higher Vocational Education. *Diary of Shenyang Institute of Engineering (Social Sciences)*, 6(1), 93–99.

Zhang, X. F. (2011). TRIZ tactics into classroom teaching. *Journal of Tianjin Normal University (Elementary Education Edition)*, 12(2), 32–35.

Liu, X. T., Zhao, C.-Y., & Xu, P. (2010). TRIZ theory and students' innovative ability cultivation. *Higher Education Forum*, 6(3), 29–31.

14

Global Innovation Problem Areas and Quality of R&D Ideas

It has never been more important to educate people and organizations how to out-imagine, out-create, and out-innovate … . The insight and experiences captured by [this book] make an important contribution toward reaching this goal.

From the Foreword by Deborah Wince-Smith
President, Council on Competitiveness

In a nutshell: Corporate innovation – and indeed any kind of innovation – is never the result of spontaneous ideas appearing for no reason. Rather, it is a process that begins with a problem or a goal and ends with the implementation of one or more ideas deemed to offer value to the organization. On those rare occasions when a researcher makes an unexpected discovery, she or he still needs to turn that discovery into an innovation – and that means they will have to start with a goal – turning the discovery into a product – or failure will usually result. Having worked with business leaders for years in the pursuit of innovation, we have come to realize that there is a fundamental reason for failure. Organizations have two modes of operation that often are viewed as incompatible – the past and the future. One mode focuses on the past and one focuses on the future, and the inability to deal with Global Innovation Problems and integrate the two explains why companies find it so hard to innovate.

Key Points

1. Because of higher expectations for innovation, coupled with shortened product life cycles, there is a constant demand for new products or services, which is challenging most organizations' existing infrastructure for new product or service development.

2. Innovation begins with ideas. Ideas generated for a known opportunity is one approach, but the continual generation of ideas that intersect with continually arriving opportunities can lead to a breakthrough or dramatically innovative solutions. Thus, there is tremendous opportunity for improving methods for generating, evaluating, and managing ideas – especially ideas that could be considered of high quality.

3. Progressive organizations will create or purchase a platform where anyone can easily contribute ideas; that is, employees, customers, users, suppliers, or stakeholders, such as the Integrated R&D Network shown in Figure 14.1.

4. Engaging people with diverse levels of experience can offer the best opportunity for generating useful creative ideas. Less experienced people tend to be bold, risk-taking, and impetuous, while the more experienced people tend to think of more rational and knowledge-based ideas. In other words, less experienced people generate more ideas while experienced people contribute higher quality ideas.

5. Methods for generating ideas

    a. Brainstorming is the most commonly used method for generating ideas.

    b. Thinking innovatively – soliciting ideas from everyone – is a challenge. There is a need for training people in asking questions, thinking of ideas, and articulating their ideas in words or graphics.

    c. Online collaboration – Instead of organizing a group in a room together, one can convene an online brainstorming or idea generation session within minutes, so members can participate remotely.

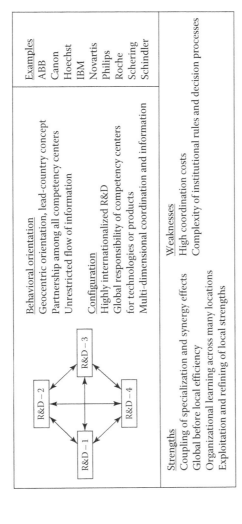

Behavioral orientation
Geocentric orientation, lead-country concept
Partnership among all competency centers
Unrestricted flow of information

Configuration
Highly internationalized R&D
Global responsibility of competency centers
for technologies or products
Multi-dimensional coordination and information

Examples
ABB
Canon
Hoechst
IBM
Novartis
Philips
Roche
Schering
Schindler

Strengths
Coupling of specialization and synergy effects
Global before local efficiency
Organizational learning across many locations
Exploitation and refining of local strengths

Weaknesses
High coordination costs
Complexity of institutional rules and decision processes

FIGURE 14.1

In an Integrated R&D Network, the coordination authority for technology and component development is allocated based on individual strengths and capabilities of R&D units. Transnational projects are a significant component in this organization; high standards of collaboration and coordination are required.

6. Evaluating ideas
   a. The first evaluation of an idea is the human response. If, after listening to an idea, the person becomes disinterested, the conversation is over. If enough people who hear the idea show no interest, then the idea needs to be rethought or reformulated – or discarded. If enough people were excited about the idea, then you may want to consider it for further evaluation. It's not the quality of the generic idea but the quality of the best idea that matters.
   b. Key attributes to evaluate an idea include; impact, sponsor, value, trade-off, usability, and cost.
   c. Idea priority index (IPI).
      i. The IPI prioritizes ideas based on the potential cost-benefit analysis, associated risks, and likely time to commercialize the idea, using the following relationship:
         1. Annualized potential impact of the idea = ($) × probability of acceptance
         2. IPI = Annualized cost of idea development ($) × time to commercialize (year)

OVERVIEW OF THE IDEA EVALUATION PROCESS

Organizational innovation is not just about generating creative business ideas. It is also about reviewing ideas in order to identify those that are most likely to become successful innovations. Unfortunately, many organizations make mistakes in their idea review processes that result in rejecting the most potentially innovative ideas in favor of less innovative ones. In some instances, the idea review process is a simple matter of a manager reading through a batch of ideas and selecting those she believes will work best for her firm. This is most often the case in smaller firms run by a single owner and manager. In most medium to large businesses, however, a structured evaluation process is necessary in order to identify the ideas that are most likely to succeed as innovations for the company. This helps to ensure that complex ideas are reviewed by people with the appropriate expertise necessary to understand what would be necessary to implement the idea – and what might go wrong. It is essential to enable a middle manager to defend the idea to senior management, stakeholders, and financial officers who may need to grant budgetary approval of the idea. Idea evaluation and management make it possible to review a large number of ideas in a resource-efficient manner. Another outcome is to improve the idea by identifying potential implementation problems and preparing suitable actions to overcome those problems.

These are more frequently performed incorrectly and are most often mismanaged due to a number of factors, namely, lack of training on proper idea selection and evaluation methods, an over-reliance on market evidence, an underuse of direct customer evidence, poor selection of evaluation tools, miscategorization of ideas, typical psychological decision biases, and a lack of an idea evaluation process.

The first idea screen should occur upon receiving the idea, which is usually conducted by employee(s) formally tasked with overseeing the ideation process. The first screen is useful in that it eliminates ideas having low market value or that would not fit the business's core competencies; yet, it can also be extremely harmful if set up wrong, in that it might weed out potentially valuable ideas, creating a self-reinforcing view that closes the organization to new ideas.

Successful companies and entrepreneurs only place barriers to ideas where they actually exist, not those based on biases in the minds of strict managers trying to keep their organization on a predictable track. After an idea passes the first screen, it then goes into a repository where it may be selected to move forward in the idea management process. The final screen of ideas is much more rigorous in nature and uses the gathered evidence and analysis results to make an informed decision with respect to the ideas; whereas, the first screen is almost a totally uninformed decision with very little or no information.

Criteria and Methods for Conducting Idea Screening

1. *Theme criteria*: Multiple themes to determine if an idea fits into those predetermined themes, such as operational improvements, branding improvements, revolutionary products. Can be used when an organization wants to focus on a few core areas. Themes have to be aligned with strategic goals.
2. *Exclusion or inclusion criteria*: Multiple general inclusion criteria (10 or more) that should be set carefully and only around the values of the company.

3. *Grouping or tiers*: Groups can be helpful in the evaluation of tiers, such as top ideas or worst ideas. Both grouping and tiers are only useful in a batch evaluation process, not a continuous process.

4. *Idea sponsor*: A person can decide to sponsor an idea. The number of ideas they can sponsor can be limited based on fairness or resource limitation. This allows executives to push ideas they see as valuable.

5. *Checklist or threshold*: An individual idea's list of attributes must match the preset checklist or threshold in order to pass (e.g., be implemented in six months, profit at least $500,000, and require no more than two employees).

6. *Personal preference*: A manager, director, line employee, or even expert is used to screen an idea based on his or her own preferences.

7. *Voting*: Individual(s) can vote openly or in a closed ballot (i.e., blind or peer review). Voting can be weighted or an individual, such as an expert, can give multiple votes to a given idea.

8. *Point scoring*: Uses a scoring sheet to rate a particular idea on its attributes (e.g., an idea that can be implemented in six months gets +5 points, and one that can make more than x dollars gets +10 points). The points are then added together and the top ideas are ranked by highest total point scores.

9. *Rating scales*: An idea is rated on a number of preset scales (e.g., an idea can be rated on a 1–10 on implementation time, any idea that reaches a 9 or 10 is automatically accepted).

10. *Ranking or forced ranking*: Ideas are ranked (#1, 2, 3, etc.) – this makes the group consider minor differences in ideas and their characteristics. For forced ranking, there can only be a single #1 idea, a single #2 idea, and so on.

The theme criterion is the most simple and valuable method for conducting a first screening. In this method, a number of themes are proposed that align with the organization's strategic aims. There are a number of common problems that occur with the first screening of ideas, usually around the submission of an idea, the individuals performing the first screening, the first screening methods, and low technology acceptance methods for storing ideas for future evaluation.

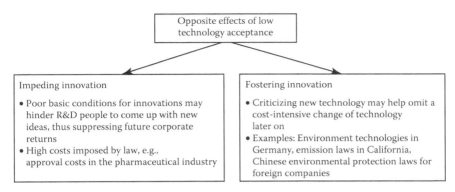

During the evidence-gathering phase, additional considerations should be given to how much of the evidence and subsequent analysis might be needed during future phases. Often, data created via first screen processes provide vital insights during later phases. However, if organizations are not purposeful in capturing and storing these additional data points, they may be unavailable for future phases, thus precluding other decision-makers from making fully informed decisions.

When venturing to gather evidence, the first distinction needing to be understood is that of primary and secondary sources of evidence. Evidence analysis is vital and required for drawing out insights, key statistics, and conclusions from the gathered evidence. When analyzing the evidence, innovation managers must select and apply the appropriate analytical methods, of which there are a great number. Thus, care must be taken in preselecting and deploying the methods and different approaches to intellectual resources between conventional and intelligent companies, as shown in the Table 14.1.

INNOVATIONS VARY WIDELY IN VALUE

Although partly realized over time, some of this heterogeneity is related to characteristics of innovations *"at birth."* The recent computerization of patent applications in the past 30 years makes it possible to exploit information on the characteristics of patents to make an early assessment of innovation quality. We model early expectations about the value and technological importance ("quality") of an idea and a patented innovation as a *latent variable* common to a set of four indicators: the number of patent claims, forward citations, backward citations, and family size.

TABLE 14.1

Different Approaches to Intellectual Resources: Conventional and Intelligent Companies

Intellectual Resource	Conventional Company	Intelligent Company
Knowledge	Power	Added-value potential
Patent	Result of R&D activity	Starting point for technology-based innovation
Market research	Justification for new product development	Starting point for innovation brainstorming
Databases	Individual support tool, controlling mechanism	Organizational and distributed knowledge of high quality
Workshop	Exchange of information and experience	Product and service development
Library, archives	(Physical) collection of books, journals, and documents	(Virtual) location for inspiration, information, and exchange

The model is estimated for four technology areas using a sample of about 8000 US patents.

Also, management of intellectual resources produces a leverage effect on R&D investment. Conventional methods of knowledge and technology creation exploit the potential of intellectual property (IP) only in a limited way. On the other hand, successful innovations are characterized by three distinct factors:

1. The correct anticipation of customer needs
2. Detailed knowledge of the supply channels
3. Intelligent application and outsourcing of external technology around technical core competencies, as shown in Figure 14.2.

All IP/resources of a company (internal and external) have to be integrated. We measure how much noise each individual indicator contains and construct a more informative, composite measure of quality. Studies show the variance reduction generated by subsets of indicators and find forward citations to be particularly important. One characterization and measure of quality is significantly related to subsequent decisions to renew a patent and to litigate infringements. Using patent and R&D data for 100 US manufacturing firms, studies find that adjusting for quality removes

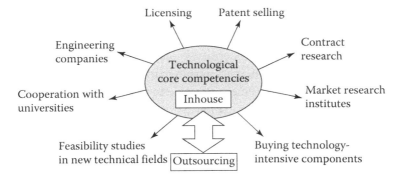

FIGURE 14.2
Outsourcing of intellectual resources to external technology suppliers.

much of the apparent decline in research productivity (patent counts per R&D) observed at the aggregate level (Table 14.2).[*]

Creative thinkers – and bear in mind that business innovation is the result of implementing creative ideas in order to generate value – turn innovation problems into creative challenges (also sometimes called "innovation challenges"). The creative challenge is then posed to a group (or in some cases to the lone creative thinker) who generates ideas to solve it. In the innovation process, this is followed by an evaluation phase to identify the ideas that offer the most value and finally by the implementation of the selected idea or ideas.

TABLE 14.2

Significance of the Top 50 R&D Investing Companies in the Triad

In US$ billion	United States	Western Europe	Japan
Total economic R&D investment	161	120	75
R&D investment of private industry	80	60	54
R&D investments of top 50 R&D spenders	55	50	43

---

[*] *The Quality of Ideas: Measuring Innovation with Multiple Indicators*, Jean O. Lanjouw and Mark Schankerman, NBER Working Paper No. 7345. See: www.nber.org/papers/w7345. Also see Table 14.2 Significance of the Top 50 R&D Investing Companies in the Triad (United States, Western Europe, Japan over a 20-year period).

Using the Model of Dominant Design

In order to turn a problem into a creative challenge, you need to deconstruct the problem so that you can identify its causes and consequences, often using Dominant Design principles, as shown in Figure 14.3. In the corporate environment, it can be extremely effective to perform the deconstruction exercise as a team in order to exploit the creative thinking of the group. Based upon the consideration of Dominant Design, organizations pursue four innovation strategies: Invention Leader, Innovation Leader, Early Follower, and Late Follower.

The dramatic fall of international telephone costs together with the Internet give well-educated engineers direct access to some of the world's most desired information. Today, knowledge and skills stand alone as the most important sources of comparative advantage, and many third world countries are now making substantial investments in training. Within a short time, cheap R&D labor in developing countries will compete with expensive engineers in developed countries: The sources of technology will be shifted from developed countries into countries with low labor costs. The need for international technology transfer is growing (Table 14.3).

Today, over 5–7 million people *work in the area of Knowledge Production* in R&D departments, which is approximately 90% of all of the scientists who have ever lived. The Information Revolution has transformed the nature of competition, and R&D is the most important element in technology-intensive organizations to source, filter, generate, and diffuse knowledge. Accordingly, R&D must be designed to selectively retain information, process knowledge, and apply know-how, for knowledge knows no boundaries.

Most companies are not using their intellectual resources up to their full potential, due to conventional barriers to innovation, information overflow, and suboptimal use of information and communication technologies. Although there is a continuous demand for increases in productivity and innovation output, a metric for knowledge management is nonexistent. There is some optimization in terms of IT infrastructure and library services, but the strategic approach is missing. Such an intelligent approach has to differentiate among types of knowledge, using

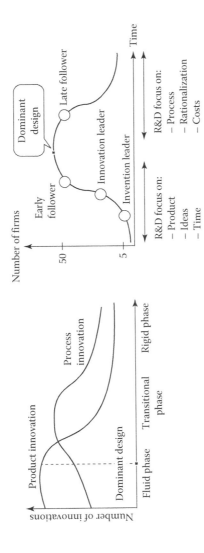

FIGURE 14.3

The model of the dominant design. (Adapted from Utterback ████.)

TABLE 14.3

US Company R&D Funds (data in %) Show the Trend Toward Services

	US$61 billion	US$109 billion
All manufacturing industries	91.6	74.8
Chemical products	8.7	6.6
Drugs and medicines	6.7	9.4
Petroleum refining and extraction	3.1	1.6
Machinery	17.2	8.9
Electrical equipment	17.0	15.7
Automotive transportation	11.7	12.5
Aircraft and missiles	9.7	5.1
Instruments	8.1	7.8
All nonmanufacturing industries	8.4	25.2
Communication services	1.8	4.4
Computer programming and related services	3.6	8.0
Research, development, and testing services	0.1	2.6
Wholesale and retail trade	N/A	6.9
Engineering services	N/A	1.1
Health services	N/A	0.7
Finance, insurance, and real estate	N/A	0.7

Source: Jankowski .

Note: Column #1 represents the average annual R&D spending over a 15-year period from 1980 to 1994; column #2 represents R&D annual spending from 1995 through 2010. The two 15-year trends clearly show the shift toward service.

instruments like technology radar, selective knowledge bases, systematic knowledge engineering, patent offices, competitor analysis, knowledge diffusion, and last but not least intrinsic motivation of R&D people. The use of Information Systems/Technology (IS/IT) as problem-solvers is essential, but alone it is not sufficient to ensure success. See Figure 14.4.

The *invention leader* is often an R&D-intensive small company (e.g., biotechnology or computer startups). Its access to capital is restricted, and it usually has little know-how in implementing and sustaining the business development of its ideas.

The *innovation leader* succeeds in bringing the invention to the market by considering technological as well as market requirements. A dominant design may be established by erecting technology barriers (patents, tacit knowledge building) and market-entry barriers (distribution channels, marketing data). Intel's microprocessor chips are a typical example.

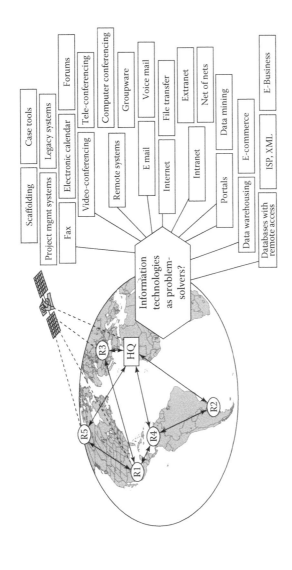

FIGURE 14.4
Use of information technology is essential – but not sufficient to ensure success.

The *early follower* imitates recently introduced products or technology once a dominant design is apparent. He differentiates himself from the innovator with superior marketing concepts, technology modifications, refined after-sales service, or simply drastic cost savings based on scale-effects.

The *late follower* enters a market characterized by mature technologies and established players. Cost leadership is the main alternative to achieve market share. This approach has been successful for insulation and plastic products.

The key to choosing the appropriate competition strategy is the ability to recognize the emergence and inherent potential of a dominant design in all important markets on a global scale (e.g., IBM PC). A dominant design is characterized by

- Decreasing market dynamics
- Decreasing number of competing firms
- Falling prices
- Convergence of the alternative product concepts toward a standard
- Reorientation away front technology toward consumer utility

It is strategically important to recognize these developments early. Appropriate tools are technology monitoring, patent research, competitor and technology analysis, as well as market analysis, and all this on a global scale. Companies have to be present with market-oriented R&D employees in the most important markets worldwide, as demonstrated in Figure 14.5.

GLOBAL INNOVATION PROBLEMS

When a company can overcome the Global Innovation Problems that it finds itself challenged with and integrate the two modes of the past and the future – while not relying too heavily on either of them – innovation has a good chance to succeed. The following is an *Importance Diagram, followed by a Matrix of Global Innovation Problems* and their relationship with the various chapters in the GISH and Innovation Tools Handbook #1, where the solutions and answers to the problems can be found.

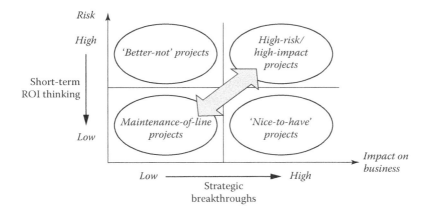

FIGURE 14.5
Multi-project-management has to balance the trade-off between tactical short-term maintenance of line projects and strategic long-term high-risk/high-impact (HIP) projects.

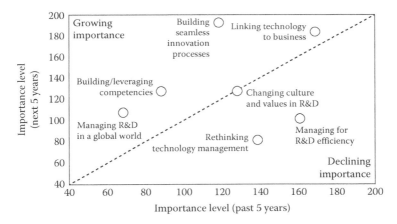

	Global Innovation Problems	GISH Handbook	Handbook of Tools #1
A	Lack of a strategy and/or framework for innovation	Chap 1, 2, 39	Chap 3, 4, 14
B	Absence of a process innovation value proposition	Chap 40	Chap 23
C	Organizational culture does not support Innovation	Chap 3, 42	Chap 8, 24
D	Science of innovation not understood or practiced	Chap 7, 8, 9	Appendix A
E	Failure to appraise roles, capabilities, and disabilities	Chap 4	Chap 12

F	The organization does not cultivate creativity	Chap 5, 6,	
G	Absence of a creativity toolkit & education	Chap 13, 15	
H	Lack of innovation/breakthrough thinking	Chap 11, 12, 25,	Chap 9
I	Absence of value networks for innovation	Chap 16, 26, 33	Chap 22
J	Unaccustomed to deconstructing problems into challenges	Chap 17, 24,	Chap 19
K	Ideas not being developed and managed effectively	Chap 20, 21, 22	Chap 15
L	Innovation methodologies not well understood	Chap 23, 27,	Chap 1
M	Lack of motive or inspiration for innovation	Chap 14, 38	Chap 17
N	Failure to match the size of organization with the size of market	Chap 34, 35	
O	Lack of focus on planning to learn vs. planning to execute		Chap 5
P	Lack of effective measurement for innovation	Chap 36, 37, 43	Chap 10
Q	Innovation is considered purely random and not systematic	Chap 28	Chap 6
R	Failure to discover insight into new and emerging markets	Chap 29	Chap 7
S	New product launch & delivery is not done properly	Chap 30, 45, 46	
T	Problems with IP and innovation	Chap 44	Chap 21
U	Importance of innovation in service & non-profits is marginalized and/or lacks a master plan	Chap 32, 34	Chap 14
V	Market research & stakeholder engagement not done/done poorly	Chap 18	Chap 13, 16
W	Design innovation lacks knowledge management	Chap 31	Chap 15
X	Innovation benchmarking not done/done poorly	Chap 10	Chap 2
Y	Failure to manage disruptive technology vs. mainstream demand	Chap 19, 41	Chap 20
Z	Financial cost structures & technology S-curves misunderstood	Chap 48, 49, 50	Chap 11
	Figure 14.6 shows the evolution of Phases of Project Management over a 50-year period		

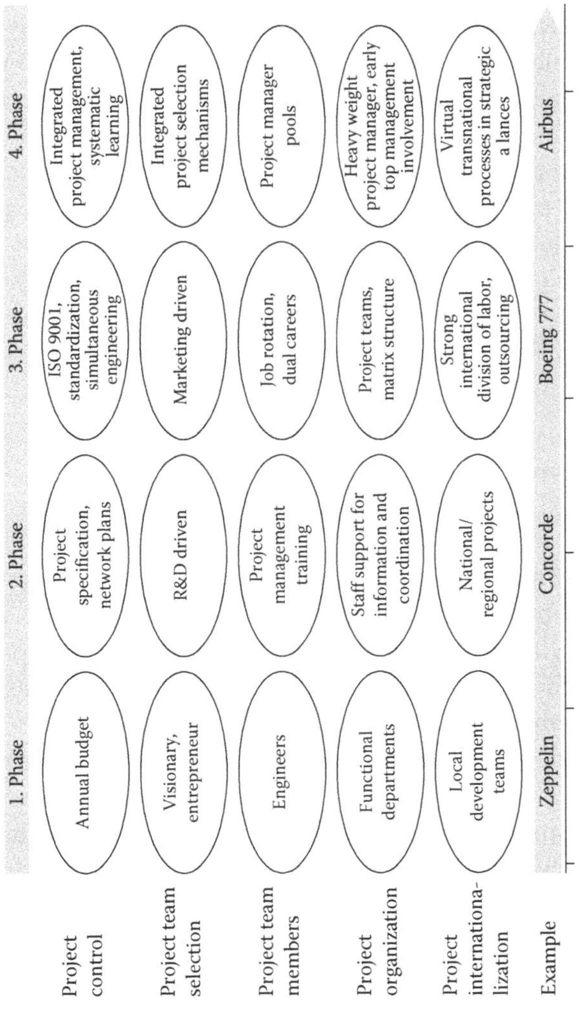

	1. Phase	2. Phase	3. Phase	4. Phase
Project control	Annual budget	Project specification, network plans	ISO 9001, standardization, simultaneous engineering	Integrated project management, systematic learning
Project team selection	Visionary, entrepreneur	R&D driven	Marketing driven	Integrated project selection mechanisms
Project team members	Engineers	Project management training	Job rotation, dual careers	Project manager pools
Project organization	Functional departments	Staff support for information and coordination	Project teams, matrix structure	Heavy weight project manager, early top management involvement
Project internationalization	Local development teams	National/regional projects	Strong international division of labor, outsourcing	Virtual transnational processes in strategic alliances
Example	Zeppelin	Concorde	Boeing 777	Airbus
	1950 — 1960	1970	1980 — 1990	2000

FIGURE 14.6

Phases of R&D project management.

One major challenge for R&D is the heritage of corporate decisions inflicted upon R&D without consulting R&D about its long-term consequences. Mergers and acquisitions have great challenges for R&D in store because they usually require dramatic changes in the way R&D is used to do its business. Typically, synergy between newly acquired R&D units and corporate R&D labs are hardly realized without major reorganizational efforts affecting all R&D units. Elimination of acquired R&D labs due to cost-cutting imperatives may destroy the human and knowledge-based resources of those labs because the top-qualified scientists tend to leave a company in this transitional period when job security is low. Should the acquired R&D organization be left intact, NIH-syndrome occurs and competition between R&D labs impedes the exploitation of potential synergy.

SUMMARY

Idea evaluation and management make it possible to review a large number of ideas in a resource-efficient manner. Another outcome is to improve the idea by identifying potential implementation problems and preparing suitable actions to overcome those problems. *Organizational innovation is not just about generating creative business ideas.* It is also about reviewing ideas in order to identify those that are most likely to become successful innovations.

Unfortunately, many organizations make mistakes in their idea review processes that result in rejecting the most potentially innovative ideas in favor of less innovative ones. In some instances, the idea review process is a simple matter of a manager reading through a batch of ideas and selecting those she believes will work best for her firm. Also, the transfer of knowledge between R&D in multinational corporations (MCNs) is almost automatically a trans-organizational and international phenomenon that must be addressed with new forms of organization and management, as every phase has different requirements, as shown in Figure 14.7.

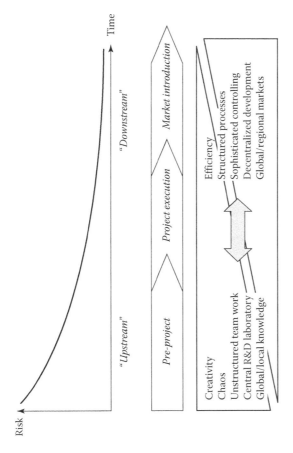

FIGURE 14.7
Every phase has different requirements.

This is most often the case in smaller firms run by a single owner and manager. In most medium to large businesses, however, a structured evaluation process is necessary in order to identify the ideas that are most likely to succeed as innovations for the company. This helps to ensure that complex ideas are reviewed by people with the appropriate expertise to understand what would be necessary to implement the idea – and what might go wrong. It is essential to enable a middle manager to defend the idea to senior management, stakeholders, and financial officers who may need to grant budgetary approval for the idea.

15

Total Innovation Management for Excellence (Time)

In a nutshell: There is a great deal of debate and disagreement between the key players in innovation methodology over how to define innovation, as we explained in Chapter 1. We have chosen to use the following definition as it is accepted by many of the leading innovation thought leaders:

Innovation is people creating value through the implementation of new and unique ideas. Innovation is how an organization adds value from creative ideas.

Innovation can take many forms. It can be an idea, an insight, or a rearrangement of present ideas and/or hardware, as long as it is new or unique, implemented, and creates significant value to stakeholders and consumers. Innovation applies to most activities including personal and organization related activities. Although the definition of innovation varies to some degree between individual thought leaders, the definition of an innovator is even more debated. Some of the same thought leaders define an innovator as "any individual who creates a new and unique idea." Others feel that an innovator is "anyone who comes up with a new and unique idea that is in line with the organization's mission." Others feel that an innovator is "anyone who takes part in the innovative process." I personally believe that there is a difference between an innovator and an entrepreneur. The difference between an entrepreneur and an innovator is that the entrepreneur does not have to originate the idea/concept. However, to be considered successful they both have to produce an output that adds value to someone other than themselves personally.

In addition, there is a difference between an innovator and a creative individual.

INTRODUCTION

The following definitions should be considered when you are defining an innovator and his/her responsibilities:

Definitions

- *Entrepreneur*: An entrepreneur is a person who organizes and manages any enterprise, especially a business, usually with considerable initiative and risk. He/she does not have to create the original concepts
- *Creative*: Using the ability to make or think of new things involving the process by which new ideas, stories, products, and so on, are created.
- *Create*: Make something, to bring something into existence

Yes, everyone can and should be creative.

This is the story about a man that was driving by an insane asylum when he got a flat tire. After jacking the car up, he removed the four nuts that hold the wheel in place. He carefully put the four nuts into the hubcap so that he would not lose any of them. As he pulled the tire off its rim, he hit the hubcap and flipped it over. The four nuts went down the sewer drain. He was stranded as he had left his cell phone at home, so he had no way of contacting AAA. One of the inmates that had been watching the struggle walked over to the fence and suggested that the driver should take one of the nuts off of each of the other three wheels and use them to hold the fourth wheel on until he could get to a garage. The driver was absolutely amazed and stated, "It's a brilliant idea. How come you are locked up in the asylum?" The inmate replied, "I may be insane, but I'm not dumb."

Innovation differs from invention in that innovation refers to the use of a better, and as a result, novel idea or method, whereas invention refers more directly to the creation of the idea or method itself.

FIGURE 15.1
A negative comparison of the number of creative ideas to innovative ideas.

Innovation differs from improvement in that innovation refers to the notion of doing something different rather than doing the same thing better.

Creativity is idea generation. Innovation is implementing the idea in a way that creates economic value to the organization and to the consumers of the organization's output. Creativity is made up of ideas that are both related to the individual and ideas that are related to the individual's employment. It has been estimated that 80% of the ideas generated by an individual are not related to the organization he/she works for. (See Figure 15.1.)

After all that the definition of innovation is fairly well understood, but it has not been completely agreed upon by thought leaders. The definition of an innovator is not important to the TIME methodology, and as a result, we will leave it up to the International Standards Association to resolve this difference of opinion.

An innovative process takes you all the way from the organization's mission to the results related to new product development. (See Figure 15.2.)

There are a number of major adjustments that need to be made when the organization swings away from a Six Sigma program, where errors were almost eliminated and risk was not tolerated, to an innovative approach where failures are considered learning experiences. In this new culture, the 20 As play a significant role in directing the organization's culture. The 20As are

1. The ability to wander, to be curious.
2. The ability to be enthusiastic, spontaneous, and flexible.
3. The ability to be open to new experiences, to see the familiar from an uncertainty point of view.
4. The ability to make desirable but unsought discoveries by accident. This is called *serendipity*.

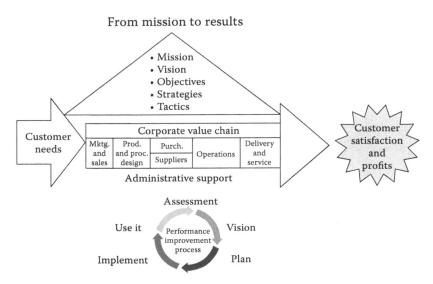

FIGURE 15.2
The beginning to end of the innovative process.

5. The ability to make something out of another by shifting functions.
6. The ability to generalize, to see universal application of ideas.
7. The ability to find disorder, to synthesize, to integrate.
8. The ability to be intensely conscious yet in touch with subconscious sources.
9. The ability to visualize or imagine new possibilities.
10. The ability to be analytical and critical.
11. The ability to know oneself and have the courage to be oneself in the face of opposition.
12. The ability to be persistent, to work hard for long periods in pursuit of a goal without guaranteed results.
13. The ability to take a risk for something you believe in.
14. The ability to put two or more known things together in a unique way, thus creating a new thing, an unknown thing.
15. The ability to do more.
16. The ability to transformed dreams into reality.
17. The ability to see new opportunities in what others view as normal.
18. The ability to learn from failure and come back running.
19. The ability to ????????
20. The ability to ??????????

You will note that 19 and 20 As are blank without a description. This was done purposely so that you could have the option to customize the list to your organization's specific needs. Our past experience proves that there are at least two abilities that are specifically related to an organization's culture and core competencies that need to be considered (As 19 and 20).

When an organization is considering making the transformation from an extremely conservative position to an innovative fast-moving culture, there are 10 specific considerations that must be addressed. These are called the 10 S transformation drivers. They are

- S1-Shared vision
- S2-Strategy
- S3-Systems
- S4-Structure
- S5-Skills
- S6-Styles
- S7-Staffing
- S8-Specialized technology – information technology systems
- S9-Systematic change management
- S10-Strategic knowledge management

There are numerous tools and methodologies used by organizations to improve their ability to innovate. In 2016, the International Association of Innovative Professionals conducted an extensive study to develop a list of these tools and methodologies. This resulted in the identification of more than 250 tools/methodologies that were being used to improve organizational innovation. Many of these tools were specific to an individual consulting firm, and a number of the tools used the same methodology but just had a name changed in order to be sold as a different product.

In an effort to reduce this large quantity of tools/methodologies down to a reasonable number of that are most frequently used and/or most effective, a second survey was conducted. The objective of this study was to reduce the list down to the 50 most effective and used innovation tools/methodologies. The results of the study did not meet the target of defining the 50 most used tools/methodologies, but we did ultimately narrow it down to the 76 most effective and used tools and methodologies. These 76 tools and methodologies were then divided into three distinct groups of approximately 25 tools and methodology in each of the groupings. (See Table 15.1), The three groups are

- Group 1 – Organizational and operational tools, methods, and techniques
- Group 2 – Evolutionary and improvement tools, methods, and techniques
- Group 3 – Creative tools, methods, and techniques

Table 15.1 details the list of the 76 most used and effective innovative tools and methodologies.

I'm sure that some of these tools/methodologies are familiar to those individuals who have been deeply involved in problem-solving. Other ones may require some study and training in order to use them effectively. All of the 76 tools/methodologies should be part of the toolkit that every individual or organization that is involved in improving innovation should be using.

Today's Problem with Innovation Approaches

❑ Teleportation
Ping Koy Lam
Australian National University
transported a beam of light

TABLE 15.1

List of the Most Used and/or Most Effective Innovative Tools and Methodologies in Alphabetical Order

	IT&M	Book III	Book II	Book I
1	5 Why questions	S	P	S
2	76 standard solutions	P	S	
3	Absence thinking	P		
4	Affinity diagram	S	P	S
5	Agile innovation	S		P
6	Attribute listing	S	P	
7	Benchmarking		S	P
8	Biomimicry	P	S	
9	Brain-writing 6-3-5-	S	P	S
10	Business case development		S	P
11	Business plan	S	S	P
12	Cause and effect diagrams		P	S
13	Combination methods	P	S	
14	Comparative analysis	S	S	P
15	Competitive analysis	S	S	P
16	Competitive shopping		S	P
17	Concept tree (concept map)	P	S	
18	Consumer co-creation	P		
19	Contingency planning		S	P
20	Co-star	S	S	P
21	Costs analysis	S	S	P
22	Creative problem-solving model	S	P	
23	Creative thinking	P	S	
24	Design for tools		P	
	Subtotal number of points	7	7	10
25	Directed/focused/ structure innovation	P	S	
26	Elevator speech	P	S	S
27	Ethnography	P		
28	Financial reporting	S	S	P
29	Flowcharting		P	S
30	Focus groups	S	S	P
31	Force field analysis	S	P	
32	Generic creativity tools	P	S	

(Continued)

TABLE 15.1 (CONTINUED)

List of the Most Used and/or Most Effective Innovative Tools and Methodologies in Alphabetical Order

	IT&M	Book III	Book II	Book I
33	HU diagrams	P		
34	I-TRIZ	P		
35	Identifying and engaging stakeholders	S	S	P
36	Imaginary brainstorming	P	S	S
37	Innovation blueprint	P		S
38	Innovation master plan	S	S	P
39	Kano analysis	S	P	S
40	Knowledge management systems	S	S	P
41	Lead user analysis	P	S	
42	Lotus Blossom	P	S	
43	Market research and surveys	S		P
44	Matrix diagram	P	S	
45	Mind mapping	P	S	S
46	Nominal group technique	S	P	
47	Online innovation platforms	P	S	S
48	Open innovation	P	S	S
49	Organizational change management	S	S	P
50	Outcome-driven innovation	P		
	Subtotal number of points	15	4	7
51	Plan-do-check-act	S	P	
52	Potential investor present	S		P
53	Proactive creativity	P	S	S
54	Project management	S	S	P
55	Proof of concepts	P	S	
56	Quickscorecreativitytest–	P		
57	Reengineering/redesign		P	
58	Reverse engineering	S	P	
59	Robust design	S	P	

(*Continued*)

TABLE 15.1 (CONTINUED)

List of the Most Used and/or Most Effective Innovative Tools and Methodologies in Alphabetical Order

	IT&M	Book III	Book II	Book I
60	S-curve model		S	P
61	Safeguarding intellectual properties			P
62	Scamper	S	P	
63	Scenario analysis	P	S	
64	Simulations	S	P	S
65	Six thinking hats	S	P	S
66	Social networks	S	P	
67	Solution analysis diagrams	S	P	
68	Statistical analysis	S	P	S
69	Storyboarding	P	S	
70	Systems thinking	S	S	P
71	Synectics	P		
72	Tree diagram	S	P	S
73	TRIZ	P	S	
74	Value analysis	S	P	S
75	Value propositions	S		P
76	Visioning	S	S	P
	Subtotal – number of points	7	12	7
	(P) priority rating	CREATIVE	EVOLUTIONARY	ORGANIZATIONAL
	TOTAL	29	23	24

IT&M in Creativity Book 29.
IT&M in Evolutionary Book 23.
IT&M in Organizational Book 24.
Book I – Organizational and/or Operational IT&M.
Book II – Evolutionary and/or Improvement IT&M.
Book III – Creative IT&M.
Note: IT&M, Innovative tools and/or methodologies; P, Primary Usage; S, Secondary Usage; Blank, Not used or little used.

James Kirk from Star Trek would define today's business as a no-win scenario. TQM, Lean, CRM, BPI, TRIZ, and the best-practice list of these methodologies goes on and on. The champions of these methodologies often report to different parts of the organization. Each of these functions considers their "favorite" as the priority activity that needs to be improved. In order to improve the organization's quality, productivity, creativity,

378 • The Framework for Innovation

profits, return on investment, market share, and so on, each function focuses on a specific improvement, such as

- Finance wants management to invest heavily in cost reduction methods like Activity-Based Costing.
- Manufacturing engineering wants management to invest heavily in automation and mechanization.
- Product engineering wants management to spend more money on basic research.
- Sales and marketing want products that are far more innovative than the competition has.
- Human resources believe that the secret to profitability is investing in our employees and training them so they have better skills.
- Field services want products that are much more reliable.
- The investor wants increased stock prices and dividends.
- The employee wants increased pay for less work along with job security.
- The consumer wants products and services to be much less expensive but function better than the more expensive products and services they are getting today.
- The consumers constantly threaten to go to our competitor if our organization doesn't meet their needs.
- Quality engineering wants – all, they want everything.

All of them want the executive team to devote all of its time to their favorite improvement approach.

The CEO knows that between 85% and 90% of his budget is only committed to things like taxes, maintenance, payroll, materials, and so on. These are the day-to-day things that are absolutely essential to keeping the organization functioning. As a result, there is only 10–15% of the budget that could be considered discretionary spending. Every function within the organization is competing for this part of the organization's budget and 100% of the CEO's time. Each of these functions promises mouthwatering results. See Table 15.2.

If these figures are correct, the CEO could invest in just three of them and make a profit without producing a product. Obviously, this is a ridiculous conclusion. As a result, there is strong competition between the individual functions to have the discretionary spending assigned to their project.

TABLE 15.2

Typical Promised (Projected) Savings

Function	Methodology	Budget Savings	Increased Profit
Finance	Activity-based costing	20%	
Manufacturing engineering	Automation	25%	
Human factors	Total resource management	30%	
Product engineering	Innovation to expanded product lines		45%
Information technology	New software packages	20%	
Quality assurance	TQM	Cycle time/costs reduction	

Total Innovation Management for Excellence Methodology

Well, it's about time for TIME (Total Innovation Management for Excellence) – a methodology that is designed to take advantage of the most positive aspects of each of the best practices that are designed to satisfy the various stakeholder desires. TIME blends together key parts of these methodologies in a manner that demonstrates to the individual stakeholders that the culture of the organization is primarily focused on improving performance and value-added to each of the stakeholders. (See Figure 15.3.) The six tiers are

- Tier I – Value to the stakeholders (the foundation)
- Tier II – Setting the direction
- Tier III – Basic concepts
- Tier IV – Delivery processes
- Tier V – Organizational impact
- Tier VI – Shared value

To accomplish this, TIME uses 16 key building blocks to construct an organizational profile designed to consider all of the individual stakeholder desires. (Note: We use the term *stakeholder desires* rather than *stakeholders' needs or requirements*.) These building blocks are strategically aligned with each other to increase the organization's efficiency, effectiveness, and

The total innovation management pyramid

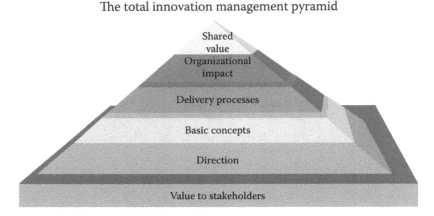

FIGURE 15.3
The six tiers of the total innovation management pyramid.

adaptability. (See Figure 15.4.) This combination of building blocks makes up a pyramid that is commonly known as the TIME Pyramid.

Tier I-Value to Stakeholders

Tier I is the foundation that is designed to support the pyramid that provides added values to Stakeholder (Stakeholder Partnerships.) It contains only one Building Block. (BB1: the foundation) that is set firmly on bedrock.

The innovation building block plays a very important role in this fast-moving, competitive environment we all are living in. The concepts and considerations that need to be addressed are extensive and outside of the scope of this book, but they will be discussed briefly.

BB1 – The Foundation

This foundation is built on bedrock to provide maximum stability to the pyramid mounted upon it. It provides assurance to the stakeholders that the organization and its activities are stable and well-constructed. Without a good foundation, no matter how elaborate the construction is, the organization is doomed to failure. Too many of the present technologies are built on a "sand" base. As such, they looked beautiful for a period of time and then slowly decayed taking the organization's culture, investors' money, and employees' jobs with it. It is absolutely essential that you invest heavily

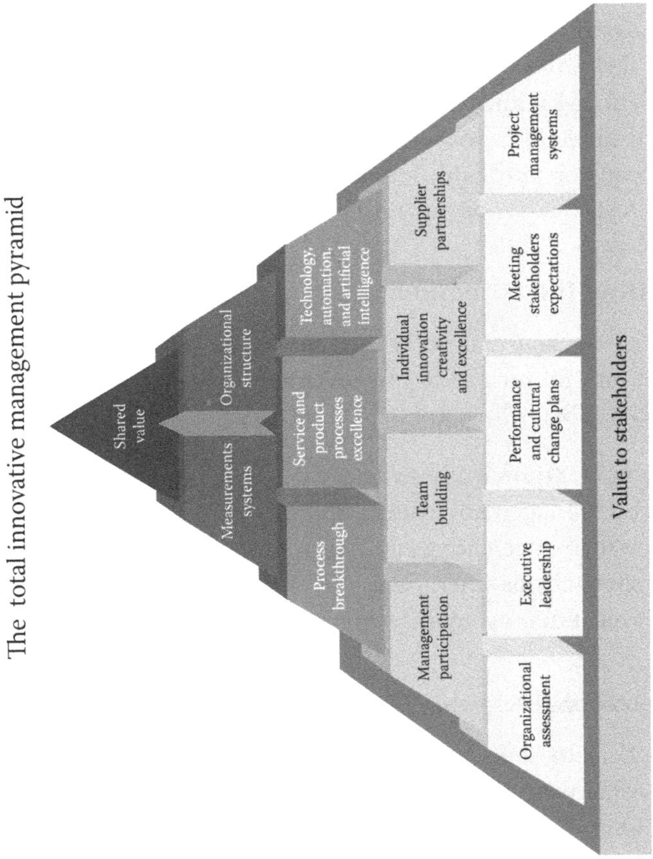

The total innovative management pyramid

Shared value

Organizational structure

Measurements systems

Service and product processes excellence

Technology, automation, and artificial intelligence

Process breakthrough

Team building

Individual innovation creativity and excellence

Supplier partnerships

Management participation

Executive leadership

Performance and cultural change plans

Meeting stakeholders expectations

Project management systems

Organizational assessment

Value to stakeholders

FIGURE 15.4

The TIME pyramid.

in building the foundation that is capable of supporting the weight of the structure that will be placed upon it even when it's subjected to shifting with time and environmental conditions (hurricanes, tornadoes, earthquakes, sandstorms, floods, etc.). The tallest skyscraper in San Francisco (The Millennium) is slowly tilting to one side because the foundation was not built on bedrock. It was the pride and joy of San Francisco residents only to turn into San Francisco's Leaning Tower of Pisa. Literally millions of dollars will be required to correct the foundation that the building was built upon. As of this date, no one knows how to correct the situation other than tearing down the upper stories of the building to reduce the weight on the foundation. I realize that investing money in the foundation looks like a waste of time and resources but let me assure you, the biggest waste occurs when you don't provide a stable foundation. The culture within your organization rests heavily on what is laid down upon for it to mature on.

Tier II – Setting the Direction

The second tier of the pyramid is used to set the innovative direction of the organization's performance improvement strategy. It consists of five building blocks (BBs), which are

- BB2 – Organizational assessment
- BB3 – Top management leadership
- BB4 – Performance/change management plan
- BB5 – External customer focus
- BB6 – Project management systems

BB2 – Organizational Assessment

It is not practical to start any type of innovative improvement without establishing what your present situation is, including its strengths and weaknesses. One of the major mistakes many organizations make is thinking that the executive team has an excellent understanding of what problems the workforce is facing. We often find out that the executive team frequently has a more positive view of the organization's operations than the employees have. In one of our surveys, we asked the individual taking the survey to list the top 10 activities that need most improvement within the organization and then to list the activities that need the least improvement. The survey typically is taken by the executive team and a sample of management and employees. One of the questions that is evaluated is, "How much trust and confidence do you have in the management team?" Almost without exception, this question is rated in the executive's list of ten things that need to be improved. It is a rare exception when it is not in the top 10 of middle management and employees' lists. It is absolutely essential that any assessment of an organization collects information related to needs, expectations, and desires of the executive team, middle management, and the employee. Once this is done, the organization is in a position to compare the organization's strengths and weaknesses as viewed from these three separate levels. (Note: It is a rare organization where a single survey and/or assessment is adequate to characterize the culture of the organization and identify opportunities for major improvement.) See Figure 15.5.

In conducting an assessment, information should be collected related to each of the 5 Cs. (See Figure 15.6). They are

1. The organization's *culture* as it varies from function to function and as a whole
2. The organization's *capabilities* based upon its resources in hard assets and people's skills
3. The organization's *competencies* based upon the organization's processes and ability to meet price, cost, and schedule targets
4. The organization's *competitiveness* based upon the level of innovation in products and services
5. The organization's ability to *communicate* both internally and externally

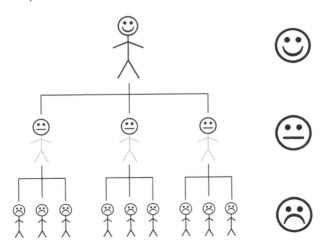

FIGURE 15.5
Three different views of the same organization.

Transformation considerations

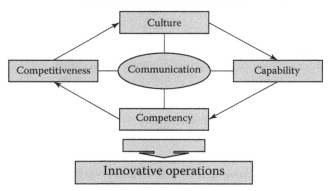

FIGURE 15.6
The 5Cs.

There is a large number of assessments available to address each of the 5 Cs. Types of typical assessment include

- Is/should be assessment
- Twelve statement assessment
- History assessment
- Employee opinion survey
- Organizational change management assessment
- Innovation assessment
- External environment current state analysis
- Task capabilities analysis
- Structure capability analysis
- People capability analysis
- Internal environment capability analysis
- Leadership for innovation capability analysis
- Stakeholder engagement capability analysis
- Innovation support capability analysis

BB3 – Top Management Leadership

"if you're going to sweep the stairs, always start at the top." My grandmother

Top and executive management must do more than just support TIME. They must be part of the process, participate in designing the process, assign resources, and give freely of their personal time. The start of any improvement process is that top management leadership requires the total executive team to make it successful.

BB4 – Performance and Cultural Change Management Plan

All employees need to understand why the organization is in existence, what the behavioral rules are, and where the organization is going. This direction must be well-communicated to the stakeholders, and there needs to be an agreed-to plan of how the organization wants to change. That is what a Business Plan does for an organization. It sets the direction of the business, what products are going to be provided, what markets are going to be serviced, and what goals need to be reached in the future. Without an agreed-to, well-understood business plan that is implemented effectively, the organization has no direction, so it meets its goal of going nowhere. It is like an automobile screaming down the road at a hundred miles per hour without a steering wheel. If the organization does have a business plan, but it is not communicated throughout the entire organization, it is not much better off. Now, management is behind the steering wheel of that car screaming down the road at a hundred miles per hour, but the steering wheel is not connected to the front wheels.

The only thing that management has control over is the environment within the organization. If we are going to improve the organization, it means that we must change the environment within the organization to produce the desired results. Environmental Change Plans first develop a set of vision statements that define the desired future environment. Individual vision statements and desired behavior patterns are developed for every influencing factor (for example, Management Leadership, Business Processes, Customer Partnerships, etc.). Then a three-year plan is developed to bring about the desired transformation. The long-term effect of changing the environment is a change in the organization's culture.

A Change Management Plan is also developed and implemented. This plan paves the road for effective implementation of the environmental changes that are required to bring about the desired environment and behaviors within the organization. It is very important to prepare the stakeholders for these changes before, during, and after their implementation. Even the very best improvement effort can be shot down if the stakeholders have not been prepared to embrace the required changes. As a result, the Change Management Plan is a crucial part of the direction-setting activities.

Whenever you do anything, you have four options. You can do the wrong thing effectively (Option I) or do it ineffectively (Option II). You can do the right thing effectively (Option III) or do it ineffectively (Option IV). In the 1980s and early 1990s, many organizations were doing a number of good things, but doing them ineffectively because they did not prepare their stakeholders to embrace the changes. Often, the losing organizations' stakeholders spent their efforts trying to define why the change would not work and/or sabotaging the change, instead of trying to make it work. As a result, many of the changes failed to meet expectations or accomplish the improvement that they should have. The winning organizations tended to prepare their stakeholders for the changes. Because the stakeholders were prepared for the changes, they embraced them and spent their efforts making the changes work. As a result, these change programs often exceeded expectations.

BB5 – Meeting Stakeholders Expectations

Every organization has an obligation to the individuals that are impacted by the organization's activities. This includes investors, management, employees, suppliers, customers, consumers, the community, the employee's family, and so on. Often, what one stakeholder expects from the organization is detrimental to another stakeholder. For example, the employees want increased benefits including salary. The investor wants decreased costs so that bigger dividends are paid. One of the biggest problems top management faces is how to balance the activities within the organization so that all the stakeholders have a win–win impression of the way the organization is managed

BB6 – Project Management Systems

One of the fastest growing professional societies in the world is the Project Management Association with headquarters in North America They just issued an updated version of their standard called "PMBOK." It is a well-prepared comprehensive document that provides detailed guidance to the professional project manager. Its contents also apply to projects that are too small to have a project manager assigned to them or are considered to not require project manager level of support. I will not try to condense it down in this technical report, and I strongly recommend that you obtain a copy of the PMBOK It is sufficient to say that any project that addresses the organization's culture should have a professional project manager coordinating it. When the culture of an organization is being changed, the risk of rejecting the concept is so high that the organization must take every precaution to ensure the project runs smoothly. Project management and change management are a critical part of this risk avoidance. To decrease the number of project failures, I recommend reading "Effective Portfolio Management Systems" (Voehl et al., 2015).

Tier III – Basic Concepts

The third tier of the pyramid is directed at integrating the basic innovative concepts into the organization. It consists of four building blocks. They are

- BB7 – Management participation
- BB8 – Team building
- BB9 – Individual creativity and excellence
- BB10 – Supplier partnerships

BB7 – Management Participation

There is a huge difference between leadership and participation. The coach of a football team provides leadership to the team. We are participating in the game if we are out on the field blocking, catching passes, being tackled, pushing, and shoving to get that extra inch. We have leaders in the football stands. They stand up and yell at the top of their lungs instructing the quarterback to throw a pass, they complain when the coach calls a play they did not like or when the guard misses a tackle. None of the players are working as hard as they could according to the coach in the stands. These are the fans that are out of breath just walking up the stairs to their seat. They are the type of person who seems to always sit beside me and spill mustard from his hot dog all over my pants.

This building block is designed to get all levels of management actively participating (out on the playing field) in the improvement effort. Having the management feel comfortable in a leadership role is essential to the success of the total process. It is important that you bring about the proper change in top, middle, and first-line managers and supervisors before the concepts are introduced to the employees. Most organizations have done a poor job of preparing management for their new leadership role. All too often the management rule is, "Do what I say – not what I do."

BB8 – Team Building

What is a team? Do I want to be in a team? Why should I be on a team? Will someone else get credit for my good ideas? Do you have a charge number for the time I spend with the team? Can I decide which team I want to be on? What part of my job will I be relieved of so that I can participate in the team? What bowling alley will the team meet in?

These are all good questions that management has to be prepared to answer based upon their activities in BB7. No, this is not an athletic team; it's a problem-solving team so do not bother to bring your bowling ball.

The use of management and employee teams to solve the organization's problems and to be involved in the organization's change process is a key ingredient in today's competitive business environment. This building block develops team concepts as part of the management process, and it prepares all employees for participating in a team environment. The team usually used a set of standard problem-solving tools selected to meet the specific requirements of the organization and definitions that everyone in the organization is trying to use.

BB9 – Individual, Creativity, and Excellence

Management must provide the environment, as well as the tools, that will allow and encourage employees to excel, take pride in their work, and then reward them based on their accomplishments. This is another key ingredient in every winning organization's strategy. You can have a *good* organization using teams, but you can have a *great* organization only when each employee excels in all jobs he/she is performing. Care must be taken to have a good balance between team cooperation and individuals who strive for excellence in all their endeavors. The two concepts need to work in tandem and not compete with each other.

BB10 – Supplier Partnerships

Winning organizations have winning suppliers. The destiny of both organizations is inevitably linked. Once the improvement process has started to take hold within the organization, it is time to start to work with your suppliers. The objective of this partnership is to help them improve the performance of their output and increase their profits while reducing the cost of their product and/or service to you.

Tier IV – The Delivery Processes

The fourth tier is the Delivery Processes Level. This tier of the pyramid focuses on the organization's processes and the output that the customer/consumer receive. It consists of three building blocks. They are

- BB11 – Process breakthrough
- BB12 – Service and product excellence
- BB13 – Technology, automation, and artificial intelligence

BB11 – Process Breakthrough

This building block uses cross-functional Process Improvement Teams (PITs) to make a quantum leap forward in the critical business processes (overhead-type activities). It focuses on making these important parts of the organization more efficient, effective, and adaptable. This building block makes use of many different streamlining techniques, including bureaucracy elimination, value-added analysis, benchmarking, and information technology all carefully woven together. This approach brings about drastic improvements in the processes to which it is applied. Improvements between 20 and 60% are being realized in a period as short as six months. Although this building block was specifically designed for performance improvement in business processes, it also works equally in product processes.

BB12 – Service and Product Excellence

This building block focuses on how to design and maintain product and services delivery processes so that they consistently satisfy external and/or internal customers and the people who consume the end product. It is directed at the product and services design activities process. All organizations, whether they are classified as service or product related, rely on process to control them. The delivery processes for products and services are very different. These differences make it necessary to apply different improvement methods, and common methods in different ways, in the delivery of service. This building block focuses on how to design, implement, and improve the service and production delivery process in the service and product industries.

BB13 – Technology, Automation, and Artificial Intelligence

Innovative use of technology, automation, and artificial intelligence has drastically changed the way our processes are designed and function. Automation has made concepts like Six Sigma practical in our manufacturing processes. Technology provides us with a new product almost on a monthly basis. Artificial intelligence provides the capacity of a computer to perform operations analogous to learning and decision-making in humans, such as by an expert system, a program for CAD or CAM, or a program for the perception and recognition of shapes in computer vision systems. In many applications, it is impossible for humans to make decisions as fast or as correctly as artificial intelligence can. The combination of innovative personnel using technology, automation, and artificial intelligence is bringing us closer and closer every day to realizing the factory of the future that will employ one person and a dog to keep him awake. His job is to turn the switch that sets the total factory into motion and turns it off at the end of the day. For accuracy, repeatability, dependability, and precision are not in the hands of a human but in the programming of the new computerized environment.

In this building block, we will show you how automation, technology, and artificial intelligence can be used to reduce costs, assist in creating new products, and reduce cycle time while improving the quality of the delivered product.

Tier V – Organizational Impact

The fifth tier of the pyramid is the Organizational Impact Level. By now the innovative performance improvement process is well underway within the organization and it will soon start to impact the organization's structure as well as its measurements. This tier consists of two building blocks. They are

- BB14 – Measurement systems
- BB15 – Organizational structure

BB14 – Measurement Systems

This building block highlights the importance of a comprehensive measurement plan in all improvement processes. It helps the organization develop a balanced measurement system that demonstrates how interactive measurements like quality, productivity, and profit can either detract from or complement each other. Only when the improvement process documents positive measurable results can we expect management to embrace the methodology as a way of life. A good measurement plan converts the skeptic into a disciple. As the process develops, the measurement system should change. When you start the improvement process, you measure activities. About six months into the process, you start to measure improvement results, and about 18 months into the process, the normal business measurement should start to be impacted.

BB15 – Organizational Structure

As the smokestack functional thinking and measurement systems begin to change to a process view of the organization, bureaucracy is removed from the processes and decisions are made at lower levels. In this new environment, employees are empowered to do their jobs and are held accountable for their actions. With these changes, large organizations need to give way to small business units that can react quickly and effectively to changing customer requirements and the changing business environment. Functions like Quality Assurance and Finance take on new roles. The organization as a whole becomes more process-driven rather than functional organization-driven. In this environment, the organization needs to become flatter and decentralized, requiring major changes to the organizational structure. This building block helps an organization develop an organizational structure that meets today's needs and tomorrow's challenges.

Tier VI – Shared Value

Shared value is at the very top of the pyramid as it provides the mortar that holds the individual building blocks together. Without enough innovative mortar, the building can collapse. As individual building blocks shift around, they cause large cracks and voids that weaken the pyramid until the house is unstable. The TIME pyramid is created to provide additional value to all the stakeholders. It is absolutely imperative that the added-value content and results are shared with the relevant stakeholders. You cannot expect an employee to suggest efficiency improvements if he or one of his friends will be laid off as a result of the suggestion. If you start a continuous improvement process and you have layoffs, what you're going to end up with is a continuous sabotage process; we like to see the organization release a no-layoff policy. For example,

"No employee will be laid off because of improvements made as a result of the TIME methodology. People whose jobs are eliminated will be retrained for an equivalent or more responsible job. This does not mean that it may not be necessary to lay off employees because of the business downturn." The organization's dollars and cents savings should be shared three ways:

1. With the customer/consumer
2. With the employee
3. With the organization

Should everyone be recognized in the same way and with equivalent value rewards? No!! All rewards and recognition systems should be capable of adjusting output based upon the contribution that the individual or team made to the organization's overall performance.

Tier IV is made up of one building block. It is BB16 Rewards and Recognition.

BB16 – Rewards and Recognition

The Rewards and Recognition process should be designed to pull together the total pyramid. It needs to reinforce the organization's desired behavior. It also needs to be very comprehensive, for everyone hears "Thank You" in a different way. If you want everyone to take an active role in your improvement process, you must be able to thank each individual in a way that is meaningful to him or her. There is a time for a "pat on the back" and a time for a "pat on the wallet." Your rewards and recognition process should include both.

Summary

There is no doubt about it. The United States is the blue-ribbon country of the world – the best place to live, work, and raise a family. We are more productive and have the best standard of living of anyone in the world. People are more satisfied with their jobs in the United States than in Canada, Europe, or Japan.

US index	40
Canadian index	39
European index	29
Japan index	16

Money magazine evaluated the *standard* of living in the 16 wealthiest nations. It compared them in five areas: health, solid job prospects, comfortable income, upward mobility, and adequate leisure time. The United States ranked #1; Japan, #7; Germany, #8; and the United Kingdom, #15. We are the envy of the rest of the world, and when you are #1, everyone is using you as a benchmark to beat. As a result of the gap between the United States and other countries around the world, everyone has targeted the United States as the gold standard. Let's face it, it is much easier, cheaper and faster if it was someone else doing and originating the idea.

I hate to complain about the United States as we are extremely lucky to live in the best country in the world. But it is up to us and the preceding generation to creatively and innovatively improve the living standards, keeping us as the benchmark country. It's up to you and me, so let's make a commitment to be more creative and innovative related to our personal life and our work environment, making the good old USA even better for our children.

"There is a time for poor planning, a time for sleeping, but now is the TIME for innovative action." H. James Harrington

How does it look for the future of the United States? We are positioned well in the products that will lead the next decade. The United States is recognized as being among the very best in microelectronics, biotechnology, new materials, civilian aviation, telecommunications, and software.

International customers are attracted to your organization for four reasons, in the following order:

Win Customers	Lose Customers
1. Capabilities	1. Trust
2. Trust	2. Quality
3. Price	3. Capabilities
4. Quality	4. Price

Product and service capability is driven by using the latest technology and/or using present technology in more creative ways. Trust is based upon experience and reputation. It reflects the faith that the customer has in your ability to meet your cost, schedule, and performance commitments. Price today ties in directly with value. Customers are looking at getting the best performance at the least cost. Quality reflects more than just the initial view of the products or services purchased. It reflects the quality of the total organization, the reliability of its products, and the capability of its sales and service personnel. You lose customers for the same four reasons that you attract them, but in a different order.

SUMMARY

For an organization to survive in today's competitive international environment, there must be improvement efforts in both the continuous and breakthrough improvement methodologies. Management needs to make the correct business decisions so that the correct products are available at the time they are needed while making the most of everyone's efforts. There needs to be a high level of cooperation between government, business, labor, and academia. Each must improve the value of its products and/or services as viewed by its customers. This means that all functions in all organizations must use the most appropriate technology to improve their effectiveness, efficiency, and adaptability. In addition, all organizations need to have a well-communicated, agreed-to plan that merges together the many improvement methodologies to provide the greatest value to all of their stakeholders.

China is now in the top five countries that the United States has the biggest trade imbalance with. If present trends continue, the United States will have a bigger negative balance of trade with China in 10 years than we have with Japan. If you think Japan is a fierce competitor, it's a pussycat in comparison to China. The other alternative to China is the European Common Market. They could come together, combining their specialties, to make a manufacturing superpower. A combination of the Soviet Union's scientific capabilities, Germany's craftsmanship, Italy's design flair, and Great Britain's financial management, would be hard to compete with.

The last and probably the most important, competitor is all the emerging industrial nations. They are modernized, upscale, and hungry. They pay lower wages, have higher work ethics, are improving at a faster rate, and their standard of living is improving faster than in Japan, Germany, and the United States. I believe there is a direct correlation between a person's work ethic and the last time he or she went hungry.

Although things in the United States today, on an average, are good and will continue to be during the 2010s, it could be a very different story by 2025. As Lester Throw, an economist at MIT, wrote, "No one at the end of the 20th century is less prepared for the competition that lies ahead in the 21st century." The United States had 70 years to prepare and today, it is not ready. It has not prepared itself as it should have. The United States. needs to be really serious about making a major improvement in the way its government, business, and schools perform.

Today, I would rate our production organizations at B- and our service organizations at C-, because they have started to improve; our government at D-, because it is not really trying; and our education system an F, because it is a dismal failure at the grade school and high school levels. We spend a higher percentage of our GDP (6.8%) on education than Japan (6.5%) and Germany (4.6%), yet only 7% of our 17-year-olds are prepared for college-level science courses.

As former President Bush put it, "A dedication to quality and excellence is more than just good business. It is a way of life, giving something back to society, offering your best to others."

Epilogue

The ISO Innovation Standard 50501 and Community Patents

On Standards, Intellectual Property Rights and Standards-Setting Process*

Abrame Walton, Ph.D., Frank Voehl and Esteban Burrone

INTRODUCTION

At present, it is virtually impossible to develop an audio or video compliance standard with a reasonable performance that does not require the use of one or, more likely, several patents.[1] This applies not only to video and audio coding, but also to a number of other products, particularly in the fields of telecommunications and electronics. Companies that are willing to manufacture products that comply with certain standards may need to use patented technology, for which prior authorization from the patent holder will most likely be required. This raises several issues and rules

---

* The genesis of this Epilogue was first published in 2000 as part of the ASQ Community Quality Technical Committee's effort to revitalize our communities. In 1999, the CQCC Public Policy Institute (PPI) started planning a set of livability reports as part of a developing AARP-sponsored index to measure community livability across the United States. Lessons learned from that project have initially inspired the creation of two companion reports, "What Is Livable? Community Preferences of Older Adults" (www.aarp. org/ppi/issues/livable-communities/info-2015/what-is-livable-AARP-ppi-liv-com.html hyperlink to article page for this report) and "Is This a Good Place to Live? Measuring Community Quality of Life for All Ages" (www.aarp.org/ppi/issues/livable-communities/info-2015/is-this-a-good-place-to-live-AARP-ppi-liv-com.html).

397

for business, patent holders and standards development organizations. This epilogue provides some insights into how IP is treated during the standard-setting process and what implications this may have for the future of the innovation management business in the years to come.*

THE ISO INNOVATION STANDARD: 50501
NEW INNOVATION MANAGEMENT

Three unassailable facts underpin the future of innovation: (1) innovation is the new mantra, whether you're involved in teaching art and design, developing new products for a blue chip consumer brand or providing public services to citizens; (2) understanding innovation requires multiple perspectives including culture and mindset, social and commercial context, and new ways of working that require new products or services; and (3) innovation is a journey, drawing on insights from around the globe is essential to accelerate our progress as an international community.

Anyone interested in innovation (student, researcher, or practitioner) will benefit from a global thought collection and an amalgamation of insights. The contributors' multiple perspectives, models, practical examples, and stories provide a sense of innovation that no single writer could ever capture. In fact, we have witnessed the formal maturation of a profession and a new field of science, broadly known as the science of innovation. As such, the future of innovation is supported by several leading institutes and organizations; the International Association of Innovation Professionals, which is the managing organization for the International Journal of Innovation Science, is the world's largest innovation association and certification body, and has produced global innovation science handbooks and journals that have been received prestigious authorship

---

* Patents play an increasingly important role in innovation and economic performance. Between 1992 and 2002, the number of patent applications filed in Europe, Japan, and the United States increased by more than 40%. The increasing use of patents to protect inventions by businesses and public research organizations is closely connected to recent evolutions in innovation processes, the economy, and patent regimes. Scientific and technological advances have created new waves of innovation, notably in information and communications technology (ICT) and biotechnology, and innovation processes themselves have become less centered on individual firms and more dependent on interactions among global networks of actors in the public and private sectors. Shifts in the legal and regulatory framework of patent regimes have resulted in more expansive domains of patentable subject matter (patent regimes in many countries now include biotechnology and software), and more robust and valuable patents.

awards (www.iaoip.org). This website, in addition to others (e.g., www. thefutureofinnovation.org), are repositories and communities where you can find even more contributions and tools that enable you to exchange, expand, elaborate, and develop your perspectives on the ISO Innovation Management Standard Series: 50500.

As the ANSI-accredited U.S. Technical Advisory Group (TAG) professional body for innovation, IAOIP was very pleased to be asked to sit on the ANSI/ISO National Technical Committee (TC 279) to share its collective and significant experience in innovation accreditation and benchmarking gained through the Basics in Innovations© and the related professional development programs. The TC 279 Committee proposed a series of standards to act as guidelines for innovation management. These standards are:

1.	Fundamentals and Vocabulary	ISO 50500
2.	Innovation Management System – Guidance	ISO 50501
3.	Innovation Management Assessment – Guidance	ISO 50502
4.	Innovation Management Tools and Methods – Guidance	ISO 50503
5.	Innovation Management Strategic Intelligence Management – Guidance	ISO 50504
6.	Innovation Management, Intellectual Property Management	ISO 50505

The first of these standards (ISO 50503) has been written up and is undergoing committee approvals. Publication of this first standard is expected in October 2018 and is to be announced in Tokyo. The IAOIP's Basics of Innovation Program is an outgrowth of this standard, and takes into consideration the TC279 standards, while providing an integrated and coherent platform for preparing an organization to meet the ISO innovation-compliancy requirements.

BACKGROUND INFORMATION ON ISO AND OECD*

Pursuant to Article 1 of the Convention signed in Paris on 14th December 1960, and which came into force on 30th September 1961, the forerunner

---

* The original member countries of the OECD are Austria, Belgium, Canada, Denmark, France, Germany, Greece, Iceland, Ireland, Italy, Luxembourg, the Netherlands, Norway, Portugal, Spain, Sweden, Switzerland, Turkey, the United Kingdom, and the United States.

of ISO – the Organization for Economic Co-operation and Development (OECD) – shall promote policies designed:

- to achieve the highest sustainable economic growth and employment and a rising standard of living in member communities and countries while maintaining financial stability, and thus to contribute to the development of national and world economies;*
- to contribute to sound economic expansion in member as well as non-member communities and countries in the process of economic development; and
- to contribute to the expansion of world trade on a multilateral, non-discriminatory basis in accordance with the international obligations of ASQ.

ISO standards influence almost every facet of our lives. They influence the food we eat, our means of communication, travel, work, play, and endless other activities. Almost every product or service available in the marketplace has been developed in compliance with one or more voluntary or mandatory ISO worldwide standards. Mandatory standards generally pertain to health, safety, or the environment, and are set and enforced by, or on behalf of, the relevant government. However, most standards are voluntary.

The International Organization for Standardization (ISO) defines a formal standard as "a document, established by consensus that provides rules, guidelines or characteristics for activities or their results." A standard, therefore, is generally a set of characteristics or qualities that describes features of a product, process, service, interface or material. A standard may also describe how properties are measured, the composition of a chemical, the properties of an interface, or performance criteria against which a product or process can be measured.

Apart from health, safety, and environmental concerns, standards are important for a number of other reasons. For example, the existence of standards makes it possible to develop compatible or interoperable products by competing firms, and allows the further technological advancement of a field. In other words, they ensure the compatibility

---

* Changes in patent policy in OECD countries over the past two decades have fostered the use and enforcement of patents with the aim of encouraging investments in innovation and enhancing the dissemination of knowledge (e.g., the U.S. based 2013 Leahy-Smith America Invents Act). Despite these reforms, few systematic economic evaluations have been carried out to better inform policy choices.

between complementary products and even between the various parts of a particular product or group of products. Product standards are often critical to the effective functioning and advancement of markets and play an important role in international trade. For consumers/users, standards provide information and serve a quality assurance function.

Complying with certain standards is generally considered to be in the overall interest of producers of goods and providers of services. By way of illustration, there are unlimited possibilities concerning the shapes and sizes of nuts, screws, and bolts which, if they were to proliferate, would mean that no standard screwdrivers or spanners could be manufactured to fit their purpose.

Similarly, in the digital world, in the absence of standards for CDs, CD-ROMs, DVDs, JPEG and a number of other systems that enable different companies to make products that are compatible, there would be insurmountable problems with the products of a company to interface with, connect to or be used in equipment made by other companies or for other markets. As with previous standards efforts, such as the ASQ-supported Standards for Interoperability, ongoing development of standards that account for and build upon the most recent governmental reforms are particularly important for network markets, such as railroads, electricity, telegraph/faxes, telephones, cellular phones, and the Internet, as well as for the continuously evolving software-embedded/software-defined product markets and technology-as-a-service business models.*

---

* ASQ, like IAOIP, is a global community of people passionate about their field of interest. They share the ideas and tools that make our world work better. Founded over 70 years ago in 1946, ASQ has its world headquarters in Milwaukee, WI. With more than 80,000 individual and organizational members in over 130 countries, ASQ has the reputation and reach to bring together diverse quality champions who are transforming the world's corporations, organizations and communities to meet tomorrow's critical challenges. ASQ is people passionate about quality and IAOIP is people passionate about innovation. IAOIP is a member community council-based operation for everyone who wants to improve themselves and the places they work and live; it supports members in nearly 100 countries (ASQ supports 130) and operates offices in Dubai, China, India, and Europe. As one of the major global voices of innovation, IAOIP provides local access to professional development, certification, knowledge, and information services, as well as to a membership community. IAOIP offers technologies, concepts, tools, training, and an active network of innovation practitioners and subject matter experts second to none. Many board members and member leaders are available to speak at meetings or events on various subjects such as the Future of Innovation Study (see the IAOIP Operations Manual pdf). Transforming our communities, transforming our world: the IAOIP Board Members are building the future of innovation. In the 21st century, the focus is on accelerating the positive, putting an emphasis on efficiency, effectiveness, and the best use of time, materials, and resources that will help us meet tomorrow's critical challenges and make the world work better. In May of 2018, IAOIP has assumed responsibility for the Administration of the U.S. TAG for TC 279, the Innovation Management Standards previously Chaired by ASQ.

402 • Epilogue

IPRS IN STANDARDS AND TECHNICAL REGULATIONS

In today's competitive context where companies invest significantly in the development of new technologies and products, which are often protected by intellectual property rights (IPRs), it is not uncommon that the best technology for a technical standard is a proprietary technology, protected by one or more patents. The development of standards more and more frequently attempts to anticipate technology rather than follow it, leading to conflicts between standards and patents. If patented technology is incorporated into a standard without the patent holder's agreement to share its patent rights, then the patent holder may be the only entity able to comply with the standard.

This conflict raises important questions for companies that own such protected technology, for individuals and companies involved in the standards-setting process as well as for all those enterprises that will then use or adopt the standard for their products or processes. Should a technology protected by IPRs be incorporated into a technical standard? Do companies willing to adopt a standard need to obtain a license from the IPR/patent holder? If so, under what terms and conditions? Do companies involved in the standards-setting process have a duty to disclose information to the other members of the standards-setting committee about their patents or patent applications? What happens if the patent holder(s) refuse(s) to provide licenses for the use of patented technology?

A patent is an exclusive right to exploit (make, use, sell, or import) an invention over a limited period of time (usually 20 years from filing) within the country where the application is made. Patents are granted for inventions that are novel, inventive (non-obvious), and have an industrial application (useful). There are other types of exclusive rights over intangible assets, notably copyright, design protection, and trademarks, but patents provide a broader protection that extends beyond the specific expression of an invention to the invention itself.

Due to this control over the technology, the patent holder is in a position to set a higher-than-competitive price for the corresponding good or service, which allows recovery of innovation, research and development costs. In return, the applicant must disclose the invention in the text of the application, which is published 18 months after application. As a patent is valid only within the country in which it is

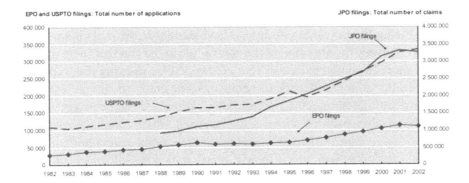

FIGURE E.1
Patent fillings at EPO, USPTO and JPO. Note: EPO and USPTO fillings correspond to total number of applications. JPO fillings correspond to total number of claims (number of claims per application mulitiplied by total number of applications) to account for the effect of the 1988 law reform allowing more than one claim per patent application at JPO. OECD patent database and USPTO, EPO and JPO annual repots. JPO figures for 2001 and 2002 are OECD estimate.

granted, it is subject to national laws and litigation settled in national courts (Figure E.1).*

The forthcoming community patent in Europe will be an exception as it will provide protection in all EU member countries and litigation will be centralized in a specialized court. International agreements, such as the agreement on Trade Related Aspects of Intellectual Property Rights (TRIPS), signed in 1994 and overseen by the World Trade Organization (WTO), tend to place restrictions on what national laws and policies can do. TRIPS introduced intellectual property rules into the multilateral trading system for the first time in an attempt to guarantee the same minimum standards of protection across countries.

Technical standards are generally developed and revised collaboratively by technical committees of Standards Development Organizations (SDOs) comprising of a number and variety of stakeholders (including consumer/ user interests and experts in the relevant technical fields). The membership

---

* Strengthening of patent systems in the European Union, Japan and, the United States has, however, raised new concerns and exacerbated old ones. There have been numerous claims that patents of little novelty or excessive breadth have been granted, allowing their holders to extract undue rents from other inventors and from customers. This has been of particular concern in software, biotechnology, and business methods where patent offices and courts have had the most difficulties in responding to rapid change, building up institutional expertise, evaluating prior art and determining correct standards for the breadth of granted patents. More basically, it has also been asked whether patentability might unnecessarily and unreasonably hamper the diffusion of knowledge, and therefore innovation, notably in these new areas.

of such committees may be open or closed, and is often by invitation only. During the development of technical standards, participants may be required to draw the attention of the committee to the fact that there may be one or more "essential patent(s)" that are needed for meeting the standard, i.e., it would be impossible for someone or some entity to comply with the standard without employing the technology protected by the patent(s). The permission of the patent holder would be needed, which could mean signing a license agreement and possibly paying royalties to the patent holder.

Obviously, even with the increase of what is generally referred to as compulsory licenses, it would not be very productive or effective to adopt a standard if an IPR holder could block the implementation of that standard by either refusing to grant a license or requiring such high royalties as to make it impossible for its dissemination and broad adoption as a standard. However, compulsory licensing strategies should not be ignored or overlooked during the examination and development of standards and how companies might employ them. Prior to the American Invents Act of 2013 companies could legally force another firm to cease production and sale of a product that infringed on IPRs. However, we are now seeing a whole host of litigation and precedent being set in the U.S. where, while courts are adjudicating in favor of infringed IPR holders, they are not always forcing the cease of operations, production or sale of said infringing product or service, but are instead assigning compensatory damage for said infringement, thusly, if not explicitly, enforcing a compulsory license between the two parties. Examples of international ISO standards that include patented technologies abound and are likely more numerous, prevalent, and fundamental than a normal consumer would anticipate, such as the MPEG-2 standard for visual and audio compression for which the number of patents required for implementing the standard is in the order of 100.

Many SDOs discourage the use of proprietary or patented technology in standards; they support it only in 'exceptional cases' where justified by 'technical reasons'. In such cases, the patent holder of a technology, considered to be crucial for meeting the requirements of a standard, may be contacted by the technical committee of an SDO to inquire whether the patent holder would agree to negotiate licenses with users of such standards on fair, reasonable and non-discriminatory terms and conditions (generally referred to as RAND terms and conditions). However, IPR policies of SDOs generally do not really explain as to what may be considered to be RAND terms and conditions. Some SDOs go beyond the RAND terms and conditions, requiring technologies to be licensed on a royalty-free basis (generally referred to as RF basis); for example, this is true of certain consortia dealing with internet standards. While SDOs work to develop standards not requiring proprietary technology, there is a dichotomy between being able to anticipate technology trends and requisite standards and building standards not requiring IPR-based technology. An alternative that has surfaced and shown significant growth in the last 15–20 years is that of Open Source Alliances (OSAs) and open source Patent Management Organizations (PMOs). These OSA PMOs sole purpose is to procure open source IPs, promote open source development, and protect the open source community from threats related to individual(s) or groups having IPRs seeking to create a technology monopoly. The IPR held by OSA PMOs can thus potentially provide an alternative solution space that, while maintaining cutting edge technology and associated patents, may be more readily willing to partner on the development of standards that might include IPR-based technology. Examples of these OSAs include some claim membership by very prominent organizations, such as the Open Handset Alliance, the Open Innovation Network, the Autonomous Vehicle Alliance, and Source Forge.*

ADOPTING THE INNOVATION STANDARD

Any company, large or small, that plans to adopt an innovation-based standard for inclusion in its products, processes, or services should first and foremost verify if there is/are any "essential" patent(s) for which a license is required and the broad terms and conditions under which the license will be granted apart or separate from the standard, and any associated fees, royalties or other costs. This information is generally available from or through the relevant SDO. If the license is to be obtained directly from

---

* It should be noted that some PMOs operate under unique business models. For instance, whether for open source purposes or for private investment, i.e., private owners, do not ever produce a product or service from the patents that are held in its portfolio. This provides an interesting business model, whereby a PMO can sue or pursue litigation against infringing firms, while minimizing retaliatory litigation because they themselves would likely not have infringed on the defending firm given they produce/sell nothing. Some examples of these PMOs have been termed 'Patent Trolls'. However, other versions of these PMOs seek to provide defensibility to smaller technology firms that, while they may not maintain a large patent portfolio, are pushing the frontier of technological advancement. Should said smaller firm be sued by a larger IPR holder, they can seek out aid from Open Source Alliances to provide patent licenses that may provide a sort of legal counter to the claimant firm.

the patent holder, then the patent holder should be contacted, a licensing agreement negotiated and signed prior to taking any concrete steps to adopt the standard for a company's products or process.*

There may also be cases in which, in order to comply with a given standard, a company may have the option of choosing from a series of alternative technologies that could be used, some of which may include the use of protected or patented technology. In all such cases, the patents would not be considered to be "essential patents" but "useful patents", as adopters of the standard have other ways of complying with the standard that does not require the use of a patent. Moreover, there may be cases in which there are a number of essential patents that may be pooled by the patent holders (i.e., a "patent pool" is established, enabling member or contributing companies to obtain licenses for a group of patents through a single agreement) to facilitate dissemination of the standard. This was the case, for example, in the case of MPEG-2.

In any case, it is crucial to understand that in order to comply with a given standard or technical regulation, a company may have to (or choose to) use one or more patented technologies. In all such cases, the company is required to obtain a license from the patent-holder and this must be done prior to using the patented technology to conform to the requirements of the standard. On occasions, patent-holders may agree to grant royalty-free licenses, but this may not always be the case. It is important to know the rules of the game so that you are able to negotiate the best possible terms and conditions for use of a proprietary or patented technology that you need for meeting the requirements of a standard.†

---

* IAOIP is working with the U.S. Chamber and the USPTO and plans on hosting a 2019 Patent Quality Community Symposium to update the public on the status of our innovation programs, to introduce some developing programs, to collect feedback and to continue the discussion from a stakeholder's perspective on what patent applicants and their representatives can do to advance innovation quality.

† The annual Technical Conference is the world's premier conference on innovation, Lean and Six Sigma, and is designed for process improvement and organizational change professionals — among others — in all industries. The conference attracts attendees with a wide range of backgrounds and experience who share best practices that attendees can use at their organizations to increase efficiencies and enhance products and services. The theme of the conference, "Sustaining a Culture of Excellence in a World of Disruption, Innovation, and Change," focuses on attention to a culture of excellence, the opportunities created by disruptive technologies changing the workforce, the markets organizations serve, and the capabilities in which they have access."We all have similar struggles to improve our organization's performance and then sustain these results over time," said IAOIP's Frank Voehl, National TAG Administrator. "The rapid rate of change in today's digital world makes that challenge even more difficult. Our Community Improvement conference is a premier event designed to address that challenge by bringing together a community of practitioners from a wide array of industries to share success stories, learn from industry experts and network with leading quality professionals from around the world."

PARTICIPATING IN THE STANDARDS-SETTING PROCESS*

In certain cases, the product specifications of a dominant supplier in the market may become the *de facto* standard for all others if they wish to enter the market. In this article, we are not concerned with these types of standards or use cases. Instead, we focus on the development and use of collaboratively developed standards, which are adopted by consensus. On occasions, however, a proprietary *de facto* standard may be adopted by consensus by the relevant standard-setting body to become the *de jure* standard.

Standards are developed at various levels by standards-setting technical committees created by international, regional, national, or subnational SDOs and/or by professional, industry, or trade associations, alliances or consortia. Most countries have a National Standards Body (NSB) like ANSI, which is accredited to the ISO. The national ANSI-NSB, in turn, may accredit a number of public and private SDOs that adhere to the criteria of the NSB (generally including on IP matters) for developing voluntary standards. A standards-setting technical committee of an SDO may have an open or closed membership. In addition to ISO, there are other multilateral bodies such as the International Electrical Commission (IEC) and the International Telecommunications Union (ITU).

THE FUTURE OF INNOVATION: THE NOTION OF A COMMUNITY PATENT AND ITS IMPLICATIONS

The strive for a Community Patent began in the mid-to-late 1970s in earnest. Although it was already possible to be covered throughout the EU by the European patent, it was felt that a Community-wide, cost efficient, new industrial property right applied without borders would ensure the

---

* The current patent system in Europe contains aspects that are both centralized and decentralized. A patent system user needs only to submit a single patent application to the European Patent Office (EPO), but when the patent is granted the result is not a single patent but a "bundle" of national patents. The patent becomes effective in each of the designated Member States once a translation in one of that Member State's official languages is filed. In addition, infringement needs to be litigated in each individual country and can become quite costly and fragmented. The question has arisen whether the lack of a Community Patent after its apparent failure in 2004 endangers the commercialization of technology in Europe.

free movement of protected goods while striding towards the creation of a genuine Single Market.* In addition, it was a generally shared belief that Europe ought to be looking at the creation of a Community Patent to meet its "innovation deficit"† as compared to the U.S. and Japan.

Communities, big or small, may wish to participate in a standards-setting committee in order to influence and steer the standards-setting process in the direction that best serves their interests. However, it may not be possible for a company to participate in the standards-setting process if the membership of the standards-setting committee is closed to, for example, members of an association, alliance or consortium.‡

While the use of an open standards-setting process usually lessens antitrust or competition concerns over the exercise of market power, open standards-setting procedures may lessen efficiency because of the need for consensus among competitors, each of whom may have its own proprietary technology. This means that companies should ensure that the standard being adopted does not make any of their own technologies irrelevant and, on occasions, companies may seek to have their own patented technology become essential (or useful) to comply with a standard. This may be especially true for a company that has complimentary assets, which could give it a competitive edge, as shown in the annual growth in Figure E.2 below.§

While there may be no duty to do a patent search of the patent portfolio of the participating company or of any other companies, the participants in the standards-setting process may be required to reveal information about IPRs, especially patents (and, in certain cases, also patent applications) that may be owned by the company and are likely to be essential for complying

---

* Official Journal of the European Communities. "Opinion of the Economic and Social Committee on the 'Proposal for a Council Regulation on the Community Patent'." (May 29, 2001).

† Hodgson p. 1.

‡ From these findings, several implications evolve for an index that aims to measure livability. An index must achieve the following: (a) Be relevant and useful to existing efforts to improve community livability; (b) Incorporate the needs of older adults into a measure of general livability; (c) Be useful for educating people about what they need as they age; (d) Help policy makers, planners, and others better understand the needs of an aging population and the steps that can be taken to improve livability; (e) Be relevant to all, no matter where they live, what their background may be, or what their income; and (f) Acknowledge data limitations.

§ Even though the growth rate of patent applications at JPO was not as high as at EPO or USPTO in those years, JPO appears to have experienced similarly high growth rates in patent protection when filings are adjusted by the growth in the number of claims. The total number of claims in applications filed in China more than doubled over the period 2010+. As the economic situation has deteriorated in OECD countries since the beginning of the 21st century, patent numbers have fallen or slowed at the EPO and JPO.

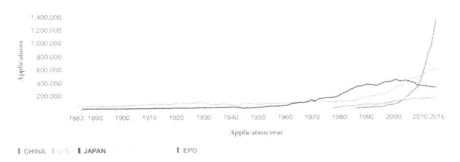

FIGURE E.2
Trend in patent applications for the top five offices. Note: EPO is the European patent office. The top five offices were selected base on their 2016 totals. Source: WIPO statistics database, septermber 2017.

with the proposed standard. The IPR policies of SDOs vary widely in this respect and have often been revised over the past years. IPRs or patent policies of SDOs follow different practices about if, when and how much information on IPRs, especially patents (or patent applications) needs to be disclosed. See the average annual growth rates of USPTO grants and EPO applications, as shown in Figures E.3 and E.4 below.*

Therefore, it is important for a company that plans to participate in the standards-setting process to be well informed about the details of the IPR policy of the relevant SDOs. It is important to note that in some cases, non-disclosure of patents or patent applications during the standard-setting

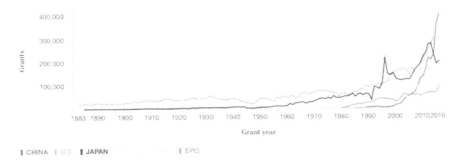

FIGURE E.3
Trent in patent grants for the top five offices. Note: EPO is the European patent office. The top five offices were selected based on their 2016 totals. Source: WIPO statistics database, September 2017.

---

* Although nearly all technology fields experienced growth in patenting over the 1990s, two con-tributed disproportionately to the overall surge in patenting: Computer Technology, and Electrical Machinery, Apparatus, and Energy.

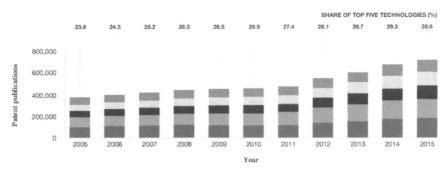

FIGURE E.4
Trend in published patent application for the top five technology fields. Note: Date refer to published patent applications. There is a minimum delay of 18 months between the applications date and the publication date. WIPO's IPC technology concordance table was used to convert IPC symbols into 35 corresponding fields of technology (see Annex A for details). The top five were selected base on their 2015 totals. Source: WIPO statistics database and EPO PATSTAT database, October 2017.

process may lead to the patent being unenforceable and/or result in investigations by the anti-trust or competition law enforcement agencies to prevent abusive use of IPRs/patents by participants in the standards-setting process. Bear in mind, however, that for some firms, being part of a standards committee that produces a usable standard that has a lifecycle for some number of years is a preferred competitive strategy to investing in their own proprietary technology that has a very limited likelihood of being adopted in broad market use. Previously, Richard Maulsby, Director of the Office of Public Affairs for the US PTO stated, "In truth, odds are stacked astronomically against inventors, and no marketing outfit can change them. There are around 1.5 million patents in effect and in force in this country, and of those, maybe 3,000 are commercially viable." That gives inventors about a 99.8% failure rate and should be taken into consideration during the formation of a corporation's strategy regarding the development and promulgation of standards vs. research and development of proprietary innovations.

There may be situations in which mere membership of an SDO (or, more specifically, membership of a technical committee) creates a 'default' licensing of a company's IPRs. It should also be borne in mind that contributions to a standards-setting process are generally not confidential; so, all technical information revealed to the members of a standards-setting committee may be considered 'prior art' for the purpose of examining or invalidating a future patent application pertaining to it.

Concerning copyright, SDOs also have different policies. Many SDOs' policies on IPRs are limited to patents and do not deal with other intellectual property rights, such as copyright, which is generally dealt with on an *ad hoc* basis. The IPR policy of some SDOs clearly states that its policy on patents also applies to any works protected by copyright, which may be required to meet the standard.*

Patenting experienced a sizeable boom in the last couple of decades. More than 1.3 million patent applications were filed worldwide in 2016, more than 850,000 in 2006 and less than 600,000 in 1996. These figures reflect the growing importance of patents in the economy. Business and public research increasingly use patents to protect their inventions and fostering this trend has been the objective of patent policy in OECD countries over the past two decades, with a view to encouraging investments in innovation and fostering the dissemination of knowledge (Figure E.5).

Other SDOs, however, have decided not to have a policy that addresses proprietary copyrighted material, such as source code. An additional issue is copyright ownership over written contributions to the standards-setting process, on which policies also vary significantly between SDOs. Similarly, the issue of copyright over the finalized standard document becomes

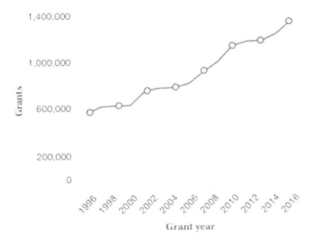

FIGURE E.5
Patent grants worldwide.

---

* Both the number of patents applied for and granted and the number of patent families have grown substantially, if not exponentially, over the past decade with no signs of slowing.

relevant if the copy of the standard is to be sold as a priced publication; the policies of SDOs vary on this question too.*

SUMMARY CONCLUSIONS

Whether your company holds patents (or has filed patent applications) that may potentially become essential or useful for meeting a standard, or whether your company intends to manufacture products or deliver services that comply with a given standard, it is imperative to become familiar with the IPR or patent policy of the relevant SDO like the U.S. Patent Office and the U.S. Chamber's Global Innovation Policy Center (GIPC). If there is a need to obtain a license from a holder of an essential patent, it will generally be necessary to contact the patent holder directly and sign a license agreement under negotiated terms and conditions that are acceptable to both the parties. Be advised, however, that seeking and obtaining licenses to IPRs is a time consuming and sometimes expensive endeavor, and, therefore, one that should not be taken lightly. There are tools, methodologies, and processes by which companies can identify those IPs that are the most germane and seminal to the technology in question. Similarly, do not ignore the content and licenses available via the open source alliances. There may be competing, if not nearly overlapping, IP that might be obtained for very little or free from the open source community. While this epilogue is not intended to serve as an instruction manual on obtaining intellectual property, it is intended to provoke thought regarding standards, strategy and the pursuit of next generation technology.

Viewed from the angle of innovation policy, patents aim to foster innovation in the private sector by allowing inventors to profit from

---

* Economic evaluation suggests that there are further possible directions of change for patent regimes that are worth exploring. Possible avenues for economic-based reforms of patent regimes include introducing a more differentiated approach to patent protection that depends on specific characteristics of the inventions, such as their life cycle or their value (as opposed to the current uniform system); making patent fees commensurate to the degree of protection provided; and developing alternatives to patenting, such as the public domain. In the near future, the patent system will be facing even greater challenges than those it has confronted in the past two decades, including increased globalization, overwhelming use of the internet as a vehicle of diffusion, and expanded innovation in services. Well-informed and more global policies will be needed to prepare the patent system to meet these new challenges so that it can continue to fulfil its role of encouraging innovation and technology diffusion.

their inventions. The positive effect of patents on innovation as incentive mechanisms has been traditionally contrasted with their negative effect on competition and technology diffusion. Patents have long been considered to represent a trade-off between incentives to innovate on one hand, and competition in the market and diffusion of technology on the other.*

However, recent evolutions in science and technology and patent policy and progress in the economic analysis of patents have nuanced this view: patents can hamper innovation under certain conditions and encourage diffusion under others. The impact of patents on innovation and economic performance is complex, and the fine tuning of patent design and issuance is crucial if they are to regain their intended effect as an effective policy instrument.

In summary, the traditional view of patents as a compromise between incentives to innovate and barriers to technology diffusion, if not incorrect, presents a rather partial picture, as patents can either encourage or deter innovation and diffusion, depending on certain conditions. Other policy or legal aspects have an impact on the patent system, including the number of damages attributed by courts in case of infringement, the conditions for exemptions for research use, whether compulsory licenses continue to be decreed, etc. Taken together, these aspects determine the strength, desirability, and value of patents.

Overall, excessively weak and narrow patents might deter business investment in R&D, as it becomes too easy for an imitator to undercut the inventor's market price. Weak and narrow patents may also encourage secrecy at the expense of publicity, and harm markets for technology, hence hindering the diffusion of technology. Furthermore, weak and narrow patents may obfuscate what the actual underlying technology is and/or does, thus circumventing the intention of a patent, namely, the right or freedom to operate at the expense of public disclosure. One of the reasons we've witnessed such an increase in patent applications is that due to the nature of technology being increasingly complex, companies and/ or inventors are creating whole families or webs of patents. As mentioned earlier, it is not uncommon to have a standard developed that requires the access or right(s) to hundreds of patents. Consider some of the larger

---

* Empirical evidence tends to support the effectiveness of patents in encouraging innovation, subject to some cross-industry variation. In a series of surveys conducted in the United States, Europe and Japan in the mid-1980s and 1990s, respondent companies reported patents as being extremely important in protecting their competitive advantage in a few industries, notably biotechnology, drugs, chemicals and, to a certain extent, machinery and computers.

societally beneficial technological advancements on the horizon; these will require access to a massive number of patents and patent families, but will also require standards such that the open market can continue to advance the field. For instance, consider hyper loop transportation or the commercialization of space, or, if you prefer, other global issues facing humanity, such as clean and renewable energy, access to clean water, etc. None of these fields are likely to be owned, developed, or promulgated by one firm nor one set of inventors alone. Similarly, in order to truly advance a field to the level of global impact, each will likely require market situations to allow for, if not promote, standards and thus advancement, refinement, and promulgation of solutions, versus an innumerable set of competing solutions.

Conversely, excessively strong and broad patents may open the door to undesired strategic behavior by patent holders, who may use their titles to appropriate revenue from existing inventions marketed by other companies. Broad or vague patents may allow for interpretation of their intent or application, and in some cases are even overturned or challenged with regard to infringement. In both cases, companies are still wise to understand the prior art or IPRs that exist, and who holds what. In particular, if the IPR is held by a PMO, who produces nothing, but has a history of litigation against infringing firms, be wary; seek standardized and/or pre-authorized licenses, open source content or accept that you may one day find yourself as the undesirable focus of a lawsuit from what is commonly referred to as a 'Patent Troll'.

The conclusions and predictions presented in this epilogue suggest a series of policy issues and options, and recommended topics for more in-depth analysis in the future. These concern the development of markets for technology and the access to basic inventions, as well as the patent system itself, its principles and the way it works. The meagerness and absence of economic evaluation of the patent system are striking. Most of the changes to patent regimes implemented over the past two decades were not based on hard evidence or economic analysis. It is necessary to develop economic analysis in this domain that would inform the policy debate, giving governments a clearer view beyond the arguments put forward by pressure groups. It is undeniable that the need for and value of patents as an economic driver of innovation is immeasurably positive. However, with technology and products becoming increasingly global in both their engineering and production, and with so many different global patent agencies and competing firms, inventors need to use caution.

On a positive note, most data scientists would agree that over 90% of the data or information our world has ever created has been created in just the past few years, meaning, our ability to invent, create, and generate new ideas and thoughts, and share them with the world has grown at an exponential speed; however, our ability to collate, aggregate, and amalgamate these ideas into a coherent analysis of prior art has not kept pace. These ideas for technological opportunities and advancement haven't always come from the traditional inventor. Instead, sometimes we see patents being overturned or denied, not due to openly competing prior art, but for reasons related to the idea existing in the prior art of movies, cartoons or other imaginative art.

In short, we agree on the value of protecting truly patentable technology to incent and reward inventors for moving fields forward. However, this epilogue is meant to provoke thought regarding how standards can and should play a role in also moving a field forward, not just for one firm or inventor, but also for communities and humanity as a whole. That is why organizations such as ISO and IAOIP exist. In particular, with regards to IAOIP and the science of innovation, such standards did not exist even a decade ago. The data is very clear on the fact that over 95% of new product development initiatives and over 50% of product improvement initiatives fail to achieve the predicted return on investment (ROI). Yet, in the U.S. alone, companies spend hundreds of billions of dollars per year on R&D and innovation. Of the 2,347 $1b market cap companies studied in a recent Harvard Business Review article, only 10 grew 5% or more for 10 straight years. It stands to reason then that, while there has been much focus on standards with regard to technology, the same focus, energym and initiative should be given to standardization regarding the science of innovation, its practices, methodologies, and processes.

That is not to say there should be, or could be, one standard innovation process, but there are scientifically proven methods and practices that can be followed to more predictably yield innovative outcomes. For instance, just as a painting requires much artistic input, one could, therefore, argue that there is no specific process for creating a painting. However, grand master painters would tell you that they have their own process that incorporates artistic practices, which, woven together over time, predictably create incredibly valued outcomes. The science of innovation and standards relating to innovation management are similar, and companies seeking to increase their return on investment would do well to study, understand, and employ these strategies.

The science of innovation, therefore, is what sets innovation management and its standards apart from any of its related or subordinate fields; it is in the intersections of business (i.e., how to make money with the idea), engineering (i.e., how to build the idea), and social science (i.e., promoting ideas humanity needs) that innovation creates its value. The balance between these three requires robust processes as well as well-honed practices, and is what separates innovators from pure inventors, pure business people or social activists.

Therefore, any future conclusions and policy recommendations or actions should rely notably on quantitative evidence: an effort to build and make available to analysts the corresponding databases has been initiated, notably by the OECD, with support from IAOIP, but this work needs to be broadened. In addition, more information is needed on the ways in which patents are used by their holders, for instance, as regards in-house implementation, licensing contracts, and business strategies. In parallel to this analytical effort, policy makers might encourage experience-sharing across countries: there are significant differences in patent regimes and many countries have experimented with various policy mechanisms, but there have been few attempts to systematize this experience and disseminate best practices across countries.

Analysis and policy messages presented in this handbook chapter also apply, to a certain extent, to developing countries with significant national innovation capacity. These countries need a unified patent system strong enough to attract foreign direct investment, to ensure inward licensing and to encourage local investment in research. However, these countries also need to protect their ability to access and digest existing foreign technology, just as developed countries used to do during their development stage. The specific features that these countries might build into their patent systems to address these various objectives is a topic for future research by IAOIP, ANSI, ISO, and other leading research organizations.

REFERENCES

Levin, R.C., A.K. Klevorick, R.R. Nelson, and S.G. Winter (1987), "Appropriating the Returns from Industrial R&D", Brookings Papers on Economic Activity: 783–820.

Mairesse, J. and P. Mohnen (2003), "Intellectual Property in Services. What Do We Learn from Innovation Surveys?", in *Patients Innovation and Economic Performance, Proceedings of the OCED Conference on IPR*, Innovation and Economic Performance, 28-29 August 2003 (OECD, forthcoming).

Martinez, C. and D. Guellec (2003), "Overview of Recent Trends in Patent Regimes in the United States, Japan and Europe", in *Patents Innovation and Economic Performance*, *Proceedings of the OCED Conference on IPR*, Innovation and Economic Performance, 28-29 August 2003 (OECD, forthcoming).

Motohashi, K. (2003), "Japan's Patent System and Business Innovation: Re-assessing Pro-patent Policies", in *Patents Innovation and Economic Performance*, *Proceedings of the OCED Conference on IPR, Innovation and Economic Performance*, 28–29 August 2003 (OECD, forthcoming).

Nuffield Council on Bioethics (2002), *"The Ethics of Patenting DNA: A Discussion Paper"*. London, UK: Nuffield Council on Bioethics, www.nuffieldbioethics.org.

OECD (2003a), *Genetic Inventions, IPRs and Licensing Practices: Evidence and Policies*, Paris, France: OECD.

OECD (2003b), *Turning Science into Business: Patenting and Licensing at Public Research Organisations*, Paris, France: OECD.

OECD (2003c), *Compendium of Patent Statistics*, Paris, France: OECD.

Quillen, C.D. and O.H. Webster (2001), "Continuing patent applications and performance of the US patent office", *Federal Circuit Bar Journal*, Vol. 11, No. 1, pp. 1–21.

Schatz, U. (2003), "Recent changes and expected developments in patent regimes: A European perspective", in *Patents Innovation and Economic Performance*, *Proceedings of the OCED Conference on IPR*, Innovation and Economic Performance, 28–29 August 2003 (OECD, forthcoming).

Sheehan, J., D. Guellec and C. Martinez (2003), "Business patenting and licensing: Results from the OECD/BIAC survey", in *Patents Innovation and Economic Performance*, *Proceedings of the OCED Conference on IPR*, Innovation and Economic Performance, 28–29 August 2003 (OECD, forthcoming).

Vonortas, N. (2003), "Technology licensing", in *Patents Innovation and Economic Performance*, *Proceedings of the OCED Conference on IPR, Innovation and Economic Performance*, 28–29 August 2003 (OECD, forthcomeing).

Walsh, J.P., A. Arora and W.M. Cohen (2003), "Effects of research tool patents and licensing on biomedical innovation, in *Patents in the Knowledge-based Economy*, Washington, DC: The National Academies Press.

Index